HONOR IN THE DUST

HONOR
IN THE DUST

Theodore Roosevelt, War in the Philippines,
and the Rise and Fall of America's Imperial Dream

GREGG JONES

NEW AMERICAN LIBRARY

New American Library
Published by New American Library, a division of
Penguin Group (USA) Inc., 375 Hudson Street,
New York, New York 10014, USA
Penguin Group (Canada), 90 Eglinton Avenue East, Suite 700, Toronto,
Ontario M4P 2Y3, Canada (a division of Pearson Penguin Canada Inc.)
Penguin Books Ltd., 80 Strand, London WC2R 0RL, England
Penguin Ireland, 25 St. Stephen's Green, Dublin 2,
Ireland (a division of Penguin Books Ltd.)
Penguin Group (Australia), 250 Camberwell Road, Camberwell, Victoria 3124,
Australia (a division of Pearson Australia Group Pty. Ltd.)
Penguin Books India Pvt. Ltd., 11 Community Centre, Panchsheel Park,
New Delhi - 110 017, India
Penguin Group (NZ), 67 Apollo Drive, Rosedale, Auckland 0632,
New Zealand (a division of Pearson New Zealand Ltd.)
Penguin Books (South Africa) (Pty.) Ltd., 24 Sturdee Avenue,
Rosebank, Johannesburg 2196, South Africa

Penguin Books Ltd., Registered Offices:
80 Strand, London WC2R 0RL, England

First published by New American Library,
a division of Penguin Group (USA) Inc.

First Printing, February 2012
10   9   8   7   6   5   4   3   2   1

Copyright © Gregg Jones, 2012
Maps by Chris Erichsen
All rights reserved

LIBRARY OF CONGRESS CATALOGING-IN-PUBLICATION DATA:

Jones, Gregg
Honor in the dust: Theodore Roosevelt, war in the Philippines, and the rise and fall of America's imperial
dream/Gregg Jones.
p. cm.
Includes bibliographical references.
ISBN 978-0-451-22904-5
1. Philippines—History—Philippine American War, 1899–1902—Campaigns—Philippines—Samar.
2. Philippines—History—Philippine American War, 1899–1902—Atrocities. 3. Philippines—History—
Philippine American War, 1899–1902—Political aspects—United States. 4. Philippines—Annexation to
the United States. 5. Waller, Littleton Waller Tazewell, 1856–1926. 6. Roosevelt, Theodore, 1858–1919.
I. Title.
DS682.S26J66 2012
959.9'031—dc23   2011033386

Set in Baskerville
Designed by Ginger Legato

Printed in the United States of America

To Don and Bonny Edmonds

ACKNOWLEDGMENTS

The debts I have accumulated in the course of writing this book are considerable, and they begin at home. I met my wife, Ali, in 1984, shortly after I arrived in the Philippines to chronicle the political upheaval in America's former colony. She was a gifted writer at a local design studio, and, with our common interests in books and world travel, we fell in love. As I completed this project, we celebrated our twenty-fifth wedding anniversary. I will be forever grateful to Ali, and our son, Chris, for their love and forbearance as I pursued this passion.

It is impossible to adequately express the gratitude I feel toward Brent Howard, my editor at New American Library. Brent saw potential from the first pitch, and he convinced his colleagues that this book was worth publishing. His enthusiasm sustained me through hard months when deadlines passed and the finish line remained far in the hazy distance. But that only begins to describe Brent's contributions. He devoted diligent weeks to my first draft, and conceived a superb road map for transforming my meandering manuscript into a compelling book. His skill and good judgment are reflected throughout.

I also want to thank New American Library publisher, Kara Welsh, who supported Brent's pursuit of this book and patiently shifted schedules as I labored on. Pete Garceau designed a striking cover. Rosalind Parry assisted with the photo insert, production logistics, and numerous other vital tasks. My thanks also to copy editor Tiffany Yates Martin and publicist Jen Bernard.

Agents are a critical cog in the publishing wheel, and I am indebted to mine, fellow writer and friend Jim Donovan. He embraced this project from the outset, taking careful notes on a napkin as I laid out the story over plates of stromboli at the Elbow Room. True to his word, he found a good home for this book.

At a time when libraries, archives, and museums are undergoing heartbreaking budget cuts, I would like to thank the dedicated professionals at the following institutions for their assistance: National Archives and Records Administration and Library of Congress in Washington, D.C.; Marine Corps Archives and Special Collections Branch, Alfred M. Gray Marine Corps Research Center and Marine Corps University Library in Quantico, Virginia; National Personnel Records Center in St. Louis, Missouri; McDermott Library at the University of Texas at Dallas; University of Texas Arlington Library; Dallas Public Library and Plano Public Library in Texas; Old Dominion University Libraries and the Norfolk Public Library in Norfolk, Virginia.

Early on, I was fortunate to sit down with Trevor Plante at the National Archives. I had admired Trevor's work in *Prologue* magazine over the years, but he was even more impressive in person. His knowledge of U.S. military activities during the Spanish-American and Philippine conflicts was encyclopedic. Even more invaluable was his assistance in tracking down various records and microfilm reels.

While the entire staff at the Marine Corps Archives and Special Collections Branch earned my gratitude, two people deserve special mention. Greg Cina was ever helpful, from the first moment I contacted him about scheduling research trips to the final minutes I spent poring over the personal papers of legendary Marines. I would also like to thank J. Michael Miller, branch head, for his kind assistance.

Special thanks as well to Michelle Brown at the National Personnel Records Center, Robert Hitchings at the Norfolk Public Library's Sargeant Memorial Room and Harry Frizzell at Old Dominion University. Roy Waller provided useful background information on Virginia's storied Waller clan. Jean Fe Wall shared rare articles and diaries as well as priceless stories about her father, Balangiga survivor Adolph Gamlin. John Reed of the University of Utah imparted keen insights on America's war in the Philippines, especially the campaigns in Panay and Samar.

Chuck Camp, a world-class writer, provided deft editing and a pitch-perfect critique as I struggled to corral the early chapters. Doug Swanson, my former collaborator and editor at the *Dallas Morning News*, was a cherished link to the outside world. I thank Doug as well as Bob Mong, George Rodrigue, and Maud Beelman for arranging a leave of absence late in this project, and for graciously accepting my resignation from the newspaper to pursue my dream of writing history.

I am grateful to longtime friend Steve LeVine, my running mate during our exhilarating days in the Philippines. When this book was still an inchoate idea, Steve spurred me on, and he and his wife, Nuri, later loaned me their apartment during a research trip to Washington, D.C. Thanks as well to filmmaker Chris Billing, who let me crash on his couch during a Washington trip and inspired me with his example. Late in the project, Gunnar Jacobson, a brilliant young writer, teacher, organic farmer, and traveler, devoted several energetic days to tying up loose ends for me at the National Archives. James Hohman helped me track down several obscure journal articles. Lori Miller of Redbird Research provided a timely assist when a missing file suddenly became available at the National Personnel Records Center in St. Louis.

Closer to home, Steve Jones has always been a terrific brother and sounding board. I'm grateful to George Getschow for his enthusiasm and encouragement. Thanks also to my Red Line Mafia cohorts—Chris Wilkins, Eddie Maguire, Pete Johnson, Keith Campbell and Gary Jacobson—for their camaraderie as I scrunched into a corner of our evening commuter train, pen or laptop in hand, and disappeared into the world of Theodore Roosevelt and America's forgotten war in the Philippines.

Finally, I wish to pay tribute to Don and Bonny Edmonds—surrogate parents, friends, mentors, and role models since we met in Virginia in 1981. Their passion for books and art and the fearless pursuit of their dreams have inspired me these past thirty years. We have shared books and stimulating conversation, exotic travels and good food, countless laughs and a few tears. Without realizing it, Don set this journey in motion in August 2007 during an evening at Casa Edmonds. I had just finished describing a book idea that I had long contemplated, about Theodore Roosevelt and the collapse of America's imperial dreams amid a war crimes scandal in the Philippines in 1902. In his cut-to-the-chase manner, Don declared, "Now that's a book I'd like to read."

It was all I needed to hear.

INTRODUCTION

A merican history captivated me from an early age, but I did not learn of the U.S. conquest of the Philippines until I was in my twenties. I wound up in the islands in the mid-1980s, a young newspaper reporter inspired to write the first draft of history as a foreign correspondent. It was while chronicling the death throes of the dictatorship of Ferdinand Marcos that I became acquainted with the bloody story of how America had acquired the islands after the Spanish-American War in 1898.

A year after arriving in the Philippines, I made a reporting trip to the island of Samar. I went there to write about the Marcos government's military campaign against Communist guerrillas, and the plight of poor farmers caught in the cross fire. I traveled into Samar's mountainous interior by dugout canoe and tramped through steamy jungles on muddy trails. I found a wild and rugged island that had changed little since American soldiers had fought a savage war with nationalist guerrillas more than eighty years earlier.

The military campaign on Samar had been the closing act in the U.S. conquest of the islands, the culmination of America's rise as a world power. But the victory had been tainted by revelations of military atrocities. The disclosures shocked the nation and staggered the young administration of President Theodore Roosevelt. After the fallout of the Samar campaign, many Americans concluded the price of empire had been too high.

I left the Philippines in 1989 and moved on to other stories, but I remained intrigued by this forgotten chapter in our nation's history. When Americans bitterly debated the Bush administration's decision to go to war in Iraq in 2003, I was reminded of our divisive war in the Philippines. The controversy over the U.S. military's use of "waterboarding" in Iraq highlighted other striking parallels with America's earlier experience in the Philippines. Some Americans justified torture in Iraq and Afghanistan as a necessary response to an elusive and treacherous enemy. It was the same argument some put forth in defense of the "water cure" and other extreme measures used by U.S. soldiers in the Philippines under Teddy Roosevelt.

On one level, *Honor in the Dust* is the story of interrelated dramas that consumed Americans in the spring of 1902: the courts-martial of U.S. military officers accused of war crimes in the Philippines, and the contentious Senate hearings on the conduct of that war. But in a larger sense, this is the story of America's emergence as a world power, and the bitter national discourse that accompanied that rise. The issues at the heart of that forgotten debate will sound familiar to anyone who has followed America's contemporary back-and-forth over military interventions in Iraq and Afghanistan. The use of U.S. power, the propriety of torture in the pursuit of American interests, the obligations of national honor— then, as now, as readers will see, Americans held passionately disparate views on these subjects.

"The fiery trial through which we pass will light us down in honor or dishonor to the latest generation."

—ABRAHAM LINCOLN

CONTENTS

HONOR IN THE DUST

Prologue

Panay Island, Philippines

I'm going to die.
The terrifying realization seized the slight, middle-aged man as he lay pinned to the convent floor by two light-skinned soldiers. A stick prevented him from closing his mouth while water poured down his throat, strangling him and swelling his stomach and intestines until surely they must explode.

Oh, how it hurts!

The *americanos* had arrived at daybreak, thundering into town with a clatter of hooves. They had summoned the man from his house and ordered him to wait while they ate their breakfast of freshly cooked eggs. Only then did the interrogation begin.[1]

A bearded officer asked the questions through a native interpreter. When the captive failed to respond as desired, a brisk command followed. Soldiers stripped the man of his jacket and shirt, tied his hands behind his back and threw him to the floor beneath a large water tank.

Ordinarily, Joveniano Ealdama surely would have protested such treatment, for he was a proud and prominent man—indeed, mayor of his town.² But fear stifled his indignation. Few who lived on the island of Panay in 1900 had not heard of the torment that the *americanos* used to loosen Filipino tongues.

Two soldiers forced Ealdama's mouth open, positioned his head beneath the tank's faucet and turned the spigot. When his stomach filled with water and became hard as a drum, the soldiers pounded his midsection with their fists. Ealdama screamed in agony, and water and gastric juices erupted from his mouth and nose. His stomach now empty, the torture began anew.

As the water did its cruel work, the American officers watched casually. Past experience left little doubt how this would end.

The Americans had slyly christened the agony that their captive was now undergoing the "water cure," for it cured Filipinos of their reluctance to betray the revolution against U.S. rule. Filipino collaborators had taught Americans the technique, but its origins resided in Spain. The "strangling torments" of torture by water had been perfected during the Spanish Inquisition, when it was forbidden by the Catholic Church to draw blood or inflict permanent injury during questioning. Water torture left no marks, but it inflicted excruciating pain and terror. Victims experienced the simultaneous sensations of drowning and of being burned or cut as internal organs stretched and convulsed.³ Confessions usually followed quickly.

After less than ten minutes, Joveniano Ealdama could endure no more. The water was stopped, and the soldiers removed the stick from his mouth. Ealdama groaned and rolled onto his side.

He would tell the *americanos* what they wanted to hear.

PART I

America Rises

CHAPTER 1

Call to Arms

A s the battleship USS *Maine* steamed into Havana Harbor, Cuba, on a muggy January night, even the lowliest sailor could see that this would be no ordinary port call. Ashore, rebels roamed the hills as Spanish soldiers watched warily from stone forts. In the bay, German warships rode at anchor, poised to capitalize on the worsening chaos at America's doorstep. Anxious officials back in Washington had ordered U.S. naval forces on high alert, then dispatched the *Maine,* one of the nation's finest warships, to this hotbed of hemispheric unrest. Every gun on deck was loaded, extra nighttime watches had been assigned and Marines were prepared to rush ashore "at any moment," seventeen-year-old apprentice seaman Charles Hamilton wrote his father back home in Rhode Island. "By the looks of things now," he predicted, "I think we will have some trouble before we leave."[1]

Officially, the *Maine* was just paying a neighborly visit to the Spanish colony ninety miles off the tip of Florida. As she lolled at anchor in the muddy harbor over the next three weeks, her officers would attend bullfights and diplomatic receptions in the city, and host shipboard banquets and tours for distinguished guests. But behind the civil display, the three-hundred-foot-long, 6,600-ton warship was clearly in Cuba for another

5

reason: The mere presence of the first American naval vessel to call on Havana in three years was a pointed reminder that the United States had more than a passing interest in the island's affairs.

America's tension with Spain had simmered for years over the European power's increasingly brutal attempts to suppress an independence movement on the island. As the year began, thousands of Cubans were dying of disease and starvation in relocation camps. Meanwhile, Washington's repeated signals to Madrid to loosen its grip went unheeded.

From his position aboard the *Maine*, Hamilton had an uncomfortably close view of this high-stakes game. Cruising just off the coast of Cuba, he and his shipmates had witnessed Spanish troops firing on the rebels in jungle encounters. As the American ship glided into Havana Bay past Morro Castle, the iconic sixteenth-century fort at the harbor entrance, Hamilton and his comrades felt the resentful stares of the Spanish soldiers. "We are in a pretty dangerous position at the present time and we hardly know when we are safe," the fledgling sailor reported. He signed off "hoping that I may be alive to see you all again."[2]

It wasn't to be.

Ten days after Hamilton posted his letter, at nine forty on the evening of February 15, 1898, just after the *Maine*'s Marine bugler had sounded taps, a tremendous explosion shattered windows across Havana, and a fireball boiled into the night sky. Twin blasts ripped through the *Maine*'s bow, detonating ammunition magazines and killing or mortally wounding 262 Americans, including Hamilton. Only eighty-nine men made it off the dying ship. Her spine shattered, the *Maine* settled into the harbor mud within minutes.

TRAGIC HEADLINES FILLED THE FRONT pages of countless American newspapers, and a black mood descended upon the nation. In Washington, D.C., flags were lowered to half-staff, and the city's high social season was abruptly suspended. Solemn crowds clustered outside the White House, awaiting word from the president. In the State, War, and Navy Building across the street, workmen quietly opened a case displaying a wooden model of the *Maine* and moved its tiny ensign to half-mast—eerily matching the Stars and Stripes that by then had been lowered on her wrecked mast in Havana Bay.

President William McKinley urged Americans to await an investigation before assigning blame. But publishing tycoons William Randolph Hearst and Joseph Pulitzer saw no virtue in calm deliberation, and their newspapers whipped public opinion into a fury long before Navy divers finished combing the *Maine*'s wreckage. In late March, five weeks after the explosion, the Navy's investigation concluded that the *Maine* had been deliberately destroyed by a mine, though it stopped short of blaming Spanish agents, as Hearst and other U.S. hawks insisted. By then, it barely mattered. Cries of "Remember the *Maine*!" were reverberating from pulpits and meeting halls across the country, and Congress was preparing for war by passing a $50 million emergency defense measure.

More than half of the new spending was set aside to increase the size of the Navy, a massive undertaking entrusted to the most energetic assistant secretary of the Navy the nation had ever seen—an asthmatic, bespectacled New Yorker by the name of Theodore Roosevelt. Almost overnight, the obscure Naval Auxiliary Board that he directed became one of the most productive offices within the vast federal bureaucracy.

The board scrambled to buy or lease scores of ships for duty as troop transports, colliers, floating hospitals, refrigeration ships, dispatch boats and patrol craft. Negotiations commenced with steamship lines, ferryboat companies and tug operators, but quickly moved on to the nation's business barons, for their steel-hulled, steam-powered yachts were some of the fastest vessels afloat. Members of the New York Yacht Club fielded offers for their richly appointed pleasure craft and retained brokers to cut deals. Some saw an opportunity for extortionate profits. The son of a Cincinnati baker and gin distiller, whose father counted President McKinley as a close friend, demanded $175,000 for the yacht *Hiawatha*—nearly double his purchase price a few years earlier. Under Roosevelt's relentless prodding, deals for five of America's finest yachts were hammered out. Among the sellers was oil and railroad magnate Henry Flagler, who, on April 6, parted ways with his beloved *Alicia,* soon to become the gunboat *Hornet.* The following week, financier John Pierpont Morgan agreed to sell his magnificent 242-foot-long *Corsair* for $225,000.[3]

One notable holdout was William Randolph Hearst, whose New York and San Francisco newspapers were busy infecting Americans with war fever. He declined to sell his storied *Buccaneer*. Only a few months earlier, it had carried Hearst's star correspondent, Karl Decker, to rescue a Cuban damsel whose imprisonment had become a cause célèbre in the United States. Now Hearst was planning blow-by-blow coverage of the war he so much favored, and he would use the swift *Buccaneer* to transport Decker and a team of Edison Company cameramen to Cuba to produce the world's first wartime newsreels for New York theaters.[4]

As spring air coaxed buds from the boughs of white oak, black walnut and tulip trees along Brooklyn Heights, the newly acquired vessels converged on the venerable New York Naval Shipyard. Better known as the Brooklyn Navy Yard, it had become overnight the center of the nation's fevered war preparations. The yard had turned out the frigate *Adams* in 1798, three years before it was an official government installation, as well as the country's first steam warship, the *Fulton,* in 1815. During the Civil War, some six thousand workers manned its foundries, shops and dry docks. Though not built there, the Union ironclad *Monitor,* which changed the very nature of warship design, was commissioned at Brooklyn. But the yard's biggest triumph in recent times had been the 1890 launch of the *Maine,* a state-of-the-art symbol of not only America's burgeoning industrial might but also its commitment to becoming a global power.

Now shouts and boat whistles mingled with the thuds, thwacks and swishes of hammers, chisels and brushes as Brooklyn crews scraped hulls to increase speed, caulked leaky seams, repaired furnaces and boilers, and camouflaged colorful hulls and smokestacks with battle gray paint. Soon an array of former merchant ships, yachts, ferries and tugs was transformed into a "mosquito fleet" tasked with defending the East Coast from Spanish attack and protecting the armada of warships converging on Key West, Florida.

Fears of a Spanish first strike unleashed a flurry of additional home defense steps. The entrance to New York Harbor was mined and studded with torpedoes. Massive twelve-inch guns were hauled onto ramparts overlooking the harbor. Rifle pits were dug and telephone and telegraph lines strung to connect a network of fortifications stretching from New

York City down to Sandy Hook on the Jersey shore. Hot-air balloons were readied for aerial surveillance.[5] Roosevelt even ordered old Civil War monitors out of mothballs for coastal duty to satisfy East Coast mayors panicked by the threat of Spanish naval attacks.

In late April, the Navy unveiled plans for an early-warning system along the Atlantic coast. Upon first sight of any Spanish ship, dozens of homing pigeons with messages attached to their legs were to be released from U.S. patrol boats. If a sighting were made 150 miles out, experts calculated, the birds could arrive at Navy yard lofts eight hours before the enemy and five hours ahead of the fastest U.S. dispatch boats.[6]

THE CUBAN ISSUE HAD HAUNTED President McKinley from his first days in office. Indigenous independence forces had renewed their rebellion against Spain during the term of his predecessor, Democrat Grover Cleveland, and by the time McKinley took over in March 1897, the protagonists had battled to a stalemate. In his inauguration address, McKinley signaled his distaste for intervention. "We want no wars of conquest," he proclaimed. "We must avoid the temptations of territorial aggression. Peace is preferable to war in almost every contingency."[7]

As he warily watched matters worsen through his first months in the White House, the president avoided addressing the Cuba problem publicly. Finally, in his annual message to Congress that December, he pledged to make Cuba a diplomatic priority, while calling for patience to allow Spain time to reform its behavior there. It was vintage McKinley, cautious to a fault.

McKinley's timid approach toward Cuba put him at odds with a majority of his fellow Republicans. Led by Senator Henry Cabot Lodge of Massachusetts and McKinley's own assistant secretary of the Navy, Roosevelt, the party's interventionists saw the Cuban revolt as a golden opportunity to expel Spain from the Western Hemisphere and establish America as a global power. The destruction of the *Maine* only strengthened their hand. As the clamor for intervention in Cuba spread across the country, McKinley found himself under growing pressure from his own party. Even at Cabinet meetings and White House socials, supposed allies

like Roosevelt and Lodge now urged him to force Spain to quit Cuba—or
go to war with the United States.

Despite his hesitation, McKinley was no pacifist. He had distinguished himself on the battlefield during the Civil War, rising through
the ranks from private to major. But behind closed doors he expressed
horror at suggestions that a conflict with Spain would be good for America. "I have been through one war," he said. "I have seen the dead piled
up, and I do not want to see another."[8] As the crisis deepened in late
February and into March, McKinley despaired over the difficult choices
he faced. Just as the nation sought leadership, its president fell silent.

McKinley's reluctance to even speak of the *Maine* disaster became
clear just a week after the explosion at an appearance at the University of
Pennsylvania. As Hearst's *New York Journal* shrilly blamed Spanish sabo-
tage for the carnage, McKinley called for calm in a speech honoring
George Washington's birthday. He reminded his audience of the first
president's cautious foreign policy credo: "Observe good faith and justice
toward all nations; cultivate peace and harmony with all."[9]

Roosevelt fumed. The president, he huffed, had "no more backbone
than a chocolate éclair." By February 25, he couldn't contain himself.
When his hypochondriac boss, Secretary John D. Long, left work at midday that Friday, Roosevelt did everything but declare war against Spain.
After conferring with Senator Lodge, his ally in favoring a muscular U.S.
response, he requisitioned guns, ordered ammunition, stockpiled coal
and asked Congress to approve the unlimited recruitment of seamen. He
also alerted the U.S. fleets in Europe and the South Atlantic to stand by
for war, and cabled the Asiatic Squadron to be prepared to take on the
Spanish in the Philippines.[10]

President McKinley was appalled, but did nothing to reverse Roosevelt's bellicose actions.

Pressure on McKinley continued to mount. On March 17, Republican
Senator Redfield Proctor of Vermont stunned the president, and the
nation, with his account of a fact-finding trip he and others had just
taken to Cuba. Before visiting the island, Proctor had supported McKinley's call for a peaceful approach. Now he stood before a packed Senate
chamber and recited a litany of facts and statistics on Cuba's sick and

starving *reconcentrados,* civilians who had been herded into fetid relocation camps by Spanish forces to deny their support to the insurgents. "Torn from their homes, with foul earth, foul water and foul food or none, what wonder that one-half have died and one-quarter of the living are so diseased that they cannot be saved?" Proctor declared.[11] As fellow senators and spectators hung on every word, Proctor called for an immediate invasion.

McKinley was still scrambling to contain the fallout from Proctor's speech a week later, when Secretary Long and four naval officers delivered the results of the *Maine* investigation—a mine in Havana Bay, not an accidental fire on board, was to blame. The president had hoped to sit on the report for a few days before passing it quietly to Congress, giving more time for negotiations with Spain, but a rebellion among congressional Republicans made that impossible. At town hall meetings and public gatherings across the country, crowds were now hissing at the mere mention of McKinley's name. Republican leaders begged him to refute charges that he was placing the interests of his business supporters above those of murdered American sailors by not taking decisive action.

The president agonized. Should the continued suffering of the Cuban people caused by inaction outweigh the lives of American boys that would be lost in a war? As stress over his decision mounted, aides were shocked by McKinley's increasingly haggard, hollow-eyed appearance. They learned he had even been rummaging through his wife's medicine cabinet at night seeking a narcotic-induced sleep.[12]

At a White House social in early April, the distraught president pulled a sympathetic Chicago newspaper editor into a room and bared his soul. "It seems to me I have not slept over three hours a night for over two weeks," McKinley moaned. "Congress is trying to drive us into war with Spain." He then wept like a child.[13]

McKinley finally came to terms with reality: He had already lost his party and was fast losing the country. On April 11, he asked Congress for authority to use armed force to end the civil war in Cuba. Spanish Prime Minister Práxedes Sagasta countered with an offer to grant limited autonomy to the island, but it was too late. On April 19, Congress adopted a joint resolution authorizing the president to intervene in Cuba.

The following day McKinley scribbled his signature on an ultimatum calling on Spain to cease operations against the independence forces in Cuba and allow America to arbitrate the conflict. The president had no doubt as to how Spain would react. Solemnly, he carried the document into the Cabinet Room, where many of the same members of Congress who had begged for this action waited. A crotchety Senator William P. Frye of Maine pressed him on how much time he intended to give Spain. Three days, McKinley replied, adding, "I suppose you'd like to give them only fifteen minutes."

Spain wouldn't need three days, or even fifteen minutes. After receiving a translation of the document in Madrid on Thursday, Spanish officials summoned the U.S. minister and announced a break in diplomatic relations with the United States.[14]

While President McKinley hoped to the last to avoid war, millions of Americans clamored to prove the nation's fighting worth to the world. Fishermen and farmers, coal miners and carpenters, steelworkers and store clerks flocked to join the Army, Navy, or Marine Corps. Bands dusted off Civil War tunes, and flags sprouted from homes and offices. Crowds gathered to cheer the arrival and departure of Navy ships and military detachments. Pent-up emotions erupted across the country.

In mid-April, a Saturday night crowd surged out of a saloon near the Navy yard in New York City and roamed the streets until dawn, finally hanging an effigy of Spanish General Valeriano Weyler, known as "the Butcher" of the Cuban conflict.[15] That same week, uptown in Manhattan, John W. Dexter, a building contractor, appeared in court on charges that he'd violated city permit laws by jumping onto a City Hall park bench and delivering a fiery prowar speech that drew hundreds of bystanders. Asked by the judge to explain, Dexter burst into verse:

> *"There's only one flag in the world for me;*
> *only one flag to light for liberty;*
> *only one flag to make the Cubans free;*
> *only one flag to make the Spaniards flee;*
> *the Stars and Stripes are good enough for me."*

The magistrate promptly freed him. "The Spaniards had no permit to starve and kill the poor Cubans," the court official thundered. "I suppose this man was making a patriotic speech and I glory in him." The room erupted in cheers.[16]

Halfway across the country, Kansas City shoemaker Thomas Collins experienced the excesses of patriotism. An outspoken opponent of war with Spain, he locked his shop, draped black crepe on the door and posted a sign that read, CLOSED IN MEMORY OF A CHRISTIAN NATION THAT DESCENDS TO THE BARBARITY OF WAR. Within minutes, an angry crowd kicked in the door. Police took Collins into protective custody and hustled him to the station, a howling mob at their heels.[17]

SUNRISE ON FRIDAY, APRIL 22, revealed the full extent of the war preparations hurtling toward a climax at the Brooklyn Navy Yard. Crews of workers cleaned and repainted ships in battle colors, overhauled engines, replaced aging decks and mounted rapid-fire guns.[18] Out in the East River, on the receiving ship *Vermont*, Army recruits were organized into groups of fifty and hustled ashore to board Florida-bound trains. At the U.S. Naval Hospital on Flushing Avenue, officers sifted through more than six hundred applications for twenty-six berths as acting assistant surgeons. Just up the river at the Mallory Line wharf, crews were loading one hundred tons of relief supplies for starving Cuban refugees and relocation camp residents into the steamer the *State of Texas*. Seventy-six-year-old Clara Barton, the revered head of the Red Cross and Civil War heroine, had agreed to escort the supplies to Cuba.[19]

At ten o'clock, as a drummer pounded out the call to formation outside the three-story Marine barracks, six companies of men in floppy campaign hats and blue woolen tunics hustled into place on the worn drill ground. Their unit, the 1st Marine Battalion, had been created only the preceding Saturday by presidential order. Throughout the week, Marine detachments had arrived from barracks along the East Coast. Some had marched through Manhattan in impromptu parades, strutting up Broadway and across the Brooklyn Bridge before cheering crowds.[20]

As the Marines finished their morning drill, a broad-shouldered, white-bearded officer strode to the head of the formation. Fifty-seven-year-old Lieutenant Colonel Robert Watkinson Huntington had been assigned to lead this critical new force.

Huntington allowed himself a moment of pride as he viewed the sharp-looking Marines before him. Then he began to speak in his slow, gentle way, praising the men for their hard work and smart appearance. For the past two days, he reminded them, they had awaited the transport ship that would carry them to war. It had arrived, and was at the coal dock taking on ammunition and provisions that very moment. They would board the transport, the *Panther,* and depart for southern waters later in the day, he said. Huntington finished his brief remarks, and the battalion was dismissed.[21]

As if on cue, the Marines erupted in wild celebration. One or two started to sing "There'll Be a Hot Time in the Old Town Tonight," and soon the entire battalion was belting out the ragtime hit. As the last strains died out, a patriotic tune was quickly taken up, and then another, and another. Marines laughed and cheered and danced as they tossed their caps into the air. "For an hour," one reporter observed, "the men acted like a lot of schoolboys who had got a holiday."[22]

For Huntington, the scene was hauntingly familiar. As a twenty-year-old newly commissioned second lieutenant in the summer of 1861, he had been assigned to a hastily assembled Marine battalion in Washington, D.C. On Sunday afternoon, July 21, along the banks of a sluggish Virginia stream known as Bull Run, Huntington was among the cocky Union troops schooled in the realities of war. The Marines broke and ran when they failed to breach the Confederate line organized by an eccentric Virginia military professor named Thomas Jackson. As darkness fell across the battlefield, "Stonewall" Jackson and the Confederate Army savored their victory while Huntington and his Union comrades fled in panic back to Washington.

Huntington survived the war and remained a Marine when the fighting ended. Over the next three decades, he navigated the internecine squabbles within the Corps and competently commanded Marines in the far corners of the world. By the time the Cuban crisis erupted in early

1898, Huntington was a gray-haired grandfather with little desire to relive the horrors he had witnessed at Bull Run. On the very day the *Maine* blew up in Havana, he confessed to Marine Corps Commandant Charles Heywood his doubts as to whether he and his peers were up for the rigors of another war.[23] Brushing aside Huntington's reservations, Heywood picked his well-traveled friend to command the new 1st Marine Battalion against Spain. Dutifully, Huntington readied his men for battle.[24]

AS THE SUN BURNED AWAY the morning chill, stevedores and gangway men swarmed over the *Panther*, filling her hold with the supplies and equipment needed to sustain the Marines for months in the field: boxes of rifle ammunition, hardtack and vegetables, tents, blankets, mosquito netting, woolen and linen uniforms, heavy and light underwear, wheelbarrows, pickaxes, barbed-wire cutters, and medical supplies.[25] The sun was fading about half past five when the *Panther* was finally loaded. As the Marines were served their final supper at Brooklyn, a buzz spread through the battalion.

Outside the mess hall, a crowd of thousands of well-wishers cheered as the Marines formed into six companies of 103 men and three officers each. Suddenly Lieutenant Colonel Huntington cantered onto the parade ground astride a magnificent black steed, followed by the Navy yard band blaring "Dixie." A reporter captured the scene: "The excitement by this time was intense, and when the color sergeant emerged from the barracks bearing the stars and stripes [sic] and the band played 'The Star-Spangled Banner' the soldiers and spectators cheered frantically."

At six o'clock, the battalion stepped off and marched through the yard's brick-columned main gate onto Flushing Avenue. The men strutted past Admiral's Row, a stretch of stately brick mansions that housed the highest-ranking naval officers and their families, and then wheeled back into the yard through the east gate. They marched past the three-story brick-and-stone machine shop, where two thousand men were overhauling ship engines and fashioning armor from steel plates. They trooped by a foundry and past the dry dock where the warship *San Francisco* was undergoing final combat preparations. As Navy yard mechanics, craftsmen, stevedores and sailors shouted, "Good luck!" and "Remember the *Maine!*" the column finally halted at the coal dock where the *Panther* now rode low in the water. The Marines formed into two lines and began boarding.

Shortly after eight o'clock, more than six hundred enlisted men, twenty-one officers and one surgeon were on board, their gear and supplies stashed below. Huntington strode up the gangplank, and the hawsers were cast off. The Marines lined the rails, shouting and waving their final good-byes. Cries echoed from crowds along the East River, and as the *Panther* slowly swung around in the fading twilight, boats in the bay tooted their whistles, and ferryboat passengers waved their hats. Among the ships the *Panther* passed as it threaded its way clear of the Navy yard were a pair of barges, the *Lone Star* and the *Shark*. They had arrived at the beginning of the week from Havana, loaded with forty tons of scorched and bloodstained wreckage from the battleship *Maine*.[26]

CHAPTER 2

"He Is No Tender Chicken"

As Huntington's Marines steamed down the Atlantic coast on the morning of Saturday, April 23, 1898, one of the happiest men in Washington, D.C., was laboring away in his second-floor office across the street from the White House.[1] Over the past year, his drooping mustache, flashing white teeth and thick spectacles had become instantly recognizable to occupants of the ornate building that housed the nation's foreign policy and national security apparatus. So had the restless energy, the rapid-fire voice and the right fist pounded into the left palm to punctuate a point. Love him or hate him, as many in Washington already did, an encounter with Assistant Secretary of the Navy Theodore Roosevelt was not soon forgotten.

The sprawling State, War, and Navy Building where he worked filled fifteen acres of prime real estate in the heart of the nation's capital. A monument to French Second Empire architecture, it had taken $10 million and seventeen years to build and was already out of style by the time it was completed in 1888. From his house on Lafayette Square, writer and resident capital crank Henry Adams, the progeny of two U.S. presidents, had scorned the rising monstrosity as an "architectural infant asylum," and the writer Mark Twain would deride it as "the ugliest building in America."[2]

Yet its European-style ostentation, price tag and vast dimensions—553 rooms, 151 fireplaces, 1.73 miles of corridors—in a perverse way symbolized America's growing wealth and global importance.[3]

In just one year Roosevelt had left an indelible mark on the building and the nation. He had become so critical to the shaping of naval policy that it was easy to forget that he had barely gotten the job.

President McKinley had followed Roosevelt's headline-grabbing work during the preceding decade on the U.S. Civil Service Commission and the New York City police board, and knew of his acclaim as a fearless reformer. But the president also saw Roosevelt as combative and self-righteous, a man who relished conflict and upsetting the status quo— useful qualities in a hard-fought political campaign, but not in the Cabinet Room. Of equal concern were Roosevelt's strident views on naval expansion, intervention in Cuba and annexation of the Hawaiian Islands—bold policy positions that the cautious McKinley had yet to embrace.

When first approached by Massachusetts Senator Henry Cabot Lodge in late November 1896 about appointing Roosevelt to the assistant secretary position, McKinley had responded warily, "I hope he has no preconceived plans which he would wish to drive through the moment he got in." A few days later, the president also conveyed reservations when a wealthy Ohio supporter made a case for Roosevelt's appointment. "I want peace, and I am told that your friend Theodore . . . is always getting into rows with everybody."[4]

Undeterred, Lodge mobilized powerful Republicans and McKinley's appointee for Navy secretary, former Massachusetts Governor John D. Long, to lobby on Roosevelt's behalf. After four months of pressure, McKinley acquiesced.

Theodore Roosevelt was thirty-eight years old when he took office on April 19, 1897.

Now, a year later, looking out on the White House South Lawn in its spring glory, Roosevelt savored his success. At that very moment, ships of the North Atlantic Squadron were about to blockade Cuba, the first step toward the invasion that Roosevelt had helped plan. Across the street in the White House, McKinley was preparing a call for 125,000 volunteers to supplement the 28,000-soldier Regular Army, further recognition that war was at hand.

Roosevelt had already secured from McKinley and Secretary of War Russell Alger the promise of an Army commission so he might fulfill his ambition of leading men into battle. He planned to raise a hybrid regiment of Harvard chums, hunting buddies and frontier characters he had befriended in a brief life as a Dakota rancher.

If these were his final days in Washington, none could have been finer. In a few weeks, heat and humidity would smother the city like a wet wool blanket. But for now, bird songs mingled in the balmy air with the scents of magnolias, dogwoods and azaleas, and Roosevelt basked in the brilliant hues of nature and the exhilarating possibilities of war.

No one had done more to persuade McKinley that a war against Spain was not only moral but necessary. And no one had done more to prepare the nation for victory. In every sense, this would be Theodore Roosevelt's war.

THERE WAS NOTHING WARLIKE, AND certainly no hint of future greatness, about the baby boy whom Martha Bulloch Roosevelt delivered in a three-story brownstone on New York City's East Twentieth Street on October 27, 1858. Martha had grown up in northern Georgia in a wealthy slave-owning family and had married well in all respects, save for her husband's embarrassing Yankee roots. Tall, handsome and athletic, the elder Theodore Roosevelt was one of five surviving sons of a millionaire New York City merchant who had made a fortune buying distressed Manhattan properties during the financial panic of 1837.

Thee and Mittie Roosevelt, as they were known to family and friends, lavished love and attention on their baby. He would need it. Theodore Junior—better known as Teedie—was a sickly child. His feeble physical appearance and generally poor health combined to create the challenge that would define his childhood and, indeed, the rest of his life: confronting and conquering fear. He was fair-headed, pale and frail, with oversize teeth and nearsighted blue eyes. Terrifying episodes of asthma plagued his early boyhood. He would wake up gasping for air, as though he were drowning in his bed. He also suffered from bouts of nervous diarrhea.[5]

From an early age, Roosevelt escaped his fear and frailties by reading. He devoured tales about Washington's ragged army at Valley Forge, other great soldiers and sailors who saved the Union, and the frontiersmen and explorers who conquered the North American continent and claimed America's "manifest destiny." Slowly, Roosevelt formed a mental picture of the man—strong, fearless, indomitable—he wished to become.[6]

As Theodore headed off to Harvard in 1876, America was celebrating its centennial and contemplating its place in the world. Unification movements had created the modern states of Germany and Italy, and they had joined Britain in a scramble for colonial possessions that provided raw materials and markets for finished goods. The United States, by contrast, was just completing its western expansion and had yet to realize the potential that would eventually propel it to world economic preeminence.

The 1880s brought a growing fear in some quarters that America could no longer cede to Europe the quest for overseas colonies if it were to continue its economic rise. At the same time, a virulent belief in Anglo-Saxon superiority was bursting forth from leading universities and churches, imbuing many with a sense of global mission. The philosophy was framed by Harvard Professor John Fiske's popular 1885 lecture on America's manifest destiny, and social evangelist Reverend Josiah Strong's 1885 book, *Our Country*, which proclaimed a sacred American duty to civilize and Christianize inferior peoples.[7]

Both of these quests—accessing distant foreign markets and exerting moral influence around the globe—hinged on control of the high seas, the reasoning went. And that required building a powerful navy that could ply the oceans without challenge, and establishing far-flung coaling stations to fuel and support such a fleet.

Roosevelt, who had taken up a dual career as a Republican politician and historian after Harvard, needed no persuading. His interest in the Navy went beyond political ambition: He had an inherited love of ships. His uncle James Bulloch, a Georgian, oversaw construction of the legendary Confederate raider *Alabama* during the Civil War. When he was a boy, Roosevelt recalled, his mother had talked to him "about ships, ships, ships and fighting of ships, till they sank into the depths of my soul."[8] While a senior at Harvard, Roosevelt began his first book, *The Naval War of 1812,* a marriage of his love of naval affairs and writing. He completed it not long after graduation, at age twenty-three.

Roosevelt presented the War of 1812 as an object lesson in the dangers of naval weakness, arguing that America's deficiencies on that score had emboldened Britain to bully the fledgling United States. His assertion was a provocative one at a particularly relevant moment. The U.S. Navy was then in a decline so dramatic that Admiral David Dixon Porter likened its collection of decrepit sailing ships and rusty ironclad monitors to "ancient Chinese forts on which dragons have been painted to frighten away the enemy."[9]

By 1885, a bald and cranky Navy captain named Alfred Thayer Mahan had taken over as the country's preeminent authority on the value of strong navies. An abysmal sea officer, Mahan found his calling as a lecturer in naval history and tactics at the Naval War College in Newport, Rhode Island. Speaking at the college in 1887, Roosevelt met Mahan and they became fast friends.

Two years later, Secretary of the Navy Benjamin Franklin Tracy finally gave shape to arguments being made by Mahan, Roosevelt and others, and called for construction of twenty first-class battleships to spearhead an entirely new, aggressive naval capability. Within months, a Navy policy board trumped that, urging construction of a battleship fleet with a range of fifteen thousand miles, enough to project U.S. naval power to any corner of the globe. But Congress was still under the sway of isolationists. It approved funds to build a mere three new warships that would match Europe's best in every facet but range.[10]

Still, the United States was serving notice: No longer would European primacy in world affairs go unchallenged.

FOR YEARS, MAHAN HAD BEEN laboring on a book that he hoped would make Americans see the need for a world-class navy. The result, *The Influence of Seapower Upon History, 1660–1783,* finally appeared in 1890. The timing was perfect. Despite its dry, academic title, the book became a bestseller, buoyed by a glowing review by Roosevelt in the October *Atlantic Monthly*. The very next month, the Navy's first armored cruiser, the USS *Maine*, one of two new ships previously authorized by Congress, was launched at the Brooklyn Navy Yard. Feverish preparations were undertaken to make that event a showcase for the country's growing "new" Navy.

On November 18, some fifteen thousand people crowded into the yard. Steel tycoon Andrew Carnegie was all smiles—his mills had turned out steel plates used in the *Maine,* and he stood to profit even more from the next ships under construction. Marines paraded in full dress uniform, while admirals and generals mingled with U.S. senators and representatives, Cabinet members, judges and ministers. Crimson-coated musicians played patriotic tunes; drums pounded; bugles blared. Civilian men in dark suits and derbies, bowlers and top hats escorted women in Sunday finery.

Finally the speeches were finished and a saw cut the last wooden restraint. On the bunting-draped platform beside the *Maine*'s bow, the sixteen-year-old granddaughter of Navy Secretary Tracy took her cue. Swinging a bottle of champagne secured to her wrist by ribbons, she called out in a clear voice, "I christen thee *Maine*," and smashed glass against steel. As champagne sprayed, the $2.5 million ship slowly slid stern-first down a track greased with five thousand pounds of tallow, soap and oil. The crowd roared. Three minutes later, cheers again rose as 6,682 tons of steel and national pride settled into the East River.[11]

Throughout the afternoon, until the last shafts of daylight faded, thousands of admirers sauntered on her decks. They marveled at her eleven-inch belt of steel armor, her enormous guns that could sink an enemy ship three miles away, her electric lights and telephones, but, most of all, at the pride and power that she embodied. "When she is finally put in commission, she will be the most thoroughly American vessel in the Navy," the *New York Times* rhapsodized. "Her materials of construction are the products of American soil, American furnaces, and American rolling mills, and last, but not least, she was built in an American navy yard."[12]

The expansion of naval power and an aggressive foreign policy were largely Republican issues, and in its 1892 election platform, the party specifically endorsed "the achievement of the manifest destiny of the Republic in the broadest sense." But that failed to fire the public imagination, and voters sent Democrat Grover Cleveland to the White House and a Democratic majority to Congress.

In mid-January, with the transfer of power to the Democrats less than seven weeks off, the mood of Washington's expansionists couldn't have been gloomier. But then, in the distant Hawaiian islands, Marines and Navy sailors marched ashore on a proclaimed mission to protect American lives and property. For a moment it looked like America was going to get into the colonization race after all.

Hawaii's fertile soil and location in the middle of the Pacific Ocean had long ago attracted U.S. pineapple and sugar growers, traders and missionaries, and in recent years acquiring the islands had become a passion of many manifest destiny advocates.

On January 14, Hawaii's Queen Liliuokalani attempted to curb the power of U.S. commercial interests in the kingdom's legislature by promulgating a new constitution. A thirteen-member coalition of Americans called the Committee of Safety angrily resisted. Two members, Judge Sanford Dole and businessman Lorrin Thurston, met secretly with U.S. envoy John Stevens and plotted to overthrow the monarchy.[13] The committee's armed militia promptly seized key buildings, triggering the landing of American troops. The group set up an ad hoc government headed by Dole "until terms of union with the United States of America have been negotiated and agreed upon." Queen Liliuokalani yielded—not to Dole's government but to "the superior force of the United States of America."

Representatives of the committee hurried to Washington to seek annexation while the lame-duck Republican administration was still in office. But time ran out. Incoming Democratic President Cleveland promptly killed their proposal and condemned the "lawless landing of the United States forces at Honolulu."

Roosevelt denounced Cleveland for a "base betrayal of our interests abroad." Still, the Hawaii experience would prove to be a milestone, galvanizing the expansionists and putting Roosevelt in the vanguard.

"I am a bit of a believer in the manifest destiny doctrine," he wrote to a fellow Republican at the time. "I believe in more ships; I believe in ultimately driving every European power off of this continent, and I don't want to see our flag hauled down where it has been hauled up."[14]

That summer, years of reckless financial practices exploded into a severe depression. Stock prices plunged, banks and businesses failed, unemployment soared into double digits and strikes and social unrest flared. For Roosevelt, Lodge and their friends, the crisis provided more grist for their argument that the nation's future prosperity and stability depended on acquiring foreign possessions. They continued stirring the pot.

In the March 1895 *North American Review,* Lodge wrote, "The great nations are rapidly absorbing for their future expansion and their present defense all the waste places of the earth," and worried that the United States was being cut out. Roosevelt hammered away on Hawaii. "I feel that it was a crime not only against the United States, but against the white race, that we did not annex Hawaii three years ago," he told the Republican Club of Massachusetts that October.[15]

The renewal of the Cuban independence movement's guerrilla war against Spain in early 1895 spurred Roosevelt to even greater rhetorical heights. He decried "the unintelligent, cowardly chatter for 'peace at any price'" that existed at institutions like Harvard, and fretted that such beliefs would produce "a flabby, timid type of character, which eats away the great fighting features of our race."

To one ally, he wrote: "The clamor of the peace faction has convinced me that this country needs a war."[16]

The presidential campaign of 1896 could not have come at a more propitious moment. Roosevelt concluded that he had accomplished all he could as New York City police commissioner. He yearned to perform on a larger stage, shaping national policy. His public image as one of the Republican Party's brightest and boldest personalities might present him with just such an opportunity, if the GOP could win in November.

The party strategy called for their bland, plainspoken candidate, Ohio Governor William McKinley, to remain above the fray at his home in Canton, Ohio, where he would deliver occasional speeches from his front porch. Railroad owners would facilitate the plan, providing free passage to supporters and undecided voters who wanted to make the pilgrimage.

The work of tearing down McKinley's oratorically gifted Democratic opponent, William Jennings Bryan, fell to a pack of Republican surrogates that included Roosevelt. Embracing his role as attack dog, Roosevelt painted Bryan and his supporters as socialists and anarchists who would plunge the United States into bloody class war, mob violence, sectional strife and economic chaos.[17] Bryan's early lead crumbled under the relentless attack, and the Republicans retook the White House in a landslide victory.

Roosevelt emerged with soaring national stature and a pile of favorable press clippings. An *Omaha World-Herald* profile, reprinted in the *New York Times,* portrayed Roosevelt as a courageous corruption fighter who embodied the frontiersman qualities that had fueled America's rise. "Roosevelt cannot see a dozen yards away without his eyeglasses, but he can do some fancy shooting that would win applause in a Wild West Show," the story gushed. He was an expert horseman, "a good man at wrestling," and "handy with the gloves," having proven to some of the biggest cowboys he crossed during his ranching days "that he is no tender chicken."[18]

UPON TAKING HIS PLACE IN the new Republican administration, Roosevelt was delighted to find he had plenty of running room. A man of limited stamina, Secretary Long frequently left the office in the hands of his eager assistant. Long also showed little interest in the intricacies of naval policy and technical questions—opening yet another door to his understudy. What Roosevelt did not know he quickly learned.

And just as the reluctant McKinley had feared, Roosevelt wasted no time in using his new job as a strategic berth from which to pursue his own agenda.

In his first week, he wrote a memo advising the president in impressive detail on the disposition and possible deployment of ships in response to a Mediterranean crisis. Roosevelt also managed to work four warnings on Cuba into those six hundred words—an opening salvo in what would become a yearlong campaign to convince McKinley and Long of the need to confront Spain in the Caribbean.

During his second week, he wrote an extraordinary letter to his friend Alfred Mahan that listed three actions he hoped to persuade McKinley to take: annex Hawaii, construct a canal across Central America and add a dozen battleships to the Navy's fleet. "I earnestly hope we can make the president look at things our way," he wrote.[19]

Behind the scenes, Roosevelt was equally assertive. "Yesterday I urged immediate action by the President as regards Hawaii," Roosevelt reported to Mahan on June 9.[20] One week later, McKinley sent Congress a newly negotiated treaty that finally would make Hawaii a U.S. territory. (Much to Roosevelt's disgust, it took Congress fourteen months to approve it.)

Roosevelt also delivered his first public address that month at the Naval War College, causing a national sensation. In describing America's destiny as a great global power, the new assistant secretary of the Navy used the word "war" sixty-two times. "No triumph of peace is quite so great as the supreme triumphs of war," Roosevelt declared in one of the defining lines.[21]

At the end of June, Roosevelt informed President McKinley that the Navy Department's updated war plan was ready. Its centerpiece was the liberation of Cuba, and it envisioned the Caribbean as the primary theater of action. But the plan also had an intriguing new provision: It called for an attack on Spain's colonial pearl in the Pacific, the Philippine Islands. The blueprint did not envision permanent occupation of Cuba, but left that question open with regard to the Philippines.

With his family still in New York during these hectic first months, Roosevelt spent considerable time at Washington's most exclusive gathering place, the stylish Metropolitan Club, where he took most meals and actively cultivated new friends. The capital's growing circle of expansionists regularly met at the club to vent their frustrations and plot strategy over lamb chops, steaks, cigars and brandy. It was an august group, but within weeks Roosevelt emerged as their undisputed leader. His voice and physique did not impress, and he lacked the battlefield feats or political triumphs that distinguished several others. But the force of his personality and convictions was unmatched. Roosevelt exuded "the inexorable coming of change," wrote one of his Metropolitan Club lunch guests, Kansas newspaper editor William Allen White, "and the passing of the old into the new."[22]

AT THE START OF AUGUST, Navy Secretary Long departed Washington for an extended summer holiday in New England. Dubbing himself the "hot weather secretary," Roosevelt roared through the department like a typhoon, issuing reports, inspecting battleships, clearing production bottlenecks. "The Secretary is away, and I am having immense fun running the Navy," he exulted to a friend.[23] He tackled red tape, unfilled positions and feuding bureaus. (He also found time to speak and write on other subjects, including an *Atlantic Monthly* article called "The Liquor Business in Politics.") "The liveliest spot in Washington at present is the Navy Department," observed the *New York Sun*.[24]

In early September, Roosevelt also left Washington—not for a vacation but for three days off the Virginia Capes with the North Atlantic Squadron. He reveled in the gunnery practice of the USS *Iowa*, the Navy's newest and biggest battleship. "Oh, Lord! If only the people who are ignorant about our Navy could see those great warships in all their majesty and beauty, and could realize how well they are handled, and how well fitted to uphold the honor of America, I don't think we would encounter such opposition in building up the Navy to its proper standard," he wrote a friend.[25]

Still, as 1897 drew to a close, McKinley seemed no closer to authorizing the intervention in Cuba that Roosevelt advocated. As the president continued to resist demands for war, Roosevelt grew more frustrated. "His weakness and vacillation are even more ludicrous than painful," he groused to his diary. Cabinet meetings, private encounters with McKinley, even White House social events became his platforms.[26] "The blood of the Cubans, the blood of women and children who have perished by the hundred thousand in hideous misery, lies at our door," he raged at one Cabinet meeting.[27]

By March, McKinley had stopped inviting Roosevelt to the White House.

Finally, worn down by a rising tide of public opinion if not Roosevelt rants, McKinley notified Congress of his willingness to go to war. At three o'clock on the morning of April 19, Congress passed a resolution calling for U.S. intervention to secure Cuban independence. It was one year to the day since Roosevelt had taken office as Assistant Secretary of the Navy.

FOUR DAYS LATER, AS MCKINLEY called for volunteers to fight against Spain, Roosevelt hurried through the tiled corridors of the State, Navy, and War Building and entered the frescoed offices of Secretary of War Russell Alger. McKinley's announcement had included an unusual provision for three regiments "to be composed exclusively of frontiersmen possessing special qualifications as horsemen and marksmen." A wealthy Michigan lumber baron in civilian life, the silver-goateed Alger knew something about soldiering. He had fought in more than sixty Civil War engagements, including Gettysburg. Now, sitting across from his desk was the nation's most celebrated frontiersman, the man who had done more than anyone to bring about the war with Spain. Alger offered command of the inaugural regiment to Theodore Roosevelt.[28]

CHAPTER 3

——————

America's Marine

On the eve of America's first foreign war in half a century, Captain Littleton Waller had already accomplished much in his career as a United States Marine. He had sailed distant seas aboard U.S. warships and left his footprints on the shores of five continents. He had saved damsels in distress and protected U.S. businessmen from bloodthirsty mobs. He had savored the pleasures of exotic ports, hunted wild boar in the hills of Morocco, and dined with Russian nobility. He had even argued, and won, a case before the United States Supreme Court.

Only forty-one, Tony Waller wanted more.

Brave and bold, Waller pulsed with pent-up energy and ambition. He had been born with a sense of destiny, the son of slaveholding Virginia aristocrats whose families evoked Old Dominion power and privilege. Although he had spurned college for a career in the Marines, his reports and letters as a Marine officer, handwritten in fine cursive, reflected literary influences that ranged from the Bible to Shakespeare.[1]

Waller stood only five feet, four inches in height, but his perfect military posture and commanding presence made him seem taller, and he exuded the confidence of a born leader. He wore his hat at a rakish angle, and removed it with a flourish. He was magnificent on horseback, and deadly with a rifle. He was equally skilled in the social graces. He was a splendid raconteur and vocalist, and it is easy to imagine his brown eyes twinkling and ruddy cheeks glowing as he spun stories around the campfire and raised his rich baritone in song.[2]

Waller could be vain, boastful and self-absorbed. He could also be charming, gracious and kind. He was a capable and dedicated officer, willing to sleep on the ground and share other hardships with his Marines in the field. He was demanding, yet earned the loyalty and confidence of his men—even as his weakness for alcohol threatened to wreck his career.[3]

For all his human frailties, for better or worse, Waller was poised to become the face of the modern Marine Corps, the cutting edge of America's unleashed global ambitions.

"I can see him, straight as a ruler, his head thrown back, his enormous nose outlined against the sky as he saluted the flag," remembered legendary Marine Smedley Butler. "Waller may have liked to talk about himself, but he had plenty to talk about."[4]

LITTLETON WALLER TAZEWELL WALLER WAS born on a York County plantation in Tidewater Virginia, on September 26, 1856, the third surviving child of Matthew Page Waller and Mary Tazewell Waller. From his great-great-grandfather Colonel John Waller, an immigrant from England in the late 1600s, Tony Waller could trace a long line of lawyers, judges, doctors and public servants—men of respected professions who managed their tobacco plantations, slaves and other investments on the side. His namesake and maternal grandfather, Littleton Waller Tazewell, was a renowned lawyer, former Virginia governor and U.S. senator who advised presidents and counseled Thomas Jefferson during the Sage of Monticello's sunset years.[5]

Waller's parents were third cousins, which accounted for the repetitious and somewhat confusing formal name they gave their child. Matt Waller was a practicing medical doctor in Williamsburg and a gentleman farmer who spent weekends and holidays on his tobacco plantation outside of town. For little Tony and his brothers, that plantation on the swampy peninsula bounded by the James and York rivers was an endless playground, with its creeks for fishing, forests full of wildlife, horses to ride and boats to sail.

When Tony was about four, Matt and Mary Waller moved their growing brood into Norfolk, the port city off Chesapeake Bay. The family settled into a house at 92 Granby Street, a stone's throw from grandfather Littleton Tazewell's two-story Georgian mansion.

For Tony and his brothers, city life curtailed the outdoor pursuits they had enjoyed on the plantation, but held its own attractions. Norfolk's waterfront was a window into an exotic world beyond America's shores. The boys could watch stevedores offloading crates of tea from China, hides and nuts from South America, sugar and rum from the West Indies and manufactured goods from Europe. From shore, they could track the comings and goings of barks and brigs, clippers and schooners, sloops, frigates, paddle wheelers and tugs.[6]

After the first shots at Fort Sumter in April 1861, troops from around the South poured into the city to guard the sea approach to the Confederate capital in Richmond. Overnight, young Tony's world became a thrilling pageant of military drills and parades, colorfully uniformed soldiers, gleaming rifles and swords, blaring bugles and pounding drums.[7]

As the first year of war drew to a close, tragedy struck the family. Matt Waller fell ill, probably with typhoid, and died two weeks before Christmas 1861 at the age of thirty-eight.[8] Mary Waller held the family together through the remainder of the war, including three years of Union occupation. By the time General Lee surrendered at Appomattox Court House in April 1865, Virginia's countryside and economy lay in ruins, and the wealth and power of the Wallers and other plantation families were forever diminished.

Fifteen years of peace found Tony Waller at a personal crossroads in the spring of 1880. He was still living on Granby Street with his mother and siblings, unmarried and employed as a clerk in a Norfolk business. Uninspired by medicine, law or business, Waller at age twenty-three began to contemplate a soldier's life. It was a logical choice. Even before the war, boys who grew up on the adventure tales of James Fenimore Cooper and other popular writers harbored dreams of chivalrous deeds and battlefield glory. During and after the war, young Southern men like

Tony Waller drew inspiration from the flesh-and-blood stories of Confederate heroes like Robert E. Lee and cavalryman James Ewell Brown Stuart. (Waller's younger brother, Robert, would later marry "Jeb" Stuart's only daughter.) Waller was an expert marksman and magnificent horseman, and no doubt would have made a superb cavalryman. Unfortunately, at five-foot-four, Waller fell one inch shy of the U.S. Cavalry's minimum height requirement.

He turned instead to the Marine Corps. A commission was secured, and on June 26, 1880, during a ceremony at the United States Marine Corps headquarters in Washington, D.C., Waller swore his oath as a second lieutenant.[9]

On land and sea, American Marines had claimed their share of glory since first seeing action in the Revolutionary War. Marines had defended American honor against North African pirates, bullying British sailors, rebellious Indian tribes and various other offenders in distant lands. In 1848, Marines had hoisted the flag over Chapultepec Castle ("the halls of Montezuma") in the climactic battle of the Mexican War. But the Civil War had stripped the Corps of much of its talent, as well as its honor. During the conflict's darkest days, senior commanders had refused to leave their desks, insisting that they were administrators, not warriors. Political patronage and nepotism had created unseemly bickering among officers. In one all too typical incident, two lieutenant colonels waged a bitter feud over the services of a prized carpenter that each wanted to be assigned to his barracks. Later one of the same officers was sacked for misusing bounty money designated for new recruits.

In the decades following the Civil War, the United States had focused its wealth and energy on settling the vast Western frontier. Congress slashed Army and Navy spending, and the tiny Marine Corps—sparingly funded during the best of times—slowly withered. The ranks were rife with alcoholism, gambling and corruption. Desertions soared. So rare were promotions and so ruthless was the competition to earn them that officers regularly initiated courts-martial against one another, alleging petty transgressions. Some members of Congress openly questioned whether the Corps' role of guarding Navy yards and policing Navy ships was worth the expense of maintaining a separate force. So desperate were the Marines to prove their worth that in the aftermath of Custer's debacle at the Little Bighorn in 1876, the Marine Corps commandant offered his men for service against the Plains Indians. The War Department declined.

Around the same time, a group of young Marine officers at the United States Naval Academy in Annapolis, Maryland, had launched a last-ditch effort to save the Corps. One of the leaders, First Lieutenant Henry Clay Cochrane, summarized the plan in a pamphlet for fellow officers. With typical candor, the former schoolteacher from Chester, Pennsylvania, excoriated the Corps as "a parasite on the body of government" and "a barnacle on the hull of the Navy." He then laid out twenty-five reforms to make the Marines "respectable and useful," including more rapid promotions based on merit, more tactical training, discharges for incompetence and disability and an end to drunkenness. It was time for either "a funeral or resuscitation," he concluded.[10]

Cochrane's proposals went too far for Marine conservatives and cost too much for Congress. By the end of the decade, the Marines' budget had been cut by a third, its number of officers slashed from ninety to seventy-eight and its enlisted ranks capped at fifteen hundred.

This was the Marine Corps that Tony Waller entered in the summer of 1880.

THE SUMMER OF 1882 FOUND Second Lieutenant Waller aboard the USS *Lancaster*, sailing the Mediterranean Sea under the tutelage of now-Captain Henry Clay Cochrane. As flagship of the Navy's European Squadron, the *Lancaster* was expected to roam northern Europe, western Africa and states along the Mediterranean, promoting good relations while protecting American commercial interests. For Waller, the cruise was an immersion in the life of a shipboard Marine officer, which, in peacetime, meant more drudgery than adventure—endless drills followed by lavish banquets and shore leaves during frequent port calls. By May, Waller had proved himself sufficiently to earn command of the Marine detachment aboard one of the squadron's gunboats, the *Nipsic*.

The following month, the U.S. fleet was ordered to Egypt, where res-
tive Muslims had risen in challenge to British rule. The arrival of a British
fleet in late May had further inflamed local passions, and on June 11, an
angry mob that included bedouin tribesmen who had poured into the city
from their outlying camps rampaged through the streets, killing scores of
Europeans.[11]

The American fleet, arriving piecemeal off Alexandria in late June
and early July, found the British in a tense standoff with a rebellious
Muslim army. Warships from Russia, Austria, Germany, Prussia, Spain,
Greece, Italy, Holland, Turkey and other countries lay about, watching
the drama play out. The British fleet opened fire on the morning of July 11,
and over the next twenty-four hours hurled more than sixteen thousand shells onto the Egyptian forts and city. As darkness fell, fires illuminated the city and a new wave of looting and killing swept the European
Quarter.

Three days later smoke was still boiling into the sky when Tony Waller
went ashore with a contingent of 132 U.S. Marines and sailors. The
native army had withdrawn outside the city walls, but looters and bandits
still roamed the rubble-strewn streets. Sporadic gunshots sounded as the
Marines advanced cautiously through the flames and smoke, past dead
bodies and the contents of shops and homes scattered by fleeing looters.
The Marines finally made their way to the Grand Square of Mehmet Ali,
in the city center, and raised the Stars and Stripes over the battered
American consulate.[12]

Over the next few days, Waller proved his mettle amid the danger and
chaos of Alexandria. He helped rescue several Greek women trapped in
a flaming hospital by rigging rope ladders from bedsheets, and led a
company of Marines through the perilous streets to save fifteen thousand
rounds of rifle cartridges from a burning warehouse. When flames threatened to drive the Marines from their stronghold on the grand square,
Waller and his men saved the day by blowing up surrounding buildings
with gunpowder. In a savvy public relations move, the Marines also provided an armed escort for reporters eager to return to their ships to file
their stories.[13] On another occasion, reports that native forces were poised

to overrun the city sent French and Italian marines scurrying back to their ships. But Waller and his men dug in for a fight. The attack never came, but the Americans earned the praise and gratitude of British commanders and the British press.

Once British reinforcements secured Alexandria, Waller and most of the Marines returned to their ships, and the American fleet soon withdrew. But the *Nipsic* revisited in early September, in time for Waller to witness the victorious conclusion of the British offensive. The experience provided Waller with storytelling grist for the rest of his days, and it also schooled him in the hard ways of total war. When Arab forces decapitated captured British Bengali cavalrymen and displayed their heads on lances, the British began summarily executing enemy captives. Years later, Waller would cite the British actions at Alexandria as justification for his own harsh treatment of enemy prisoners.[14]

BY THE LATE SUMMER OF 1883, Waller had been at sea for two years. He had gotten a whiff of the excitement and peril of war, but for the most part it had been an educational and at times gloriously entertaining hitch—days and nights filled with banquets and luncheons, drunken celebrations, sightseeing, hunting expeditions and other pleasing pursuits.

He had earned good marks from his commander and mentor, Captain Cochrane, save for two blemishes on his record: an embarrassing (and painful) incident in Le Havre, France, when he shot himself in the hand during a drunken celebration; and another nasty (and probably alcohol-fueled) accident when he fell down a flight of stairs during a port call in Copenhagen, Denmark.[15] His initiation into the brotherhood of Marine officers complete, young Waller was ready to return home. In the summer of 1884, at his request, he was reassigned to the Marine barracks in Norfolk, Virginia.

WALLER NOW BEGAN A SLOW, methodical rise in the Marines. Sedentary shore assignments alternated with a series of overseas tours, mainly to

Central and South America. He found time to get married in 1885, and his Norfolk home would soon resound with the cries and laughter of three boys.

By the mid-1890s, Waller had crafted a reputation as a capable and aggressive field commander. He had also begun to win attention for his poise and skill in another arena, as a Marine judge advocate prosecuting cases in the military justice system. In April 1895, though untrained in the legal profession, Lieutenant Waller rose before the Supreme Court of the United States to argue the government's case against a Navy yard paymaster's clerk convicted of embezzlement. The clerk had won an appeal on the grounds that he should have been tried before a civilian court during peacetime. With hundreds of cases riding on the outcome, Waller eloquently laid out the argument for continued military court jurisdiction over military defendants, even in times of peace. Three weeks later, the justices ruled in Waller's favor. Praise rained down on him from the highest levels of the Navy and the Department of Justice, and a commendation was followed by a coveted assignment in the Navy Judge Advocate General's office in Washington.[16]

In September 1896, Waller celebrated his fortieth birthday. He recently had been promoted to captain and assigned to the USS *Indiana*, the first battleship in the Navy's growing arsenal of modern warships. His future as one of the most powerful men in the Marine Corps—perhaps even a future commandant of the corps—seemed secure.

That autumn, Waller was serving yet again as judge advocate in a controversial naval court of inquiry. In his prosecutorial sights this time was a Navy lieutenant commander accused by junior officers of despotic and capricious conduct. In court one day, Waller worked himself into a self-righteous fury at senior Navy Department officials who had reprimanded a junior officer for leveling the allegations against the senior commander. The acting secretary of the Navy (Theodore Roosevelt's Democratic predecessor) had used his power in a tyrannical, "repugnant" way, Waller railed—"a thing we could expect in an absolute monarchy." He likened the acting secretary to Britain's Charles I, who was deposed and beheaded in 1649 "for just that sort of thing."[17]

It was a reckless choice of words, and foolhardy, given that his insult was directed at a senior official in his military chain of command. This time, unlike his drunken accidents of the distant past, Waller's offense was too public, too personal, to go unpunished. On January 28, 1897, Secretary of the Navy H. A. Herbert formally reprimanded Waller and barred him from appearing before any naval court or board for one year.

WALLER'S BANISHMENT HAD ENDED ON the eve of the *Maine*'s destruction at Havana in February 1898. Two months later, when the American fleet was mobilized for combat against Spain, he headed off to war for the first time in his twenty-seven years as a Marine.

It was a fortuitous turn of events for Waller, for a war offered the prospect of redemption. Just like Theodore Roosevelt, Waller needed war to achieve his ambitions of glory and senior command.

Late on the afternoon of Friday, April 22, 1898, Spanish lookouts in Morro Castle at the mouth of Havana Harbor spotted wisps of black smoke on the horizon. A red lantern was hoisted, and three cannon blasts fired to sound the alarm: The American fleet was approaching.[18] Panic-stricken Havana residents braced for the bombardment that was sure to follow, but the ships of the U.S. Navy's North Atlantic Fleet dispersed in a formidable blockade line along Cuba's northern coast without firing a shot. Now searchlights stabbed the sultry air and patrol boats tacked through the darkness, on the prowl for blockade runners and Spanish warships.[19] Gentle waves slapped the steel hull of the battleship *Indiana*, and a feathery breeze carried faint scents from shore, the tropical tang of Cuba. Among the American naval officers and Marines aboard the *Indiana*, peering at the dark landmass that loomed in the half-light of a full moon and contemplating their destinies as warriors, was Marine Captain Tony Waller.

CHAPTER 4

Manila Bay

Off the Philippine island of Luzon, the cruiser USS *Olympia* steamed southward through glassy seas, eight other ships of the U.S. Asiatic Squadron fanned out in her wake. Only five years old, the steel-hulled *Olympia* was one of the Navy's elite warships, bristling with rapid-fire cannon and machine guns, and crowned with the latest long-range guns set in armored turrets and barbettes. She weighed more than five thousand tons, nearly as much as a battleship, yet her powerful twin engines could drive her through the water at a remarkable twenty-two knots.[1]

Finished originally in gleaming peacetime white and buff, like other U.S. warships the *Olympia* was now flat gray, a sober reminder of the job ahead. On board in a wood-paneled stateroom, Commodore George Dewey, squadron commander, anxiously awaited the arrival of the captains he had summoned to his flagship from the trailing fleet.[2] He was about to launch America's first foreign war in half a century.

The sixty-year-old Dewey seemed an unlikely choice to strike the first blow against Spain. Only three years from retirement after forty years of duty, he had logged an unremarkable career since graduating from the Naval Academy in 1858. He remained trim and fit, but his graying hair signaled his age—and the approaching end of a career. Over the years,

38

Dewey had impressed his peers as a capable officer, but hardly the equal of great naval warriors like John Paul Jones or David Farragut. Genial and averse to controversy, he lacked obvious fighting qualities. Before taking command of the Asiatic Squadron four months earlier, he had not been to sea in eight years.

But now, as evening approached the Philippine coast, Dewey would waste no time in announcing his plan. "We shall enter Manila Bay tonight," he told the captains and their aides.[3]

As the meeting broke up, an officer approached Dewey and saluted. It was his nephew, Lieutenant William Winder from the cruiser *Baltimore*. Like many others, Winder was worried by nagging reports that the Spanish had seeded the entrance to Manila Bay with deadly mines. He proposed heading the column with a smaller craft to chart a safe path for the *Olympia* and the other big ships. Dewey did not have to be reminded about the ignominious place in naval history that awaited him should his flagship strike a mine or his entire fleet stall in a minefield without firing a shot. But he didn't waver.

"I've waited for sixty years for this opportunity," the commodore declared. "Mines or no mines, I am leading the squadron in myself."[4]

AS A YOUNG NAVAL ACADEMY graduate during the early years of the Civil War, Dewey had had the good fortune to serve under the Union's greatest admiral, David Farragut. In March 1863, in the campaign against Vicksburg, Dewey was aboard the USS *Mississippi* when it ran aground. Under punishing Confederate fire, he remained on deck long after the order to abandon ship, setting fires and spiking guns to render the immobilized sloop useless to the enemy. Finally jumping into the Mississippi River, he saw a wounded comrade struggling nearby. Dewey grabbed the sailor with one arm and a floating spar with the other, and as bullets whizzed overhead he paddled to safety.[5]

Dewey idolized Farragut, extolling him as the "ideal of the Naval officer, urbane, decisive, indomitable." Throughout his career, Dewey would later say, he applied a simple test in moments of crisis: What would Farragut do?[6]

For most of his post–Civil War life, Dewey had no opportunity to employ the Farragut test. Indeed, from the beginning of the 1880s through the eve of the war with Spain, he spent only four years at sea. His reputation was that of a skilled desk officer, not a sailor or fighter.

Dewey was at his best during those years as a denizen of the Washington social scene. Though only five-foot-six, he cut a dashing figure, with his expertly tailored white uniforms, trim physique and immaculate handlebar mustache. A widower, Dewey made no secret of his fondness for the company of pretty women. In one telling incident in 1893, Dewey was escorting two attractive ladies aboard a warship when he bumped into his college-sophomore son—and promptly introduced the youth as his younger brother.[7]

Dewey held a seat on the board of the capital's elite Metropolitan Club, where he spent leisurely lunch hours and evenings with friends, playing chess and pontificating on the day's events. Though pleasing company, he impressed few with his ideas or intellect. Indeed, at a time when the capital's strategic thinkers and naval strategists were locked in vigorous debate over the merits of a world-class navy and overseas expansion, his views remained something of a mystery.[8]

Suddenly in June 1896, a month after his promotion to commodore and with mandatory retirement looming, Dewey applied to become commander in chief of the Asiatic Squadron. On paper, he was a long shot. But he had learned well the value of connections. One of the new friends he had cultivated at the Metropolitan Club was Assistant Secretary of the Navy Theodore Roosevelt. The two often rode horseback together and shared meals and conversation at the club.

At some point Dewey may have intimated that he held views similar to Roosevelt on expansion and related topics—though nothing in his official or private communications confirms that. In any event, Roosevelt backed Dewey as his choice for the Asia post.[9]

When it appeared in late September that a more senior candidate was about to get the job, Roosevelt engineered an end run. With his boss, Navy Secretary Long, out of town, he dispatched Dewey to the office of Vermont's Senator Redfield Proctor. An old Dewey family friend and a man of reliable expansionist beliefs, Proctor also had President McKinley's

ear. He promptly headed to the White House. Long returned to Washington the following day to find a memo from the president on his desk
recommending Dewey. Roosevelt's man got the job.

A few weeks later, on the eve of Dewey's departure for Asia, his
friends feted him at the Metropolitan Club. Twenty-two places were set
with the finest china, and a collection of Washington's most powerful men
arrived to pay homage. After a sumptuous dinner, speeches and toasts,
Colonel Archibald Hopkins rose to read a poem composed for the occasion. The final stanza prophesied great achievements for Commodore
Dewey:

> And when he takes the homeward tack
> Beneath an Admiral's flag,
> We'll hail the day that brings him back
> And have another jag.[10]

———

On New Year's Day, 1898, Dewey boarded the *Olympia* in Japan's Nagasaki Harbor to take command of the United States' Asiatic Squadron.
The fleet consisted of a handful of ships that patrolled Asia's eastern rim,
their primary mission being the protection of Americans in the event of
riots or rebellions in the crumbling empires of China and Korea. It
boasted only two cruisers at that point: the *Olympia* and the *Boston,* the
latter noted for putting Marines ashore in Hawaii to help overthrow
Queen Liliuokalani in 1893.

The U.S. force paled in comparison to other powerful fleets already
operating in the area. Russia, Germany and a rising Japan were vying
for control of Korea and China, and the British and French were also angling
for greater influence. To Dewey, a mere bit player in the drama, an Asian
war of some sort seemed imminent. "Affairs are very unsettled here," he
wrote his son. "The Germans, English and Russians and Japanese are playing a big game of bluff since it remains to be seen who will take the pot."[11]

But at this moment, Spain was foremost in the minds of Dewey and
his Navy Department patron, Roosevelt. On February 11, with tensions
between the countries rising, Dewey departed Japan with the *Olympia* and

the gunboat *Concord,* headed for the British colony of Hong Kong. From there he could keep closer tabs on the Spanish fleet in Manila Bay, six hundred miles to the east. Shortly after arriving, Dewey received word that the battleship *Maine* had blown up in Havana Harbor. Ordering the *Olympia's* flags lowered to half-mast, he dusted off his charts and intelligence reports on the Philippines.

The mountainous, palm-studded islands had long been Spain's Pacific jewel, stretching a thousand miles across the South China Sea. Since Ferdinand Magellan's fatal layover in the Philippines in 1521, Spain had oppressed and plundered the archipelago, extracting timber, sugar, coconuts and hemp used in making high-quality rope and ship's riggings.

Navy planners had recognized the importance of the islands years earlier, as they began gaming possible conflicts for a more assertive United States. When in the mid-1890s unrest over Spanish misrule lit the fuse of revolution there, the Office of Naval Intelligence started polishing a more specific plan for a possible war with Spain. It called for a "purely naval war of blockades, bombardments, harassments, raiding on exposed colonies, and naval actions." Through the summer and fall of 1897, Assistant Secretary of the Navy Roosevelt advocated an even bolder role for the Asiatic Squadron: the seizure of Manila.[12]

On the morning of February 26, a coded telegram from Roosevelt in Washington was ferried out to the *Olympia* in Hong Kong Harbor. In urgent succession, it directed the commodore to consolidate his fleet in Hong Kong, take on coal, and prepare for war. "In the event of declaration of war [with] Spain," the telegram continued, "your duty will be to see that the Spanish squadron does not leave the Asiatic coast, and then offensive operations in Philippine Islands."[13] In a stroke of breathtaking audacity (and questionable authority), Theodore Roosevelt had just set in motion America's conquest of the Philippines.

DEWEY'S PREPARATIONS FOR WAR QUICKLY became the talk of Hong Kong. Spanish spies tracked his every move. So did a slight twenty-eight-year-old Asian man who had taken up residence in the colony several weeks earlier. Known in the Filipino community as *"el presidente"* or "*generalissimo,*" Emilio Aguinaldo y Famy had taken control of the tumultuous Philippine revolutionary movement that had launched a war against Spanish rule eighteen months earlier. As part of a peace agreement with Spanish authorities, Aguinaldo now was in exile in Hong Kong with nineteen trusted commanders and aides, waiting to see whether Spanish authorities introduced promised reforms in the Philippines.

Like the rebellion in Cuba, the armed revolt in the Philippines had grown out of more than 350 years of Spanish exploitation and misrule. In the 1860s and 1870s, a Filipino nationalist movement demanded equal rights with Spanish citizens, only to be crushed by authorities. In the 1880s, Filipino expatriates in Madrid and Barcelona renewed the cause, cranking out pamphlets, newspapers and magazines advocating equal rights back home. One of the writers, a young man named José Rizal, captured the plight of his countrymen in a pair of popular melodramatic novels that Spanish officials quickly banned as subversive. Returning from Europe in 1892, Rizal was exiled to the distant southern island of Mindanao, and an organization he founded—La Liga Filipina, or the Philippine League—was summarily outlawed.

It was too late to stifle the movement, however. One of those drawn to La Liga Filipina's first and only meeting was Andres Bonifacio, a self-educated Manila nationalist of working-class roots. He promptly founded a militant underground organization. By 1896, Bonifacio's supporters, known to native speakers as the Katipunan, were stockpiling weapons stolen from Spanish arsenals and sharpening spears and machetes. On August 29 of that year, Bonifacio launched a revolt in Manila. Thousands of Filipinos joined in, but the ragtag army was bloodied in a chaotic attack on a Spanish warehouse. In response, authorities accused Rizal of masterminding the uprising and executed him.[14]

The budding revolution that had been so long in coming once again seemed in peril. But hope was rekindled in the swampy jungles of Cavite province on Manila Bay's southern shore, where Emilio Aguinaldo and his rebel units scored a stunning series of victories against the Spanish army.[15] Aguinaldo, who was then mayor of his hometown, Cavite el Viejo, and best-known for his success in the family cattle business, had secretly been a member of the Katipunan over the preceding four years. When

Bonifacio declared war, the ambitious Aguinaldo swiftly took control of three towns, making himself the new hero of the struggle. By the following May, Aguinaldo had gained undisputed control of the revolution, and Bonifacio was dead, executed by his comrades after losing a power struggle with the newly elected *presidente*.[16]

The fall of 1897 found Aguinaldo and his faltering army hunkered down in the mountains and caves northeast of Manila, beyond the reach of Spanish forces. Their situation was dire, but Spain's was no better. The rebellion in Cuba was worsening, as were tensions with the United States. In an attempt to settle the Philippine conflict so it might focus on Cuba, Madrid opened peace talks. In December, Aguinaldo agreed to surrender his arms, renounce the rebellion and leave the Philippines. The Spanish governor-general, Fernando Primo de Rivera, agreed to pay him eight hundred thousand pesos and consider a list of demands, including parliamentary representation for Filipinos and curtailment of Catholic religious orders that controlled most of the land, exacted taxes and dominated daily life.

Two days after Christmas, Aguinaldo and his top aides left Luzon's Lingayen Gulf on a ship headed for Hong Kong. The revolutionary leader carried with him four hundred thousand pesos, half of the agreed Spanish payment. He deposited the money in a local bank and sat back to await Rivera's promised reforms back in the islands. By late February 1898, it was clear the bargain was unraveling. Aguinaldo tapped the bank account to buy arms and ordered his guerrilla forces in the Philippines to resume their war.

DEWEY, MEANWHILE, HAD BEGUN EXECUTING Roosevelt's directive to ready for war. Chief among his preparations was the collection of intelligence on Spanish defenses at Manila Bay and the status of Aguinaldo's on-again, off-again insurgency. The U.S. consul general in Manila, a balding fifty-four-year-old Republican political appointee from New York named Oscar Williams, threw himself into his role as America's eyes and ears. He began hiring agents and charming Spanish officials to glean details about troop strength, naval deployments and shore defenses. To confound prying Spanish eyes, he disguised his reports to Dewey as personal letters to one of the commodore's aides.[17]

By April, Manila seethed with unease and intrigue as Spain hurtled toward a showdown with the United States. A trickle of defections by native soldiers to the revolutionary cause was becoming a flood, and authorities imposed martial law. Ambulances carrying wounded and maimed soldiers rumbled through city streets. As Spanish officials increasingly resorted to harsh tactics, including the execution of prisoners, a growing sense of desperation gripped the colonial regime.[18]

No longer limiting his reports to Manila's defenses or the spreading insurgency, U.S. Consul General Williams began to advocate an ambitious agenda. "Daily the cry arises, 'if the U.S. or Great Britain would only have taken these islands, how happy we would be,'" he wrote Dewey. In fact, the insurgents "would gladly aid our fleet and submit to our flag," he asserted. "If I could command you and your fleet, I would capture every Spanish merchant and battleship and annex the islands before next Sunday."[19]

Dewey had launched his own initiative to find out what the insurgents wanted, ordering Captain Edward P. Wood, commander of the U.S. gunboat *Petrel*, to open a dialogue with Aguinaldo. A bearded forty-nine-year-old Ohioan, Wood promised the revolutionary leader American arms and advice. He also confided what was obvious to everyone in Hong Kong: Dewey was about to sail to Manila to attack the Spanish fleet. Intrigued, Aguinaldo pressed for a statement of American intentions: What exactly did the U.S. plan to do with the Philippines after Spain's defeat? "The United States, my general, is a great and rich nation," Wood soothingly replied, "and neither needs nor desires colonies."[20]

In late April, Aguinaldo received the same pledge from the ranking American diplomat in Singapore. An air of secrecy surrounded their nighttime rendezvous at an out-of-the-way pub in a suburb of the British colony. U.S. Consul General Spencer Pratt began the meeting with the dramatic announcement that the United States and Spain were now officially at war. "Now is the time for you to strike," he exhorted Aguinaldo. "Ally yourself with America and you will surely defeat the Spaniards!"[21]

Aguinaldo asked for a document spelling out the terms of a U.S.–Philippine alliance. Pratt demurred—only Commodore Dewey could sign such a paper, he said. But as Captain Wood had done earlier in Hong Kong, Pratt assured the Filipino that he need not fear American objectives. Indeed, he noted, Congress had just disavowed U.S. territorial interests in Cuba once the Spanish were defeated.

"As in Cuba," Pratt proclaimed, "so in the Philippines."

 The Filipino leader and the American diplomat shook hands.

 As Dewey steamed toward the Philippines, Aguinaldo prepared to return to the islands "and fight side by side with the Americans."[22]

IN THE PREDAWN HOURS OF Saturday, April 30, the *Olympia*'s lookout had made out Cape Bolinao on the northwest coast of Luzon, the main Philippine island. Dewey dispatched the cruiser *Boston* and the gunboat *Concord* ahead to scout Subic Bay for any sign of the Spanish fleet. Throughout the day, the squadron cautiously made its way south. "You cannot imagine the suspense we are in," Seaman Charles W. Julian recorded in his diary.[23] Finally, minutes after three p.m., the *Boston* and *Concord* appeared in the tropical haze. Signal flags flashed: no Spanish ships at Subic Bay.

On the bridge of the *Olympia*, Dewey could not conceal his relief, for he did not relish the prospect of combat in Subic's cramped confines.[24] Manila Bay, however, presented its own challenges. He would have to thread his way past antiquated muzzle-loading cannon on the island of Corregidor and nearby shores, and a handful of modern guns the Spaniards had placed on Caballo Island and a small rocky outcropping known as El Fraile. Even more worrisome was the threat of underwater mines in the bay's main entrance, Boca Grande. At a farewell banquet in Hong Kong, British officers had toasted Dewey and his men while privately predicting disaster for the Americans.[25]

At nine forty-five p.m., as the *Olympia* led the darkened American squadron through the muggy night, Dewey ordered his crews to quarters. The dark shape of the volcanic Bataan Peninsula now loomed off to port, faintly illuminated by a moon that hovered behind scudding clouds and distant lightning flashes. Anxious men dozed at their battle stations, cooled by passing showers.

Ten miles from the entrance to Manila Bay, a signal light flashed on

Corregidor, and a Spanish warning rocket soared into the night sky. The element of surprise had been lost, but Dewey did not flinch. Around eleven thirty p.m., he quietly gave an order, and the *Olympia* turned to port, into the Boca Grande channel.

The American flagship crept along at a sluggish eight knots, far below top speed, to allow the squadron's slow supply ships to keep pace. The night was calm and nearly windless, favorable to Spanish lookouts. Dewey and his men peered anxiously into the darkness, awaiting the explosion of a mine or the flash of a Spanish gun that would signal the beginning of a desperate fight.[26]

Seconds ticked by. Jagged El Fraile, with its lethal battery of modern artillery, lay ahead. The *Olympia* glided past within a half mile, engines throbbing, screws driving, yet still the Spanish guns remained silent. Cruisers *Baltimore* and *Boston* cleared El Fraile. The last ships had nearly completed the passage when a fireman on the *McCulloch*, a cutter escorting the supply ships, ordered scoops of soft Australian coal shoveled into the vessel's furnace. A shower of sparks shot up through the smokestack, illuminating the American squadron in a shaft of ragged light.[27]

Off to the west, a Spanish bugle sounded. A sharp flash broke the blackness, and an artillery piece boomed. Two more followed, and Spanish shells splashed off the *McCulloch*'s stern. The *Raleigh*, *Boston* and *Concord* opened fire, and then the *McCulloch*. The Spanish batteries fired three more rounds, then, inexplicably, fell silent. Without a single casualty or even a scratch, Dewey and his ships entered Manila Bay.

The first hurdle cleared with unexpected ease, Dewey now ordered a course set for Manila on the far eastern shore, thirty miles ahead. The nine American ships moved cautiously through the darkness, "creeping, creeping, creeping with invisible mines below us and an invisible fleet ahead," one of Dewey's officers recalled.[28] About three a.m. the lights of the Spanish colonial capital became visible. Twenty minutes later an order to "stand easy" was passed, and men slumped to the deck to await the dawn.

First light revealed the enemy fleet was not lying off Manila, as Dewey had expected. A lookout quickly solved the mystery. Spyglasses swung to the south, in the direction of the Cavite naval station. There, unmistakable in the dim light, a cluster of Spanish warships lay at anchor. Dewey had found his adversary.

DRUMS BEAT TO QUARTERS AND the Stars and Stripes fluttered from mastheads as the American squadron began a slow turn to the south. Moments from his first combat in more than thirty years, Dewey sat placidly on the bridge of the *Olympia* in a wicker armchair, immaculate in his white duck uniform and golf cap. Occasionally he rose to scan his surroundings with a telescope. In the rising tropical heat, the fleet swept past Manila, where spectators perched in church towers and on city walls, and swung in the direction of Cavite and Admiral Patricio Montojo's aging Spanish fleet.[29] Enemy ships and shore batteries opened fire, but Dewey seemed unconcerned. He calmly studied his enemy through his telescope. Finally, he ordered signal flags run up to communicate with his squadron. Cheers erupted from a thousand American throats as the message was translated: "Remember the *Maine*."[30]

The Spanish guns now thundered and snapped. Still, Dewey pressed on. Two explosions ripped the water off the bow of the cruiser *Baltimore*, shooting geysers of mud and water into the air—the first of the feared Spanish mines. Sailors and Marines whispered prayers. The *Olympia* had closed within 5,500 yards when Dewey leaned over the rail and casually called down to the ship's skipper, Captain Charles V. Gridley, "You may fire when you are ready, Gridley."[31] The frail Gridley, dying of cancer, gave the command, and a forward eight-inch gun began the American response. It was five forty-two a.m.

Dewey's squadron began to maneuver in a revolving oval, allowing each ship to bring its broadside guns to bear on the enemy fleet. On the commodore's orders, fire was concentrated on the Spanish flagship, and shell after shell ripped into the *Reina Cristina*. A direct hit on the pilot-house wounded the helmsman and the crews of the forward rapid-firing guns. The next salvo disabled the *Cristina*'s steering gear and destroyed her hospital, killing most of her wounded sailors and medical personnel. At seven forty a.m., with his ship wrecked and half his crew dead or dying, Admiral Montojo ordered his men to abandon ship and transferred his flag to the gunboat *Isla de Cuba*.[32]

The Spanish gunners matched the Americans shell for shell, but their aim was poor. Enemy shells that found their marks somehow failed to inflict serious damage. One Spanish shell was on a line to take out Dewey and other senior American officers on the *Olympia*'s forward bridge when it exploded about a hundred feet from its intended target. One piece of the shell sawed the rigging just over the heads of the American officers, while another gouged a long sliver of wood from the deck beneath Dewey and his command group. A third fragment smashed the bridge gratings. "All around and about and above us there was the sputter and shriek and roar of projectiles," one of Dewey's officers recalled.[33] Miraculously, not a single American was killed.

With each pass, the superior American firepower and aim took an ever deadlier toll. By midday, the battle was over: The smoldering ruins of twelve Spanish warships wallowed in the mud of Manila Bay, and a white flag fluttered over the Cavite naval station; 381 Spaniards had been killed or wounded. Only one American had died—from heatstroke, not enemy fire—and six had been slightly wounded.

By late afternoon, as a spectacular sunset cast a golden glow over Manila Bay, hundreds of Spaniards and Filipinos hastened to the water's edge to catch a glimpse of the victors. When a crowd clustered on the ramparts of a waterfront battery that had shelled the Americans earlier, Dewey magnanimously ordered the *Olympia*'s band to play "*La Paloma*" and other Spanish airs. In the fading light, as a sea breeze carried the melodies ashore and announced the arrival of a new world power, the Spanish battery's distraught commander placed a gun to his head and pulled the trigger.[34]

CHAPTER 5

Guantánamo Bay

News of Dewey's victory unleashed frenzied celebrations across America, the likes of which had not been seen since the conclusion of the Civil War. One hundred thousand people crowded into New York's Madison Square for a raucous gala fueled by fireworks, brass bands and patriotic speeches. Parents christened newborn babies Dewey. Hawkers sold hats, cigarettes, canes, candlesticks, paperweights, spoons and other souvenirs emblazoned with Dewey's name and likeness. Songwriters and poets dashed off tributes. Congress passed a resolution of thanks and reserved a rear admiral's slot for the hero of Manila Bay. (Eventually, Congress would also present Dewey with a jeweled sword from Tiffany & Co. of New York and the lifetime position of admiral of the Navy.[1]) Among the hundreds of congratulatory telegrams that poured into the Hong Kong cable office was one from Assistant Secretary of the Navy Theodore Roosevelt. After noting his role in arranging Dewey's Asian assignment, Roosevelt gushed: "Every American is in your debt." Dewey did nothing to discourage the accolades. "The Battle of Manila Bay is one of the most remarkable naval battles of the ages," he wrote his son.[2]

As much as Dewey was America's man of the hour, sixty-two-year-old

Army General William Shafter was fast becoming the national goat.
Gouty and nearly immobile at 320 pounds, the former Michigan schoolteacher and Civil War veteran had been handed the plum assignment of
conquering Cuba. Yet forty days had passed since Dewey's triumph, and
Shafter's invasion force sat sweltering in its chaotic Florida bivouac.

Shafter was not entirely to blame (although Roosevelt would have
suggested otherwise). President McKinley and his advisers feared that
Admiral Pascual Cervera's elusive Spanish fleet might suddenly appear
in the night to bombard New York City or sink an American invasion
force on the open sea. The frantic search for the Spanish flotilla had
finally ended in late May with the discovery of Cervera's warships in
southeastern Cuba's Santiago Bay. Commodore Winfield Scott Schley's
"Flying Squadron" had sealed off the bay, but powerful Spanish shore
guns prevented the American ships from replicating Dewey's bold stroke.
The stalemate would have to be broken by a ground campaign against
the garrison city of Santiago—if only Shafter's army could get ashore.

Channeling the nation's impatience, William Randolph Hearst took
matters into his own hands. On June 2, screaming headlines in his *New
York Evening Journal* reported that five thousand American troops had
started for Santiago and that ten thousand more were poised to follow.
(In truth, Shafter's army still hadn't left Tampa Bay.) On June 6, the paper
breathlessly described how the first five thousand U.S. troops had stormed
ashore "under terrific fire" at Playa de Aguadores, Cuba. The following
day the *Journal* described another landing by U.S. forces twelve miles east
of Santiago. And on June 10, the paper announced the capture of Santiago by the imaginary American invasion force.[3]

Hearst's fertile imagination aside, the wheels of invasion had finally
begun to turn. By early June the Navy had discovered a superb deepwater
anchorage forty-seven miles east of Santiago that could serve as the invasion fleet's logistical base. The bay had long been favored by pirates and
European mariners—Columbus had christened it Puerto Grande when
he anchored there in 1494, and eighteenth-century British sea captains
had variously charted it as Walthenham Bay or Cumberland Harbor.[4]
Under Spanish colonial sway, the blue-water haven had become known

as Bahía de Guantánamo. Now Lieutenant Colonel Robert Huntington's 1st Marine Battalion was on its way from Key West to secure the beaches and hills around Guantánamo Bay as a prelude to Shafter's landing.

AT TWO O'CLOCK ON THE afternoon of June 10, 1898, the bands aboard the gathered American warships belted out a rousing ragtime tune as the sweating men of Company C of the 1st Marine Battalion clambered into low-slung cutters for the journey ashore. An impressive collection of U.S. warships rode easily in the shimmering turquoise waters of Guantánamo Bay: the cruiser *Marblehead*; auxiliary cruisers *Yankee* and *Yosemite*; and assorted gunboats, supply ships and press boats. Most impressive of all was the mighty USS *Oregon*, newest of a trio of seagoing battleships authorized by Congress in 1890.[5] The *Oregon* had just joined the fleet after a record-breaking 13,792-mile journey from America's Pacific Northwest, racing down the South American coast, through the gale-buffeted Strait of Magellan and back up into the Caribbean—an epic sixty-six-day voyage that millions of Americans had anxiously followed on newspaper front pages.

History would later record the landing at Guantánamo as a turning point in the annals of the United States Marine Corps, but Huntington and his men were concerned only with their immediate objectives: seize the high ground, scatter any Spanish troops, and secure the bay as a safe haven for U.S. warships.

In a matter of minutes the landing craft surged into the gravelly shallows off Playa del Este. The Marines plunged into the warm waters and, without firing a shot, splashed ashore singing the jaunty anthem of an ascendant America: "There'll Be a Hot Time in the Old Town Tonight."[6] As Huntington observed, "We went ashore like innocents. . . ."[7]

The Marines hustled up the beach into a small fishing village of palm-frond huts. Orders were passed to destroy the village, lest U.S. fighting men contract yellow fever or other diseases from its inhabitants. Torches were lit and smoke soon curled from the flimsy houses.

Huntington's men struggled up a two-hundred-foot hill and, upon reaching the crest, spread out in a skirmish line. As his comrades scanned the chaparral and ridgelines for enemy troops, Sergeant Richard Silvey planted the American flag on Cuban soil. Cheers erupted from the Navy ships below.

With the high ground overlooking the beach secured, three more companies came ashore, stacked their rifles and began unloading supplies. The Marines sweated heavily in the tropical heat as they lugged ammunition and stores up the steep trail to the campsite. Tents were pitched and perimeter outposts established.

As the sun sank below the horizon, the thrill of establishing the first American beachhead on Cuba gave way to anxiety. At eight p.m., a jittery advance picket sounded an alarm. Off in the darkness, "the steady tramp of men and the noise of rolling stones down the mountain side indicated the approach of the enemy," Huntington recorded.[8]

With weapons close at hand, the Marines fell into a fitful sleep.[9]

IN THE EARLY-MORNING LIGHT of Saturday, June 11, the Marines surveyed their surroundings. Their camp offered a breathtaking view of the blue Caribbean a few hundred yards to the south and the shimmering bay that unfolded below them on the west. To the north the pine-forested Sierra Cristal rose sharply in the distance, while to the east and northeast the closer Cuzco Hills topped out at about five hundred feet. The terrain was dry and rugged, a jumble of steep hills and plunging ravines covered with rough vegetation that included cactus and palms. Limestone and granite cliffs rose a hundred feet or more in places, broken by occasional strips of pebbly beach and mangrove swamps.

The weeks at Key West had given Huntington time to size up the mix of old hands and raw recruits that comprised his battalion. The Marine Corps had yet to become an institution with national appeal, and a large share of its enlistees still came from East Coast cities where Marine detachments were a fixture in local holiday parades. The Corps was a magnet for the urban unemployed, struggling immigrants and young troublemakers—many of whom had "little idea of obeying orders," Huntington observed.[10] Almost all of the Marines now encamped on the heights above Guantánamo Bay had been born and raised within a few hundred miles of the Atlantic Coast.

That was true of one of the first Americans ashore at Guantánamo, Sergeant John Henry Quick of Company C. Just ten days shy of his twenty-eighth birthday, Quick was born in Charles Town, West Virginia, in the state's eastern panhandle. A quiet, serious young man, he had joined the Marines when he was twenty-two, enlisting in Philadelphia in August 1892. As he rose through the ranks he became skilled at semaphore, the visual equivalent of Morse code in which messages were spelled out through the use of flags "wig-wagged" in each hand. When the new Marine combat battalion was formed, Quick was assigned to Company C as a signalman.

Another of Huntington's noncommissioned officers was Sergeant Charles Hampton Smith. The third of eight children, Smith was born in 1867 on a farm in Carroll County in western Maryland, forty miles from Quick's hometown. At the age of twenty-one the curly-haired young man with deep blue eyes left farm life for the big city of Baltimore. He found work with an insurance firm, starting as a canvasser and collector and working his way up to an assistant superintendent's position. When financial panic rocked the nation in 1893, Smith left the firm and enlisted in the Marine Corps. He was twenty-six.

Smith reveled in the life of a globe-trotting Marine. "I have made friends in all parts of the world that I have been in," he wrote home in January 1898. "Turks, Greeks, Italians, Spanish, Moors, Austrians and English." Three months later, he became a charter member of the Marine battalion formed to fight the Spanish.[11]

The last of Huntington's six companies had safely come ashore late Saturday afternoon when shots rang out. Several hundred yards from camp, privates William Dumphy of Portsmouth, New Hampshire, and James McColgan of Stoneham, Massachusetts, had been preparing to eat supper at their forward outpost when Spanish soldiers crept through the underbrush and surrounded their position. Too late, the Americans grabbed their rifles. A thunderous volley ripped through the chaparral and the Marines crumpled to the ground.[12]

The Marines at the hilltop camp nervously scanned the hillsides and ravines but failed to spot the Spanish attackers in the fading light. Conversations soon resumed, and some of the men made their way to the beach to bathe after the hard day's labor. Once again, the sharp crack of rifles sounded, and Spanish Mauser bullets spattered dust, sheared tree branches and slapped the water.

As Huntington directed fire at the unseen enemy, a group of naked Marines dashed up from the beach, grabbed rifles and fell into line. Some of the men worked their way down the hill toward the sound of the enemy rifles, while comrades behind them poured rounds into the thickets. On Huntington's command, clothed and unclothed Marines alike charged into the thorny undergrowth. Once again, the Spanish soldiers had slipped away.[13] Over the next one hundred hours, the pattern would be repeated again and again: Spanish soldiers would creep close to the Marine camp, unleash furious fire, and melt into the brush.

It was a brusque initiation into combat for the battalion's assistant surgeon, John Blair Gibbs. Forty years old, balding, with a bushy mustache, Blair Gibbs, as he was known to family and friends, was a graduate of Rutgers College and the University of Pennsylvania medical school. When tensions with Spain came to a head in the spring, Gibbs, the son of a U.S. Cavalry officer, quit a thriving practice in Manhattan and volunteered for the Navy. After joining Huntington's battalion at Key West in May, he made friends easily.[14]

Shortly after going ashore at Guantánamo, Gibbs fell into conversation with a young war correspondent along to cover the action. Affectionately known as "Little Stevey," twenty-six-year-old Stephen Crane was an unimposing five feet, six inches, with delicate and finely chiseled facial features, sad blue eyes and a shock of light hair across his high forehead. Shy and serious, he possessed "the smile of a man who knows that his time will not be long on this earth," observed British writer Joseph Conrad, a good friend. Another friend, legendary correspondent Richard Harding Davis, would later praise Crane as "the coolest man, whether army officer or civilian, that I saw under fire at any time during the war."[15]

Crane had already achieved fame and success as a novelist and short-story writer in the United States and Great Britain, most notably for *The Red Badge of Courage*, a searing account of Civil War combat—even though he had never witnessed any battle himself. Writing about men at war unleashed in Crane a desire to experience combat firsthand, and he decided to chronicle the insurrection in Cuba. In January 1897, Crane nearly drowned when a boatload of mercenaries he was accompanying to the island sank in a storm off the Florida coast. After hearing of the *Maine*'s destruction, Crane attempted to enlist in the Navy but was rejected because of poor health. He finally landed a job as a war correspondent for Joseph Pulitzer's *New York World*.

At Key West, Crane had wangled a spot aboard a press boat headed for Cuban waters, then talked his way onto the cruiser *New York*. He filed dispatches on the U.S. blockade before joining several other reporters on the *Three Friends,* Pulitzer's chartered tug. The boat and its load of correspondents arrived at Guantánamo Bay just ahead of Huntington's Marines.

On their first night ashore at Guantánamo, Crane and his fellow correspondents had been disappointed by the lack of action. Crane wandered through the Marine camp in search of stimulating company, and found it in the person of Blair Gibbs. The pair passed the evening in pleasant conversation.[16]

Amid the escalating Spanish attacks of the second night, Crane set out after midnight to find Gibbs. Suddenly, heavy fire raked the exposed camp from three directions. Crane threw himself onto the ground, "feeling the hot hiss of the bullets trying to cut my hair." In the nearby medical tent, Gibbs was bandaging a private's wounded hand when lamplight momentarily framed the doctor in the doorway. A Spanish bullet smashed into his left temple, and Gibbs collapsed to the ground. Hugging the dirt less than ten feet away, surrounded by "a wild storm of fighting," Crane could only listen to the terrible death throes of his new friend. "He was dying hard," he later wrote. "Hard. It took him a long time to die."[17]

To AVOID BEING OVERRUN, HUNTINGTON ordered his signalmen to request artillery support from the warships anchored in the bay. Sergeant John Quick had positioned himself and three other signalmen on a prominent point overlooking the bay, from which they could "wig-wag" flags in daylight or wave lanterns at night to communicate with the U.S. ships below. It was perilous duty, especially in darkness, when the signalman had to stand behind one lantern and swing a second one left and right— all while presenting a tempting target to enemy riflemen.

Whenever Quick or one of his men would jump into place, position his lanterns and begin flashing the message, "the bullets began to snap, snap, snap, at his head while all the woods began to crackle like burning straw," Crane reported. He marveled at the courage of Quick and his men, and wondered how the four Marines "were not riddled from head to foot and sent home more as repositories of Spanish ammunition than as Marines. . . ."

With the message received, American ships poured fire into the dark hills while Huntington's Marines pounded away "at every flash or any noise." A launch from the *Marblehead* pushed up the bay and sprayed the chaparral with its Colt machine gun, and Navy searchlights played over the hills, catching fleeting glimpses of Spanish soldiers as they maneuvered closer to the Marine lines. At one point enemy soldiers attempted to overrun the Marine camp, but Huntington's men beat back the attack. The Marines began to pray for daylight. "Utterly worn to rags, with our nerves standing on end like so many bristles, we lay and watched the east," Crane wrote. As the half-light of dawn finally arrived, the gunfire tapered off and then stopped altogether.[18]

The Spanish struck again shortly after daybreak, firing from several directions before breaking off the attack. Casualties from the long night had been surprisingly light for the Marines, but among the dead was Sergeant Charles Hampton Smith. The Marine from Maryland who had made friends around the world had taken a bullet in the chest and died alone in the darkness.[19]

SHAKEN BY THE FEROCIOUS SPANISH fire and the uncertain fate of a patrol he had dispatched into the chaparral the previous evening, Huntington requested permission to abandon the hilltop camp and withdraw his Marines to the offshore ships. When the appeal was strenuously rejected by the ranking naval officer on the scene, Commodore Bowman "Billy Hell" McCalla, Huntington came to the sobering realization that "our salvation rests in our own hands." He put his men to work. Bullet-riddled tents were moved from the exposed peak to the hillside overlooking the beach. Trenches and rifle pits were dug, and Colt machine guns and Hotchkiss field pieces dragged up to commanding positions with the aid of news correspondents.

Forty Marines and two more machine guns came ashore from the *Texas*, and another small detachment arrived from the *Marblehead*.[20]

Early that afternoon, a group of sweating men appeared on the hilltop lugging a ship's spar. It was a gift from Commodore McCalla: a permanent flagpole for the fortress now bearing his name, a none too subtle reminder from the crusty commander that Americans would not be surrendering this sunbaked chunk of Cuban soil if he had anything to do with it. At one fifteen, the Stars and Stripes was run up the spar and the Marines roared three times—"Hip, hip, hooray!" The celebration spread through the fleet out in the harbor, and cannon boomed and whistles tooted.[21]

The Spanish attacks continued through the afternoon and another long night, but the Marines would not be shaken. They fought back from trenches and rifle pits and launched swift thrusts into the underbrush to keep the Spanish off balance. On one foray Lieutenant Wendell Neville, a future Marine Corps commandant, and thirty Marines braved heavy enemy fire and overwhelmed a small stone fort held by the Spanish. Three of Neville's men were wounded, and one was fatally injured when he fell off a cliff in the darkness. The Spanish troops left behind fifteen dead.[22]

By daybreak on June 13, the Marines were exhausted from sixty hours of nearly continuous combat, but had gained the upper hand. To Crane, who would go on to witness all the major battles of the Spanish-American War, nothing matched those harrowing first nights at Guantánamo Bay: "The noise; the impenetrable darkness; the knowledge from the sound of the bullets that the enemy was on three sides of the camp; the infrequent bloody stumbling and death of some man with whom, perhaps, one had messed two hours previous; the weariness of the body, and the more terrible weariness of the mind, at the endlessness of the thing, made it wonderful that at least some of the men did not come out of it with their nerves hopelessly in shreds."[23]

THE QUESTION OF HOW LARGE a force he was up against had vexed Huntington from the start. Now Cuban guerrillas reported that the Spanish force consisted of four companies of regulars and two companies of Cuban loyalists, about five hundred men in all. More important, they said the attackers were operating from a camp on the coast southeast of the Marines, at the base of the rugged Cuzco Hills. In the center of the camp was Cuzco Well, the only source of potable water for miles around.

Cuzco Well lay only a few hundred yards from the coast in a horse-shoe-shaped valley, cooled by sea breezes even as the surrounding arid hills baked in the sun. The Spaniards had built a blockhouse on a gentle slope that afforded a commanding view of the valley and the sea beyond. A little village of tropical houses and shacks had sprung up. A windmill sat over the well itself, pumping freshwater up from a subterranean aquifer. With the American blockade preventing resupply from the sea, the Spanish were running low on food and had begun slaughtering and eating their horses. Without a reliable source of water, they could not survive.

At nine o'clock on the morning of June 14, 1898, two companies of Marines under the command of Captain George Elliott started down the hill from Camp McCalla and into the brush. Beside Elliott was Stephen Crane, footsore in his knee-high leather shooting boots, yet game for another encounter with the enemy. The gunboat USS *Dolphin* tracked the progress of the Marines offshore, ready to provide support, should the Spaniards try to ambush the advancing units.

In a straight line, the Spanish camp and its all-important well were less than two miles away. But getting over the jumbled Cuzco Hills meant six miles of hiking on hard trails through the hills and ravines. The temperature was rising steadily toward a hundred degrees, and heat waves shimmered from the cactus-studded scrub. About two and a half miles from Cuzco, Elliott sent a platoon of Marines with two dozen Cubans north to cut off any Spanish pickets and cover the advance of the main body. While climbing a steep hill, the advance group stumbled onto a Spanish outpost, and the enemy soldiers dashed off toward the base camp.[24]

A desperate scramble ensued as Marines and Spanish soldiers raced to the crest of a high hill overlooking the Spanish camp. A few Spanish soldiers arrived first, and poured fire down at the advancing Americans. Red faced and soaked with sweat, the Marines and their Cuban allies drove the enemy soldiers from the crest and held it under heavy enemy fire until the rest of Elliott's column arrived.[25]

As the battle stretched into the afternoon, the Marines began to run low on water, and many were overcome by heat. A former Cuban army colonel who had joined the operation added to the chaos, wounding one of his own men while wildly firing his pistol. But the most critical issue was a group of enemy soldiers concealed in a thick grove of sea grape trees about two hundred yards below the crest, positioned between the Marines and the Spanish command center.

The *Dolphin* was signaled, and soon its shells ripped through the grove. Tree limbs, stones and soil spewed into the air. Other shells smashed into a blockhouse down the valley, triggering cheers from the Marine lines. Small groups of Spanish troops began to flee the grove, running for their lives. "We set our sights on the rifles at 1,200 yards," recalled Private Frank Keeler, "and fired volley after volley. . . ."[26]

Back at camp, Huntington heard the heavy firing and grew concerned that his men might be overwhelmed by superior numbers. He ordered Lieutenant Louis J. Magill to take forty Marines and ten Cuban guerrillas and reinforce the initial force as fast as possible. Magill's men approached Cuzco Well from the north, and clawed their way up a hill several hundred yards off the left flank of Elliot's line.

Mistaking the reinforcements for Spanish troops, the *Dolphin*'s gunners turned their fire on the new arrivals. Elliott desperately yelled for a signalman, and Sergeant Quick found a long, crooked stick, tied his blue polkadot neckerchief around it and selected a conspicuous place atop the ridge. As Spanish riflemen fired furiously at the solitary Marine silhouetted against the sky, Quick focused on his work. "Escape for him seemed impossible," Crane wrote. "It seemed absurd to hope that he would not be hit."[27]

But Quick completed his task unscathed, and the guns of the *Dolphin* fell silent. Magill and his men were saved.

After three hours of fighting, Spanish troops began sprinting into the eastern hills. The firing died away by shortly after three p.m., and forty Marines scrambled down the slope to burn the enemy headquarters and fill the well with rocks. Dead and dying Spanish soldiers littered the valley— about sixty had been killed and 150 wounded. Only two Marines had been wounded by Spanish fire and another twenty-three overcome by heat.

When the wounded were safely aboard the *Dolphin* and eighteen Spanish prisoners taken away by a Navy cutter, the weary Marines fell in for the long hike back to Guantánamo Bay. Night had fallen when Elliott and his men marched into their camp, bone-tired, but flush with victory.[28]

The victory at Cuzco Well crippled the Spanish military in the area, and ended the attacks on the Marine outpost. More important, it secured Guantánamo Bay as a logistical base for the long-delayed invasion. Although the Army's campaign would ultimately decide the war, those five days in the hills above Guantánamo Bay, in the words of Marine historian Allan R. Millett, would prove of "incalculable importance for the Marine Corps."[29]

Indeed, Americans viewed the Marines in a different light after reading the dispatches of correspondents like Stephen Crane. The Marines might have been a small force, but they were nimble, they fought hard—and they were first. On June 17, the *New York Times* captured the tone of the accolades pouring forth across the country. "When the history of this war comes to be written it will contain many bright spots," the paper proclaimed, "but none brighter than that which describes the gallantry and the spirit of patriotic self-sacrifice which marked the Marines who landed on the shores of Guantánamo Bay."

LATE ON THE AFTERNOON OF June 14, as the Marines finished their work at Cuzco Well, a string of thirty-one transports crowded with more than sixteen thousand Army soldiers weighed anchor in Tampa Bay, Florida. Twice in the previous week bands had played and crowds had cheered their departure, only to see the anchors dropped at the last minute because of rumored threats from marauding Spanish ships. Now, as the transport *Yucatán* cleared Tampa Bay and turned south toward Key West, the men of the 1st U.S. Volunteer Cavalry broke into the jaunty chorus of "There'll Be a Hot Time in the Old Town Tonight."

Among the cavaliers on deck, outfitted in a uniform specially tailored by Brooks Brothers in New York, was a short man with thick eyeglasses and oversize teeth that flashed like piano keys when he smiled. Lieutenant Colonel Theodore Roosevelt had dreamed of battlefield glory since he was a boy, and now, finally bound for Cuba, he was determined to write his own chapter.

CHAPTER 6

"It Was War, and It Was Magnificent"

Starlight spangled the great fleet as buglers blew reveille and bleary-eyed soldiers rolled from their bunks to begin final preparations for the first invasion by U.S. armed forces since 1845. It was three o'clock on the morning of June 22, 1898. On the overcrowded transports hugging the southern coast of Cuba, American soldiers pulled on woolen blue uniforms and gray slouch hats, looped blanket rolls across their necks and fastened hundred-round ammunition belts and full canteens around their waists. Completing each soldier's kit was a haversack crammed with three days' rations and a nine-pound bolt-action Krag-Jørgensen rifle.

Never before had America assembled such a fleet. Civil War–era paddle-wheelers and flat-bottomed scows mixed with torpedo boats and colliers. There was a floating hospital and even a tank ship full of drinking water. Most important of all, there were thirty-one transports crammed with 819 officers, 15,058 enlisted men, 30 civilian clerks, 89 newspaper correspondents, 11 foreign military observers, 272 teamsters and packers, 959 horses and 1,336 mules.[1]

The combined firepower of this army-in-waiting was formidable: In addition to each soldier's Krag-Jørgensen rifle, a Norwegian-designed weapon that fired a .30-caliber slug at an effective range of three thousand feet, the ships carried light artillery batteries, seven-inch howitzers, Gatling guns and assorted cannon and mortars. To feed this massive force, ten million pounds of rations had been loaded—hardtack and coffee, of course, along with slabs of greasy bacon, tinned fruit and crates of canned meat so foul-tasting that an outraged Congress would later investigate.

The six-day passage to Cuba had been agreeable enough for the officers residing in airy first-class accommodations. But belowdecks, enlisted troops experienced conditions "unpleasantly suggestive of the Black Hole of Calcutta," in the colorful description of Lieutenant Colonel Theodore Roosevelt, deputy commander of the 1st U.S. Volunteer Cavalry Regiment. They slept in claustrophobic rows of splintery bunks, breathing air that reeked of sweat, seasickness and manure. Horses and mules, unable to escape the searing heat, had begun dying shortly after the flotilla cleared the Florida coast. Soon a trail of carcasses bobbed in the column's wake.

The American fleet had arrived off the coast of southern Cuba two days earlier with plans still unsettled. The much-maligned commander of the invasion force, General William Rufus Shafter, had settled on a landing site only after conferring with Admiral William Sampson, commander of U.S. naval forces for the campaign, and a Cuban insurgent leader, General Calixto García. Shafter had ruled out a landing at Guantánamo Bay, which would have required a forty-seven-mile overland march to the Spanish stronghold at Santiago. An invading British army had attempted the feat in 1741, Shafter learned from his readings on the voyage from Florida, and the campaign had ended badly. The British column of five thousand soldiers was forced to quit sixteen miles short of the city after suffering two thousand casualties from heat, rain and tropical diseases.[2]

García had recommended two possible landing sites. Daiquirí, eighteen miles east of Santiago, was the location of the Spanish-American Iron Company, a New York–based iron ore mining and export business whose shareholders included oil tycoon John D. Rockefeller. Siboney, seven miles nearer the city, was where the coastal road turned and climbed inland. It was quickly agreed that the initial landing would be at Daiquirí, which had a marginal beach and a small wooden wharf, while the remaining troops would disembark at Siboney. Both groups would then march to just outside Santiago, where, on a ridge named San Juan, they would confront the enemy.

Shafter was told to expect resistance from three hundred Spanish troops dug in with heavy guns on the high ground above Daiquirí. Though far less than the seven thousand that War Department intelligence reports estimated would greet the Americans, the enemy force clearly was large enough to inflict heavy casualties. Indeed, the Spanish commander had boasted of his ability "to resist any attack at Daiquirí, either by land or sea."[3]

A steamy dawn broke over the Cuban coast with Shafter's invasion force still stuck on the fetid transport ships. At nine forty a.m., the Navy's big guns finally opened fire on the heights above Daiquirí, while lighter cannon and machine guns on smaller ships raked a twenty-mile stretch of coast east of Santiago. Whenever a Navy shell struck a Spanish blockhouse or other fortified position, soldiers on the transports cheered. "It was war, and it was magnificent," an Associated Press correspondent wrote.

It was also all for show: The Spanish had pulled out before dawn.

After a half hour, the shelling stopped and Shafter ordered the landing boats ashore. As a ragged troop of Cuban rebels galloped down the beach, men clambered down Jacob's ladders and ratlines into landing craft wallowing in the choppy seas. Impatient coxswains cursed and scorned the frightened soldiers, who "fell and jumped and tumbled from the gangway ladder into the heaving boats that dropped from beneath them like a descending elevator or rose suddenly and threw them on their knees," correspondent Richard Harding Davis reported.

Navy steam launches then plunged into the clouds of artillery smoke, towing trains of landing craft toward the beach and Daiquirí's decrepit dock. Following close behind were the newspaper yachts filled with correspondents, creating a scene that to Davis looked "strangely suggestive of a boat race." Some craft reached the dock, and soldiers leaped onto the planking to avoid pitching into the sea. Others ran aground and troops tumbled out, cursing and thrashing their way up the beach. As fast as companies and regiments safely reached dry ground, they formed up and marched away to join the swarm of blue-uniformed soldiers in the expanding American perimeter.[4]

Among the first ashore was a six-foot-four, broad-chested Hoosier, Brigadier General Henry Ware Lawton. A Civil War veteran famed for his epic pursuit of Geronimo in 1886, Lawton had seen his hair and bushy mustache turn iron gray, but his energy was undiminished—along with his habit of commanding from the front lines, a dangerous practice that endeared him to his men.

The landing plan had called for General Lawton to lead his Army regulars onto the beach first, but the ever-impatient Lieutenant Colonel Roosevelt had other ideas. He coaxed a former naval aide passing by in a converted yacht to send a local pilot to his transport, the *Yucatán*, and the Cuban gently edged the ship into shallow water. Roosevelt's Rough Riders, as correspondents had christened them, scrambled into the water carrying their rifles, ammunition belts and haversacks, becoming the first cavalrymen ashore. (Most of Roosevelt's troopers were cavalry-men in name only: Shafter had decreed on the eve of departure that the transports would have room for only eight of the twelve Rough Rider units and that only senior cavalry officers could take their personal mounts. Incensed by the decision, Roosevelt would later excoriate the American commander: "Not since the campaign of Crassus against the Parthians has there been so criminally incompetent a General as Shafter."[5]) Roosevelt and his men made it ashore with only one casualty: One of Roosevelt's two mounts had drowned during a botched attempt to winch the horses to safety in a specially fitted harness.

About five o'clock, shouts swept the beach and all eyes turned to the bluff overlooking the village. "Outlined against the sky, we saw four tiny figures scaling the sheer face of the mountain up the narrow trail to the highest blockhouse," reported Davis, accompanying the Rough Riders at Roosevelt's personal invitation. "Then . . . the American flag was thrown out against the sky, and the sailors on the men-of-war, the Cubans, and our soldiers in the village, the soldiers in the longboats, and those still hanging to sides and ratlines of the troopships, shouted and cheered . . . and every steam whistle on the ocean for miles about shrieked and tooted and roared in a pandemonium of delight."[6]

By sunset, more than six thousand soldiers were setting up tents, dry-ing clothes over campfires, or chasing huge land crabs that scuttled through the underbrush. General Lawton had skillfully expanded the American beachhead without firing a shot by dispatching a detachment to the west toward Siboney and positioning another in the hills overlooking the village. Roosevelt and the Rough Riders, meanwhile, pitched camp a few hundred yards off the beach, alongside a palm-fringed pool. As night fell, the soldiers stretched out on rubber ponchos and, serenaded by the pounding surf, fell asleep under the starry Cuban sky.[7]

THE NEXT MORNING, GENERAL LAWTON and five regiments of his 2nd Division seized Siboney without a fight. As the remaining U.S. troops came ashore there and at Daiquirí and supplies were unloaded, Lawton engaged in a brief skirmish with Spanish troops as he pressed up the road toward Santiago.

Early in the afternoon, the Rough Riders broke camp and prepared to head for Siboney as well. Their departure from Daiquirí had been ordered by a man praised by Roosevelt as "a regular game-cock," the expedition's hard-driving cavalry chief, Major General Joseph Wheeler. More than thirty years earlier, "Fighting Joe" had been a Confederate cavalry commander. Now the old warhorse was Congressman Wheeler, and, with his white beard, he vaguely resembled the revered leader of the Lost Cause, Robert E. Lee. Though sixty-two, Wheeler was back in the saddle to underscore regional unity in America's crusade against Spain— and also to grab his share of glory. On this day, Wheeler wanted his 2nd Cavalry Brigade under Brigadier General Samuel B. M. Young to hustle to the front while he schemed how to score the Army's first victory. The Rough Riders fell in at the rear of Young's column heading west.

They set out on a hilly jungle trail "so narrow that often we had to go in single file," remembered Roosevelt. Under the merciless Cuban sun, the heavy bedrolls and haversacks the men carried "were like lead," recalled Private Ogden Wells of D Troop. "At last we could stand it no longer and we began to throw away our blankets; after the blankets went cans of meat, then our coats and underclothes, until some only had their guns and ammunition left, for these were essentials."[8]

The Rough Riders staggered into Siboney long after nightfall, marching past Lawton's puzzled infantry units that had landed there that morning. In the darkness, fires were hastily lit and the men wolfed down a meal of coffee, pork and hardtack just before a tropical downpour lashed their camp. When the rain stopped, fires were relit and the Rough Riders peeled off waterlogged uniforms and dried them over the flames.[9]

While Colonel Leonard Wood, the Rough Riders' commander, huddled with General Wheeler, Roosevelt strolled over to the camp of L Troop. Their lead officer, Captain Allyn Capron, the son of an artillery captain who at that very moment was serving in Lawton's division, and his trusted aide, Sergeant Hamilton Fish, the grandson of President Grant's secretary of state, were broad-shouldered men of extraordinary strength and endurance. "Two finer types of the fighting man, two better representatives of the American soldier, there were not in the whole army," Roosevelt admiringly observed. Listening to Fish and the younger Capron speculate on how the coming battle might unfold, Roosevelt sensed a familiar desire: The two men burned "with eager longing to show their mettle."[10]

Around midnight Colonel Wood returned from his meeting with General Wheeler. Pulling Roosevelt aside, he softly informed his deputy: They would attack at dawn.

CONTEMPORARY CRITICS QUESTIONED WHY THEODORE Roosevelt would set aside a promising political career, leave an ailing wife and risk his life as a soldier. His most severe detractors whispered, as they did throughout his rise, that it was yet another sign of mental instability. Those closest to him understood.

The simple answer is that Roosevelt, unlike so many hawks before and since, firmly believed that a man who advocated war should fight. "I have always intended to act up to my preachings if occasion arose," he declared in a letter to the *New York Sun*. "Now the occasion has arisen, and I ought to meet it."[11]

But it was more complicated than that. Although he deeply loved and respected his father, Roosevelt had obsessed over Theodore Senior's decision not to fight in the Civil War. When questioned publicly, young

Theodore, not surprisingly, mentioned nothing of that. Privately, however, he viewed his father's failure to serve as a stain on the family name that he could purge by proving his own courage as a soldier.

Although Secretary of War Alger had offered him command of the 1st U.S. Volunteer Cavalry in April, Roosevelt had realized his limitations and recommended that his friend Colonel Leonard Wood lead the unit. Lieutenant Colonel Roosevelt was content to serve as second in command—at least on paper.

Roosevelt received twenty-three thousand applications for membership in his regiment. He also personally solicited friends and acquaintances acquired at various points in his rich and well-traveled life. Typical was a telegram to an aristocratic bear- and foxhunting buddy in Lexington, Kentucky, asking him to raise a company of a hundred Kentuckians. The final roster included a member of New York's gilded Tiffany clan, the reigning U.S. tennis champion, a legendary Harvard quarterback, and the ex-captain of the Columbia University rowing crew. It also boasted a full-blooded American Indian, the former mayor of Prescott, Arizona, and several rough-hewn characters Roosevelt had met as a Dakota rancher and big-game hunter.[12]

At their training camp in San Antonio, Texas, Roosevelt's first meeting with his new regiment momentarily unnerved some of the hard-boiled frontiersmen who had never met the man. It wasn't so much the fawn-colored Brooks Brothers uniform with its canary yellow trim. It was the fact that their deputy commander wore glasses.[13]

Roosevelt's celebrity, coupled with his recruits' reputations, immediately fired the imagination of news correspondents, and they spun romantic portraits of a "cowboy regiment" and "rough riders from the West." A flattering New York Times profile hinted that Roosevelt and his men might not even have needed the nation's Regular Army to whip Spain. "They have their own mounts, their own arms, and, what is more, know how to take care of themselves, live under any circumstances, and fight all the time," the reporter wrote. "They need no drilling or inuring to hardship, but can give lessons in endurance and soldierly qualities to the veterans of the regular Army."[14]

Smitten reporters and headline writers competed to coin the unit's perfect name: Teddy's Texas Tarantulas; Teddy's Terrors; Teddy's Riotous Rounders; Teddy's Gilded Gang; Teddy's Cowboy Contingent. Roosevelt's Rough Riders stuck.

Under Wood's firm guidance in Texas, Roosevelt learned the ropes of Army command. He was a quick study. When Roosevelt bought his men beers at a local watering hole after a particularly hot day, Wood lectured him on the proper distance a military commander needed to maintain from his men. That evening, a chastened Roosevelt apologized profusely to his mentor. At other times Wood willingly abetted Roosevelt's penchant for violating the rules.

At Tampa on departure day, Wood and Roosevelt had cleverly navigated the chaos at the docks to snag space on a transport—the *Yucatán*—that had been assigned to two other regiments. Roosevelt marched his men double-quick to the pier "just in time to board her as she came into the quay." He then refused to budge when the two other units arrived a few minutes later. Recalling the incident afterward, Roosevelt could barely contain his glee. The late-arriving units, he boasted, were "a shade less ready than we were in the matter of individual initiative."[15]

FROM SIBONEY, THE ROAD TO Santiago plunged inland through rising foothills. A mile to the west, a jungle trail offered a rugged shortcut that rejoined the road about four miles away, at a place called Las Guásimas. There, dug in and waiting for the Americans, were two thousand troops of the Spanish 4th Army Corps under Major General Arsenio Linares.

Linares's men had studded the high ground around Las Guásimas with stone breastworks and blockhouses. Snipers and pickets waited in thick brush. But the rapid American advance of the day before had convinced Linares to consolidate his forces at the main Spanish lines outside Santiago. He ordered his men at Las Guásimas to resist the Americans, but only enough to permit an orderly retreat.[16]

At first light on June 24, Wheeler started General Young up the road toward Las Guásimas with 470 men from the 2nd Cavalry. About fifteen minutes later, Colonel Wood set out along the jungle trail with five hundred dismounted Rough Riders. About eight o'clock Young opened fire

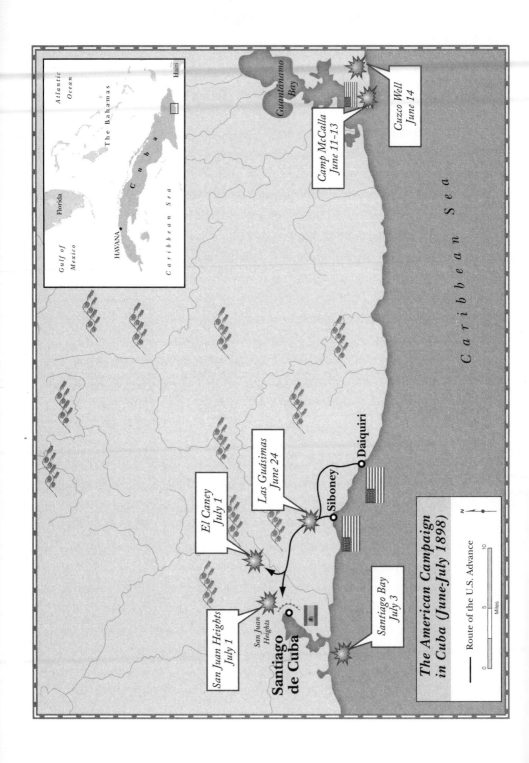

The American Campaign in Cuba (June-July 1898)

on the Spanish positions with one-pound shells from his rapid-fire Hotch-kiss guns. Under heavy fire, he urged his men forward in a skirmish line until they were close enough to the enemy's positions to hear shouts in Spanish.

The Rough Riders, meanwhile, found the going tough as they angled up a steep hill on the jungle trail. The trail leveled out on a ridgeline, and the Rough Riders noisily threaded their way in and out of thick jungle and pleasant glades. "They wound along this narrow winding path, babbling joyously, arguing, recounting, and laughing," wrote Stephen Crane, "making more noise than a train going through a tunnel." Roosevelt, an amateur botanist, admired the royal palms and brilliant red-blossomed royal poinciana, and noted the calls of wood doves and a great brush cuckoo.[17]

Suddenly, a volley ripped through the jungle ahead. Jumping up and down with excitement, Roosevelt ordered his men forward, toward the gunfire.

At the head of the column, Captain Capron's L troop had walked into an ambush. Sergeant Fish and three of his four men in the lead were killed in the first flurry of shots. Capron was hit in the chest, and died a few minutes later. A lieutenant took over, but almost as quickly fell wounded. As Rough Riders cursed the concealed Spaniards, Colonel Wood coolly led his horse along the line. "Don't swear," he scolded. "Shoot!"[18]

Rough Riders farther back in the column crumpled to the ground as enemy riflemen found the range. Roosevelt narrowly escaped death when a bullet sliced through the trunk of a large palm that he was using for cover. His left eye and ear were scoured with dust and splinters, but the future president was otherwise unscathed.

Still not fully aware of what was happening at the front, Roosevelt and his men scanned the jungle, trying to pinpoint the source of the deadly fire. Finally correspondent Richard Harding Davis spotted through his field glasses the straw hats of Spanish soldiers poking through the underbrush. Three or four of Roosevelt's best marksmen trained their fire on the spot, and soon others joined in. Several Spaniards broke from their hiding places and disappeared into the jungle.

Roosevelt now began to run up the trail toward the fleeing Spaniards, his sword flapping awkwardly between his legs. He passed the lifeless body of Hamilton Fish, a bullet through his heart, and finally reached the column's lead elements. Assuming command of a leaderless troop, he launched an attack on several red tiled ranch buildings about five hundred yards ahead. With bullets humming over their heads, Roosevelt and his panting men reached the enemy stronghold to find the Spaniards had fled, leaving behind heaps of empty cartridges and two dead comrades.

The orderly withdrawal that General Linares had envisioned now disintegrated, and Spanish soldiers scuttled down the road and through the jungle toward Santiago. Watching the rout unfold from his position on the far right of the American line, "Fighting Joe" Wheeler, the old Confederate commander, was ecstatic. "We've got the damn Yankees on the run!" he howled—forgetting for a moment that his current adversary was the Spanish army.

In military terms, Las Guásimas was a minor skirmish with major implications. The Americans had shown they were more than a match for the Spanish army. And at the cost of sixteen killed and fifty-two wounded, they had cleared the road to Santiago.

News accounts of the battle gave top billing to the Rough Riders (although Crane and others dimmed the luster by reporting that the celebrated volunteers had rather amateurishly stumbled into an ambush). It was precious validation for Roosevelt. For much of his life he had dreamed of battlefield valor as the ultimate test of manhood and honor. Now Theodore Roosevelt and his Rough Riders had proven beyond question their courage under fire.

OVER THE NEXT WEEK, GENERAL Shafter rested and resupplied his men. Malaria and other tropical illnesses had already begun to ravage the invasion force, and rainy season downpours made it excruciating for Army teamsters to get their six-mule supply wagons out to the soldiers beyond Las Guásimas.

The day after the battle, the Rough Riders moved a couple of miles beyond Las Guásimas and camped close to a mountain stream. A number of foreign military attachés—some of them Roosevelt's friends from

Washington—made their way up the muddy road to pay their respects. They found Roosevelt in especially good spirits. General Young had fallen ill and Colonel Wood had been promoted to take over Shafter's cavalry brigade—leaving Roosevelt in sole command of the Rough Riders.

Seven miles down the road, the Spaniards waited in their trenches on the heights overlooking Santiago. The American naval blockade had created acute shortages of food and medicine in the city, but a relief force of eight thousand Spanish soldiers was rumored to be marching from Manzanillo. With the Spanish column confronted by the same bad roads and rain that plagued the Americans, as well as constant harassment from Cuban guerrillas, it was an open question as to when or whether it would arrive.

Late on June 28, with the Spanish reinforcements on pace to reach Santiago within four or five days, Shafter laid out a plan that was as simple as it was unimaginative. The bulk of his army would march down the Santiago road and attack the San Juan Heights head-on. Simultaneously, General Lawton would take a division of infantry and a light artillery battery and capture an enemy outpost called El Caney, six miles north of Santiago.

On June 30, the Rough Riders struck camp about noon and formed up behind the 1st Cavalry. Roosevelt fumed as regiment after regiment marched by—regular infantry and volunteers, white units and black, artillery batteries, ragged bands of Cuban guerrillas, mule trains with ammunition. When the cavalry finally got under way, progress was slow. Darkness fell, and still Roosevelt and his men pushed on through steamy jungle and ragged clearings. Around eight o'clock, the Rough Riders trudged up a hill known as El Pozo. From there, little more than a mile away, they could make out their objective: the San Juan Heights, now held by about ten thousand entrenched Spanish troops.

MORNING'S FIRST GRAY LIGHT REVEALED scenes of deceptive tranquillity. Ribbons of smoke rose from cooking fires in the thatched cottages of El Caney, while cattle grazed in the valley nearby. "Around us on three sides," wrote a British army observer with General Adna Chaffee's brigade, "arose tier upon tier, the beautiful Maestra Mountains, wearing delicate pearly tints in the first rays of the rising sun. . . ."[19]

On El Pozo, teams of horses dragged four light field guns up the slope, urged on by foulmouthed, whip-swinging artillerymen. The artist Frederic Remington made quick sketches of the scene. Nearby, thirty-seven-year-old Lieutenant John J. Pershing of the 10th Cavalry gazed across the valley to the San Juan Heights, which arced around the city of Santiago in the shape of a half-moon.

The Spanish commander, General Linares, had created a dilemma for Shafter by deploying 520 men in a stone fort, wooden blockhouses, and trenches at El Caney, three miles north of El Pozo. Shafter was intent on eliminating that threat off his right flank before proceeding with the main assault. At six thirty-five a.m., an artillery battery commanded by Captain Allyn Capron Sr.—the father of Roosevelt's fallen troop commander—opened a leisurely bombardment of El Caney.

At eight o'clock, American artillery on El Pozo began shelling the San Juan Heights, and after a few minutes the Spanish guns responded. Atop El Pozo, Roosevelt heard "a peculiar whistling, singing sound in the air, and immediately afterward the noise of something exploding over our heads." A second shell burst above them, and a piece of shrapnel struck Roosevelt on the wrist, "raising a bump about as big as a hickory nut." He hustled his men to shelter.

Meanwhile, the road leading down from El Pozo was filling with American troops moving forward for the assault. The Rough Riders soon found themselves caught in a crush of men, artillery, and mule-drawn Gatling guns, all creeping toward the San Juan Heights under increasingly deadly Spanish fire. Twigs and leaves showered down on the troops as enemy bullets sliced through the forest canopy. "It seemed that if one stuck out his hand, the fingers would be clipped off," recalled Private Charles Post of the 71st New York Regiment. "We huddled within ourselves and bent over to shield our bellies."[20]

A shell exploded and twelve men fell to the ground. Just ahead of Post a soldier stumbled and dropped dead. "We stepped over him," Post recalled. "The man beside me lurched a little and sank down: 'Je-e-sus!'

he grunted. Four bullets had caught him between knee and thigh." The column wound past the body of a young lieutenant. Ants were already swarming his head as sobbing, hysterical soldiers pushed forward. "Cover him up! He's an officer! Cover him up, goddammit!" a major standing over the lifeless body shouted to the terrified soldiers scurrying past. "Cover him up yourself, you son of a bitch!" came a reply. The column moved on.[21]

A HAIL OF BULLETS AND shrapnel now pelted the American troops bunched up where the road traversed a branch of the San Juan River. Already the blood of dead and dying men glistened in the mud and stained the water. Roosevelt hurried his men across. Moving through a glade of waist-high grass, they reached a sunken lane and crouched behind its protective bank. The Rough Riders now anchored the right flank of the American line, which was pinned down several hundred yards short of the San Juan Heights. Spanish fire "swept the whole field of battle up to the edge of the river, and man after man in our ranks fell dead or wounded," Roosevelt recalled. He ordered his troops to spread out, "taking advantage of every scrap of cover."[22]

Rough Rider Captain Bucky O'Neill, insisting it was an officer's duty to inspire his men by exposing himself to enemy fire, strolled the line, smoking a cigarette and ignoring pleas to get down. "A bullet is sure to hit you, sir," a sergeant warned. O'Neill brushed him off. "Sergeant, the Spanish bullet isn't made that will kill me." Moments later, a slug struck O'Neill in the mouth and ripped through the back of his head.[23]

Shafter's plan was now in danger of unraveling. The assault on the San Juan Heights was supposed to begin only after Lawton overran the forward Spanish position at El Caney. Yet Lawton's men had yet to take El Caney after six hours of fierce fighting. In the meantime, American soldiers at the base of the heights burrowed into the tall grass and flattened behind bushes while awaiting the order to advance. "The situation was desperate," Richard Harding Davis wrote. "Our troops could not retreat, as the trail for two miles behind them was wedged with men. They could not remain where they were, for they were being shot to pieces. There was only one thing they could do—go forward and take the San Juan hills by assault."

Roosevelt was poised to attack of his own volition when an order granting his request to advance arrived. He leaped onto the back of his horse Little Texas. "And then," as he famously wrote, "my 'crowded hour' began."[24]

THREE BROWN LINES OF ROUGH Riders surged ahead. Dissatisfied with the pace, Roosevelt spurred his horse through one line, then another, and another, "until I found myself at the head of the regiment." Riding back and forth, he exhorted the men to keep moving. They quickly covered a hundred yards and fell to the ground behind the 1st Cavalry Brigade. Roosevelt told one of the brigade's officers that he was supposed to attack. The confused cavalryman hesitated. "Then let my men through, sir!" Roosevelt demanded. The Rough Riders resumed their charge with the regulars following.[25]

Spurred on by Roosevelt, the Rough Riders pushed ahead through waist-high grass. Ahead of them, the Spanish trenches and blockhouses atop Kettle Hill and the heights beyond "roared and flashed with flame." Roosevelt's men were so few in number at first that "it seemed as if someone had made an awful and terrible mistake," recalled Richard Harding Davis. Watching the scene unfold from El Pozo, a mile and a half away, a crowd of foreign military observers quickly agreed the American assault was doomed to failure. "It is very gallant, but very foolish," said one. And another: "It is slaughter, absolute slaughter."[26]

But Roosevelt's charge was gaining momentum, and other units joined in. Black troopers of the 10th Cavalry pressed forward on the left, led by Lieutenant John J. Pershing, forevermore known as "Black Jack" for the skin color of the troops he led. A bullet grazed Roosevelt's elbow, but did not slow him.

When a barbed-wire fence halted his progress, Roosevelt leaped off Little Texas, vaulted the obstacle and continued up the hill on foot.[27] American troops soon swarmed the crest of Kettle Hill—Rough Riders and regulars, white skinned and black.

To the left, Brigadier General Jacob F. Kent's 1st Infantry Division was now striding up San Juan Hill, heading for a Spanish blockhouse as Roosevelt's men fired supporting volleys. A fresh wave of blue-shirted infantry burst from the undergrowth to join the charge. They were led by Lieutenant Jules Ord of the 6th Infantry, son of General Grant's close Civil War aide, who clutched a saber in one hand and a revolver in the other. As his men crested the hill, retreating Spanish troops fired a few parting shots, and Ord fell dead.

With San Juan Hill now also in hand, Roosevelt led hundreds of dismounted cavalry up the next ridge. Two Spanish soldiers jumped up, fired and turned to run. Roosevelt fired two shots from his revolver, a relic recovered from the battleship *Maine*. The first missed, but the second dropped one of the enemy soldiers. Roosevelt charged ahead, past ranch buildings the Spaniards had just fled and through a palm grove. When he finally paused to get his bearings, the red tiled roofs of Santiago lay below him.

By two p.m., the Americans controlled the San Juan Heights, but the battle was not over. Spanish riflemen and artillery raked the ridge from the outskirts of Santiago, five hundred yards away. Exhausted soldiers sprawled atop the just-captured crests, their silk cavalry guidons, regimental flags and the Stars and Stripes fluttering in the breeze.

Finally, around four fifteen, the battlefield fell silent. At San Juan and El Caney, the Americans had achieved their objectives at the cost of 205 dead and 1,180 wounded. The Spaniards suffered 215 dead and 376 wounded. Later, summing up the day that would become an icon for his legendary life, Roosevelt was uncharacteristically subdued. "The Spaniards made a stiff fight, standing firm until we charged home," he wrote. "On this day they showed themselves to be brave foes, worthy of honor for their gallantry."[28]

NIGHTFALL BROUGHT LITTLE REST FOR the Americans. The battle had underscored the need for shelter on the exposed ridgeline, so the weary soldiers spent hours digging trenches and rifle pits and throwing up parapets. It was after midnight when they fell asleep on their rifles. Three hours later, Spanish skirmishers opened fire, followed by an enemy artillery barrage. The shivering, haggard Rough Riders stumbled into trenches they had just completed to await an attack, but it never came.

The Spanish signaled the arrival of dawn with renewed fire. Snipers had crept up the ridge during the night and now peppered the trenches from the tall grass and trees. Anxieties soared. Behind the American front lines, rising casualties from unseen gunmen fueled rumors that the jungle at the base of El Pozo was infested with snipers. Fresh troops destined to reinforce the thin front lines were held back to search for Spanish holdouts. At Shafter's headquarters, the mood darkened even more as casualty reports rose and seasonal rains paralyzed efforts to resupply the front. Worse still, the Spanish relief column was reported to be less than a day's march away.

By evening, with scuttlebutt of an American withdrawal sweeping the heights, Shafter summoned his senior officers. Debilitated by fever and heat stress, the obese commander was carried into the war council on a door that had been removed from an abandoned farmhouse. Shafter informed his generals that the Spanish relief column was believed to be nearing Santiago, and an additional twenty thousand or more enemy troops were within striking distance. Raising the possibility of an immediate withdrawal, he polled his generals. By a vote of three to one, they recommended holding the line. Shafter paused, then announced his decision: They would hold in place for another twenty-four hours.[29]

On the front lines, Roosevelt had heard the rumors of retreat, and he had vigorously urged General Wheeler to oppose such a move. He had even volunteered the Rough Riders to lead an assault on the Spanish lines. But the bravado hid growing doubts, and as Shafter and his generals debated, Roosevelt pondered the potential catastrophe that confronted the Americans.

As he often did in times of crisis, Roosevelt now confided his worst fears in a letter to his friend Henry Cabot Lodge. "Tell the President for Heaven's sake to send us every regiment and above all every battery possible," he grimly wrote in his tent atop the San Juan Heights. "We are within measurable distance of a terrible military disaster."[30]

CHAPTER 7

The Eagle Spreads Its Wings

A thousand miles to the north, President William McKinley continued to be haunted by his own fears and doubts. In the three months
since agreeing to go to war, McKinley had thrown himself into his role
as commander in chief. He had a second-story White House office transformed into a war room equipped with fifteen telephone lines and twenty
telegraph wires, putting him in ready contact with his far-flung military
commanders. On the walls, maps of the United States and the Caribbean
bristled with colored flags marking the location of troops and ships.[1] Once
General Shafter's army landed in Cuba, the president began spending
most evenings in his war room, awaiting cables from the front.

McKinley had been disturbed by news dispatches from Cuba suggesting that American troops had been needlessly sacrificed at Las Guásimas.
Some of the more critical reports depicted the battle as the bloody result
of General Wheeler's lust for personal glory. Anxieties soared on Friday,
July 1, when the War Department announced that Shafter's troops were
in combat on the outskirts of Santiago.[2]

Just before midnight, a cable finally arrived from Shafter. The general
confirmed that his troops had taken El Caney and the outer defenses of
Santiago, but at the cost of more than four hundred casualties. McKinley

was still digesting that news when a more ominous cable arrived about two a.m. "I fear I have underestimated today's casualties," Shafter wrote without further explanation. "A large and thoroughly equipped hospital ship should be sent here at once to care for the wounded."[3] With the weight of that disconcerting report on his mind, McKinley retired for the night.

The president awoke the next morning to find there was no further news from Cuba, and so he settled into the war room with Secretary of War Russell Alger to await developments. McKinley's closest friend and adviser, millionaire Senator Mark Hanna of Ohio, joined the vigil, but hours ticked by without word from Shafter.

By Saturday afternoon, speculation filled the news vacuum. Dark rumors about staggering American casualties and an unfolding military disaster unsettled the White House and War Department. The Associated Press and several afternoon newspapers reported that General Shafter and General Wheeler were seriously ill, and that dreaded yellow fever was ravaging the American camps outside Santiago.[4]

Night fell without news from Santiago, and McKinley and his advisers began another long vigil. At one a.m., after nearly twenty-four hours of silence, Alger fired off a pointed telegram to the American commander: "We are waiting with intense anxiety tidings of yesterday." McKinley and his men stood by for another three hours, but the telegraph machine remained silent. At four a.m. the president gave up and went to bed.[5]

IN THE PREDAWN DARKNESS OF Sunday, July 3, the USS *Indiana* rode easily in calm seas off the entrance to Santiago Bay. All night her broadside guns had been trained on the canyonlike channel through which the Spanish fleet would have to pass should it attempt an escape. Nearby, her sister battleships, the *Iowa* and *Oregon*, illuminated the mouth of the bay with powerful searchlights.

The *Indiana* had missed Friday's action in the hills above Santiago. She had been taking on coal at Guantánamo Bay, but hurried back to her place in the blockade line after General Shafter appealed for a naval bombardment of Santiago to relieve pressure on his troops along the San

Juan Heights. With coal dust "still thick on the deck and on the faces of the officers and crew," wrote Captain Henry Taylor, the men of the *Indiana* "sprang to their stations with a cool exultation of spirit."[6]

At midnight Saturday, the *Indiana* pulled into position outside the entrance to the bay with a heightened sense of urgency. Throughout the day plumes of smoke had risen from the shielded cove where Admiral Cervera's fleet was anchored. The Spanish warships were getting up steam, but why? Were they preparing to run for it? Or was Cervera repositioning his ships to bombard American ground forces?

Sunrise seemed to answer the first question, at least. Admiral Sampson and his commanders were quite certain that if Cervera attempted to break out, it would be in darkness.

FIFTY-NINE-YEAR-OLD ADMIRAL PASCUAL CERVERA Y Topete arose before dawn on Sunday morning, slipped on his lavishly medaled uniform, and steeled himself for the heartbreaking assignment that awaited him. A bearded, music-loving graduate of the Spanish Naval College, he had ascended to become one of Spain's most experienced and versatile admirals, decorated for bravery in combat in the Philippines and praised for his meticulously crafted nautical charts. When the war with America began, Cervera found himself in command of a decrepit squadron with orders to save his country's possessions in the Caribbean.[7]

Cervera had argued that his ships were no match for newer American battleships in speed, armaments and armor, but to no avail. In late May, he crossed the Atlantic and put in at Santiago for coal and repairs, only to be trapped there by Admiral Sampson's American fleet. In the weeks since, Cervera had resisted pressure from Madrid to fight his way out of the bay and had sent his sailors ashore to assist in the defense of Santiago. But as Shafter's army closed in, the supreme Spanish military commander on Cuba, Captain General Ramón Blanco, issued Cervera a direct order: Break out of Santiago Bay—or die trying.[8]

On Saturday, Cervera recalled his sailors from the trenches and readied his fleet for departure. He sealed his official documents, letters, and telegrams in a package and sent it ashore for safekeeping with the

Archbishop of Santiago, to be delivered to Cervera's relatives in the event of his death.

Constant probes of the American blockade had convinced the Spanish admiral that there was nothing to be gained by a nighttime escape attempt, so he decided to gamble on a daylight run. Perhaps the American sailors might let their guard down on a Sunday morning. With luck, he would reach open water before the American warships could react.

THE MORNING OVERCAST QUICKLY GAVE way to brilliant blue skies off Santiago. Pulled back into a half circle around the entrance to Santiago Bay was the might of America's new navy, the magnificent trophies conjured by Alfred Mahan, Theodore Roosevelt and Henry Cabot Lodge— the battleships *Indiana*, *Iowa* and *Oregon*. Big guns jutted menacingly from armored barbettes and turrets on the steel-sheathed, steam-powered leviathans.

The *Indiana* held the distinction of being the first of this new generation of warships, launched in early 1893. At the time, she was the most expensive ship ever built for the Navy, but proponents had insisted that her $3 million cost was a modest price for national greatness. Three years later, as the ship was about to be commissioned, the *New York Times* reinforced that view, proclaiming the *Indiana* "a wonder" after her official speed tests off the Massachusetts coast. She averaged 15.61 knots per hour over four hours, beating the Navy's fifteen-knot contract requirement and earning her builder a $50,000 bonus.[9]

But the art of battleship design was rapidly evolving, and the *Indiana* soon revealed her flaws. She rode too low in the water and even in normal conditions tended to roll, putting her decks awash. Her round, steam-powered turrets lacked counterweights to offset their heavy gun barrels, causing the ship to list in the direction the massive weapons were pointed. To compensate, gunners had to add elevation to their target calculations. Then in early 1898, though she was only five years old, her boiler tubes began leaking so badly during one exercise that she had to be taken in tow.[10]

Despite these problems, Captain Henry C. Taylor whipped his ship and crew into fighting shape by the time war was declared in April.

With the sun now fully up, any attempt at a breakout by the Spanish fleet seemed out of the question. At nine a.m., the flagship *New York* pulled away, carrying Admiral Sampson to a meeting with General Shafter.

Aboard the *Indiana*, at half past nine, a bugle interrupted the leisurely Sunday-morning pace with the call to quarters. Officers and crew— among them Captain Tony Waller and the ship's contingent of Marines— made their way to the main deck for muster and inspection. Church services were to immediately follow.

"The weather was quiet, the sea smooth," Captain Taylor later recalled. "There was nothing to indicate the startling event that was about to occur."[11]

The crack of a light gun off to the west shattered the calm. All eyes turned toward the sound. A gentle breeze unfurled a signal flag from one of the masts of the *Iowa*, the closest ship to the bay channel: enemy ships coming out.

Taylor and his officers shouted a flurry of orders.

"Sound the general alarm!"

"Clear ship for action!"

"Bugles call to general quarters!"

One hundred seventy men in the powder division bunched up at the narrow hatches leading belowdecks. Sailors frantically threw themselves down the steep ladders and, bruised and bleeding, limped across the ammunition deck to their stations.

On the gun deck, men crowded toward the scuttles and ports of the thirteen-inch and eight-inch turrets, the *Indiana*'s mightiest guns. Sweating heavily, they stripped to the waist and prepared to fire. From the bridge, Captain Taylor shouted down to the men on the forecastle and around the forward turrets.

"Get to your guns, lads! Our chance has come at last!"

Cheers swept the ship.[12]

STANDING AT THE BRIDGE OF his flagship, the cruiser *Infanta María Teresa*, Admiral Cervera led his fleet single file out of Santiago Bay. Ten minutes behind him was the cruiser *Vizcaya*, followed by the cruisers *Colón* and

Oquendo and the destroyers *Furor* and *Plutón*. Red-and-gold battle flags snapped from the masts of the black-hulled ships, and their polished brasswork gleamed in the sun. Buglers sounded the call to battle.[13]

The *María Teresa* emerged from the bay to find the American ships arrayed in an eight-mile semicircle, smoke spewing from their stacks as crews frantically tried to coax more steam out of dampened boilers. The Americans were already beginning to close on Cervera's flagship, like a quiver of deadly spears converging on a single target. They had spent weeks calibrating ranges by sextant and stadiometer, using the venerable Morro Castle, perched on a cliff above the channel, as their guide. Now the *María Teresa* had emerged into a killing zone.

Shells from the American ships began to smash into the Spanish flagship. On the *Indiana*, at the eastern end of the line, Captain Waller and his Marines hammered away at the lead ship with their secondary guns—the last great naval battle using Marine gunners on U.S. Navy ships.[14] To the west, the battleship *Iowa*, cruiser *Brooklyn* and second-class battleship *Texas* raked the Spanish cruisers, while to the east the *Gloucester*—until recently the J. P. Morgan yacht *Corsair*—engaged the enemy destroyers.

The Spaniards returned spirited fire, but their aim was poor. The exception was a pair of superb shots fired by the *Colón* at the *Iowa*. The first punched through the American ship's starboard side forward of the bridge and exploded in the dispensary, shattering medicine bottles but miraculously sparing nearby crewmen. The second tore a jagged hole at the waterline amidships—the highlight of the day for the Spanish fleet.

The battle quickly became a replay of Dewey's triumph at Manila Bay. Shells smashed into the *María Teresa*, ripping away chunks of steel and igniting her ornate woodwork. The other Spanish ships suffered similar punishment. Blood and body parts soon littered the Spanish decks, and smoke from raging fires billowed from hatches.

Around ten thirty a.m., an hour after leaving the bay, Cervera ordered the doomed *María Teresa* to strike colors and turn for shallow water along the shore. The *Oquendo*, on fire fore and aft, her boilers destroyed and her commander mortally wounded, soon followed, but sank before reaching the beach. The *Vizcaya* made it farther down the coast, but she, too, was forced to strike colors and turn to shore.

On the doomed and burning ships, the shrieks of Spanish sailors carried across the water. Some men, their uniforms ablaze, threw themselves into the sea. Burned and bloodied sailors thrashed in the water as sharks moved in. Survivors who dragged themselves onto the beach found themselves under fire from Cuban insurgents until the Americans silenced their eager allies.

The *Colón* now fought on alone. After a two-hour chase, the *Oregon* bracketed the fleeing cruiser fore and aft with shells from its heaviest guns. His fate sealed, the *Colón*'s skipper turned to shore and scuttled his ship.

After less than four hours, the battle of Santiago Bay was over. Only one American died in the fighting, a sailor on the *Brooklyn*, decapitated by a Spanish shell. Cervera lost 323 men killed and 151 wounded. Another 1,670 were taken captive.

On the American ships, line officers, surgeons and chaplains sprang into action to save the Spanish sailors. Captain Taylor of the *Indiana* dispatched two volunteer relief parties to rescue men from the burning Spanish wrecks. Marine Captain Tony Waller led one of them, setting out in a small boat with several other men, including the ship's surgeon, carrying water, hardtack and medical supplies. Ignoring the exploding ammunition and raging fires, Waller and his men headed toward the *María Teresa* and *Oquendo*. They worked to save burned and wounded Spaniards past dark, aided by ghostly light from the burning ships and a bonfire built by American sailors on the beach. From the shadows, gaunt Cuban insurgents watched curiously as the Americans carefully tended to Spanish sailors who only hours earlier had been their mortal enemies.[15]

Among those who surrendered onshore was Cervera. The *Gloucester* carried him out to the *Iowa*, where he found the American battleship's officers mustered on one side of the quarterdeck and rescued officers and crew from the vanquished Spanish cruiser *Vizcaya* on the other. The *Iowa*'s men crowded turrets and the superstructure to watch a Marine guard present arms and buglers blast flourishes in a show of respect for the Spanish admiral. As the Americans burst into cheers, the bareheaded and shoeless Cervera bowed in thanks.[16]

THE DESTRUCTION OF CERVERA'S FLEET ended the threat to Shafter's army, and effectively concluded the war in Cuba. On Sunday morning, July 17, General Shafter was hoisted onto his horse, and at eight forty-five a.m. led his commanders and an honor guard of a hundred soldiers down the slopes of El Pozo toward Santiago. They trotted across the valley where their troops had fallen, splashed through the river fords that ran red with American blood and made their way up the San Juan Heights. American regiments, drawn up beside their trenches, watched as Shafter and his entourage cantered toward the Spanish lines for the brief surrender ceremony.

Afterward, Shafter and his guard rode into Santiago to formally take control of the shattered city. As the clock on the old cathedral tolled noon, three U.S. soldiers—among them Lieutenant Joseph Wheeler Jr.—hauled the Stars and Stripes up the flagpole on the central plaza. A military band played "The Star-Spangled Banner" while, on the heights overlooking the city, an artillery battery commanded by Captain Allyn Capron Sr., the grieving father of the fallen Rough Rider, fired a twenty-one-gun salute. Along seven miles of trenches, American soldiers cheered.

AS THE WAR IN CUBA sputtered to a close, newly minted Admiral George Dewey was presiding over a precarious state of affairs in the Philippines. The day following his Manila Bay victory, Dewey had dispatched a contingent of Marines to secure the Spanish arsenal at Cavite. But Spanish troops still held Manila, and Emilio Aguinaldo's revolutionary army controlled the countryside. As if that weren't worrisome enough, Dewey found himself having to fend off threatening actions by the German navy while parsing rumors of an approaching Spanish fleet. Privately, he could only hope that U.S. ground forces arrived before the situation spun beyond his control.

McKinley had ordered an expeditionary force to the Philippines on

May 2, even before news of Dewey's victory had reached Washington. He had placed the troops under the command of Major General Wesley Merritt, a handsome West Pointer from New York City who had earned his first star as a twenty-three-year-old Union Army cavalryman on the same day as George Armstrong Custer. Unlike Custer, Merritt had burnished his reputation during the Indian campaigns of the 1870s, and by the time war was declared against Spain, he was the Army's second-ranking officer.

Merritt had departed for the Philippines in June without a clearly defined mission. He had tried, without success, to pin President McKinley down on whether he should merely seize and secure Manila or "subdue and hold all of the Spanish territory in the islands." It took McKinley seventeen days to draft a vague reply that laid out America's "twofold purpose" in the Philippines: "reduction of Spanish power in that quarter" and the introduction of "order and security to the islands while in the possession of the United States." McKinley, as historian Stanley Karnow has noted, failed to specify whether America's custody of the islands "would be permanent or temporary."[17]

When he reached Manila Bay in late July, Merritt found an even murkier situation. Dewey had arranged for Emilio Aguinaldo to end his Hong Kong exile and return to the Philippines on a U.S. vessel in mid-May. After an hour-long meeting aboard the *Olympia*, Dewey had sent the revolutionary leader ashore with weapons and instructions to attack Spanish forces.

Dewey later denied Aguinaldo's claim that he had pledged support for an independent Philippine republic in return—indeed, Dewey dubiously testified before the U.S. Senate in 1902 that he was even unaware that Aguinaldo desired independence when he brought him back to the islands. In any event, Dewey proved shrewd in his dealings with the Filipino. When Aguinaldo invited Dewey to attend a ceremonial declaration of Philippine independence in his Cavite hometown on June 12, the American admiral begged off, citing the demands of mail delivery for his fleet. While Dewey watched and waited, Aguinaldo's army surrounded Manila and captured key towns on Luzon and outlying islands.[18]

As Merritt's force steamed across the Pacific, the intrepid U.S. diplomat Oscar F. Williams assured administration officials in Washington that a majority of Filipinos would welcome the Americans as liberators. Williams had accompanied Dewey's fleet back to Manila, and he had been warmly received by Filipinos when he went ashore in Cavite. "Few United States troops will be needed for conquest," Williams reported, "and fewer still for occupancy."[19]

But the native hospitality that Williams promised began to fade soon after the lead elements of Merritt's troops landed south of Manila in late June. At first Aguinaldo shared maps and intelligence with the Americans and allowed U.S. soldiers to pass through his lines to reconnoiter Spanish positions. But when still more American troops came ashore in July, a wary Aguinaldo ordered the local population to withhold supplies, food and transportation from the foreigners unless expressly approved by his headquarters. Only after American officers threatened confiscations from the local citizenry did Aguinaldo resume grudging cooperation.[20]

Relations frayed even further when General Merritt arrived on the scene in late July. After rejecting any personal dealings with Aguinaldo, Merritt dispatched a subordinate to persuade a frontline Filipino commander to vacate his position in exchange for four artillery pieces. Aguinaldo approved the arrangement, and his troops withdrew as agreed. Merritt's men promptly took control of the trenches, but refused to deliver the artillery pieces. A distraught Filipino general rushed to Aguinaldo to protest the betrayal. "If we're not careful," he cried, "they will soon be replacing our flags with their own all over the country!"[21]

 On August 13, with 8,500 troops ashore, Merritt launched a joint sea and land attack on Spanish forces in Manila. Unknown to the American soldiers and their erstwhile Filipino allies, secret talks overseen by Merritt and Dewey had predetermined the outcome: The Spaniards would surrender after token resistance, allowing their commanders to claim an honorable defense in the face of overwhelming enemy force.

The plan nearly went awry when Filipino forces tried to join the attack and were rebuffed by U.S. troops. Merritt's agreement with the Spaniards expressly barred the entry of Aguinaldo's men into the city, and he warned the revolutionary leader that he would use force if necessary. Furious Filipino fighters surged into the suburbs, and an armed confrontation with U.S. soldiers appeared imminent. After a standoff lasting several hours, Aguinaldo's forces angrily returned to their trenches.[22]

Three days later, a message arrived from Washington announcing the signing of a peace protocol between the United States and Spain. While plans were laid for negotiations to decide the fate of the Philippines and other matters, Merritt's troops and Aguinaldo's soldiers kept a distrustful eye on one another.

THROUGHOUT AUGUST AND SEPTEMBER, TRANSPORT ships bearing the soldiers of Shafter's triumphant army arrived in East Coast ports. The naysayers had been spectacularly wrong about Theodore Roosevelt's decision to resign his Navy Department position to chase battlefield glory in Cuba. Far from ruining his political career, Roosevelt was now hailed across America as the hero of San Juan Hill. New York Republican bosses handed him the party's nomination for governor in the November election.

The war had also been a turning point for the embattled Marine Corps. After returning to Portsmouth Naval Shipyard in southern Maine on August 26, Colonel Huntington and his 1st Marine Battalion were feted at parades and clambakes, and their glorious deeds at Guantánamo Bay and Cuzco Well celebrated. Even the health of the bronzed Marines enhanced their image as America's new superheroes. Navy spokesmen and newspaper reporters waxed about the hale condition of Huntington's men, while none too subtly noting the Army's heavy losses to malaria, yellow fever and dysentery.[23]

One final curtain call remained. On September 22, at President McKinley's request, three officers and 164 Marines who had served under Huntington on Cuba marched in review in Washington. Despite heavy rain, a large crowd cheered as the Marines strutted down the capital's boulevards. Afterward, Sergeant John Quick was presented with the Medal of Honor for his "cool and gallant conduct" at Cuzco Well, and surgeon John Gibbs, one of the first casualties at Guantánamo Bay, was posthumously honored.

Talk of abolishing the Marines had been silenced, and Commandant Charles Heywood was preparing his case for expanding the Corps as a quick-strike force suited to policing America's new overseas possessions. It would take several more months, and trouble in the Philippines, but President McKinley and Congress would support Heywood's request. In the meantime, the Corps was content to bask in its newfound glory. "They have performed," McKinley declared, "magnificent duty."[24]

NOT QUITE FOUR MONTHS HAD passed since Congress had granted a reluctant president the authority to make war on Spain, but in that short time America had charged into a new era. The "splendid little war," as Secretary of State John Hay famously described it, had been decisively won at the cost of little American blood or treasure. With its powerful ships and brave soldiers, its material wealth and industrial might, the United States had humiliated a once-great European power. Its claim to world-class status no longer in doubt, America marched confidently onto the global stage.

Events could not have turned out more to the satisfaction of Theodore Roosevelt and his fellow expansionists. The war that Roosevelt had so vigorously advocated had expanded America's reach around the world, with possession of Cuba and Puerto Rico in the Caribbean and Manila and the island of Guam in the Pacific. The summer's patriotic fervor had even moved Congress to annex Hawaii, fulfilling another expansionist goal.

But with victory came profound questions that the nation had only begun to ponder. Should America return to isolation within its shores, content with having liberated Cuba and the Philippines from oppressive rule? Or should it permanently claim its new possessions to support a larger world role? Formal treaty negotiations with Spain would not begin until the fall, but already across America the winds of a bitter and divisive debate had begun to blow.

PART II

Imperial Glory

CHAPTER 8

"White Man's Burden"

B rass bands blared and drums pounded as thousands of excited Hoo-
siers converged on downtown Indianapolis, Indiana, for the kickoff
rally of the fall political campaign. It was Friday, September 16, 1898,
and in the gathering twilight a raucous procession approached Tomlinson
Hall. Two hundred Republican activists waving torches and red lanterns
drew near the stately brick auditorium, and a roar swept through the
crowd as a carriage came into view. The object of the sudden excitement
sat serenely in the coach, a handsome thirty-six-year-old Republican
attorney whose spectacular oratorical skills had made him a national
political celebrity. Tucked in his vest pocket was the most important
speech of his career, for on this evening, Albert Jeremiah Beveridge was
poised to set America on the road to empire.[1]

Beveridge had long bridled at America's failure to aggressively com-
pete with Britain and Germany in the quest for colonies and overseas
markets. In his analysis, the nation's destiny would be determined by its
success in a global industrial and commercial competition. Asia would be
the pivotal battleground, with China the grand prize. And now, in a
divinely ordained flurry of events, the United States had an outpost on

China's very doorstep—if only it would claim the Philippines as its permanent possession.

In the spring, Beveridge had been the first prominent Republican to forecast the territorial windfall that awaited the United States in a war with Spain. "We will establish trading posts throughout the world as distributing points for American products," he had prophesied in a Boston speech. "Great colonies, governing themselves, flying our flag and trading with us, will grow about our posts of trade. And American law, American order, American civilization, and the American flag will plant themselves on shores hitherto bloody and benighted."[2]

Now, as Beveridge prepared to address the Republican faithful in Indianapolis, President William McKinley was weighing just how much he should demand from Spain in the peace talks scheduled to open in Paris in a few weeks. Particularly vexing was the disposition of Spain's largest overseas colony, the Philippines. Germany had made clear its interest in the islands, as had Britain and Japan. Should the United States demand part of the archipelago from Spain, or all of it? Or should it grant Filipinos their wish for self-rule? As usual, McKinley was playing his cards close to the vest.

To Beveridge, the choice was clear, as he was about to reveal. A thunderous ovation greeted his introduction and he briskly made his way to the platform. A man of only average height, Beveridge appeared taller because of his erect military posture. His shoulders were broad, his upper body muscular. His face was lean and handsome, his blue-gray eyes expressive.

For a full two minutes, he stood at the lectern and let the cheers and applause roll over him. And then, on his gesture, the crowd fell silent and Beveridge began to speak, softly at first, each word perfectly enunciated, as he had trained himself to do as a barefoot boy plowing his family's Illinois farm.

"The burning question of this campaign," Beveridge said, "is whether the American people will accept the gifts of events; whether they will rise as lifts their soaring destiny; whether they will proceed upon the lines of national development surveyed by the statesmen of our past; or whether, for the first time, the American people, doubting their mission, will question Fate, prove apostate to the spirit of their race, and halt the ceaseless march of free institutions."

He brusquely dismissed the critics of American expansion. "The opposition tells us we ought not to rule a people without their consent," he said, but liberty could be extended "only to those who are capable of self-government."

So what was to be done in the Philippines? America could not in good conscience return the islands "to the savage, bloody rule of pillage and extortion from which we have rescued them," he said. Nor could it "abandon them to their fate, with the wolves of conquest all about them—with Germany, Russia, France, even Japan, hungering for them." As for granting self-rule to the little brown-skinned Filipinos, he proclaimed, "It would be like giving a razor to a babe and telling it to shave itself."

The crowd roared with laughter.

America had a long tradition of territorial expansion, Beveridge assured his audience: the Louisiana Purchase of Thomas Jefferson, America's "first imperialist," as he approvingly described the nation's third president; the acquisition of Florida from Spain; the war with Mexico that delivered Texas, the Southwest and California into American hands. Each acquisition had been fulfillment of America's divine destiny, Beveridge insisted, the inexorable "march of the flag."

Economic self-interest now made expansion more important than ever, Beveridge said. American farmers were "raising more than we can consume," and factory workers "making more than we can use." Overseas colonies were the solution to the nation's mounting challenges.

Beveridge now soared to his conclusion, his voice rising, the crowd cheering every sentence. Expansion transcended material concerns, for it was a matter of national honor and duty, he cried. It was America's destiny "to set the world its example of right and honor," for "we cannot fly from our world duties. We cannot retreat from any soil where Providence has unfurled our banner. It is ours to save that soil, for liberty and civilization."

As a deafening ovation shook the hall, Beveridge bowed and took his seat.

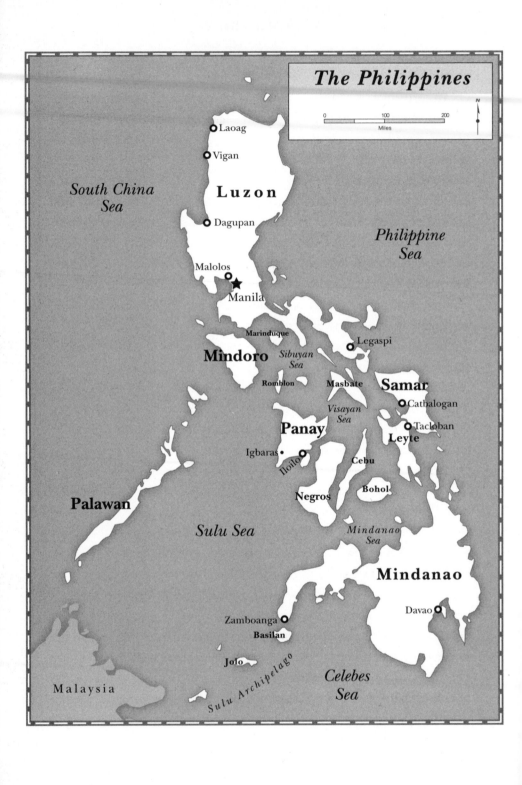

ON THE OTHER SIDE OF the world, fifteen thousand American troops were settling into their role as an occupying army in the steamy Philippine Islands. The docks of Manila bustled with U.S. Army transports offloading troops, ammunition and tons of supplies. Passenger steamers disgorged a civilian army of American speculators, swindlers, prostitutes, gamblers and adventurers converging on Manila. Scores of new saloons, whorehouses, gambling halls and opium dens sprouted along the narrow streets.

It was the height of the rainy reason season in Manila, and the American soldiers—a mix of army regulars and militia from nearly a dozen states—were soon exposed to the travails of tropical monsoons. Trenches filled with water, wet uniforms mildewed, boots and shoes rotted. Tired of wearing sopping uniforms, troops drilled in their underwear. Some fell ill from malaria, dengue fever, dysentery, cholera and other tropical diseases.

Despite the discomforts and dangers, Will Christner, a good-looking, mustachioed corporal in the 10th Pennsylvania National Guard Regiment, found Manila to his liking. He and other soldiers were smitten by the beautiful, dark-skinned women in their sheer dresses made of delicate pineapple fibers. The leisurely pace of occupation duty gave Christner "plenty of time to look over the city," and, as he wryly noted, "a boy of my prying disposition can find many things to interest him in an oriental town." One of his interests, the daughter of a Filipino store owner, encouraged his flirtations by washing and mending his clothes for free and plying him with cigars, lemonade and fruit.[3]

If American soldiers were enchanted by the exotic women, they tended to loathe Filipino men, especially the native soldiers dug in around the city. Distrust between the two armies was mutual. Revolutionary leader Emilio Aguinaldo and his soldiers had hoped to share in the occupation of Manila, until the secret deal American commanders arranged with the Spaniards denied the Filipinos their prize. Now Aguinaldo's soldiers seethed with anger and resentment in their trenches surrounding the city.

Demeaning treatment of Filipinos by the Americans fueled resentments. U.S. soldiers commonly referred to the dark-skinned Filipinos as "niggers," an insult so vehemently expressed that it quickly transcended language barriers. James J. Martin, a member of the 10th Pennsylvania, wrote home in late 1898 that "the way the soldiers are using the natives is enough to make them hate the American people." Thefts, assaults and rapes were not uncommon. As the weeks passed, simmering tensions between American and Filipino soldiers sometimes flared into violence. "We killed a few to learn them a lesson," Will Christner wrote his father after one incident, "and you bet they learned it."[4]

The Americans had inherited a starving, filthy, disease-ridden city from the Spaniards. An influx of refugees had swollen Manila's population from ten thousand to seventy thousand. Many of the weakened inhabitants were living in the streets. Hospitals and churches overflowed with the sick and the wounded. Garbage and human waste clotted the narrow streets and canals, and putrid smells permeated the steamy air.

Fulfilling President McKinley's directive to uplift the Filipinos, American officers brought an evangelical zeal to the task of revitalizing the run-down city. A police force was created. Military courts were established. Schools were reopened and roads repaired. The wanton dumping of garbage, swill and human excrement into city streets was forbidden, and Filipino teamsters were hired to collect refuse and cart it away for disposal. Health clinics were opened and children immunized against smallpox and other diseases.[5]

Overseeing the massive effort was the recently promoted commander of American forces in the Philippines, Major General Elwell Stephen Otis. On paper, the sixty-one-year-old Otis was an impressive choice to preside over America's first imperial outpost: A decorated veteran of the Civil War and Indian campaigns, Otis was also a Harvard Law School graduate and founder of the Army's staff school at Leavenworth, Kansas. Anyone who had served under the portly, muttonchop-whiskered general could also attest to a less impressive side: a fussy, pompous micromanager who obsessed over every minute detail of his command. A Civil War head wound had left him an insomniac, and so, from dawn to midnight, he could be found at his desk, shuffling papers and "counting the beans," as one aide put it. Major General Arthur MacArthur likened him to "a locomotive bottomside up on the track, with its wheels revolving at full speed."[6]

Otis performed ably in the administrative work of bringing law and order to Manila and getting the city back on its feet. But he was singularly ill suited to the delicate task of managing America's fraying relationship with the Filipinos. Utterly incurious when it came to dealing with the people whose fate he now held in his hands, Otis had little contact with Filipinos and never even bothered to meet Aguinaldo. That did not prevent him from forming strong opinions. He accused Aguinaldo of "duplicity" and dismissed Filipinos in general as "robbers" who sought to "drive the Americans into the sea, and kill every white man in Manila."[7]

Otis had inherited a muddled military situation that derived from President McKinley's vague characterization of Major General Merritt's mission. On August 29, Merritt formally handed command of U.S. forces in the Philippines to Otis. With fifteen thousand regulars and volunteers at his disposal, Otis assured his superiors he would handle the restless Filipinos with a little "delicate manipulation."[8]

There was nothing delicate about the general's handling of his first crisis in early September. Filipino troops remained in several Manila suburbs, and their proximity to American positions presented both a constant source of conflict and a military threat in the event of war. Otis alerted Washington that he planned to eject the Filipinos, and warned that his action might trigger violence. The War Department cabled its approval. After placing his troops on full alert, Otis sent Aguinaldo a legalistic letter on September 8, ordering Filipino forces to vacate the suburb in one week—or face "forcible action."[9]

Still hopeful of a favorable outcome for his cause at the peace talks in Paris, Aguinaldo hinted at acquiescence to Otis's command, if only the general would soften his language. Otis resubmitted his demands in the form of a request, and on September 14 some two thousand Filipino soldiers marched out of their trenches in the Manila suburbs, pausing to salute the Stars and Stripes as it was raised over their former positions.[10]

Afterward, Otis was in a buoyant mood as he sat at his desk in Manila's riverside Malacañang Palace and drafted another long status report for his superiors in Washington. The U.S. military government in Manila was "being perfected gradually," he wrote, the city cleaned up and policed and order restored. Trade and commerce had resumed (including the importation and sale of opium). Tax receipts were on the rise.

On the military front, the threat of imminent war with the Filipinos had diminished, Otis reported. Aguinaldo and his political and military leaders were in an "excitable frame of mind," but most were "amenable to reason." Confidently, he concluded, "Based upon present indications, no further force [is] required."[11]

Otis had badly misread the situation. By mid-September, any trust that had existed between the Filipino revolutionaries and the Americans had been shattered. Within Aguinaldo's inner circle, Apolinario Mabini, a disabled intellectual and militant nationalist, had gained sway with his view that further cooperation with the Americans was futile. "The conflict is coming sooner or later," Mabini darkly predicted, "and we shall gain nothing by asking as favors of them what are really our rights."[12]

ON A CRISP AUTUMN DAY in late September, a slight, well-dressed Asian man in a stylish bowler hat made his way from one of Chicago's train stations to Lincoln Park on the city's north side. Arriving at the leafy lakefront green, he hurried on foot to one of Chicago's most famous pieces of sculpture: a life-size bronze Abraham Lincoln, deep in thought, rising from an eagle-emblazoned chair, about to deliver a speech. As a lake breeze rustled through trees splashed with autumn colors, the visitor approached the silent figure and bared his head in tribute to the Great Emancipator. Momentous events beckoned the Asian man eastward, to what he hoped would be a White House meeting with America's current president. After ten or fifteen minutes, he hurried back to the train station and resumed his journey across the United States.[13]

Thirty-eight-year-old Felipe Agoncillo had arrived in America less than a week earlier, stepping onto the docks at San Francisco as the chief diplomatic representative of Emilio Aguinaldo's revolutionary government. His orders were to proceed to Washington, D.C., and seek an audience with President McKinley. There he was to plead the case for Filipino independence—or, at the very least, representation at the peace talks scheduled to begin in Paris in a few days.

It was an awesome responsibility for such a boyish-looking man from the hinterlands of a Spanish colonial backwater, unschooled in the intricacies of international diplomacy. Agoncillo had been born in 1859 to a family of means in Batangas province, along the coast of southern Luzon. But unlike many of his privileged peers, he had not gone abroad to Europe to pursue his education. He had earned his undergraduate and law degrees in Manila before returning to Batangas to pursue a career in law.

By 1885, Agoncillo had risen to a post equivalent to an assistant attorney general in the Spanish colonial government in Batangas. He held the position for much of the next decade, when he was caught up in the Spanish backlash against rising Filipino nationalism. Agoncillo's transgression had been providing free legal advice to the poor and advocating equal rights for Filipinos. Accused of "antipatriotic" and "anti-Catholic" activities, he was denounced as a *filibustero*—a subversive—by Spanish authorities and Catholic friars. In February 1896, orders were signed for his deportation to the remote southern island of Jolo.

Agoncillo slipped away before the order could be executed and found refuge in Manila with the followers of an underground revolutionary group, the Katipunan. With their assistance, he arrived in Japan in April 1896, and from there made his way to the British colony of Hong Kong, where he joined a growing community of Filipinos plotting to overthrow Spanish rule in their homeland. A committee was set up to direct and support revolutionary activities in the Philippines, with Agoncillo as a member.[14]

In December 1897, after the arrival of Aguinaldo and his aides as part of the short-lived peace agreement with Spanish authorities, the Hong Kong revolutionary committee was transformed into a ruling junta. Aguinaldo returned to the Philippines at the behest of the Americans in May 1898, leaving Agoncillo and others behind in Hong Kong to continue their work. After revolutionary forces were excluded from the occupation of Manila, Aguinaldo designated Agoncillo his chief diplomat and directed him to secure foreign recognition of their fledgling republic. In early September, Agoncillo set sail for the United States.

While Agoncillo steamed across the Pacific, President McKinley agonized over what Americans had come to know as "the Philippine

Question." Germany's interest in the islands had warmed McKinley to the expansionist cause. He had praised the long-delayed annexation of Hawaii by Congress in July, and later that month took his Cabinet on a three-day Potomac River cruise to decide the fate of the Philippines.

There was no shortage of opinions for McKinley to consider. British expert John Foreman had asserted in a recent treatise that Filipinos were incapable of self-rule. Self-appointed authorities like Albert Beveridge proclaimed the Philippines an invaluable source of raw materials and potential consumer of American products. U.S. diplomats and strategic thinkers like Alfred Mahan prized the islands as a base for projecting U.S. power into Asia—propitiously, just as European powers were poised to carve up China.

Agoncillo was nearing American shores in mid-September when President McKinley hosted a farewell banquet for his peace negotiators on the eve of their departure for Paris. In a long sermon that echoed the Indianapolis speech of Beveridge two days earlier, the inscrutable McKinley finally staked out a position on the Philippine question—behind closed doors, at least. The capture of Manila had presented the United States with "new duties and responsibilities, which we must meet and discharge as becomes a great nation." Spain must cede the entire Philippine island of Luzon to the United States, he instructed his negotiators, or there would be no peace.[15]

Landing in San Francisco, Agoncillo joined Brigadier General Francis V. Greene and his staff on the journey across America by rail. Greene, who until recently had commanded New York militia forces in the Philippines, planned to brief President McKinley on the political and economic situation in the islands.

After a stop in Chicago, the group arrived in Washington on September 27. Greene was welcomed to the White House later that afternoon for the first of several discussions in which he urged the president to annex all of the Philippines.

On the afternoon of October 1, Agoncillo was finally ushered into the White House Cabinet Room for his meeting with McKinley. At the first opening, the Filipino diplomat began to state his people's case to the president in florid Castilian Spanish. As an interpreter struggled to keep pace,

Agoncillo juxtaposed the despotic excesses of Spanish colonial rule with the virtues of the American system, the model "which the Philippine people will follow when they are independent." He recalled Emilio Aguinaldo's meetings with Dewey and other American representatives, and asserted that each of the U.S. emissaries had pledged support for Filipino self-rule.

McKinley listened politely, and then it was his turn to speak. Ignoring the issue of previous American commitments to the revolutionaries, he rejected the request for Filipino representation at the peace talks in Paris—the Spaniards would not hear of it, McKinley explained. Furthermore, he said, Agoncillo's command of English was too poor to plead his case personally with the U.S. negotiators. McKinley thanked Agoncillo for stopping by and escorted him to the door. Perhaps, he solicitously suggested, Agoncillo could give the State Department a memorandum summarizing his views.[16]

MUCH LATER, AFTER MCKINLEY'S ASSASSINATION in 1901, a member of a Methodist missionary society that had visited the White House during these weeks revealed how the president supposedly arrived at his decision to retain the Philippines. McKinley told the group that he had paced the White House nightly as he agonized over the Filipinos, at times falling on his knees to pray to God "for light and guidance." One night, his prayers were answered, and it became clear: America could not return the islands to despotic Spain, or leave them to the greedy Germans or French, or permit the "anarchy and misrule" of Philippine self-government. The only honorable course was to annex every last one of the islands, "educate the Filipinos, and uplift and Christianize them, and by God's grace do the very best we could by them, as our fellow men for whom Christ died."[17]

It may be true that McKinley received divine guidance, but other considerations certainly influenced his decision to annex the Philippines. McKinley was a masterful politician, with instincts keenly attuned to the popular will. He kept his ear so close to the ground, Congressman Joe Cannon wryly observed, it was full of grasshoppers.[18] Those skills enabled McKinley to grasp the electoral implications of the expansionist mood sweeping the nation.[19]

As if the political stakes were not high enough, a potential Republican rival for the White House in 1900 now turned up the pressure. Theodore Roosevelt kicked off his campaign for New York governor on October 5 with a stirring call for American expansion. "We cannot avoid facing the fact that we occupy a new place among the people of the world, and have entered upon a new career . . . ," Roosevelt proclaimed to a roaring crowd at Manhattan's Carnegie Hall. "The guns of our warships in the tropic seas of the West and the remote East have awakened us to the knowledge of new duties."[20]

With Roosevelt's words reverberating across the country, and three hundred thousand copies of Beveridge's "March of the Flag" speech circulating through America's heartland, McKinley headed to the Midwest to gauge grassroots support for retaining the Philippines.

Over two weeks, McKinley made fifty-seven public appearances in Illinois, Iowa, Nebraska and Missouri, and delivered major speeches in Omaha, St. Louis and Chicago. A presidential stenographer stood in the wings, carefully noting the enthusiasm with which McKinley's remarks on expansion and anti-imperialism were received.[21] As the days passed, and the public zeal for expansion became clearer, his rhetoric became nearly indistinguishable from that of Roosevelt and Beveridge. The war with Spain "was no more invited by us than were the questions . . . laid at our door by its results," he assured his audiences, but Americans now had "moral obligations" to carry out the overseas duties that God had laid at their feet.

In Chariton, Iowa, he told a cheering crowd, "Territory sometimes comes to us when we go to war in a holy cause, and whenever it does the banner of liberty will float over it and bring, I trust, blessings and benefits to all people." And in Nebraska, a state he had narrowly lost in 1896, he asked an audience, "Shall we deny to ourselves what the rest of the world so freely and justly accords to us?" In unison the crowd roared, "No!"[22]

McKinley returned to Washington reassured that he had accurately interpreted the public mood. On October 28, he cabled his peace negotiators new instructions regarding the Philippines: "The cession must be of the whole archipelago or none. The latter is wholly inadmissible, and the former must therefore be required."[23]

SPANISH NEGOTIATORS BALKED AT THE new American demands, insisting that domestic political considerations precluded the loss of their largest remaining overseas colony. But the Americans crafted a face-saving compromise: The United States would pay Spain $20 million for the Philippines. Financially ruined and militarily impotent, Spain accepted.[24]

Felipe Agoncillo watched the bargaining with dismay. After his rebuff at the hands of President McKinley, he had sailed to Paris and checked into an apartment on the same floor of the Hotel Continental where the U.S. peace commissioners were ensconced. For the next six weeks he tried to convince the negotiators to support Filipino self-rule. In desperation, Agoncillo granted an interview to the *New York Times* in late November. He warned that the United States was repeating the mistakes of Spanish colonial authorities, and offered a grim prediction: "I am afraid the Filipinos will never again submit to the yoke of a colonial government. Rather than live again as slaves, they will fight to the bitter end in defense of their rights and freedom."[25]

The pleas and warnings of the Philippine Republic's chief diplomat never gained a serious hearing. On December 10, Spanish and American negotiators signed the Treaty of Paris, ending Spain's three centuries of dominion over the Philippines. Excluded from the ceremony, Felipe Agoncillo filed a strongly worded protest with the peace commission, recalling the past promises of American officials and President McKinley's earlier disavowals of territorial ambition. Afterward, he boarded a steamer bound for America.[26]

The U.S. Senate would have the final word on the fate of the Philippines.

THE ZEAL FOR EXPANSION THAT McKinley had witnessed in the Midwest was genuine, but powerful forces were coalescing in opposition to America's quest for empire. In time, the opposition would cut across lines of party and class, attracting the industrialist Andrew Carnegie and labor leader Samuel Gompers, former presidents Grover Cleveland, a Democrat, and Benjamin Harrison, a Republican, bestselling writer Mark Twain and social activist Jane Addams. But in these early months, the movement was largely confined to aging New England reformers and Northeastern political mavericks, veterans of previous national crusades against slavery and, more recently, Gilded Age political corruption. On November 19, the most outspoken of these men gathered in Boston to create a new organization they christened the Anti-Imperialist League. Their stated mission was to prevent the liberation of Cuba "from being perverted into a war for colonial spoils."[27] Their immediate objective was the defeat of the Treaty of Paris in the U.S. Senate.

If the anti-imperialists found support for their crusade lacking at home, they received much encouragement from abroad. In Germany, France and Britain, politicians, military leaders and newspaper editors condemned America's sudden lust for colonies—conveniently overlooking their own charter membership in the imperial club.

But the view from abroad was not uniformly critical of American expansion. Watching the angst-ridden debate unfold from across the Atlantic, British writer Rudyard Kipling dashed off a poem aimed at fortifying America's will. He sent an advance copy to a good friend, the newly elected governor of New York, Theodore Roosevelt.

"Take up the White Man's Burden," Kipling exhorted,

> *Send forth the best ye breed—*
> *Go bind your sons to exile*
> *To serve your captives' need;*
> *To wait in heavy harness,*
> *On fluttered folk and wild—*
> *Your new-caught, sullen peoples,*
> *Half-devil and half-child.*

For seven stanzas the poem waxed in that vein, enjoining Americans to fulfill their duties as a colonial power and embrace "the savage wars of peace." Roosevelt passed the unpublished poem to his friend Henry Cabot Lodge, who needed all the moral support he could muster as he prepared to lead the Senate fight for the treaty.[28]

So uncertain were the treaty's prospects as the year drew to a close that President McKinley decided to strike a preemptive blow. On December 21, he issued an executive letter of instruction in which he proclaimed U.S. sovereignty over the Philippines and directed that American military government be extended throughout the islands. Mindful that his order would not be welcomed by Aguinaldo and his revolutionaries, McKinley pledged to protect the rights of Filipinos. Rather than conquest, the United States merely sought "the benevolent assimilation" of the Filipino people.[29]

AT TWELVE FIFTEEN P.M. ON Monday, January 9, 1899, a distinguished gentleman with white hair and a round face rose to the floor of the U.S. Senate to formally open the debate over the Treaty of Paris. A Republican since the party's birth, seventy-two-year-old George Frisbie Hoar was the senior senator from Massachusetts, and a veteran of righteous causes. Four decades prior, he had earned his political spurs in the fight against slavery. He had been an early and consistent supporter of women's rights. And, as political corruption and patronage had threatened to undermine American democracy, he had fought for civil service reform and clean government. Now, torn between party loyalty and principle, Hoar laid out the case against annexation of the Philippines.

There were practical considerations, unintended consequences such as the threat of tropical diseases that would be transported to American shores and the unknown results of assimilating alien races, Hoar warned. But the paramount issue was the threat the treaty posed to the American constitution and ideals. The United States had been founded on the ideal of the "consent of the governed," he reminded his colleagues. And without the consent of Filipinos, the United States could never justly or constitutionally purchase the islands and rule its people, he argued.

Hoar's speech provoked debate across the country. Supportive telegrams and letters flooded into the Senate. Steel magnate Andrew Carnegie sent $1,000 so Hoar might widely distribute his speech. (The senator returned the check.[30]) But Hoar's belief that his fellow senators would see the danger and reject the treaty quickly evaporated. The administration was "moving Heaven and earth" to win passage, offering patronage plums and other incentives in exchange for votes, he charged.[31]

On January 24, Henry Cabot Lodge, the junior senator from Massachusetts, delivered the administration's response. Aloof and imperious, Lodge fancied himself a visionary who possessed singular insight into America's role in the new century ahead. And now he would share his wisdom with his colleagues and the nation.

Lodge rejected the anti-imperialist arguments that territorial expansion would violate the U.S. Constitution and undermine American democracy. Even more important were the practical reasons why the United States must claim the Philippines. Rejection of the treaty would subject the president to international humiliation, he warned. It would also subject Filipinos to further oppressive rule by Spain. Worst of all, America would have to resume its war with Spain.[32]

Lodge's words may have lacked the lofty idealism of Hoar's antitreaty crusade, but his arguments were backed by the power of the presidency. As the date of the vote neared, McKinley and Lodge used patronage and persuasion to pick off Republican opponents to the treaty. Democratic opposition—largely based on a racist aversion to burdening American taxpayers with another ten million brown-skinned wards—eroded when party leader William Jennings Bryan suddenly urged his members to support the treaty to prevent a resumption of war.

 Still, the vote was close. When the count was tallied on the afternoon of February 6, 1899, the Senate had approved the treaty fifty-seven to twenty-seven—one vote more than the two-thirds margin required for passage.

PRESIDENT MCKINLEY HAD WON THE treaty fight, but his pledge of "benevolent assimilation" in the Philippines was about to be put to the test. On Saturday evening, February 4, a little more than forty-eight hours before the Senate vote, fighting between Aguinaldo's troops and American soldiers had broken out in a Manila suburb and quickly spread around the city. By the time Vice President Garret Hobart banged his gavel and declared the Treaty of Paris approved on Monday afternoon, the trenches around Manila were piled high with the bodies of dead Filipinos.

CHAPTER 9

Spring Victories, Summer Stalemate

Frederick Funston came of age at a time of national anxiety over the decline of America's pioneering spirit, but no one would ever accuse the diminutive Kansan of succumbing to the soft life. As the Western frontier officially faded into oblivion in the century's final decade, Funston molded himself into a contemporary Kit Carson. He joined botanical expeditions into the remote reaches of the Dakota badlands and Death Valley and blazed a new trail through the Yosemite Valley. After a restless stint as a Kansas City newspaper reporter, he headed for Alaska, where he spent two years studying the flora and paddling fifteen hundred miles down the Yukon River. Making his way back across the continent, Funston was in New York City in 1896 when he heard the one-legged Civil War General Daniel Sickles deliver a speech in support of Cuba's revolutionary movement—and promptly enlisted in the Cuban army.

In his nearly two years with the Cuban revolutionaries, Funston fought in twenty-two battles. He had seventeen horses shot out from under him, was seriously wounded through the lungs and one arm, and nearly died from malaria. He returned home to Kansas in early 1898, coughing up blood, eighty pounds of skin and bones. Later that spring, after the United States entered the war against Spain, Funston's Cuban exploits won him an appointment as commander of the newly formed 20th Kansas Volunteer Regiment. The Kansans missed the fighting in Cuba. But in October, after five tedious months of drilling at the Presidio in San Francisco, Colonel Fred Funston led his men aboard an Army transport bound for the Philippines.

Funston turned thirty-three during the Pacific crossing and arrived in Manila with his regiment in early December, as the treaty negotiations with Spain were concluding. He and his men feared they had missed all the excitement, but a few days on the ground convinced them otherwise. In Manila, the friction between American and Filipino soldiers had reached the point of open contempt.[1] By early February 1899, as the U.S. Senate prepared to vote on the Treaty of Paris, Funston and his Kansans braced for war.

The spark that ignited the smoldering tensions was struck on Saturday night, February 4. In the city's eastern suburb of Santa Mesa, the 1st Nebraska Volunteers had traded insults and occasional shots with Filipino forces for weeks in a disputed wedge of land at the confluence of the San Juan and Pasig rivers. Shortly before eight o'clock that evening, Private Willie Grayson and three comrades warily probed the thickets beyond their forward outpost. Grayson spotted movement and yelled a challenge. When the shadowy figures continued to approach in the darkness, Grayson shouted again, "Halt!"

"Halto!" a Filipino voice mockingly replied.

Grayson and his comrades opened fire, and the three Filipino soldiers fell. The Nebraskans scurried back to their outpost and sounded the alarm. Muzzle flashes flared along the lines, and soon the firing spread around the outskirts of Manila.

In the city, Colonel Funston and his wife of four months had just retired for the evening when someone pounded on their door.

"Come out here, Colonel," one of Funston's officers shouted. "The ball has begun."[2]

AT DAWN ON SUNDAY, FEBRUARY 5, U.S. volunteers and regulars on a sixteen-mile front surged from their trenches in attack. They splashed through swamps and creeks, picked their way through bamboo groves and charged across sunbaked rice paddies—lines of shouting men in blue, surging headlong toward rows of enemy trenches. After months of mindless duty in the tropical heat and humidity—tormented by flies and mosquitoes, drenched by monsoonal rains, ravaged by fevers and diarrhea—Wyoming volunteer Robert Crosbie summed up the attitude of many: "I would not have missed the fight we had on the 5th of Feb for a thousand dollars."[3]

The rattle of small arms and rumble of cannon unleashed a flurry of activity in Manila. General Robert Hughes, the city's provost commander, positioned his police companies at strategic points, and early Sunday morning they opened fire on Aguinaldo's urban guerrillas as they attempted to mass for an attack. Sporadic sniper fire and knife attacks kept American soldiers in the city on edge. An Army colonel was driving down a street when a sword-wielding Filipino guerrilla jumped into his carriage. Drawing his pistol, the American felled his attacker with a single shot and continued on his way.[4]

Along the front lines, the American volunteers quickly silenced any doubts as to their courage under fire. In the gritty suburb of Tondo, volunteers from Pennsylvania and Montana drove their adversaries back in house-to-house fighting. General Arthur MacArthur's 2nd Division dislodged enemy troops from behind the headstones and crypts of a Chinese cemetery and seized the high ground of Santa Mesa Ridge.

At the first alarm on Saturday night, Funston had hurried to 2nd Division headquarters and laid out for MacArthur his plan for ending the war with one bold stroke: He would slip through enemy lines with a single platoon and capture Aguinaldo. MacArthur gently rejected the proposal, but made sure that Funston got an early shot at glory. In Sunday's fighting, Funston and his men had so enthusiastically charged and overrun the Filipino trenches to their front that they found themselves a thousand yards beyond the main American line when they finally stopped.

By nightfall, the U.S. forces had driven Aguinaldo's army back from the network of trenches they had spent weeks fortifying. It would prove to be the war's biggest and bloodiest day of fighting. The U.S. forces had suffered 238 casualties, including forty-four killed in action or mortally wounded. Filipino losses were estimated at more than a thousand.

After five days of setbacks that had separated his forces into bloodied halves, north and south of Manila, Aguinaldo attempted to rally the northern portion of his army at the town of Caloocan. At the same time, he handed command of the army to General Antonio Luna, a native of northern Luzon's Ilocos region who had studied in Europe and fancied himself a military expert. Aguinaldo also ordered all males aged sixteen to fifty-nine throughout the islands to join a local militia unit and arm themselves with long knives known as bolos. Finally, he called for the creation of a guerrilla organization under the auspices of town and village officials.

The moves did nothing to slow the American advance into Central Luzon. "Fighting Fred" Funston's Kansans had become the 2nd Division spearhead, smashing through each Filipino trench and fortification in its path as the Americans drove toward the republican capital at Malolos. MacArthur proudly watched as his protégé wrapped them both in glory. "There goes Kansas," MacArthur exclaimed as the spirited regiment charged on yet another enemy fortification, "and all Hell can't stop her." At Caloocan, Aguinaldo's newly reorganized Army of Liberation broke and ran under the relentless pressure of the better-trained and -armed Americans. Once again, the Kansans ignored orders to halt. They roared through the town, in hot pursuit of Aguinaldo's army.

As THE U.S. FORCES ROLLED northward, the capital seethed with rumors. Aguinaldo had infiltrated scores of trained fighters into the city with instructions to rise from their hiding places and overwhelm the American occupiers. Sporadic sniper fire, attacks by knife-wielding assailants and acts of arson served as a constant reminder of the enemy's shadowy presence in Manila.[5] On February 9, U.S. soldiers captured a chilling order issued two days earlier by General Luna, calling for the Army of Liberation's urban militia to launch a "war without quarter" on the Americans.[6]

On the evening of February 22, the uprising began. At nine o'clock, a fire erupted in a brothel in the city's Santa Cruz district, near the barracks

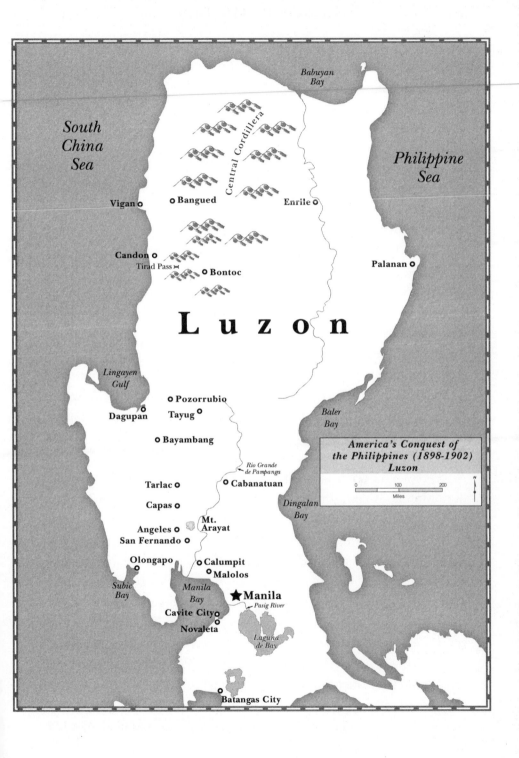

South
China
Sea

Philippine
Sea

*Babuyan
Bay*

Central Cordillera

Vigan ○ ● Bangued

Enrile ○

Candon ○
Tirad Pass ✕ ● Bontoc

Palanan ○

L u z o n

*Lingayen
Gulf*

○ Pozorrubio

Dagupan ○ Tayug ○

*Baler
Bay*

○ Bayambang

*Rio Grande
de Pampanga*

Tarlac ○ ○ Cabanatuan

Capas ○

*Dingalan
Bay*

America's Conquest of
the Philippines (1898-1902)
Luzon

0   100   200
Miles

N

Angeles ○ Mt.
Arayat
San Fernando ○

Olongapo ○ ○ Calumpit
○ Malolos

*Subic
Bay*

*Manila
Bay* ★ Manila
Pasig River

Cavite City ○
Novaleta

*Laguna
de Bay*

○ Batangas City

of the 10th Pennsylvania Volunteers. A stiff breeze soon engulfed an entire block in flames. When firefighters arrived, snipers opened up, while other Filipino fighters and their sympathizers tried to slash the fire hoses with their bolos. American troops exchanged shots with the snipers and beat back saboteurs with rifle butts and bayonets.[7]

As the drama unfolded in Santa Cruz, another fire broke out near two American police stations in Tondo, along the north bank of the Pasig River where it emptied into Manila Bay. Firefighters found their way blocked by five hundred Filipino guerrillas who had barricaded the streets and houses with foundation stones and railroad iron.

By midnight, General Hughes faced a critical situation. Another major fire had broken out, and it threatened to consume vast quantities of U.S. Army supplies. At the same time, American troops in Tondo were under heavy attack by guerrillas firing from rooftops and walled gardens. The spreading flames, the rising gunfire and surreal bugle calls of the Filipino fighters panicked the city's foreign residents. Rumors spread that Aguinaldo's troops had broken through the American lines and were poised to recapture the city and slaughter non-Filipinos. Terrified foreigners poured out of their hotels and houses, only to be stopped at gunpoint by nervous American troops and ordered back to their residences.

At dawn on February 23, black smoke still curled into the pink sky over Manila as companies of exhausted U.S. volunteers and regulars prepared to retake Tondo. Under the command of Major G. A. Goodale of the 23rd U.S. Infantry, three columns of American soldiers began fighting their way into the crowded district, house by house and street by street. When frontal assaults did not work, the Americans set fires to drive snipers from houses. Thirteen dead enemy fighters were found in one small yard. In another block, a 2nd Oregon officer counted thirty-four dead Filipinos. As resistance crumbled, scores of enemy fighters attempted to flee up the coastal road and beach, only to be cut down by the machine guns of the U.S. Navy gunboat *Callao*, lying just offshore.[8]

Beyond the burned-out suburban streets, the advancing American troops skirted swamps and bamboo groves and engaged in sporadic firefights with the Filipino survivors. At four fifty p.m., the Americans reached the headquarters of Funston's 20th Kansas. Their mission accomplished, Goodale and his hollow-eyed men retraced their steps to Manila, where they were hailed as the city's saviors. Once again, American casualties had been remarkably light—only two men killed and twelve wounded.[9]

Luna had confidently predicted that Filipinos in Manila would fall on the Americans when his troops launched the uprising. It was an idle boast. Most of the city's inhabitants had sought shelter in the American-controlled areas. Aguinaldo's urban organization suffered devastating losses and never seriously threatened Manila again.[10]

THE OPENING DAYS OF THE war revealed the harsh tactics that both sides were prepared to use in the pursuit of their aims. McKinley had ordered the "benevolent assimilation" of the Filipinos, but on the ground U.S. field commanders modeled their tactics after the Army's unsparing campaign against the Indian tribes of the American West. The prevailing view among American officers and soldiers held that the Filipinos were savages, unworthy of civilized treatment.

Historian Brian Linn, a scrupulously neutral scholar on the U.S. war in the Philippines, has noted that the first weeks of American operations around Manila revealed "clear evidence of troop misconduct, brutality, criminal activity, and atrocities." Months of resentment toward Filipinos—much of it racially motivated—had been unleashed. Soldiers fired indiscriminately on civilians and summarily executed prisoners. So excessive were the acts of violence and destruction that even cold-eyed General Robert Hughes recoiled. "It is not," he declared, "our usual way of making war."[11]

The U.S. soldiers blamed their Filipino adversaries for setting the tone. Enemy troops were accused of firing on ambulance litter bearers and Red Cross workers, and were said to continue fighting after raising white flags. In an incident cited repeatedly by the American military, Filipinos were accused of torturing to death a wounded U.S. doctor in the fighting around Manila. One American soldier expressed the sentiment that inspired subsequent U.S. military operations throughout the islands: "We would have no pity for the savages who finished off our wounded in this barbarous way."[12]

IN MANY WAYS, THE ARCHIPELAGO that the Americans now claimed as national territory had changed little since Ferdinand Magellan had planted the crimson-and-gold standard of Spain on a sun-dappled beach in 1521. Over half of the seven million inhabitants lived on Luzon, the largest of the archipelago's seven thousand islands, at the far northern end of the sprawling chain. Luzon was the location of Manila and home of the Tagalogs, the largest of five major linguistic groups that inhabited the islands. Aguinaldo was a Tagalog, as were most of his commanders. Luna, who hailed from the Ilocos region of northwestern Luzon, was the notable exception.

In addition to the linguistic divisions, the Americans found their unwilling colonial subjects fractured along social and economic lines. Under Spanish rule, a Filipino aristocracy had taken root and flourished. While the Catholic Church was the largest landholder, wealthy native planters also controlled vast tracts in the countryside. The majority of Filipinos were impoverished farm laborers who grew rice on rented land or tended plantations of sugar, coconuts and hemp. With little to lose, the laboring classes embraced the revolutionary cause in large numbers. Wealthy landowners and merchants, on the other hand, watched and waited. While independence appealed to many elites, preserving the existing social order was their paramount goal.

When the Americans occupied Manila, upper-crust Filipinos ingratiated themselves with General Otis and his generals. They convinced the U.S. commander that the revolution was strictly a Tagalog affair, and that if he defeated or captured Aguinaldo, the non-Tagalog population would embrace American colonial rule. On that belief, Otis formulated his plan: He would contain the revolutionary forces south of Manila, then strike northward to smash Aguinaldo's army.

In the safety and comfort of Washington, the generals and politicians pored over their outdated maps of the Philippines and concluded that, as in Cuba, American forces were poised for quick and easy success. All Otis had to do was move his army a short distance over flat terrain, and engage and destroy an inferior enemy force.

On the ground, Otis found a far different reality. For months, the tightfisted general had assured Washington that he had enough troops to handle any trouble. After the initial battles around Manila, it had become clear that he did not have enough troops to garrison the capital and nearby towns, secure his lines of supply and communication and push deeper into Central Luzon. Three regiments of U.S. Army regulars were on the way, but until their arrival Otis would have only eleven thousand men available to pursue Aguinaldo. Compounding his problem, over half of his troops were state volunteers whose military obligations were scheduled to end with ratification of the peace treaty with Spain on April 11. Five weeks before the deadline, Congress passed legislation that allowed the American commander to retain state volunteers in the Philippines. The legislation also provided for expansion of the Regular Army to sixty-five thousand men, and recruitment of a separate thirty-five-thousand-man force of U.S. volunteers for duty in the islands.

The crisis over manpower was resolved for the moment, but Otis faced other problems beyond his control. By March, Luzon was baking in the dry-season heat, with daily temperatures soaring into the nineties. The rainy season would arrive in May or June, transforming the dusty roads and dry rice paddies into a sea of sticky mud. Meanwhile, the tropical heat and humidity incubated deadly bacteria and diseases, and typhoid, cholera, malaria and dysentery soon were claiming more American lives than enemy bullets and bolos. Though not as deadly, low-grade fevers, skin diseases, rashes, rotting feet and tropical ulcers further ravaged the American ranks.

Few of the American soldiers had an inkling of the miseries that awaited them on the islands. U.S. military units arrived with "absolute ignorance of the Philippine archipelago in respect to geography, climate, people and the general aspects of nature," Major General Arthur MacArthur later acknowledged. What little orientation there was did not hearten the troops. "One writer to whom we had access advised all travelers to carry coffins," MacArthur recalled, "as few returned alive from Manila."[13]

THE FIRST PHASE OF OTIS's plan for ending resistance called for securing his southern and eastern flanks from the revolutionary forces that remained around Manila. This job fell to a provisional brigade of regulars and volunteers under the command of Brigadier General Lloyd Wheaton. A sixty-two-year-old Army veteran with a legendary capacity for foul language, Wheaton had been wounded at Shiloh during the Civil War, and then won the Medal of Honor for heroics in storming a Confederate fort. As with most of his peers, his career had stalled in the postwar doldrums, only to be revived at the last possible moment by the war with Spain. Now Wheaton found himself in the Philippines, the clock ticking as he played out the last hurrah of his military career.

Wheaton's objective was to push up the Pasig River from Manila, sever the lines of communication between the northern and southern elements of Aguinaldo's army, and end the harassing attacks by enemy forces scattered through the foothills between Manila and a large inland lake, Laguna de Bay. Over five days of sometimes heavy fighting, he drove the revolutionary forces back from Manila, captured three nearby towns and secured the northern and western shores of Laguna de Bay.

Infuriated by the stiff resistance he encountered at the town of Taguig, Wheaton ordered his men to burn houses and fields for several miles along the lake road. Boats used to transport crops—and, potentially, enemy troops—were also thrown into the flames. Schooled under General William Tecumseh Sherman, Wheaton left a trail of destruction that would have made Uncle Billy proud.[14]

THE AMERICAN DRIVE ON MALOLOS began at dawn on the morning of March 25, 1899, when lead elements of MacArthur's 1st Brigade—Funston's 20th Kansas and the 3rd Artillery—plunged into the Tuliahan River under heavy fire from enemy fighters dug in on the opposite bank.

Funston and his men waded through neck-deep water and swam at times, then swarmed up the slippery bank to hit the Filipinos head-on. Quickly overrunning the enemy trenches, the Kansans killed or wounded all but one of the defenders. By nightfall, MacArthur's brigade had made impressive progress at the cost of sixty-eight men killed and wounded.

For the next four days, the American troops fought their way across one river after another and through steamy patches of dense jungle, bamboo groves, swamps, marshes and streams. Back in the United States, newspapers tracked the offensive as if it were a football game. "Like a Flying Wedge," a headline in the *Chicago Daily Tribune* announced, describing one unit's charge on enemy trenches. "KANSANS' CYCLONE CHARGE," the *Los Angeles Times* trumpeted in banner headlines.[15]

Meanwhile, the Kansans continued to distinguish themselves with their courage and initiative. Again and again, with Funston in the lead, blazing away with his revolver, they charged into the teeth of enemy fire. "When I tell them to charge," Funston boasted, "the trouble is not to get them to come on, but to keep from being run over by them."[16]

By the night of March 30, MacArthur's division had reached the outskirts of the enemy capital at Malolos. As a heavy rain fell, weary soldiers wrote final letters home and fell into a fitful sleep.

The following morning, MacArthur's artillery opened the action by pounding the enemy trenches. As American troops massed for their assault, Filipino civilians could be seen fleeing Malolos in all directions. Smoke began to curl from bamboo huts on the outskirts, and soon a black cloud rose from the town.

The Americans reached the first line of enemy trenches, and found them abandoned. A second line was also deserted. General MacArthur ordered Funston to send a reconnoitering party into town, and, in typical fashion, the aggressive colonel led the probe himself. A few minutes later, Funston marched into Malolos with two squads. As the Kansans approached the convent that Aguinaldo had used as a residence, the Filipino rear guard opened fire from behind a street barricade. Funston's men fired two volleys, then charged. The enemy fighters broke and ran, and Funston quickly secured the town plaza. As American troops poured into Malolos, the Stars and Stripes was hoisted into the smoky sky on an

improvised flagstaff. The rebel capital had fallen, but once again Aguinaldo and his army had escaped.[17]

In mid-April, after two weeks of rest and recuperation, the Americans
resumed their northward thrust in the torrid dry-season heat. Rivers and
streams coursed like capillaries through this part of the fertile Central
Luzon plain, and Luna forced the Americans to fight their way across most
of them. He scattered small units to snipe and spring ambushes from bamboo thickets and jungle, while concentrating four thousand men at the town
of Calumpit and another three thousand at the nearby town of Baliuag.
There his men awaited the Americans in a formidable network of trenches
and breastworks along the Río Grande de Pampanga and two tributaries.

On the morning of April 25, General Wheaton opened the battle for
Calumpit with Funston's 20th Kansas and the 1st Montana advancing on
either side of the railroad line that led northward through Central Luzon.
The American troops were joined by an armored train that General
MacArthur had outfitted with three Gatling and Colt machine guns and
a six-pound naval cannon. The train had already proven useful in enfilading enemy entrenchments and terrorizing Filipino troops, and now it
set to work raking Luna's lines. Three field guns of the Utah Artillery
joined in, showering explosive rounds along a row of bamboo huts on the
outskirts of the town. Up and down the line, American volunteers opened
fire with their smoke-belching Springfield rifles. They lay on their bellies
in the blazing sun, small piles of shells beside them to speed their firing.

The American advance was halted at the Bagbag River by heavy fire
from Filipino troops dug in along the north bank. Funston called for
volunteers, and, as enemy bullets sliced the air, the little colonel led ten
men in a mad dash for a steel railroad bridge. The Filipinos had removed
the rails and ties, forcing Funston and his soldiers to pick their way across
on four-inch girders. They came to a broken span, and the colonel and
four men dropped into the swirling waters and swam the rest of the way
to the far bank. They emerged from the river "barefoot, unarmed and
dripping," and rushed into the enemy trench to find the defenders had
fled, leaving behind their dead and wounded.[18]

By the following evening, the American forces had advanced through the burning ruins of Calumpit to the banks of the Río Grande de Pampanga. Luna's men waited four hundred feet away, behind field fortifications carved into the river's northern bank. Loopholes had been cut into the breastworks to allow the Filipino riflemen to fire without exposing themselves. Three artillery pieces and a rapid-fire Maxim machine gun further complemented their defenses.

Funston had been itching to lead his men in a headlong rush across a railroad bridge that anchored the enemy line, but a scouting report convinced him that casualties would be too heavy. Around midday of April 27, he led his men about six hundred yards downstream, where bamboo thickets along the north bank could screen his movements. He positioned a hundred sharpshooters along the river's edge to keep the enemy soldiers pinned in their trenches, then asked for volunteers willing to swim across the river.

From a dozen men who stepped forward, Funston picked two: Private Edward White and Corporal William Trembley. Stripping off their uniforms and underwear, the men slipped into the treacherous river and began swimming toward the opposite shore with three hundred feet of rope in tow. Enemy soldiers opened fire, but the pair reached the north shore just twenty feet from an enemy emplacement. Crawling on all fours, the naked Americans dragged the rope up the bank and tied it to a post on the enemy breastworks.

Funston and eight men now climbed aboard a crude raft and began pulling themselves across the Río Grande. They joined their two comrades on the far bank, and sent the raft back for another eight men to cross. The routine was repeated until Funston had three officers and forty-five men with him on the north bank.

On the colonel's command, the band of Americans charged into the Filipino trenches and headed upstream. The enemy's Maxim gun slowed Funston's advance, but after a half hour fight he and his men had worked their way to within a few hundred feet of the bridge. As General MacArthur and General Wheaton watched from across the river, the Kansans once again drove the last enemy defenders from their trenches. American troops poured across the river to resume their thrust.[19] For their heroic actions at the Río Grande de Pampanga, Funston and the two men who had carried the rope across the river would be awarded the Medal of Honor.

A week after the dramatic crossing, Funston was in the thick of the fighting around the town of San Tomas when a bullet smashed into his hand. The colonel's luck once again prevailed: The bullet sliced cleanly through the flesh without shattering any bones. After a few days of recuperation in Manila, he rejoined his regiment in Central Luzon as a newly promoted brigadier general.

As the dry-season heat reached its zenith on the Central Luzon plain, the paramount question became whether the Americans could capture Aguinaldo and destroy his army before the rainy season ended offensive operations. The men of MacArthur's 2nd Division pushed northward as fast as the spongy terrain would allow, suffering in the searing sun and humidity as they forded rivers, fended off ambushes and fought running battles. Luna's forces engaged in increasingly desperate tactics to slow the Americans. They fouled water holes—sometimes with corpses— and seeded roads and trails with camouflaged pits lined with bamboo spikes. Still, the Americans marched on.

On May 5, MacArthur's weary troops launched an attack on the enemy lines before the important crossroads and commercial center of San Fernando. A flanking move by two Iowa battalions panicked the demoralized Filipinos, and their retreat quickly became a rout. Several dozen enemy soldiers tied their white linen shirts to their rifles and surrendered.[20]

The capture of San Fernando and San Isidro, another of Aguinaldo's temporary capitals, on May 17 once again brought the Americans to the brink of victory. But weeks of marching and fighting in the brutal heat and soggy terrain had crippled the U.S. forces. In the campaigning of April and May, MacArthur's division had suffered thirty-two killed and 219 wounded. Nearly half his men who were still in the field were sick, and the other half exhausted or suffering from combat fatigue. They could go no farther.

The arrival of the rainy season in late May found U.S. forces in control of a narrow forty-mile corridor along the railroad line from Manila to San Fernando in Central Luzon. The revolutionary army had suffered great losses, and Luna was dead, assassinated by Aguinaldo loyalists after a long-running feud with *el presidente*. But individual Filipino units kept MacArthur's forces under constant pressure by attacking isolated outposts and ambushing patrols and resupply trains.

With the onset of the monsoon rains, the window of opportunity for the Americans to quickly crush the rebellion had closed. On top of his casualties to combat and disease, General Otis was about to lose sixteen thousand state volunteers to the domestic political demands to bring the troops home. Now he would have to wait for autumn, and the arrival of reinforcements and better weather, before making another attempt to secure U.S. rule in the Philippines.

As proof of America's munificent intentions toward the Philippines, President McKinley in January 1899 had announced the appointment of a panel to study the islands and their problems. The three civilian members of the Philippine Commission—Cornell University President Jacob G. Schurman, University of Michigan Professor Dean Worcester, and former U.S. Minister to China Charles Denby—arrived in Manila in March, after war had already broken out. Their first order of business, with little cooperation from the commission's two military members, Admiral Dewey and General Otis, was to convince the natives to stop fighting.

Four days after the fall of Malolos, with hopes high among American observers that the revolt was in its death throes, the commission issued a proclamation that laid out the benefits of American rule. A U.S. colonial administration would deliver civil rights, religious freedom and self-government while promoting public works, education and foreign trade. "The purpose of the American Government is the welfare and advancement of the Philippine people," the document proclaimed. Copies were printed in English, Spanish and Tagalog and distributed in areas under American control. Fleeting peace talks got under way but soon ended, with little progress having been made, in part because of Otis's insistence on unconditional surrender.[21]

Otis thought 30,000 was enough by 4/18/99 He said He needed 40,000 men

Otis, meanwhile, confronted other problems. Since assuming the Philippine command in the late summer of 1898, he had assured the War Department that he could conquer and hold the Philippines with thirty thousand men. But in the spring of 1899, he was forced to acknowledge that he would need more troops to destroy Aguinaldo's army and occupy key towns and villages—perhaps as many as forty thousand, he informed the War Department. He also abandoned another fiction he had peddled to the War Department for months and admitted that the overwhelming majority of state volunteers had no intention of reenlisting. Already hard-pressed to replace the departing volunteers, the War Department suddenly confronted an even more critical shortfall.

Otis remained less than forthcoming when it came to informing his superiors about troop morale. Many of the state volunteers who had enlisted to free Cuba and the Philippines from Spanish rule openly questioned why they were waging war against the people they were sent to liberate.[22] News correspondents in the Philippines filed stories about the darkening mood of the American soldiers, their struggles with tropical diseases, heatstroke and exhaustion, and the tenacious enemy resistance. But Otis kept the stories from reaching American readers. In addition to censoring the reports of U.S. correspondents, he shuttered "treasonous" local publications while inundating correspondents and his superiors with upbeat press releases.

In July, eleven correspondents of leading U.S. news organizations drafted an open letter that revealed the unpleasant realities that military censors had suppressed for months. Otis's communiqués "have presented an ultra optimistic view that is not shared by the General officers in the field," the correspondents wrote. He had downplayed the tenacity of the Filipino resistance and misled the American people into believing "the Insurrection can be speedily ended without a greatly increased force." And he had withheld full reports of field operations that had gone badly and generally suppressed "complete reports of the situation."[23]

When the letter was smuggled to Hong Kong and published by U.S. newspapers, Otis threatened to haul the correspondents before a court-martial. But the damage was done. The letter had stirred a political controversy in the United States that Otis could not suppress through intimidation. Anti-imperialists seized on the allegations to raise doubts about the war and U.S. policy in the Philippines. Fearing a political backlash as he prepared to seek reelection, President McKinley ordered the War Department to end the censorship, and the dispute faded away.

The mood in Manila was not so easily addressed. Arriving reinforcements were taken aback by the unease that gripped the city. "An air of gloom prevails everywhere and even the city is deemed unsafe," observed one American officer in August 1899. "Although we have over 30,000 troops about Otis seems to have failed entirely."[24]

AMID THE RISING CONCERNS, THE silver-tongued champion of U.S. imperialism strode ashore in the Philippines. Albert Beveridge had ridden the soaring rhetoric of his "March of the Flag" speech to an improbable victory for a seat in the U.S. Senate in February 1899. With his term not scheduled to begin until the following January, he set out for the Philippines, determined to become the Senate's expert on the islands.

Arriving with his wife on May 1, Beveridge embraced his work with missionary zeal. He interviewed scores of expatriates and a few Filipinos about potential business opportunities and effective colonial government, scribbling quotes and observations in a red pocket notebook. He showed even greater interest in the welfare of America's men in uniform. Armed with a pistol and a military escort, he made his way to the field headquarters of his fellow Hoosier, the recently promoted Major General Henry Lawton. Twice Beveridge rode into battle beside the daredevil commander.[25] He joined General MacArthur's division in time to witness the fall of San Fernando, and spent an anxious evening with the command group, listening to the howls of wild dogs across the rice paddies as they awaited an enemy counterattack. Finally, he made his way to the camp of the 20th Kansas, where he soaked up the hard-line views of Fred Funston.

After covering the Central Luzon front, Beveridge boarded an Army transport and spent most of June touring the central and southern islands. On Panay, where U.S. soldiers were engaged in a difficult campaign against revolutionary forces, he donned a soldier's uniform—slouch hat, blue flannel shirt, khaki trousers, and leggings—and set off on horseback in a tropical downpour for a visit with troops from Tennessee. At each stop, he delivered pep talks to soldiers and American civilians, exhorting them to finish the job and "come back with flying colors." On the central island of Cebu, he made his way through American lines to chat with a local revolutionary leader—one of his few encounters with a Filipino opposed to U.S. rule.[26]

By the time he left the islands in July, Beveridge was more convinced than ever that the United States had done the right thing in retaining all of the islands. Arriving back in America in August, the senator-elect maintained an uncharacteristic silence about his travels. Brushing off the reporters who hounded him at every stop, he made his way to Washington, where he briefed President McKinley and other top officials. On his way home to Indiana, he stopped in New York to present his findings to Theodore Roosevelt.

Beveridge merely reinforced what arch-expansionists had been saying for the past year: The Philippines would enrich America, with an effective government under U.S. control. But first, the rebellious natives must be brought to heel. The Filipinos understood only force, Beveridge lectured his audiences, quoting a Spanish Jesuit priest he had interviewed in the Philippines. The war against Aguinaldo and his followers must be pursued "ceaselessly and remorselessly."[27]

CHAPTER 10

"The Filipino Republic Is Destroyed"

After the disasters of the war's opening months, Emilio Aguinaldo welcomed the rainy season of 1899. The downpours brought respite from American attacks, and an opportunity to consolidate and reorganize his battered forces. He had established a new capital in the Central Luzon town of Tarlac, thirty-five miles north of General MacArthur's headquarters in San Fernando, and had deployed six thousand men behind a new defensive line that blocked the northward path of the Americans. The revolutionary leader hoped to hold out long enough for arms shipments to arrive from Europe, or for his adversaries to weary of war in the tropics. For either to occur, Aguinaldo and his men would have to survive the second act of the American offensive.

Tarlac province was home to large sugarcane plantations, and its wealthy planters were members of a privileged class whose support Aguinaldo desperately needed to finance the revolution. Increasingly, however, the demands of feeding and supplying an ill-disciplined army had alienated him from Tarlac's leading citizens. Like so many of their moneyed compatriots in Manila, the landed aristocrats of Central Luzon were warming to the prospect of U.S. sovereignty—as long as it prolonged their place atop Philippine society.

A letter written by a wealthy Tarlaqueño to a friend in Manila that July underscored the flagging appetite for revolution. "For some days, I have been trying to get into your city and leave the band of thieves, but with my numerous family it is impossible to travel off the road and they watch us here so closely that it is impossible to get away, which I very much regret," the wavering patriot wrote. Many in Tarlac "long for the American troops to advance, for everyone is desperate with so much savagery committed by our army. Quiet citizens are never left in peace, nor anyone in fact who has as much as a grain of rice to put aside. . . ."[1]

Aguinaldo and his commanders desperately needed a victory to shore up their eroding support. For the revolutionaries, the fall dry season offered a last chance to save their republic.

THE RAINS WERE STILL FALLING from leaden skies over Central Luzon when General MacArthur began to lay the groundwork for a final offensive against Aguinaldo's forces. In mid-August, MacArthur dispatched the 12th Infantry to seize the town of Angeles. His men quickly overran the enemy trenches, positioning the Americans only a two-hour march from Aguinaldo's main line.

In October, after the dispersal of Filipino forces south of Manila and the arrival of new U.S. volunteer regiments, General Otis ordered a three-pronged strike: MacArthur's division would hold Aguinaldo in place in Central Luzon, while fast-moving columns of cavalry and infantry led by General Lawton and General Wheaton encircled the Army of Liberation to the north and east. MacArthur would then drive Aguinaldo's line against the blocking forces of Lawton and Wheaton. "The Great Roundup," as the plan was known informally within Army circles, would end the war.

The first phase got under way on October 12, when General Lawton led a column of infantry and cavalry east from San Fernando. Unusually late rains had turned the roads into a gumbo, tormenting men and beasts. With wagons nearly immovable in the mud, Lawton attempted to use the Río Grande de Pampanga as a supply line, but fluctuating water levels and enemy attacks made the river route unreliable as well.

Forming the point of Lawton's spear was the 3rd Cavalry Regiment, commanded by Theodore Roosevelt's former comrade in Cuba, Brigadier General Samuel B. M. Young. At six feet, four inches and 250 pounds, the tough and cranky Young was an imposing figure. He had begun the Civil War as a private and ended it as a brevet brigadier general in the Army of the Potomac. Wounded three times in the same arm, he earned five brevets for bravery, including one for leading an assault across the stone bridge at Antietam.

A year after the war ended, Young entered the Regular Army as a second lieutenant of infantry. Over the next thirty-two years, his assignments ranged from fighting Indians to overseeing the nation's new national park at Yellowstone. The outbreak of war with Spain thrust Young back into the limelight. His 3rd Cavalry Regiment played a pivotal role in breaking the Spanish defenses at Las Guásimas, an achievement largely overlooked because of the publicity accorded Roosevelt and his Rough Riders. When Young was incapacitated by tropical fever, Roosevelt wound up in sole command of the Rough Riders, to the New Yorker's eternal gratitude.

On October 19, Lawton's infantry routed nine hundred enemy fighters at San Isidro, a town he had briefly held before the rainy season. Another ten days of miserable marches along bad roads, contested river crossings and running battles across soggy rice paddies brought the lead elements of Lawton's column to the important crossroads of Cabanatuan, twenty-five miles due east of Aguinaldo's capital at Tarlac. With his supply line now completely severed by washed-out bridges, Lawton placed his division on half rations of bread and meat. Engineers arrived to oversee the construction of new bridges—only to see their work swept away within two days.[2]

In early November, Young's men captured a proclamation by Aguinaldo announcing the imminent transfer of his capital to the mountains of Nueva Vizcaya province, seventy-five miles north of Lawton's current position. Aguinaldo and his army would have to pass just north of Lawton, through mountain passes the American general intended to block—if he could get his wet and hungry men moving again.

Young stepped up with a bold proposal. He asked Lawton to allow him to forge ahead with a fast-moving detachment and seal off the mountain passes. He would live off the land, as General Sherman had done during his march across Georgia in 1864. Lawton gave his blessing.

On November 7, carrying little more than ammunition, hardtack and coffee, Young set off with about a thousand infantry, cavalry and native scouts. Through rain and mire, the column marched northward. Ahead and along their right flank towered Luzon's spectacular Central Cordillera, the island's mountainous spine. At the town of Tayug, a 3rd Cavalry detachment intercepted Aguinaldo's main supply train as it rumbled toward the new mountain capital. Lost to Aguinaldo were supplies vital to his war effort: 270,000 pounds of rice, 3,000 pounds of sugar, 25,000 pounds of salt, 1,000 pounds of coffee and 4,000 ball cartridges.[3]

Over seven grueling days, Young's column covered 120 miles on abysmal roads. Constant wetness rotted the leather and stitching in shoes, forcing some of the infantry to march barefoot. At night, soldiers shivered in wet uniforms. Malarial fevers, chills, fungal infections and skin rashes tormented the men. Yet each morning, Young's column pressed ahead, tightening the noose on Aguinaldo and his crumbling army.

As Young's men were embarking on their trek, Wheaton's force of twenty-five hundred troops landed at San Fabian on Lingayen Gulf without opposition. The following day, General MacArthur moved against Aguinaldo's main force in Central Luzon. MacArthur had hoped to end the war himself, but heavy rains slowed his attempts to envelop the Filipino forces in Tarlac. By the time MacArthur's men reached the town of Capas, Aguinaldo's army had slipped away. On November 12, American forces captured Tarlac, Aguinaldo's most recent capital, without a fight.

The following day, twenty-six miles to the north, Aguinaldo convened a council of war with his general staff. Nine months of defeats had made it painfully clear to the commanders that they could not win a conventional war. From this moment forward, Aguinaldo decreed, they would utilize tactics that placed a premium on their familiarity with the local terrain and the population, a war without fronts or fixed positions. Filipino soldiers would exchange their uniforms for the clothes of simple farmers, and they would blend in with villagers and townsfolk, awaiting opportune moments to strike. If the Americans wanted the Philippines, they would have to win a guerrilla war.[4]

AGUINALDO'S IMMEDIATE CONCERN WAS ESCAPING the American trap that was rapidly closing around him. MacArthur's division was twenty-five miles to the south and advancing. General Wheaton's blocking force was twenty miles to the north. General Young's column was about twenty-five miles to the northeast. The only route of escape was a narrow corridor between Wheaton and Young. But now, only hours from ending the war, the hard-charging Wheaton inexplicably dawdled.

Standing between Wheaton and the crowning glory of his career were inexperienced troops commanded by Aguinaldo's youngest general, twenty-two-year-old Manuel Tinio. A handsome young man with a long and angular face and an impressive military bearing, Tinio was a Tagalog, born into affluence in Nueva Ecija province. As a high school student in Manila, he had joined the Katipunan revolutionary society. When the uprising against Spain broke out in the summer of 1896, Tinio had returned to Nueva Ecija and joined the local revolutionary forces. Rising through the ranks, he was personally commissioned by Aguinaldo as a colonel in June 1897. Before the year was out, at the tender age of twenty, he had earned a brigadier general's star.[5]

Tinio had been one of the commanders who had accompanied Aguinaldo into exile in Hong Kong in December 1897. He had returned to the Philippines on an American warship the following spring, and headed home to recruit a brigade of volunteers. As tensions with the Americans had worsened during the fall, Aguinaldo had named Tinio commander of all revolutionary forces in Northern Luzon. Tinio had remained in the north as the revolutionary army had suffered its string of defeats in Central Luzon. In late September 1899, with the Americans preparing their dry-season offensive, Aguinaldo directed Tinio to confront U.S. forces should they attempt a landing to his rear at Lingayen Gulf.

As Aguinaldo had anticipated, Wheaton's force went ashore at San Fabian on November 7. He routed several hundred Filipino defenders in a brief fight, then did virtually nothing for two days. When Wheaton finally started inland, his men quickly ran into opposition. On November 10, just east of San Fabian, elements of the 33rd U.S. Volunteer Regiment, crack Texans commanded by Major Peyton C. March, defeated six hundred Filipino troops. The following day, near the town of San Jacinto, Wheaton's men again found their way blocked by an entrenched enemy force.

The Filipino soldiers who awaited the Americans were the greenest men under Tinio's command, yet they fought with valiant resolve. Only after bringing up a Gatling gun and raking the Filipino trenches with a deadly scythe of bullets did the Americans gain the upper hand. When Tinio's men finally withdrew, they left behind 134 dead. Wheaton had suffered seven killed, including a battalion commander, Major John H. Logan, and fifteen wounded. Perhaps unnerved by the ferocious resistance, Wheaton halted his troops, only twenty miles from blocking Aguinaldo's escape.

On the evening of November 13, after ordering his forces across the Philippines to disperse into small bands and begin guerrilla warfare, Aguinaldo prepared to leave his temporary capital at Bayambang. The fate of the Philippine Republic hung in the balance, but Aguinaldo also carried the weight of personal tragedy. His infant daughter, Flora, had died of fever during the retreat from Tarlac, and he had just presided over hurried burial services. With no time to spare, Aguinaldo gathered his family, three Cabinet ministers and the presidential guard and boarded a special train headed north. Arriving in the dead of night in the town of Calasiao, less than ten miles from Wheaton's troops, Aguinaldo and his entourage set out on foot in a desperate attempt to thread their way through the converging American forces. The group reached the town of Santa Barbara at dawn on November 14, and there Aguinaldo was joined by the most famous of his "boy generals," twenty-three-year-old Gregorio del Pilar.

Splitting his force, Aguinaldo set out in the rain with twelve hundred troops, del Pilar and his men in the van and Tinio and his battered brigade as the rear guard. Their destination was the town of Pozorrubio, at the edge of the mountains. Aguinaldo and his group managed to elude the roving American forces, but a trailing contingent that included Aguinaldo's mother and son was cut off and captured.

By now, Wheaton should have held Pozorrubio, but he had hardly moved since the battle at San Jacinto. Even after the lead elements of Young's force had informed him on November 14 that Aguinaldo was only a few miles away, Wheaton procrastinated. Not until the following day did he order troops to Pozorrubio.

Even with Wheaton's lapse, Young's exhausted, mud-spattered cavalry nearly captured their quarry. Led by a native guide, the Americans arrived at the outskirts of Pozorrubio late on the afternoon of November 14—only to discover that their escort was an Aguinaldo loyalist who had led them to the wrong village.

Aguinaldo and his weary companions were resting in Pozorrubio the following morning when the sound of rifle fire announced the arrival of Young's troops. As the firefight raged, the revolutionary leader and his entourage hurried out of town, toward the mist-shrouded hills.

FOR ANOTHER TWO WEEKS, AGUINALDO and his group trudged up the Northern Luzon coast, keeping just ahead of their pursuers. As they passed through towns and villages, cheering crowds and brass bands turned out to greet them. (Some of the same crowds and bands would similarly welcome the Americans a few days later.) Climbing into the foothills, the revolutionaries found the way even harder. "It rained continuously, and it was very muddy," recalled Colonel Simeon Villa, an officer in Aguinaldo's column. "A strong wind and the cold air made our teeth chatter as we climbed [and] when we reached an altitude of more than 500 meters, we thought we were high up near heaven. . . . We were all wet but we could not change, for our clothes [were] with the soldiers of the rear guard."[6]

On November 21, at the town of Candon, in Ilocos Sur province, Aguinaldo and his group turned eastward. They slogged across a muddy coastal plain, and then began the arduous climb into Luzon's Central Cordillera. The trail crossed fast-flowing streams and wound through rice fields that stair-stepped up the mountainsides in spectacular terraces. Clouds closed in around them, and at 4,440 feet, they reached the summit of Tirad Pass. With the Americans no longer on their trail, the Filipinos made a leisurely descent to a picturesque town along a rushing mountain river.

While Aguinaldo and his entourage rested, sixty men handpicked by the dashing Filipino General Gregorio del Pilar set to work transforming Tirad Pass into an impregnable fortress. They constructed a stone barricade across the twisting footpath, and carved parallel rows of trenches into the boulder-strewn slope.

With the trail gone cold, Young had rested his weary men and horses while awaiting supplies and reinforcements at Candon. Their spirits were lifted by the arrival of Major Peyton March and his battalion of crack-shot Texans, assigned to assist Young's pursuit of Aguinaldo and other Filipino forces. The tall and athletic son of an English professor at Lafayette College in Easton, Pennsylvania, March had graduated from West Point in 1888. During the Cuban campaign against Spain, he had commanded a volunteer artillery battery funded by the New York millionaire John Jacob Astor. Ordered to the Philippines later in 1898, March had caught the attention of General MacArthur during the opening battle against Aguinaldo's forces when he had volunteered to lead a charge against an enemy blockhouse. March took the position with fifty artillerymen armed with revolvers, beginning a rise that would culminate nineteen years later with his promotion to major general and the youngest Army chief of staff in history.

As the Americans rested in Candon and pondered their next move, an informant arrived with information about Aguinaldo's route. Young ordered Major March to take three hundred men and head into the mountains to the east, where Aguinaldo had supposedly fled.

Late on the afternoon of December 1, del Pilar's lookout on the summit frantically signaled the approach of enemy soldiers. Atop the pass that evening, del Pilar confided his thoughts in his diary: "The General has given me the pick of all the men that can be spared and ordered me to defend the Pass. I realized what a terrible task has been given to me. And yet I feel that this is the most glorious moment of my life."[7]

On the morning of December 2, del Pilar's riflemen opened the battle when the American column came within range. "A sharp clatter of Mausers was heard, and bullets began singing overhead," wrote newspaper correspondent John T. McCutcheon, who had joined March and his men for the trek. March double-timed up the trail with two companies while another sprinted through a rice field in search of an alternate route to the top. As they picked their way up the narrow path, two Americans fell wounded. At the head of the column, March found his lead company pinned down by heavy enemy fire. Scanning the summit with his field glasses, he spotted a Filipino officer standing exposed on the rocks, directing fire down on the Americans.[8]

Ignoring Aguinaldo's suggestion to leave the defense of Tirad Pass to his subordinates, del Pilar had taken personal command of the sixty Filipino soldiers who stood between the Americans and his president. During three years of war, the gallant officer had narrowly averted death on more than one occasion. Handsome and charismatic, del Pilar had earned a reputation for bravery matched only by his renown as a ladies' man, and his travel bags were said to be stuffed with the perfumed letters of female admirers.[9] Now del Pilar exhorted his men to hold their ground.

Studying the formidable enemy position, March ordered a dozen sharpshooters to make their way across a deep gorge to a hill that overlooked the trail to the left of the enemy position. He also commanded a sergeant major named Thompkins to take a company back down the trail to scale a peak that towered over the pass.

As the day wore on, fire from the enemy fortress tapered off. The Filipinos had begun to run low on ammunition, and so they rolled stones down the slope onto March and his men, huddled on the ledges below. Around midday, March's sharpshooters appeared on the hilltop to the left and began to pick off enemy fighters behind the stone barricade. Later in the afternoon, after scaling a sheer cliff face, Thompkins and his men opened fire from the peak above the pass. March ordered his soldiers to charge, and they rushed up the trail and scrambled over the barricade. Only eight defenders had survived "the Filipino Thermopylae," as March christened the battle. Among the Filipino dead, his body picked clean of souvenirs by the American soldiers, was Gregorio del Pilar.

Fifteen miles up the trail, at the town of Cervantes, Aguinaldo received word of del Pilar's death in the waning twilight. The daylong defense of Tirad Pass had given Aguinaldo a head start on his pursuers, but it was little solace. Afterward, as *el presidente* and his weary party climbed higher into the craggy mountains, word arrived that a force in Nueva Vizcaya they had hoped to join had surrendered on the day of del Pilar's last stand. Grim tidings of more capitulations followed in the days ahead.

By December 7, March and his men were once again closing in on Aguinaldo, and the Filipino leader was forced to flee a temporary sanctuary in the high mountains of Bontoc province. But the Americans could go no farther. Many were shoeless and sick, worn down by the weeks of reduced rations and hard hiking along difficult mountain trails. March gave the order for his men to turn back.[10]

Though no longer hounded by his relentless pursuers, Aguinaldo faced a desperate situation. Cut off from his armed forces, the revolutionary leader headed into the territory of head-hunting Igorot tribesmen. As they pressed deeper into the dangerous mountains, the beleaguered revolutionaries ate horses, cats and dogs to survive. Spear-throwing Igorots attacked the column, forcing Aguinaldo and his men to expend precious ammunition. Combat and disease soon pared Aguinaldo's security force from more than 2,000 men to less than 150 and a dozen officers.[11]

For the American high command in the Philippines, Aguinaldo's retreat and the disintegration of his army were cause for celebration. It had not been neat and easy, like the war against Spain, but after a year of hard campaigning, the end was surely near. In a triumphant telegram to General Otis, General MacArthur declared victory: "The so-called Filipino Republic is destroyed."[12]

CHAPTER 11

"A Nasty Little War"

At his palace headquarters in Manila, General Otis devoured the upbeat reports that poured in from the field. Night after night he worked late, transforming the telegrams and letters from subordinates into even more positive cables for his superiors in Washington. From his first days in command in the Philippines, Otis had cast the situation on the ground in a rosy light. Now, with his forces sweeping across Luzon in the waning weeks of 1899, he fattened the profits of transpacific cable operators with accounts of his army's triumphs.

Otis had little firsthand knowledge of what was going on, even in Manila, much less in the far-flung corners of the archipelago. He rarely ventured outside the walls of his riverside palace, and shunned the daily social rituals of his senior commanders and ambitious junior officers— late-afternoon promenades through Luneta Park, carriage rides along the bayfront boulevard, and evening banquets and balls. When he left Manila after nearly two years in the islands, it would be written that Otis "has never been seen on the Luneta, like the other officers, and only two or three times has he been seen in society."[1] Instead, he preferred to cloister himself in his office, fussing over the minute details of logistics and administration and preparing his daily reports to Washington.

Through November and into December, Otis bombarded his superiors with news of Aguinaldo's flight and "disintegrating" enemy units. Most encouraging to President McKinley and his new secretary of war, former Wall Street lawyer Elihu Root, were the assurances that U.S. commanders had all the troops they needed to subdue the crumbling resistance. Around the islands, U.S. forces were being greeted as liberators and given "all possible aid," Otis proclaimed, while Aguinaldo was so reviled that his captured mother and son were under American protection "to prevent their murder by natives." He scoffed at Washington's intelligence reports that the revolutionaries had purchased arms in Europe that were now headed his way. There was "no longer any insurgent government or authorities," so even if the rebels got the weapons ashore, they were "too late."[2]

With the fighting winding down, Otis ordered his army to implement the benevolent program promised by President McKinley twelve months earlier. After a year of fighting, McKinley had felt compelled to restate the policy in his annual message to Congress on December 5. "We shall continue . . . to make these people whom Providence has brought within our jurisdiction feel that it is their liberty and not our power, their welfare and not our gain, we are seeking to enhance," he declared.[3] Fired with what historian John Gates has described as a sense of "duty to uplift the world's 'retarded' peoples and bring them the joys of law, order, and 'civilization,'" U.S. soldiers built schools and bridges, vaccinated children and organized municipal governments.[4]

Progressive American officers like Captain Joseph B. Batchelor Jr. fervently believed that McKinley's approach would transform Filipinos into "faithful, loyal, and law-abiding subjects." On the other hand, Batchelor warned, if Filipinos "be treated with weakness and cruelty; if bad faith be shown; if they be exposed to a course of insult and robbery, a fire will be kindled which it will take thousands of men to extinguish."[5]

Across the islands, the fire was already smoldering.

EVEN AS THE MANHUNT FOR Aguinaldo had played out, scattered Filipino forces on Luzon had begun to regroup and launch attacks on U.S. troops.

One of the boldest occurred on December 4, when two hundred soldiers under the command of General Manuel Tinio attacked Vigan, the elegant provincial capital of Ilocos Sur. Tinio's fighters had slipped into town in the predawn and taken up positions in the Catholic church, bishop's palace, convent and hospital grounds. They had hoped to surprise the American garrison in their quarters, but a spy had betrayed their plans. In more than four hours of close-quarters combat, eight U.S. soldiers died and three were wounded. By midmorning, the bloody streets and plazas of Vigan were strewn with the bodies of forty Filipinos.[6]

Five days later, U.S. troops badly mauled Tinio's brigade in a running battle. Tinio and his men fled into a forest rather than surrender, and there, in a pattern repeated across the islands in the days and weeks that followed, he broke his battered brigade into bands of twenty to thirty men. Within days, the newly formed guerrilla units began attacking American garrisons, ambushing patrols, and assassinating Filipino collaborators.

Closer to Manila, America's first year of war in the Philippines ended with an even more shocking testament to the resolve that burned within the Filipino nationalists. A week before Christmas, General Henry Lawton led his brigade out of Manila in a raging typhoon, in search of a guerrilla band operating in the foothills northeast of the city. Early on the morning of December 18, Lawton found his prey dug in at San Mateo, along the north bank of the Marikina River. The Filipinos opened fire, and Lawton deployed his men in flooded rice paddies along the opposite shore. As the battle intensified, the towering Lawton paced the paddy dikes where his men had sought cover, directing fire and barking orders— a conspicuous figure in his trademark British cork helmet and yellow rain slicker. Suddenly, the big American clutched his chest and sank to the muddy ground. An enemy bullet had pierced his lungs and sliced an artery. As an aide gently cradled Lawton's head, one of the most celebrated American soldiers of the late nineteenth century—the captor of Geronimo and victor at El Caney—bled to death in a Philippine rice paddy.[7]

ON FEBRUARY 4, 1900, THE first anniversary of the war in the Philippines passed without formal celebration. Over the preceding weeks, the

conventional conflict had sputtered to an unofficial close with the surrender of more enemy commanders and the occupation of the remaining
major cities. One of the last campaigns had covered far southern Luzon
and neighboring islands to the south, a White House–ordered expedition
to restore the flow of cheap hemp exports to America's rope and twine
industry and Midwest farmers—important Republican constituencies.
The Americans now occupied all the major towns and cities of Luzon,
the major ports of the central Visayan Islands, and the predominantly
Muslim southern island of Mindanao, second in size only to Luzon. But,
as U.S. troops would soon learn, the war had merely entered a new and
deadlier phase. The Filipinos no longer sought to defeat U.S. forces in
battle, but aimed to bleed them until they wearied and went home.

    A year of less strenuous conventional warfare had already taken a
heavy toll on American soldiers. Veteran units had seen their numbers
decimated by tropical diseases, diarrhea, dysentery, intestinal parasites
and skin maladies. Those who had not succumbed to an enemy bullet or
illness had been worn down by months of operations in tropical heat and
humidity.[8] A typical weekly casualty report cabled to Washington in early
January 1900 offered a grim snapshot of the growing perils American
soldiers faced in the islands: Of thirty-four U.S. military deaths during
the week, five soldiers had been killed in action, six had drowned, seven
had succumbed to typhoid fever, four had died of malaria, four had suffered dysentery and one had committed suicide.[9]

    Along with the casualty lists, Otis had begun to inundate his superiors
with reports on schools built and municipal governments established—all
measures of the growing acceptance of U.S. rule by Filipinos, he asserted.
At the same time, Otis downplayed in his communications a disconcerting
trend that had begun to emerge by February 1900. Communiqués from
U.S. field commanders announcing enemy surrenders had tapered off,
and in their place, piling up on Otis's desk, were disturbing reports of
ambushes, raids and assassinations carried out by shadowy Filipino forces.

McKINLEY'S ANNUAL MESSAGE REFOCUSED THE Army's efforts to the work
of pacification, and on December 20 Otis had named hard-charging

General Samuel Young to assume responsibility for winning Filipino hearts and minds in northwestern Luzon. Within three months, Young reported the creation of town councils and native police forces in sixty-three towns. More than two hundred schools had been established, and barefoot Filipino children were learning the mother tongue of their new colonial masters.[10]

Assisting Young was a thirty-five-year-old lieutenant colonel from Texas named Robert Lee Howze. The strapping West Pointer had won the Medal of Honor in 1891 for holding off an attack by Brule Sioux Indians following the Army's bloody deeds at Wounded Knee, South Dakota. Howze had served with distinction in Cuba before his assignment to the Philippines, where he commanded a battalion during the pursuit of Aguinaldo. Afterward, he was named provincial commander of Ilocos Norte.

Howze had only five companies of troops to secure the province, but it seemed enough in the early weeks. Armed resistance to American rule had evaporated overnight, and newly appointed town presidents assured Howze that their people welcomed the Americans.

By early March, however, Howze had begun to doubt the friendly smiles and cooperative attitudes. Convoys were suddenly being ambushed and telegraph lines mysteriously cut. Army intelligence reported that a provincial priest, Father Gregorio Aglipay, had used native clergy to establish an underground organization with a large irregular military component. The guerrillas had formed their own shadow governments and had co-opted American-appointed officials through threats and intimidation. After the murder of a pro-American town chief and two Filipinos suspected of spying for the occupation army, local officials were afraid to be seen with U.S. troops, and some refused to collect salaries and municipal funds from the new colonial administration. "There is a strong undercurrent of bad spirit," Howze reported to Manila, "and preparations for a revolt."[11]

THE PREPARATIONS, IN FACT, WERE under way across the islands. While the Americans had focused their energies on colonial rule and reconstruction, nationalist forces had organized a guerrilla army with full-time regulars and part-time militia. Cells of the Katipunan, the underground organization that had launched the revolution against Spain nearly three years earlier, were revived in towns and villages to conduct espionage, raise funds and report on troop movements. Shadow governments funneled supplies to guerrilla units and punished spies and collaborators.[12]

In each town, the revolutionary committee formed a unit known as the *sandatahan,* a company-size unit armed with bolo knives that assisted with military operations and carried out nighttime assassinations of pro-American officials, prominent citizens, spies and informants. One such company in Ilocos Sur killed about thirty *americanistas* around Vigan in 1900. Operating secretly at night, members of the unit seized victims one at a time and took them to a designated spot along the grassy beaches. The captives were forced to kneel at the edge of a grave dug by other team members, then stabbed to death with swords and bolos and buried. Their work done for the night, the *sandatahanes* would slip away to their respective homes and civilian lives.[13]

General Young had initially dismissed the violence as the work of "murderers, thieves and robbers" and assured Otis that he would cleanse the region of this scourge within two months, "or sooner with more troops." Young got his reinforcements, but still could not stem the violence. Alarmed by the rising pace of guerrilla activity in his area, he called off the pursuit of Aguinaldo to focus on this new threat. He recruited native scouts, but that did little to stop the flurry of raids and ambushes. Badly shaken, Young would eventually endorse ruthless measures to crush the guerrillas, including martial law, summary executions and the concentration of civilians in camps—tactics condemned by Americans when employed by the Spaniards in Cuba.[14]

As American and allied casualties mounted, so did Young's contempt for the native population. There were two classes of Filipinos—"the actively bad" and "the only passively so"—in his jaundiced view. "I have been in the Indian campaigns where it took over 100 soldiers to capture each Indian," General Young observed, "but the problem here is more difficult on account of the inbred treachery of these people."[15]

As the situation in the countryside deteriorated, Otis continued to assure Washington that all was well. But in early April, an Associated Press dispatch from Manila tripped alarms in the War Department and the White House:

> General Young . . . has made several requests for reinforcements, representing that his force is inadequate; that the men are exhausted by the necessity of constant vigilance; that he is unable to garrison the towns in his jurisdiction; that the insurgents are returning to the district and killing the *amigos,* and that it is necessary for him to inflict punishment in several sections before the rainy season begins. General James Bell, who is commanding in Southern Luzon, has made similar representations. He says his forces are inadequate and that he merely holds a few towns, without controlling the territory.[16]

Secretary of War Root urgently cabled Otis for an explanation.

Otis again downplayed the threat posed by the resistance and suggested that his subordinates had overreacted. "Robberies and murders have been committed, and have always been committed throughout these islands," he said, implying that the latest violence was nothing more than a continuation of Spanish-era lawlessness. "Now guerrillas and *ladrones* murder each other, and occasionally rob and murder peaceable citizens."

With a hint of condescension, Otis explained why he was so confident the end was near for the resistance: All the important towns, and many smaller ones, were safely in American control; the guerrillas were capable of attacking only in remote areas; and U.S. troops were capturing enemy firearms every day. Furthermore, Filipinos had begun providing the Americans with information on the insurgents, "which until recently they feared to do." Once again, Otis assured Secretary Root that he had enough men "to meet any anticipated emergencies." Indeed, he concluded, "We no longer deal with organized insurrection."[17]

Less than a week later, Ilocos Norte exploded in violence.

On April 16, Father Aglipay led six hundred fighters in a daylong attack on the town of Batac and its thirty-man garrison of 34th Infantry soldiers and 3rd Cavalry troopers. The guerrillas advanced in three waves: a file of women used as human shields, followed by bolo men armed with wooden swords, then a line of riflemen. When some of the women fell wounded, the others threw themselves onto the ground to make way for the fighters behind them. The bolo men charged the American positions "like the descent of the Mahdi's fanatics upon Kitchener's squad at Khartoum," an eyewitness reported. "They kept coming on faster than the soldiers could shoot them down, until they were so close that our cavalrymen had no time to fire and load, but went through them with clubbed carbines."[18] Aglipay's riflemen joined the assault, and the outnumbered Americans found themselves in "a desperate and terrible fight," Army Captain C. J. Rollis reported. "Three times the town was cleared of insurgents but they persistently returned." The Americans finally drove the attackers back in hand-to-hand fighting that left Aglipay seriously wounded. Daylight revealed the one-sided nature of the carnage (or perhaps a highly sanitized American casualty report): 180 dead Filipinos, versus two Americans.[19]

That evening, hundreds of guerrillas attacked the nearby town of Laoag. Again, the bravery of the guerrillas exceeded the sophistication of their weaponry and tactics, and they lost scores of fighters in another suicidal assault that claimed the life of only one American soldier.

Afterward, Howze gave the guerrillas four days to surrender. When the deadline passed, he went on a rampage that devastated the countryside around Batac. The destruction and carnage culminated on April 24, when an American cavalry troop surrounded three hundred guerrillas and killed 125 of them.[20]

The Americans had inflicted heavy casualties on the resistance forces, but the high command in Washington was hardly reassured. The very size and ferocity of the attacks called into question Otis's repeated claims that the war was over and pacification progressing nicely. In fact, the rising violence in Ilocos Norte and elsewhere revealed formidable opposition to American rule.

Otis accepted none of this. "Young has plenty [of] troops and will have little further opposition," he assured the War Department in an April 24 cable. "Affairs at other Luzon points [are] improving."

THE CLAIMS OF AN "IMPROVING" situation would have baffled beleaguered U.S. troops in the Bicol region of southeastern Luzon, who by April found themselves in a stalemate with local guerrillas. Inadequate troop levels forced the Americans to fight for the same towns again and again. When they moved on to the next hot spot, the revolutionaries immediately reclaimed the vacated town, killing Filipinos who had given information or shown friendship to the Americans. "We are governing just the spots we sit upon," Lieutenant Samuel P. Lyon wrote from Bicol.[21]

As was true elsewhere in the islands, U.S. forces in Bicol outgunned their enemies—the guerrillas were armed with bolos, bows and arrows, and only a few rifles—but the superior organization and tactics of the Filipinos blunted the American advantage. The sounds of water buffalo horns and bamboo tom-toms tracked American patrols, leading one Army officer to complain that any nighttime movement of his men was broadcast ahead within ten minutes. Slogging along trails that snaked through jungle-clad hills, American soldiers found their progress slowed by mantraps, spring-triggered spears and other deadly snares. The guerrillas kept occupied towns on edge by launching attacks when patrols were out, and infiltrating assassins, like the harmless-looking Filipino who whipped out a long knife from a basket one day and decapitated an American sentry.[22]

The guerrillas financed their activities through an underground system of tax collections and contributions. Planters contributed a portion of their hemp or rice harvests, while in other instances guerrillas harvested hemp belonging to suspected collaborators and sold it to middlemen. Requests by outraged U.S. field officers to close the hemp ports and ban the trade were rejected by Otis and his superiors in Washington—the potential political fallout for McKinley and the Republicans in the November elections trumped the concerns of troops on the ground.

Adding to the American hardships and misery were Army logistical failures that denied troops adequate food and medicine and deprived them of pay for months at a stretch. An officer of the 47th U.S. Volunteers painted a dire picture of the deterioration of his regiment after only a few months of guerrilla warfare in Bicol. "The condition is not altogether due to the climate, but is largely due to the intense strain they have been under," the officer reported. "Some [soldiers] have been rendered nervous and unfitted by it, others seem to have grown callous and indifferent, willing at any time to take undue risks. . . ."[23]

GENERAL MARCUS MILLER HAD WATCHED his men undergo the same physical and psychological decline during operations against guerrillas on the central island of Panay in mid-1899. In response, he had proposed a solution that eschewed McKinley's promised benevolence: "All measures of a bitter war should be used."[24]

Miller's recommendation had been favored by many U.S. field officers from the beginning of the war, but the discussion of a harsher reply to resistance had intensified after the collapse of Aguinaldo's conventional forces. In late 1899, after learning of Aguinaldo's order to begin guerrilla warfare, General MacArthur had urged Otis to offer remaining enemy fighters a chance to surrender before shifting to a no-tolerance policy. The killing of an American soldier would be regarded as murder under MacArthur's plan, and the Filipinos who pulled the trigger as well as their commanders would be treated as common criminals. Otis rejected the extreme measures as unnecessary and impractical, but the debate was only beginning.[25]

The surge in guerrilla activity in early 1900 sharpened the American discussion over tactics, and an informal consensus, at least among field officers and rank-and-file soldiers, coalesced around MacArthur's severe policy. A convergence of factors hardened attitudes: beliefs that guerrilla tactics were illegitimate; that Filipinos were "niggers" and savages who responded only to force; and, perhaps most decisively, that Filipinos had forfeited humane treatment by their own brutal actions.

Historian Brian Linn has noted that neither side sanctioned torture, summary executions or other extralegal tactics at the high command level. It was a far different story in the field. The behavior of Filipino forces, like that of American troops, would vary from island to island and even province to province. American field officers and their men, however, tended to exhibit isolated atrocities by their adversaries as the norm. Although many U.S. prisoners of war reported humane treatment by their Filipino captors, every incident of abuse was seized on as the true measure of a cruel and dishonorable enemy. Consequently, just as Custer's doomed troopers at the Little Bighorn had preferred a quick death, even at their own hand, to the horrors that awaited them in Indian captivity, U.S. soldiers in the Philippines lived in terror of capture.

Among the cautionary tales that circulated through the ranks was the case of three Americans who fell into enemy hands during a chicken-stealing expedition near their camp in Pampanga province in November 1899. The captives were taken off to an enemy hideaway on the slopes of Mount Arayat, an extinct volcano that towered above the rice paddies and sugarcane fields of Central Luzon. There they endured six hellish weeks of starvation and mock executions. In January, when American troops approached the enemy camp during a sweep, the guerrillas cut the throat of a Filipino collaborator, then shot and slashed the three Americans with their bolos. Two of the badly wounded prisoners survived to recount their terrifying ordeal.[26] Similar stories and rumors circulated elsewhere in the archipelago. Three missing soldiers on the island of Panay were reported to have had their throats cut on orders of a parish priest. On Leyte, insurgents were said to have beheaded an American prisoner of war.[27]

By the spring of 1900, with guerrilla attacks spiking across the islands, an ethos of reprisal had been embraced by many American officers. Enemy attacks, ambushes and assassinations were routinely punished by burning houses or entire villages, destroying crops and livestock, and torturing suspects. Captured guerrillas were frequently shot "attempting to escape." An Army lieutenant in La Union province reported to his superiors, with grudging admiration, the case of one tough town president who had refused to reveal guerrilla secrets, "even after being strung up three times by the neck, about six inches clear of the ground."[28] Preparing for a spring operation in Laguna province, near Manila, Colonel Benjamin F. Cheatham, commander of the 37th U.S. Volunteers, sought permission for his troops to "burn freely and kill every man who runs." Permission was denied in this instance, but the fact that Cheatham would make such a request in writing is a telling measure of American frustrations in the field—and a forewarning of even more drastic measures.[29]

Only three years earlier, such Spanish tactics had been cited by Theodore Roosevelt and other prominent Americans as justification for U.S. military intervention in Cuba. Most Americans considered their troops to be more humane than their European counterparts, yet by the spring of 1900, American field commanders up to the general officer level had come to accept the legitimacy of these practices.

AMONG THE PRACTITIONERS OF THE eye-for-an-eye tactics in the early months of 1900 was the war's quintessential American hero, Frederick Funston. The heroic Kansan and his sunburned troops had been hailed by adoring crowds when they stepped off a train in Topeka in early November 1899.[30] Funston was still savoring the parade-and-banquet circuit a couple of weeks later when a War Department telegram arrived, ordering him back to the Philippines in command of one of the new regiments of U.S. volunteers. He reached Luzon in time for the final push against Aguinaldo.

When the Army began its local pacification campaign, Funston was chosen to whip into shape General Tinio's home province of Nueva Ecija. Sprawling from the eastern edge of the Central Luzon plain into the foothills of the Cordillera Mountains, the province seemed placid enough in the first weeks after Funston's arrival. Guerrilla attacks and assassinations, however, soon shattered the tranquillity, and Funston found himself fighting "a nasty little war."[31]

Scarcely hiding his disdain for the benevolent policies of McKinley and Otis, Funston focused his energies on smashing guerrilla military capabilities. He personally led strikes on guerrilla hideouts, relying heavily on a native cavalry force recruited from the Pampanga town of Macabebe. Early in the war the Macabebes were known for their military prowess and their animus toward the Tagalogs, but they soon became better known for their brutal tactics, including the liberal use of a Spanish torture known as the "water cure," in which victims were subjected to simulated drowning.

Combining relentless pressure and aggressive tactics, Funston soon halted the spread of guerrilla activity in Nueva Ecija. He set the tone with his swift and severe response to each convoy ambush or telegraph-line cut: He would start by arresting the chief of the nearest village and burning houses nearest to the cut; if it happened again, he burned the entire village. As guerrilla activity escalated, Funston adopted even more draconian responses while allowing the torture and summary execution of suspects by his native forces.[32] One of Funston's lieutenant colonels was later accused of beating to death several Filipino officials accused of providing a tip that resulted in the death of an American lieutenant in an ambush. Although Funston would later face questions as to whether he had ordered the execution of twenty-four prisoners in retaliation for the ambush, a cursory military investigation had already concluded that the Filipinos were killed while attempting to escape.[33]

In late March, Funston was leading his men back to his base in San Isidro after an operation when his column encountered a guerrilla band that had captured several Macabebe scouts. After a brief fight, one of Funston's sergeants appeared with two guerrillas he had captured in the act of butchering two Macabebes with bolo knives. Funston asked the two guerrillas "if they could give any reason why the penalty of death should not at once be inflicted for having violated the laws of war in attempting to kill prisoners to prevent their escape," he later recounted. "They replied that they could say nothing that would help their case." Funston ordered the execution of both guerrillas on the spot. "Two picket ropes were called for," he recalled, "there was a tree near at hand, and within ten minutes after the commission of their brutal crime the two had paid the only appropriate penalty."[34]

FUNSTON WAS HARDLY ALONE IN adopting the hard approach that spring. Around the same time, the commander of the 13th Infantry in Central Luzon, Colonel William Henry Bisbee, was being warned by his commanding officer for revealing in his operational reports the use of property destruction and physical coercion of suspected guerrillas. Another incident that Bisbee had not reported had raised concerns with a member of Otis's staff. In this case, an officer had hanged a Filipino man suspected of hiding arms. When the rope broke, the officer then threatened to shoot the native, and fired his pistol close to the frightened Filipino. The officer then raked some leaves against the man's house and lit a match. The native broke down and revealed the hiding place of thirteen guns.

The commanding officer, Brigadier General J. Franklin Bell, sympathized with the difficulties faced by Bisbee and other field commanders. "I fully believe that such methods are necessary and justifiable under the circumstances," he wrote Bisbee. By the same token, he "would not be able to protect any officer whose employment of such methods became a matter of complaint or scandal."[35]

By May 1900, abuses by U.S. troops had become so commonplace that General Lloyd Wheaton felt compelled to remind his commanders in the Department of Northern Luzon that Civil War–era legal guidelines for dealing with irregular forces and civilians still applied. Privately, Wheaton was among the hardest of the hard-liners. "You can't put down a rebellion," he huffed, "by throwing confetti and sprinkling perfumery."[36]

EMILIO AGUINALDO HAD ENDURED SIX months on the run in the cold mountains, the disintegration of his army and government, the capture of his mother and son and the surrender of his wife and top aides. Now, as sporadic reports of widening guerrilla resistance reached him in the spring, he was heartened by the knowledge that his revolution lived on. In mid-April, he had received an encouraging briefing from General Tinio, the first time they had been able to meet since the previous November. The guerrilla war was going especially well in Ilocos Norte, Tinio reported.[37] Indeed, in a six-week span, guerrillas had cut American telegraph lines twenty-three times, killed fifteen American soldiers in ambushes and assassinated fifteen native policemen.

Aguinaldo barely had time to savor the reports when his old nemesis, Major Peyton March, picked up his trail again.

On the afternoon of May 20, at a mountain village called Asibanglan, a column commanded by March caught up with Aguinaldo's group. The revolutionary leader's guards had been depleted by sickness, and part of his security forces had been separated from the presidential party when the shooting started. The Americans were within seconds of capturing Aguinaldo when the general fled through a closing cordon of American troopers "amidst a hail of enemy bullets," Aguinaldo's aide, Dr. Simeon Villa, recalled.[38] A force of thirty Filipinos held off 150 Americans while Aguinaldo again made his escape.

By late May, after another hard march through the mountains, Aguinaldo had put forty miles between his group and his American pursuers. Inspired by his meeting with Tinio and the news that the guerrilla war was proceeding apace, and reinvigorated by another escape from the American dragnet, he was once again acting as commander in chief, issuing proclamations and circulars to commanders, and organizing stragglers into new guerrilla bands. On the night of May 28, he reached the town of Enrile, in the far northeastern corner of Luzon. In his honor, local citizens organized an impromptu ball. For a few hours, the worries of war were forgotten. Sixty young ladies of the local aristocracy had turned out to pay their respects, and the general and his hosts danced until dawn.[39]

IN THE TWENTY MONTHS SINCE Elwell Otis had assumed command in the Philippines, Manila had taken on the flavor of an American city. Baseball games pitted Marines against the Army. Golfers chipped and putted at the newly formed Manila Country Club. Military officers entertained lavishly at the Army and Navy Club, where they and their civilian guests dined on Australian steaks, French and Spanish wines, freshly churned ice cream and local cigars.

Ships from the United States still arrived daily, disembarking eager passengers into this newest of American frontiers—schoolteachers and social workers, missionaries and temperance activists, businessmen and speculators, prostitutes and swindlers. The Spanish were gone, but corruption still flourished. Among the many illicit opportunities available to dishonest American officers was a thriving black-market trade in Army goods. An Ohio crony of President McKinley, Major H. O. Heistand, set his sights higher, hatching a scheme to corner the lucrative hemp trade.

In April 1900, against this backdrop, Otis abruptly asked to be relieved from command in the Philippines. As he prepared to leave the islands, news of more guerrilla attacks arrived. On Samar, twenty American soldiers died when their garrison was besieged for five days and nearly overrun by guerrillas. On Panay, four American soldiers were killed and sixteen wounded when their patrol was ambushed.[40]

The statistics that Otis tossed around so freely in his cables, if analyzed carefully, called into question his portrait of resounding success: Over the last four months of 1899, U.S. forces had suffered 69 killed and 302 wounded in 329 engagements. During the first four months of 1900, casualties had surged to 130 killed and 325 wounded in 442 encounters. April would be the bloodiest month yet for U.S. forces.

Yet to the end, Otis perfumed his reports to Washington with unbridled optimism. He even publicly proclaimed victory in an interview with the influential *Leslie's Weekly.* "The insurrection ended some months ago," he declared, "and all we have to do now is to protect the Filipinos against themselves and to give protection to those natives who are begging for it." Speaking as though the rising guerrilla attacks were imagined, he concluded, "You will see that there will be no more real fighting of any moment. What there is will be but little skirmishes which amount to nothing."[41]

ON THE MORNING OF MAY 5, 1900, Otis settled behind his desk in Malacañang Palace as he had nearly every morning for the past twenty months. He pored over the latest reports from the field and the sheaves of paperwork generated by an army of more than 2,100 commissioned officers and 60,700 enlisted men. On this, his final day in Manila, the American-owned *Manila Times* would praise Otis for devoting himself to his paperwork "with his accustomed energy," but in fact, breaking with his joyless routine, he did more socializing than work. For a few more hours, he would remain the most powerful man in America's Pacific outpost, and a parade of Army officers, colonial administrators, Supreme Court justices and other prominent officials and citizens arrived to pay homage.

At four o'clock, Otis made his way across the palace lawn one last time, and descended a set of stairs to a dock along the banks of the Pasig River. Accompanied by several aides, he boarded a steam-powered launch, and the craft cast off and chugged downstream through the throbbing heart of the city. Emerging from the mouth of the Pasig into Manila Bay, the launch set a course for the U.S. Army transport ship *Meade*, anchored in the shallow waters.

As the vessel steamed past the walls of the old Spanish city, two Army regiments positioned along the shore presented arms, and a military band struck up "Auld Lang Syne." A shore battery boomed a major general's salute, and the warships in port responded in kind. The launch pulled alongside the *Meade*, and Otis and two aides climbed aboard. Within minutes, the transport weighed anchor and steamed toward the setting sun, past Corregidor and into the South China Sea.[42] America's nasty little war in the Philippines was now the problem of Major General Arthur MacArthur.

CHAPTER 12

"Men of a Bygone Age"

Psident William McKinley was at work in his White House office on Saturday evening, February 4, 1899, crafting a speech about his vision for America's overseas expansion, when an aide handed him a news dispatch from Manila: fighting had broken out in the Philippines.[1] The specter of U.S. soldiers killing freedom-seeking Filipinos shocked Americans, and the dismay and confusion that swept the nation convinced even the famously reticent McKinley to quickly rally public support for his policies. Eleven days later, the first anniversary of the *Maine* tragedy, he headed north by train in a heavy snowstorm to the cradle of the anti-imperialist movement.

More than nineteen hundred guests had paid for the honor of dining with the president at the Home Market Club of Boston on February 16, 1899, and another thirty-eight hundred spectators packed the sumptuously decorated balconies to await the evening's speech. Flags and bunting festooned the hall. Behind the speaker's table hung large portraits of Washington, Lincoln and McKinley, over a one-word caption: "Liberators."[2] Given the deaths of more than a thousand Filipinos at the hands of U.S. soldiers over the previous twelve days, it was a debatable claim for McKinley. But he boldly made his case.

The president did not break new ground, or offer fresh strategic thinking. Instead, in language sometimes pugnacious and other times pious, he restated all the arguments for why he had been compelled to claim the Philippines. From the beginning, "our concern was not for territory or trade or empire, but for the people whose interests and destiny, without our willing it, had been put in our hands." America was performing "a great act for humanity" by attempting to civilize and democratize those benighted islands, obeying "a higher moral obligation" that "did not require anybody's consent."

Amid frequent applause, he rebuked those who had questioned his policy—the anti-imperialist doubters who would do nothing, as well as the Democratic warmongers who had pushed him into the confrontation with Spain in the first place. "No imperial designs lurk in the American mind," McKinley assured his audience. "They are alien to American sentiment, thought, and purpose. Our priceless principles undergo no change under a tropical sun." The violence was tragic, he allowed, invoking "the blood-stained trenches around Manila, where every drop, whether from the veins of an American soldier or a misguided Filipino, is anguish to my heart." But glorious days lay ahead.

With the gathered thousands now shouting their approval, McKinley conjured the future of the Philippines, when the guns had fallen silent and the gifts of American rule had been fully bestowed. Filipinos would blaze a path for other Asians to follow, "a people redeemed from savage indolence and habits, devoted to the arts of peace, in touch with the commerce and trade of all nations, enjoying the blessings of freedom, of civil and religious liberty, of education, and of homes," striving ever forward "in the pathway of the world's best civilization."[3]

It was McKinley at his earnest best, inspiring his audience, calming their fears. His words would have a similar effect across the nation, steadying the nerves of the Republican faithful and silencing his critics, at least momentarily. Biographer Margaret Leech rated the speech "a landmark in McKinley's utterances as President." Historian Lewis L. Gould credited McKinley's words that evening with giving form to the modern presidency and setting the stage for the muscular leadership of Theodore Roosevelt and Woodrow Wilson. He could not make the

Philippine conflict popular, Leech writes, but McKinley "had armed the people with patience to accept a bitter phase of transition, and restored their faith in the purpose and the ultimate beneficence of the national conduct."[4]

RANK-AND-FILE REPUBLICANS HAD SEEN THEIR faith in McKinley's policy restored, but a vocal minority of moderate Republicans, Democrats and independents remained repelled by the idea of the United States as an imperial power. Their efforts to force America's withdrawal from the islands in the years ahead would vary widely, reflecting the disparate elements drawn to the anti-imperialist cause. Adherents ranged from socialists to conservative Southern Democrats who feared that U.S. stewardship of the Philippines would attract a new and unwelcome wave of dark-skinned immigrants. A broad range of social reformers rallied to the cause, including aging antislavery activists and corruption watchdogs; and then there were assorted other Americans, driven by outrage and fear that this sudden lust for empire had betrayed the nation's founding principles and undermined the republic. The fractious nature of the antiwar movement ultimately weakened its national impact, but, in the meantime, it forced the Republican administration and the nation as a whole to consider the political, moral and historical consequences of America's increasingly bloody quest for empire.

The public face of war opposition—and the principal target of outrage vented by the McKinley administration and the military—was the Anti-Imperialist League, a New England–rooted organization that by early 1899 had opened offices in several cities in the East and Midwest. The League's organizers were all members of the Massachusetts Reform Club, which had led the fight for clean government in the corruption-stained 1880s and 1890s. At its inception in November 1898, the group had pledged to do all in its power to prevent the ostensibly humanitarian war with Spain from being transformed into a war for colonial spoils. By the spring of 1899, U.S. annexation of the Philippines and the conduct of the war had become the organization's focus.

The league's founding constitution pledged nonpartisanship and welcomed "all who would join the battle against imperialism and the extension of American sovereignty over noncontiguous territory."[5] But even this all-inclusive credo had not been enough to attract the membership of America's most respected anti-imperialist, seventy-two-year-old George Frisbie Hoar. The senior U.S. senator from Massachusetts, a staunch Republican from the days of Lincoln, was personal friends with many of the league founders. They had worked in common cause during the fight for African-American rights in the post–Civil War South and the crusade against government patronage and corruption. But Hoar was a loyal party man, wary of his fellow New Englanders' history of political insurgency. He soldiered on alone in the Senate fight against expansion, rebuffing repeated invitations to join forces. Now, as the war rekindled national debate over the Philippines, the anti-imperialists were not the only ones keeping a close eye on Hoar. President McKinley feared a hard reelection campaign in 1900, and the cherub-cheeked senator from Massachusetts was a source of growing concern.

HOAR BEGAN HIS POLITICAL CAREER as a twenty-four-year-old fledgling lawyer in Worcester, Massachusetts, making a name as a Free Soil Party activist and antislavery organizer. He denounced the aging Daniel Webster and his fellow Whig aristocrats for their willingness to allow slavery in the Western territories. At the same time, Hoar was fervid in his belief that change should come through political and constitutional mechanisms, and not through the extralegal tactics of William Garrison and his fellow radical abolitionists.[6]

When the Republican Party was given life by the slavery debate in the mid-1850s, Hoar had found his political home. He campaigned vigorously for Abraham Lincoln in 1860 and helped deliver the ticket's decisive victory in Worcester. After much agonizing, he turned down a commission to fight with the Union Army, concluding he could better serve the cause as a patriotic speaker and fund-raiser for the local volunteer regiment.

Elected to Congress in 1869 as an advocate of "Radical Reconstruction" of the South, the slender, sandy-haired, sideburned freshman representative served as a House champion of Massachusetts Republican

Senator Charles Sumner's initiatives on African-American rights and a national system of primary education. He further burnished his reputation as a reformer by embracing the causes of women's suffrage and labor rights and opposing Republican patronage excesses in the 1870s and 1880s.[7]

Hoar's tenure in the U.S. Senate began in 1877, as Congress confronted an array of policy questions spawned by rapid industrialization, foreign immigration and urbanization. Simultaneously, the Republican Party was racked by an internal struggle that pitted against each other two powerful factions: the Stalwarts and the Half-Breeds. Hoar was one of the original Half-Breeds, exemplifying the faction's modest reform tendencies and rejection of personality-driven politics.

When Republicans split over the nomination of corruption-tainted James G. Blaine in 1884, a group of more liberal reformers known as Mugwumps broke away in protest. Hoar remained true to the party, despite his distaste for Blaine, and bitterly denounced the Mugwumps (many of whom were longtime New England associates). In the end, Democrat Grover Cleveland won the election, and Hoar never forgave the Mugwumps. Outraged by the election of "that hippopotamus Cleveland," Hoar called for loyal Republicans to recommit themselves to their sacred mission: political and social equality for blacks in the South.[8]

In 1896, Hoar turned seventy years of age. A veteran of nearly thirty years of Washington legislative battles, he no longer resembled the young man who had arrived at the Capitol in the shadow of the Civil War. His sandy hair had turned white, his lean face round, and his slender torso rotund. He had long since shaved off the bushy sideburns and abandoned attempts to grow a mustache. His clever wit, sweet disposition, honesty and integrity had won him the love and respect of his colleagues and friends. Yet, increasingly, he was ridiculed as a relic by his younger peers. A new generation of Republicans harbored little enthusiasm for Hoar's devotion to African-American rights, especially with the party losing electoral support in the rising Jim Crow South. The cause of foreign expansion, not downtrodden African-Americans, had stirred the imagination of young Republican lions like Theodore Roosevelt and Henry Cabot Lodge.

To sympathetic observers of the Washington scene, Hoar indeed belonged to a different era, but was it so terrible to personify the party that had emancipated the slaves and saved the Union? The impatient Roosevelt dismissed Hoar and his ilk as "men of a bygone age," but many Americans saw in the aging senator a dignity and righteousness too rare in public life. As the century drew to a close, and America contemplated its rise to global power, George Frisbie Hoar charted an increasingly lonely path within the Republican Party.[9]

THE INAUGURATION OF WILLIAM MCKINLEY as president in March 1897 was embraced by Hoar as a welcome development. The earnest, sweet-tempered president embodied many of the senator's political and personal qualities. On the policy front, Hoar found common ground with McKinley in at least two important areas: a commitment to high protective tariffs, and a distaste for the overseas expansion agenda promoted by Roosevelt.

Hoar also shared the same agonized soul-searching on Cuba that had reduced McKinley to tears. Ultimately, Hoar had reached the same conclusion as McKinley in the spring of 1898: War against Spain was a humanitarian necessity. Initially, he naively insisted that America had gone to war without the slightest thought of territorial gain. By summer, he feared the nation's rising lust for world power. "America's time of temptation," he confided to a friend, "will come after victory."[10]

As Washington newsboys touted great U.S. victories on Cuba in early July 1898, President McKinley moved quickly to channel the nation's patriotic spirit into the long-delayed annexation of Hawaii. Twice he summoned Hoar to the White House to ask for his support. And twice the senator refused to commit.

On July 5, as the Senate prepared to vote on the Hawaii resolution, Hoar announced his decision. Explaining his intention to vote for annexation, Hoar insisted that he was not abandoning his opposition to foreign expansion. Hawaii was a special case, he said, because of its importance to U.S. national defense, its long-standing ties with America and sudden Japanese interest. He drew a sharp distinction between the case of Hawaii and the desire of some Americans to annex the Philippines, Cuba and Puerto Rico. Annexation resulting from military conquest "has been the ruin of the empires and republics of former times," he argued, and was "forbidden to us by our Constitution, by our political principles, by every lesson of our own history and of all history."

Hoar had convinced himself that the president would never allow America to betray its founding principles by taking on a colony. His self-deception continued into September, even as McKinley offered him an appointment as U.S. minister to Great Britain on the eve of peace talks with Spain—suspicious timing, given Hoar's stated opposition to further overseas expansion and the brewing political debate on the subject. Hoar declined the position, and then watched with alarm as McKinley dispatched to Paris a negotiating team that was heavily tilted toward the expansionist view. By October, McKinley's support for annexation of the Philippines was no longer in doubt.

The following month, Hoar turned down an invitation to attend the charter meeting of the Anti-Imperialist League in Boston. He could not bring himself to sit around the same table with prominent Mugwumps who had condemned him for supporting Blaine in the 1884 campaign. Hoar rebuffed all pleas for a united front against the treaty, and watched with dismay as it won Senate approval with one vote to spare on February 6, 1899.

IN THE WEEKS THAT FOLLOWED, the Anti-Imperialist League stepped up its attacks on the administration. On March 13, two dozen prominent members issued a manifesto calling on President McKinley to declare an armistice and convene peace talks with Filipino representatives in Washington. They also called for Philippine independence "as soon as proper guarantees can be had of order and protection to property." The document's signatories included such noted Republicans as former U.S. Senator Carl Schurz, industrialist Andrew Carnegie and former Secretary of State John Sherman.[11]

McKinley and U.S. military commanders brusquely dismissed the proposal: There would be no talks until the rebels surrendered to American authority.

The rejection enraged hot-blooded anti-imperialists such as Massachusetts Mugwump Edward Atkinson. Like many of his like-minded comrades, Atkinson based his views on a mix of beliefs. His business background persuaded him that America's colonial experiment would trigger soaring taxes and stunted economic growth back home. His moral and political beliefs convinced him that annexation was evil.[12]

Among his many talents, Atkinson was a prodigious pamphleteer, and within weeks after fighting erupted he had cranked out several anti-imperialist tracts with provocative titles such as "The Cost of a National Crime," "The Hell of War and Its Penalties," and "Criminal Aggression: By Whom Committed?" In them, Atkinson advised soldiers to demand to be sent home from the Philippines, and he counseled officers as well as enlisted men to refuse immoral orders.

His savvy business instincts led Atkinson to a brilliant plan to simultaneously publicize his work and provoke the administration. Atkinson mailed copies of his pamphlets to McKinley's secretary of war, Russell Alger, explaining that he wished to "send a large number . . . to the officers and privates in the Philippine Islands." Innocently, he asked: Could he send them directly through the War Department? Or should he use regular mail?[13]

As Atkinson expected, he received no reply. So he dropped copies of two pamphlets in the mail, addressed to four senior military commanders in the Philippines, including Admiral Dewey and General Lawton, two civilian members of the administration's Philippine Commission and the Manila correspondent for *Harper's Weekly*. The pamphlets got as far as San Francisco, where McKinley's postmaster general had them removed from the Manila-bound mail.[14]

The seizure of the tracts briefly became a national sensation. Atkinson denounced the McKinley administration's "rape of the mails," while the president and his Cabinet accused Atkinson of treason and sedition. In Chicago and other cities, administration supporters held rallies to condemn Atkinson and his fellow anti-imperialists and cheer America's annexation of the Philippines. Pro-administration newspapers across the nation attacked Atkinson as "an uncompromising radical" and a traitor who had provided "aid and comfort to the enemies of their country." Embarrassed by the backlash, the Anti-Imperialist League disavowed Atkinson.[15]

Atkinson, not surprisingly, was pleased by all the attention. In a letter to Hoar, he declared that his actions had revealed the brutish nature of the McKinley administration and its willingness to violate the Constitution to suppress dissent. Demand for his pamphlets soared tenfold.[16]

The controversy had only reinforced George Frisbie Hoar's determination to maintain his distance from the Anti-Imperialist League, though his horror over the war mirrored that of Atkinson and his friends. "The blood of the slaughtered Filipinos" as well as "the blood and wasted health and life of our own soldiers" rested on the head of the expansionists, he wrote in a letter made public in April. He called for America to grant independence to the Philippines. "Let us do what we pledged ourselves to do for Cuba—compel other nations to keep their hands off, and keep our hands off as well."[17]

THEODORE ROOSEVELT HAD LISTENED TO the anti-imperialists rail against expansion since his return from Cuba, and by early 1899 his anger had reached volcanic intensity. How any red-blooded American could wish to undo the nation's global ascension was a mystery to him. As to the motivations of the anti-imperialists, he had no shortage of theories. Hoar was "senile," the Mugwumps "idiots." The whole lot of them, he seethed to his friends, were "unhung traitors."[18]

Roosevelt had publicly sparred with the anti-imperialists since his campaign for New York governor in the fall of 1898. As he delivered speeches across the state at county fairs and urban rallies, candidate Roosevelt proclaimed it America's duty to retain overseas posts its fighting men had fairly won.

New York's most prominent anti-imperialist, former U.S. Senator and Lincoln friend Carl Schurz, denounced Roosevelt and his fellow expansionists for promoting "a vulgar land grabbing [scheme] . . . glossed over by high-sounding cant about destiny and duty and what not." Schurz was encouraged in his efforts by fellow Republican and strident anti-imperialist steelmaker Andrew Carnegie. "You have brains and I have dollars," he wrote Schurz. "I can devote some of my dollars to spreading your brains."[19]

Roosevelt prevailed over Schurz's brains and Carnegie's dollars in a close race, and on the bitterly cold day of January 2, 1899, the brash Rough Rider took the oath of office in Albany. Although he had his hands full in New York, trying to wrest control of state government from the political machine of Republican Senator Thomas Platt, Roosevelt agonized over the looming treaty vote. Commiserating with Lodge over the uncertain outcome, he offered to have the New York state legislature pass a resolution in support of the treaty. When the treaty passed, Roosevelt fired off congratulatory letters to Lodge and other expansionists.

Roosevelt's pride over America's rise quickly gave way to a dark mood over the widening war in the Philippines and congressional attempts to block higher military appropriations. The opponents of expansion "are quite as potent forces for evil as the most corrupt politicians," he railed to one friend.[20] To Lodge, he fumed about the actions of Hoar, Maine Republican Senator Eugene Hale and their congressional allies. "We may have serious work in Cuba and the Philippines, and I only hope that in doing it we shall not display the qualities displayed by the democratic opposition, by Hoar, Hale and the peace-at-any-price men. . . ."[21]

In April, after concluding his first legislative session as governor, Roosevelt headed west on a speaking tour that was to eventually take him to New Mexico for a Rough Riders reunion. The war in the Philippines, and America's wavering spirit in the face of this momentous trial, weighed heavily on Roosevelt as his train rolled into Chicago. There, drawing on his vast powers to lead and inspire, he delivered the signature speech of his career on April 10.

His audience as he gazed out from a flag-draped stage was the membership of the city's prestigious Hamilton Club, but in truth he was speaking to all Americans. The nation stood at a pivotal moment in its history, Roosevelt declared. Never had America been so prosperous, yet prosperity too easily achieved threatened the very future of this great people. Frontier challenges had once forged the inhabitants of the United States into a tough and resourceful nation, but those challenges were now gone, replaced by easy living and urban comforts. Americans, he warned, faced a peril that had been the downfall of every great nation: They risked growing soft as a people. The solution, as Roosevelt saw it, was to shun the easier path and, as individuals and Americans, to pursue a "strenuous life."

At that very moment, America faced such an opportunity in the Philippines, he continued. "The guns that thundered off Manila and Santiago left us echoes of glory, but they have also left us a legacy of duty. . . ." And that duty was unmistakable. America "cannot avoid the responsibilities that confront us in Hawaii, Cuba, Porto [sic] Rico, and the Philippines," he declared, for the "splendid ultimate triumph" would go "not to the man who desires mere easy peace, but to the man who does not shrink from danger, from hardship, or from bitter toil."

As Roosevelt framed it, Americans confronted a stark choice: the glory of global power, or the disgrace of retreat. He had long ago made his choice. Now he exhorted his countrymen to join him in the march to claim America's destiny. "Let us shrink from no strife, moral or physical, within or without the nation, provided we are certain that the strife is justified," he urged, "for it is only through strife, through hard and dangerous endeavor, that we shall ultimately win the goal of true national greatness."[22]

AS HE WORKED HIS WAY westward, Roosevelt remained uncertain as to whether the nation would heed his call and hold steadfast in the Pacific. He confided his hopes and fears to his good friend and fellow Rough Rider General Leonard Wood, serving with U.S. occupation forces in Cuba: "In the Philippines we still seem to be having ugly work, but if only our people stand firm and take a little punishment and send if necessary a few tens of thousands of reinforcements there, we will have the islands absolutely pacified once and for all in a short time. I most earnestly pray that there will be no backing out."[23]

Greeted by tumultuous crowds across the Midwest, Roosevelt soon found his concern over the state of affairs in the Philippines tempered by his surging presidential ambitions. In Kansas, he paid tribute to the state's newest hero, Frederick Funston, and, in turn, was feted by William Allen

White, the influential editor of the *Emporia Gazette,* who was promoting Roosevelt as the Republican standard bearer in 1900. Though flattered by White's labors on his behalf, Roosevelt also instinctively understood the political risks of an unsuccessful challenge. Reining in his ambitions, he publicly endorsed McKinley's reelection.

Roosevelt returned from the West in late June, heartened by the adoring throngs, but still anxious about his political future. His reception had been encouraging, but, as he observed to Lodge, "I have never yet known a hurrah to endure five years."

For the moment, there was nothing Roosevelt could do regarding his political prospects, and so he turned his attention to America's shaky imperial venture in the Philippines. On the evening of June 30, he dined at Sagamore Hill with General Wood and retired Major General Francis V. Greene, a West Pointer who had commanded New York militia in the Philippines during the war against Spain. They discussed at length the problems that American troops confronted overseas.

The following day, Roosevelt penned a twenty-four-hundred-word letter to Secretary of State John Hay, laying out how President McKinley could end the uprising in the Philippines and avoid a "political cataclysm" that could cost the Republicans the 1900 election.[24] He recommended two actions to save the day: a surge in troop strength, and the appointment of a new supreme commander over U.S. forces in the islands. He urged that General Greene be given the position and dispatched to the islands "with instructions not simply to defend Manila, but to assume aggressive operations and to harass and smash the insurgents in every way until they are literally beaten into peace."[25]

McKinley politely ignored the advice, but that did not discourage Roosevelt. A prodigious letter writer throughout his life, he had expanded his circle of correspondents to include a number of American military officers in the Philippines, including his former commander in Cuba, General Samuel Young, and Frederick Funston. Late that summer, when General Young wrote to suggest that Henry Lawton should replace General Otis as supreme U.S. commander in the Philippines, Roosevelt immediately approved. "With you and Lawton I know there is no delay, no carelessness, no hesitancy in taking the initiative, no failure to appreciate that the enemy must be hit and smashed and followed up on the run and smashed again," he wrote Young. "We must have a man in command who is continually at the front and who means hard hitting and the finishing up of the whole business."

Roosevelt promised to do all he could to orchestrate a change in command in the Philippines.[26]

BY THE FALL OF 1899, the war in the Philippines had created a fault line that increasingly divided Americans into expansionist and anti-imperialist camps. The attempts by General Otis to censor unfavorable news reports from the Philippines had fueled the claims of critics that the war was going badly, and that the McKinley administration was hiding the ugly truth from the American people. Even Republicans fretted about the stories of harsh U.S. tactics, sick and exhausted American soldiers and stiffening Philippine resistance. Pro-administration newspapers warned McKinley that more missteps in the Philippines could spell defeat in the 1900 election.

The tenor of the public debate had deteriorated throughout the spring and summer. In March and April, the journal *Puck* ran cartoons depicting anti-imperialists as skirt-wearing "Aunties," bowing before Filipino clowns or blocking the way of gallant U.S. soldiers. Pro-administration newspapers and politicians denounced the anti-imperialists as traitors and "Copperheads," the pejorative applied to Northern antiwar forces during the latter stages of the Civil War. At its annual encampment in the summer of 1899, the Grand Army of the Republic—the Civil War veterans group—pronounced Anti-Imperialist League members "unworthy of the name of American citizens."

The anti-imperialists, in turn, continued to depict the war against Filipino nationalists as a betrayal of America's founding principles of liberty and self-government. In speeches and literature, anti-imperialists lionized the Filipino nationalists as liberty-loving freedom fighters in the mold of America's founding patriots. Boston anti-imperialist Gamaliel Bradford, addressing an August peace conference in Connecticut, called for a "moral alliance with the Filipinos." Congressman John J. Lentz, at a meeting of "Peace Democrats" at Cooper Union in New York in September, hailed Aguinaldo as an Asian Patrick Henry.[27]

With the arrival of the fall political season, the back-and-forth intensified. Addressing the annual dinner of the Republican Club of Massachusetts in October, Theodore Roosevelt cast the rebellion in the Philippines as a test of America's manhood—one that the Democrats would miserably fail should the country return them to power. "We have got to put down the insurrection," he declared. "If we are men, we can't do otherwise."[28]

President McKinley stirred from his summer torpor and traveled to Pittsburgh to welcome home the 10th Pennsylvania Volunteers from the Philippines. It was a prelude to an extended campaign swing through the Midwest in October, where he defended his colonial policy. To resounding cheers, McKinley vowed that the war would not end until the Stars and Stripes "shall float triumphantly in every island of the archipelago under the undisputed and acknowledged sovereignty of the republic of the United States."[29]

Back in Washington, McKinley provided a platform to like-minded soldiers and civilians who had just returned from the Philippines. Among them was a sharp-tongued "soldier priest," the Reverend Robert McKinnon of the 1st California Volunteers. McKinnon emerged from his White House audience to denounce the Filipino insurgent leaders as murderers, convicts and horse thieves and to excoriate the anti-imperialists for sustaining the rebels with their encouragement.[30]

Lest Americans, after the months of fractious debate, doubt the value of their Pacific islands or the necessity of continuing American control, the White House on November 2 released the preliminary report of the commission that President McKinley had dispatched to study conditions in the Philippines. The commissioners reached unsurprising conclusions: U.S. occupation had saved the Philippines from chaos and foreign occupation, and was the only path to sustainable self-government in the islands.[31]

Optimism within the administration soared as the fall offensive by U.S. troops shattered Aguinaldo's army and forced the Filipino revolutionary leader into the mountains of northern Luzon. As Americans prepared to celebrate the Thanksgiving holiday, Secretary of War Elihu

Root declared, "I think the rebellion will be thoroughly crushed out before Christmas."[32]

The victory pronouncements did nothing to quell the anger of administration opponents. Anguished by recent news of the death of Aguinaldo's infant daughter and capture of his son and mother by U.S. forces, one of New England's leading anti-imperialists, businessman Erving Winslow, penned a caustic Thanksgiving note for William McKinley. He accused the commander in chief of conferring on America "her first Thanksgiving of shame," and prayed that in the weeks and months ahead, the American president would "be brought to repentance and a better mind."[33]

As AMERICA'S FIRST YEAR AS a world power drew to a bloody and divisive close, Albert Beveridge arrived in Washington to take up his seat as the new United States senator from Indiana. Beveridge strode briskly into the Capitol with an overweening ego and outsize ambitions, already envisioning himself as president of the United States within a few years. But first, he intended to carve out a position as congressional overlord for America's new overseas empire in the Caribbean and the Pacific.

Beveridge had lobbied for a vacant seat on the Senate foreign relations committee, but had to settle for a spot on Henry Cabot Lodge's new Committee on the Philippines—not the chairmanship, as Beveridge presumptuously requested, but a seat nonetheless, "which I think he was fortunate to get," Lodge stiffly apprised one of Beveridge's backers, Theodore Roosevelt.[34] The young Hoosier's vanity and ambition quickly irritated many within the staid Republican hierarchy. Even the genial McKinley found Beveridge "sometimes tiresome," observing that the senator "was hurting his standing here by his unwise methods of securing recognition."[35]

Unfazed, Beveridge set off at a gallop. On January 4, 1900, he introduced a Senate resolution reaffirming America's rightful possession of the Philippines. He also announced his intention to break a Senate tradition of yearlong silence by freshman members so he might share his observations on the Philippines with the American people.

Just after midday on January 9, Beveridge rose to the Senate floor.

Every seat in the galleries was filled, and a long line of disappointed spectators stretched through the Capitol's marbled corridors.[36] Beveridge was smaller and thinner than many in the audience had imagined, and he appeared nervous and pale. But when he began to speak, his charismatic appeal became apparent. For two hours, his remarkable voice, "clear and musical as a bell," filled the great room.

He began with a declaration of America's imperial destiny so brash and uncompromising that it shocked many of his colleagues. "The Philippines are ours forever: 'territory belonging to the United States,' as the Constitution calls them," he said. "And just beyond the Philippines are China's illimitable markets. We will not retreat from either. We will not repudiate our duty in the archipelago. We will not abandon our opportunity in the Orient. We will not renounce our part in the mission of our race, trustees under God, of the civilization of the world."[37]

With the divine nature of America's mission established, Beveridge explained the practical reasons that demanded annexation of the Philippines. The archipelago, as he had personally witnessed, was "a revelation of vegetable and mineral riches"—fertile fields of rice, coffee, sugarcane, tobacco and hemp, lush groves of coconut and banana, enough fine wood to "supply the furniture of the world for a century to come," "mountains of coal," "great deposits of copper," and gold strewing the banks of streams.

The fact that the islands sprawled on China's doorstep made the Philippines even more valuable. America's trade with China would be "the mightiest commercial fact in our future," and now, by holding the Philippines, the United States held "a base at the door of all the East." Beyond the commercial exigencies were strategic considerations, he declared: "The power that rules the Pacific is the power that rules the world," and by holding the Philippines, "that power is and will forever be the American Republic."

At times, Beveridge held the little red notebook he had carried with him during his travels through the islands. He reminded his audience that his words were based on firsthand interviews and observations—not the half-cocked assertions and wishful thinking of those opposed to America's colonial venture.

His travels had left no doubt that the idea of self-government by Filipinos was preposterous. "My own belief is that there are not a hundred men among them who comprehend what Anglo-Saxon self-government even means, and there are over five million people to be governed." As for the bloodshed, Americans desired peace in the islands, but peace required "overwhelming forces in ceaseless action until universal and absolutely final defeat is inflicted on the enemy."[38]

Beveridge ended as he began, with a call for America to meet its divine destiny. It was America's duty to "establish system where chaos reigns," to "administer government among savages and senile peoples." End the debate once and for all, he urged Congress and the nation, for America had "saving, regenerating, and uplifting work" to do with its "deluded children" in the Philippines.

As the gallery erupted in thunderous applause, Beveridge settled back into his seat to accept the congratulations of his colleagues. And then, as the roar died away, the senior senator from Massachusetts asked for the floor.

George Frisbie Hoar had not arrived at the Senate with the intention of challenging Beveridge, but he could not allow the battle cry for American empire to go unchallenged. He offered a brief and polite rebuttal.

Hoar was appalled by the glittering lure of material prosperity that Beveridge offered as justification for the nation's bloody colonial venture. To a descendant of New England Puritans, it sounded like Satan's temptation of Jesus. His young friend had offered an "eloquent description of wealth and glory and commerce and trade." He had said much "to excite the imagination of youth seeking wealth, or the youth charmed by the dream of empire." But the senator from Indiana, Hoar solemnly pointed out, had not even paid lip service to the cherished ideals of America's birth—"those words which the American people have been wont to take upon their lips in every solemn crisis of their history," the ideals of liberty, freedom and self-government.[39]

As WINTER GAVE WAY TO spring, the Senate continued to debate America's war in the Philippines. Beveridge had quickly alienated party elders, and so responsibility for defending American honor and administration policy fell chiefly to Henry Cabot Lodge. In his aristocratic style, so cold that mocking colleagues sometimes turned up their collars and shivered as he walked past, Lodge brusquely dispensed with the constitutional and moral questions. The commercial and strategic rewards of planting America's flag in the Philippines were paramount in the Lodge worldview.

In April, Hoar rose once again to address the Senate on America's forced annexation of the Philippines. Drawing on his considerable intellect and decades of experience in the fight for human liberty, Hoar had carefully prepared his "supreme effort in the anti-imperialist cause," writes historian Richard E. Welch Jr., a speech that stretched over more than three hours and presented all the constitutional and moral arguments against America's conquest of the islands.[40] "Drunk with the lust of empire," Hoar declared, Republicans had abandoned the principles of Lincoln, the ideals that had made the party synonymous with liberty and equal rights, and had now started down a dangerous slope. Many Republicans no longer even questioned the disenfranchisement of African-Americans in the South, he sadly noted. If America so readily denied the rights of the lowliest of its own citizens, not to mention its sovereign subjects in the Philippines, where would it end?[41]

CHAPTER 13

"Brave Hearts and Bright Weapons"

Captain Tony Waller had returned from Cuba in the fall of 1898 slightly deaf in his left ear from the roar of naval guns, and a minor hero after his role in the battle of Santiago Bay. Back in the States, the forty-three-year-old Waller took an assignment as a recruiter at the Marine barracks in Norfolk, Virginia. It allowed him to spend time with his wife and their three young sons, but for the moment, Waller's shot at battlefield glory had seemingly passed.

In the spring of 1899, as Frederick Funston dazzled America with his feats of derring-do in the Philippines, Waller was preoccupied with his mundane recruiting duties. Two battalions of Marines were formed and dispatched to help pacify the islands, yet Waller remained chained to his Norfolk desk. In October, with U.S. forces poised to launch a final offensive against Aguinaldo and his army, the newly promoted Major Waller finally received his coveted orders to lead a battalion of Marines to the islands.

Fortune favored Waller and his men during their monthlong Pacific passage, and on December 15, 1899, they steamed into Manila Bay and anchored off Cavite, near the sunken Spanish fleet of Dewey fame. When they went ashore, the local *Manila Times* correspondent was impressed with the new arrivals. "The boys are large," he wrote, "well drilled and looking healthy."[1]

ALTHOUGH THE MARINES HAD ACQUITTED themselves well in their combat debut at Novaleta, Cavite, in October 1899, their showing did not lead to a more prominent role in the fall campaign against Aguinaldo. General Otis had planned "the Great Roundup" as an Army affair and so, while his boys grabbed the glory, the Marines guarded military supplies at the Cavite naval station and sparred with smugglers and thieves. In late November, a company of Marines was finally dispatched to northern Luzon to occupy the port of Vigan, which they accomplished without firing a shot. A few days later, the Army marched into town and the Marines were sent packing.

Waller and his fifteen officers and 325 enlisted men went ashore at Cavite to find their comrades mired in tedium as they kept watch over the Navy yard coal pile, lighthouse and other facilities. There were fleeting moments of excitement, like the night shortly after Waller's arrival when the Marines received word that a foreign spy had checked into the International Hotel in Cavite City. Fifteen or twenty Marines with bayonets fixed hurried to the hotel and pounded on the door of the suspected agent. A groggy Romanian Jew by the name of H. S. Deurns appeared, and soon found himself behind bars at the Marine barracks, accused of espionage. After ten harrowing days of interrogation and threats of execution, the terrified Romanian was released and caught the first boat back to Manila.[2]

The Marines at Cavite remained insulated from the guerrilla conflict spreading through the islands in the early months of 1900, but some of their comrades had gotten a taste of the new style of warfare. In December 1899, Captain H. L. Draper led a force of 120 Marines from Cavite to occupy the town of Olongapo, site of the old Spanish naval station on Subic Bay. There they began the dangerous work of clearing the jungle-clad hills and ravines of insurgents and bandits. The Marines also did their part to fulfill President McKinley's call for benevolent assimilation of the Filipinos, and by March, Olongapo boasted a smoothly functioning municipal government and an English-language school—courtesy of the United States Marine Corps.[3]

THOUGH SPARED THE TRIAL OF guerrilla war, the Marines at Cavite could not avoid the health perils of the tropics. Malaria, dengue and other mosquito-borne illnesses became chronic afflictions for the men. By February 1900, fevers, diarrhea and other intestinal ailments had so debilitated his ranks that Colonel Robert L. Meade, the new Marine commander at Cavite, suspended all morning drills, exercises and ceremonies. He also limited guard duty and assemblies and, acting on the recommendation of his regimental surgeon, ordered his men "not to drink water in the native houses and to avoid the so-called soda water and lemonade."[4]

By late March, Tony Waller had fallen ill with the dreaded "intermittent fever" and chills that afflicted most of the Marines. Over the next three months, he would struggle with bouts of the malarialike symptoms, and his fever would soar as high as 105 degrees. As with many of his comrades, Waller was sidelined on the regimental sick list for days at a stretch.[5]

In the meantime, Waller had begun to forge lasting relationships with several of the rising Marines under his command. His budding friendship with Lieutenant Smedley Butler, the son of a Pennsylvania congressman influential in military affairs, would prove especially beneficial to his career. The young Butler, in turn, would come to revere Waller as a father figure. Thirty years later, Butler would recall Waller as "the greatest soldier I have ever known."

Sometime after his baptism of fire at Novaleta, Butler had walked into a local tattoo parlor in Cavite to memorialize his glorious blooding in the Philippines. The artist went to work with his needles, and, after several painful sessions, Butler stepped from the parlor with a huge and colorful Marine Corps emblem tattooed across his chest. "I blazed triumphantly forth," Butler recalled, "the Marine from throat to waist."[6]

Waller and Butler shared similar aspirations of finding battlefield glory in the Philippines, but their dreams remained unfulfilled as General Otis declared the war all but over in the late spring of 1900. Nearly six months after leading his battalion ashore, Waller still had not seen a single Filipino *insurrecto* or fired a shot in anger. Indeed, he had seen more action as a fledgling second lieutenant in Egypt seventeen years earlier.

And then, without warning, fate dealt an even crueler blow. A cable arrived from Corps headquarters in Washington, ordering Waller to assume command of the Marine detachment on the island of Guam. Waller's reaction can be fairly imagined, for the reputation of Guam among Marines as "the island of misery" had spread throughout the Corps. "But for the [Navy] band," a Marine posted to Guam in 1900 reported, "we would have gone crazy." A sun-scorched flyspeck in the middle of the Pacific, Guam was a place of deadly fevers, killer typhoons and devastating earthquakes, a hellhole where horrified Marines encountered lepers "walking the streets without hands or eyes or noses." A few months earlier, a Marine first lieutenant had fallen into such a depression during his Guam deployment that he had been placed on a Manila-bound hospital ship. Somewhere between Guam and the Philippines, he jumped overboard, never to be found. On Guam, there was no war, and no glory.[7]

Waller and his unfortunate men were preparing to depart for their new assignment in mid-June when the spirit of resistance to Western domination that had sustained the independence movement in the Philippines exploded in China in the form of antiforeign violence. Waller was ordered to lead a battalion of Marines to China to join a gathering multinational expeditionary force. It was a stroke of unbelievable luck. Hours away from exile, Waller was headed instead to the number one global hot spot.

ON THE MORNING OF JUNE 20, 1900, the gate of the German Legation swung open and two sedan chairs borne by pigtailed natives emerged onto the streets of the foreign quarter of Peking, China. Seated in the lead sedan was Germany's handsome, blue-eyed envoy to China, forty-six-year-old Baron Clemens von Ketteler, and in the second rode his personal secretary and interpreter, Heinrich Cordes. The destination of the German diplomats on this humid Friday morning in the Chinese capital was the imperial government's Office for the Management of the Business of All Foreign Countries, about a mile away. After weeks of escalating threats and violence directed against the city's non-Chinese residents, fear gripped the foreign diplomatic compounds. Yet the debonair German diplomat affected an air of untroubled calm. Rather than packing a pistol, von Ketteler had armed himself with a good book and a fine cigar.[8]

To Chinese nationalists, the shabby building that beckoned the diplomats with urgent business was a hated symbol of the foreigners and their humiliating treaties, military bases and trading concessions, all imposed on China's crumbling Ch'ing Dynasty over the previous sixty years. Peking's foreign quarter occupied a similar place of revulsion, for it was home base of the "foreign devils" in their escalating competition to strip China of its sovereignty and territory.

Anger toward the growing foreign presence had combusted over the previous months, exploding into violent outbursts by a shadowy group of disaffected Chinese calling themselves the Society of Righteous and Harmonious Fists. Members embraced an incendiary brand of nationalism, and they performed martial rites that they claimed made them invulnerable to foreign bullets. Foreigners who had witnessed the routines had nicknamed the rebels Boxers.

Wearing red headbands, red aprons and red leggings, the Boxers had begun their bloodletting on the last day of 1899 by beheading a Christian missionary from England. In the months that followed, the Boxers left a bloody trail across the countryside of north China. Spring brought a brazen escalation as the Boxers began threatening foreigners and proselytizing recruits in the cities of Tientsin and Peking.[9]

Meanwhile, Western powers ratcheted up their pressure on Peking's fractious imperial court to stop the violence. In April, a great armada flying the flags of the world's most powerful nations had gathered off the Chinese coast near Tientsin. When that failed to curb the attacks, the United States in late May dispatched fifty U.S. Marines and sailors with an automatic gun to secure Peking's diplomatic quarter.

The first days of June had seen a flurry of ominous developments. The Boxers had cut rail and telegraph service to Peking, and, on the night of June 12, set fires across the city and painted red symbols on the doors of Chinese Christians. The next day, thousands of Boxers poured into the city through the Hata Gate, just east of the foreign quarter, shouting incantations and waving swords and spears. They attacked the Austrian compound and threatened the American Legation, but fled for cover when Marines hurried out into the street with their Colt automatic guns. Late in the afternoon, Boxers set fire to foreign missions and churches, and as night fell, they began slaughtering Christian converts and other Chinese with ties to the foreigners. "Awful cries in the west part of the city all through the night," British journalist George Morrison scribbled in his diary. "The roar of the murdered. Rapine and massacre."[10]

On June 17, the foreign armada lying off the coast at Taku had seized the Chinese forts guarding the mouth of the Pei River. The Chinese government responded by ordering the foreign diplomats and their families to leave Peking by four o'clock on June 20. Fearing a massacre, the foreigners asked for more time.

With the deadline less than twelve hours away, the diplomats gathered at the French Legation on Friday morning to discuss the government's silence to their request. When someone suggested patience, Baron von Ketteler erupted: He would proceed to the foreign office and remain until Chinese officials responded. And with that, the German diplomat and his secretary climbed into their sedan chairs.

The Germans had gone several blocks through the strangely quiet streets when they encountered a group of Chinese soldiers. Suddenly, an officer stepped forward, thrust his rifle nearly to the window of the lead sedan, and assassinated von Ketteler with a shot to the head.[11]

News of the shocking attack spread quickly through the foreign quarter. Security details and civilians stockpiled food and medical supplies and strengthened breastworks and barricades. By late afternoon, about four thousand people from eighteen countries, including three thousand Chinese Christians, waited within the walls of the foreign quarter.

As the sun settled into the western sky, gentlemen gathered on the lawn of the British Legation, pocket watches in hand, counting down the minutes to the Chinese deadline. In the southwest corner of the quarter,

Captain John T. Myers waited at the American Legation with his Marines, pondering the reports of his spies: Boxers were pouring into the city through all gates, welcomed by government troops.[12]

Promptly at four o'clock, the Chinese opened fire on the foreign quarter.

As his comrades in Peking took cover from Chinese bullets, Major Tony Waller and his undersized battalion of 130 Marines were ninety miles to the southeast, pushing inland from the coast. The Marines had arrived off China late on June 18, steaming into the midst of the international armada. Steam launches, tugs, lighters and Chinese junks chugged through the waters, carrying supplies, men, mules and horses from the forty-odd warships to the docks at Tongku, four miles up the Pei River. Bands played and soldiers waiting to debark cheered as troops from the various nations headed ashore.[13] With the assistance of a German admiral, Waller and his men hitched a ride aboard a German freighter, and stepped into the chaos on the Tongku docks.

The first goal of the foreign military forces was to save their besieged citizens, but strategic considerations weighed heavily, especially for the Americans. Since taking over the State Department for President McKinley in 1898, John Hay had made Asia a focal point of administration foreign policy. With McKinley's blessing, Hay had dispatched a series of diplomatic missives regarding China in the fall of 1899. The "Open Door" notes accepted spheres of influence in China claimed by England, Russia, Germany, France, Italy and Japan, but also staked for the United States and other powers free-trade privileges in those zones. Now the arrival of Waller and his Marines underscored America's intention to claim its share of the China spoils.[14]

Geopolitical considerations aside, Tony Waller's objective was to get his Marines inland to join the multinational rescue of foreign citizens in Peking and Tientsin. About thirty miles up the Pei River from the coast, Tientsin had been under siege by Boxers and Chinese troops since June 15, and the situation was growing more dire by the day. Waller loaded his men aboard a train of flatcars stacked with rails, ties, spikes, telegraph poles, wire and other equipment to make repairs as needed, and set off up the line. By late afternoon, the Marines had advanced to within twelve miles of Tientsin when they encountered a regiment of Russian infantry accompanied by galloping Cossack outriders. With night fast approaching, Waller and the colonel commanding the Russian regiment agreed to bivouac for the night.[15]

At two a.m., Waller was awakened with the news that the Russian colonel had decided to force his way into Tientsin. After registering a protest, Waller sent his Colt machine gun and its crew to the head of the column. The remainder of the Marines fell in behind the Russians and marched through the darkness toward the Chinese city.

Around seven a.m., on the southern outskirts of Tientsin, the Russians and Americans came under fire. Marine sharpshooters had silenced a line of enemy skirmishers when an entrenched force of two thousand Chinese troops opened an even heavier attack. Waller headed off a flanking maneuver by enemy forces, and then rallied his men as the Boxers mounted a furious charge, "waving their swords and banners frantically." The Marines held steady, and the assault was broken at about five hundred yards.[16]

Casualties mounted and the fight grew increasingly desperate for the Marines. When the Russians fell back on the right, Waller and his men came under heavy enfilading fire. In danger of being overrun, Waller finally ordered a withdrawal. For the next four hours, the Americans fought a running battle with the advancing Chinese as small knots of bleeding, sweat-stained Marines fell back under the covering fire of comrades.[17] The Marines finally reached the safety of their new base at two p.m. They had left four dead comrades on the field of battle and lost their two artillery pieces, but, unlike the Russians, the Marines had fought well against a superior enemy force. Though it was hardly a glorious victory, Tony Waller had held his Marines together in an ill-advised engagement and had prevented a perilous retreat from becoming a rout.[18]

The following day Waller and his men retraced their march to the outskirts of Tientsin with a more formidable force of two thousand allied troops. At four o'clock on the morning of June 24, the international troops launched an all-out attack on the Chinese siege lines southeast of the city.

In eight hours of hard fighting that culminated with a bayonet charge, the Marines and their foreign comrades broke the enemy lines. As bugles blasted "There'll Be a Hot Time in the Old Town Tonight," and haggard foreigners (including future American President Herbert Hoover and his wife) cheered, Waller and his Marines led the column into Tientsin's battered foreign quarter.[19]

THE EXPLOITS OF WALLER AND his Marines were headline news back in America as the dramatic events continued to unfold. In league with a unit of Welsh Fusiliers, the Marines rescued an allied column that had been trapped for two weeks in a Chinese arsenal eight miles north of Tientsin. The Marines and their British comrades escorted scores of sick and wounded troops back to Tientsin. "Our men have marched 97 miles in the five days, fighting all the way," Waller reported. "They have lived on about one meal a day for six days, but have been cheerful and smiling always. . . . They are like Falstaff's army in appearance, but with brave hearts and bright weapons."[20]

On July 9, Waller's Marines and their British allies were thrown into a fight to prevent Chinese troops from flanking the foreign force. Waller was given command of a column composed of his Marines, a contingent of Japanese sailors and a British Royal Navy unit, and advanced under heavy shell fire. While Japanese cavalry smashed Chinese positions on the allied left, Waller's men captured an enemy arsenal complex about fifteen hundred yards from the walls of the old Chinese city. Waller's performance once again won praise from their allies. Japanese Major General Yasumas Fukishima presented the American with a captured field gun and a note of thanks written in French. The overall British commander, Vice Admiral Edward Seymour, credited the Marines with saving the British from "a good many casualties."[21]

On the eve of the allied attack on the old Chinese walled city, Waller relinquished overall command of the Marines in China to the heavy-drinking, rheumatism-racked Civil War veteran Colonel Robert L. Meade, newly arrived from the Philippines with another Marine battalion. The allied attack got under way in the predawn darkness of July 13.

While Russian troops converged on the Chinese redoubt from the north, U.S., British, Japanese and German troops attacked from the south. Anchoring the far left of the allied line, U.S. Marines and Royal Welsh Fusiliers advanced in rushes, throwing themselves behind grave mounds and rice paddy dikes to avoid deadly enemy fire from atop the city walls.[22] By eight a.m. the Marines had advanced eight hundred yards, nearly halfway to their objective, when a large pond and heavy enemy fire halted their progress. Chinese infantry poured out of the city and opened fire into the left flank of the Marines. Among the Marines who fell was Lieutenant Smedley Butler, who took a bullet through the thigh when he dashed into the open to help a wounded comrade.[23]

For twelve hours, the Marines remained pinned down on the bullet-swept plain as shells exploded overhead, and a brutal sun beat down. Twice Chinese forces sprinted out of the city's south gate to cut off the Marines, only to be driven back in desperate fighting. As the afternoon wore on, ammunition ran low and canteens ran dry. Wounded Marines begged for water.[24]

Off to the right, the fifteen officers and 423 men of the newly arrived 9th U.S. Infantry Regiment found themselves in even worse straits. In a desperate advance under heavy enemy fire, five officers and seventy enlisted men were killed or wounded.[25] The regimental commander, Colonel Henry Liscum, marched boldly toward the enemy fire, urging his men forward. When the regiment's color sergeant, an Irishman named Edward Gorman, collapsed to the ground with a severe wound, Liscum grabbed the Stars and Stripes, "holding them erect and fearless." And then the colonel fell, mortally wounded in the stomach. "Keep up the fire, men," Liscum commanded, and then he died.[26] The attack faltered and the survivors hunkered in ditches and shallow pools of water as murderous Chinese fire raked the landscape.

Night arrived and the Marines and men of the 9th began to pull back in small groups, dashing between grave mounds, paddy dikes and ditches as naval guns thundered overhead. It had been a costly day, with total allied losses numbering several hundred. The Chinese fighters remained at their battlements, their great fortress unbreached.

Japanese soldiers at the center of the allied line on the south front had tenaciously held their ground and maintained fire on the city walls into the night. During the early hours of July 14, a team of Japanese sappers blew the massive south gate of the city wall from its hinges, and allied troops poured into the city. Most of the Chinese defenders had already slipped away. Of 5,650 allied troops involved in the assault on Tientsin, more than two hundred had been killed and about six hundred wounded. Twenty-four Americans had been killed, including six Marines, and ninety-eight wounded.[27]

The campaign to liberate Tientsin had ended with Waller and his Marines the toast of the allied army. "Foreign officers have only the highest praise for their splendid fighting qualities," Rear Admiral Louis Kempff wrote of Waller and his men. Equally generous accolades came from Colonel Meade: Waller had shown "untiring zeal" and proven himself "a fine soldier," earning "high praise everywhere" among the allied forces. A brevet promotion to lieutenant colonel would be Tony Waller's reward.[28]

WALLER AND THE MARINES HAD covered themselves in glory at Tientsin, but the liberation of the besieged foreigners in Peking remained—if it was not too late. On July 16, the London *Daily Mail* carried a horrifying story on the massacre of foreign citizens in Peking. The following day, the staid London *Times* published an even more harrowing account of the terrible end met by the city's foreign citizens. "They have died as we would have had them die," the newspaper reported, "fighting to the last for the helpless women and children who were to be butchered over their dead bodies. . . ."[29]

An ominous uncertainty lingered on August 4, when an international relief force of twenty thousand men marched out of Tientsin, bound for Peking, ninety miles to the west. The American contingent of about twenty-five hundred men, now under the command of Major General Adna R. Chaffee, U.S. Volunteers, had been reinforced by the arrival of the 14th U.S. Infantry and additional Marines. Throughout the day, columns of soldiers representing the world's finest armies tramped into the Chinese countryside—U.S. Marines, Japanese infantrymen, French

Zouaves, Russian Cossacks, Royal Welsh Fusiliers (wearing their Bunker Hill battle ribbons), Italian Bersaglieri, and British and French colonial troops from India and Indochina.

For ten days, a great column of dust marked the progress of the international force through the Chinese countryside. Imperial infantry and cavalry slowed the advance in a series of sharp engagements, but the greatest threat to the international army was the heat of the Chinese summer. Waller led a successful attack on several villages on the morning of August 6, but left an entire company behind in a cornfield, overcome by heat. (As it turned out, the only Marine death during the fighting was due to heatstroke.) So it went, day after grueling day. A trail of blankets, ponchos and other military equipment snaked through the countryside as men desperately tried to lighten their loads. Nightfall brought a parade of exhausted stragglers stumbling into camp.[30]

On August 14, allied troops fought their way into Peking. Two companies of the 14th U.S. Infantry scaled the city wall at the northeast corner and drove Chinese defenders from the massive east gate. Gradually, the Americans worked their way westward, toward the Hata Gate and the besieged foreign legations.[31]

The Marines had joined the assault after a twelve-mile, all-night march through mud and rain. As they neared the Tungchow wall of the outer city, a Chinese bullet struck Smedley Butler in the chest and knocked him to the ground. The round had flattened the second brass button on his uniform blouse and driven it into his chest, but, fortuitously, had not caused more serious injury. He would cough blood and carry a painful bruise for several days, but Butler's only lasting damage was losing a piece of Latin America from his Marine Corps tattoo.[32]

By three o'clock, Chaffee's troops had fought their way to the foreign quarter, and soldiers of the 14th Infantry entered the walled settlement. They found scenes of terrible destruction, but the haggard residents were very much alive. They had endured fifty-five days of shelling and rifle fire from Boxers and Chinese imperial troops, subsisting on little more than horse and mule meat and rice. Sixty-six foreigners had died, including seven Marines, and 150 were wounded. Only twelve American soldiers had been wounded in the fight to liberate the legations.[33]

Later in the afternoon, the Marines arrived to join the celebration under way in the foreign quarter. "There was a lot of hand-shaking and though we were filthy with mud, grime, and sweat from our ten days on the march, some of us were soundly kissed by the women of the party much to our embarrassment," one Marine later recalled. Butler, true to his Pennsylvania Quaker upbringing, offered a more modest summation: "All the hardships were forgotten when we gazed on the women and children we had saved."[34]

THE FOLLOWING DAY, AS AMERICAN troops fought their way into Peking's Imperial City, Tony Waller stood atop the Chien Gate alongside General Chaffee and Captain Henry J. Reilly, commander of a four-gun artillery battery. As Reilly directed fire at the next gate of the imperial enclave, a Chinese sharpshooter trained his sights and fired. A bullet entered Reilly's mouth and exited through the back of his head, and the American officer fell dead. Below, American soldiers captured two more gates before stopping at the walls of the fabled Forbidden City, home to Chinese emperors.[35] The Boxer Rebellion had been broken.

In the weeks that followed, allied reprisals would leave a trail of blood across northern China. "It is safe to say that where one real Boxer has been killed since the capture of Peking, fifty harmless coolies or laborers on farms, including not a few women and children, have been slain," observed General Chaffee, an old Indian fighter who was no bleeding heart. The harsh agreement that the allied powers imposed on China as the price for withdrawing their troops, including payment of a $333 million indemnity, only deepened antiforeigner bitterness.[36]

Allied troops took their revenge in other ways as well, systematically plundering the ancient palaces of Peking. One French officer shipped home no less than ten crates of booty. American troops helped themselves to furs and silk robes and treasures of porcelain and jade. One of Waller's subordinates described the spoils in the Marine officers' quarters at the Palace of the Eighth Prince, where "piles of loot" grew bigger and bigger, and "more Chinese trunks and chests were added to each officer's room."[37]

On August 28, the allied forces completed their humiliation of the Chinese by staging a military parade into the heart of the Forbidden City.[38]

WITH THE U.S. PRESIDENTIAL ELECTION only two months away, and America's imperial adventure in the Philippines already causing political problems for the Republicans, President McKinley on September 29 ordered the drawdown of U.S. troop levels in China. On October 4, in a cold rain, Waller and his Marines boarded a train in Peking and headed east to the coast, where Navy ships waited to ferry them back to the Philippines.

The Marines had dispatched forty-nine officers and 1,151 enlisted men to China. Thirty-three enlisted men would be awarded the Medal of Honor for their bravery during the campaign. But the Marine whose star had shone brightest in China was Tony Waller. In the critical early days of the campaign, Waller and his men had won the admiration of the world's finest armies. Now, at a critical moment in America's faltering conquest of the Philippines, the Marines were returning in triumph to the troubled islands.

BOXER REBELLION LASTED FROM 6/15/1900 AND ENDED ON 10/4/1900

CHAPTER 14

The Election of 1900

The China crisis had seized America's attention like a streaking comet, but Republican and Democratic strategists remained convinced that another subject would decide the presidential election of 1900. "The Philippines [will] be the paramount and dominating issue in the campaign," President McKinley had privately predicted in May. Democrats concurred at their national convention six weeks later, proclaiming imperialism "the paramount issue of this campaign."[1]

For more than a year, the war in the Philippines had cast a pall over the Republican Party. Rising U.S. casualties and misdeeds by American soldiers had prompted the pro-Republican *San Francisco Call* in the spring of 1900 to warn of "danger signals" for the party in November. "The Filipinos are not conquered," the newspaper declared. "Their spirit is not broken. Their capacity for resistance has not begun to be exhausted." A Manila-based businessman and writer friendly to the McKinley administration, Phelps Whitmarsh, predicted the war would drag on for "years, not months"—unless the administration sanctioned even more extreme measures.[2]

Steel magnate Andrew Carnegie, one of the nation's wealthiest Republicans, foresaw a day of reckoning for his party in November. "I think that we are now finding out the truth of what others saw months and months ago: that you may suppress 8 million people for a time but that you can't hold them down without an army of 70,000 men," Carnegie said. "How long the American people are going to hold them down is a question which the people must answer."[3]

REPUBLICANS WERE CONSUMED BY A different question as they gathered in Philadelphia for their national convention in June: Who should be nominated as McKinley's running mate? Since the death of Vice President Garret A. Hobart the previous November, Henry Cabot Lodge had tried to convince his good friend, New York Governor Theodore Roosevelt, to make a play for the number two spot on the Republican ticket. Roosevelt had professed disinterest: He preferred to become America's first governor-general in the Philippines while waiting for McKinley to vacate the White House. Or perhaps he would run for a second term as New York governor.

Lodge, meanwhile, had persuaded McKinley to name him convention chairman, and when the gathering convened he set to work lining up delegates in support of Roosevelt's candidacy. Momentum for Roosevelt built, despite the strenuous objections of McKinley's close friend and fund-raiser Senator Mark Hanna. "Don't any of you realize that there's only one life between this madman and the presidency?" Hanna pleaded with fellow party power brokers. It was no use. Chants of "Teddy! Teddy!" echoed through the hall on June 19 as delegates nominated Roosevelt for the vice presidency.[4]

Roosevelt needed no convincing that America's conquest of the Philippines was the campaign's salient concern. He had already prepared a two-part narrative to defuse the issue: First, he would argue, U.S. soldiers had already won the war; and second, America's duty as a world power demanded retention of the islands. Roosevelt had polished the arguments at the New York Republican state convention in April, and hammered them home in his address before the national convention in June. "Is America a weakling, to shrink from the work of the great world powers?" he demanded.[5]

The guerrilla war's rising toll of American casualties presented the

Republicans with inconvenient facts, but Roosevelt was the perfect pitch-
man for selling administration policy in the Philippines. He had spent
much of the past year studying the subject and corresponding with military and civilian authorities on the scene. His belief in the righteousness
of America's imperial quest was sincere. Under American tutelage, "that
beautiful archipelago shall become a center of civilization for all eastern
Asia and the islands round about," he wrote after being chosen as McKinley's running mate. "A great future lies before the Philippines, and it can
only be marred if this country is so unwise as to listen to those who would
let us let the islands fall back into chaos. . . ." Roosevelt did not intend to
allow that to happen. "I am as strong as a bull moose," he declared, rar-
ing to hit the campaign trail.[6] In his view, the nation faced its most important election since the Civil War, with nothing less than America's future
as a global power riding on the outcome.

ROOSEVELT KICKED OFF THE CAMPAIGN on July 17 before the annual
meeting of the National League of Republican Clubs in St. Paul, Minnesota. Eleven days earlier, Senator George Frisbie Hoar had ended the talk
of party schism by announcing his support for McKinley's reelection—the
danger of Democratic domestic policies, Hoar had declared, outweighed
the damage of administration actions in the Philippines. Now the spotlight
shifted to Roosevelt, and he seized the moment in trademark fashion.

Teeth flashing, fist pumping, a roaring crowd feeding off his manic
energy, Roosevelt delivered a pugnacious speech that would become his
template for the fall. He appealed to loyal Americans—Democrats as well
as Republicans—to reject Democratic candidate William Jennings Bryan
and his policies that "stand for lawlessness and disorder, for dishonesty
and dishonor, for license and disaster at home and cowardly shrinking
from duty abroad." A Bryan victory would spell economic ruin, social
upheaval and international humiliation for America—"misery so widespread that it is almost unthinkable and a disgrace so lasting that more
than a generation would have to pay before it could be wiped out."[7]

Turning to the crux of the campaign, Roosevelt ripped the Democratic
platform's position on the Philippines. The Democrats had attempted to

tread a middle path by promising eventual independence for the islands under a U.S. protectorate. "They have invented the imaginary danger of imperialism," Roosevelt sneered. "Yet so conscious are they of the hollowness of their attack, so well aware that to follow out their professions would mean to trail the American flag in the dust, that they are obliged to pretend that really after all they are for expansion."

Under Republican leadership, Roosevelt reminded his audience, America had surged to "the forefront of the great nations of the earth." Under the Democrats, everything would be undone. "Woe if we fail to do our duty, because the first step seems hard to the weaklings and men of little heart."

ROOSEVELT'S CONTEMPT FOR HIS OPPONENTS was a constant throughout his political career, but William Jennings Bryan was a target of particular vehemence. The two men stood at opposite ends of America's political mainstream in 1900: Roosevelt, the child of old Manhattan money and privilege, the worldly intellectual steeped in the classics of history and literature, versus Bryan, the son of a rural Illinois lawyer, an anti-intellectual who owed his worldview to *The Jeffersonian Cyclopedia* and the Bible.

Bryan was born in March 1860, two years after Roosevelt, and while the Harvard-educated New Yorker was establishing himself as a rising Republican politician, the young man from backwater Illinois was an obscure lawyer in Lincoln, Nebraska. The economic and social upheavals of the 1890s propelled both men to the pinnacle of American politics, and although each claimed to represent the common man, their philosophies diverged sharply. Roosevelt championed the American melting pot, offering compromise and conservative reforms to bridge the divide between business and labor, civil rights to cleanse the stain of slavery, and overseas expansion to fulfill America's manifest destiny. Bryan painted on a canvas of more modest proportions, preaching an uncompromising, Christianity-inspired populism as the salvation of his dispossessed followers, mainly struggling farmers across the South and Great Plains, and assorted other white-skinned outsiders who feared the growing power of big business and Wall Street bankers.[8]

Bryan compensated for his lack of intellectual gravitas with inspiring oratory, a gift that had enabled him to captivate crowds from early childhood. Four years earlier, he had dispensed with the gentlemanly tradition of pawning off presidential campaigning to surrogates and had plunged into the fray with evangelical fervor. With his mellifluous baritone voice and empathetic smile, the Great Commoner, as he was affectionately known, had attracted enthusiastic crowds in his losing effort. Now, with McKinley again watching the fray from his Ohio porch, the campaign of 1900 became an unprecedented head-to-head contest between America's political heavyweights: Bryan versus Roosevelt.

From the beginning, Bryan struggled under the weight of a fractious coalition formed around three major issues: imperialism, currency reform and the regulation of big business. Unfortunately for Bryan, few of his supporters cared about all three. His signature issue in 1896, replacement of the gold standard with silver, had been offered as the antidote for the depression that had plunged millions of farmers into debt. Eastern bankers and other Republicans denounced the "Free Silver" proposal as financial witchcraft, and even "Gold Democrats" deserted the party in droves, but Bryan went down to defeat touting the silver standard—his sacred promise to struggling farmers.[9]

In the four years following McKinley's election, urban Democrats had promoted the regulation of big industrial trusts as the party's salient domestic issue. But when party delegates convened at their national convention in Kansas City in July, overseas expansion had overshadowed both "Free Silver" and business regulation. The Democratic national committee had quickly pronounced "imperialism" as the campaign's "paramount issue," and a succession of speakers railed against the evils of the administration's expansionist policies. Only on one critical point did the Democrats pull their punches: Fearful of being labeled unpatriotic, they refused to condemn the war in the Philippines.[10]

The Democrats departed Kansas City amid professions of unity, but in reality the party was deeply conflicted by the Philippine issue. Nowhere was that truer than the South, where attitudes fractured along fault lines of race, history and self-interest. There, at one end of the spectrum, resided men like Senator John T. Morgan of Alabama, who believed the

South's continued rise from the devastation of the Civil War hinged on the acquisition of overseas markets and colonies. At the other extreme were die-hard anti-imperialists like Senator Benjamin "Pitchfork Ben" Tillman of South Carolina, who were repelled by the thought of dark-skinned Asian immigrants polluting America's racial purity. It was difficult for Democrats to claim the moral high ground in the expansion debate when Tillman was proclaiming that the white man would forever "walk on the necks of every colored race he comes into contact with."[11]

Amid these surging crosscurrents, William Jennings Bryan on August 8 delivered his acceptance speech before an enthusiastic crowd of fifty thousand in Indianapolis, Indiana. In his heart, Bryan still held silver as the issue that bound him to his agrarian base, but party leaders had persuaded him that anti-imperialism would translate into a Democratic victory.

As a hot breeze stirred the summer air, Bryan unleashed a stinging attack on the immorality of America's quest for empire. He drew on the defining influences of his life—Jefferson and Jesus—as he painted the war in the Philippines as an abuse of American power and a betrayal of national principles. Even if Jefferson had never written the Declaration of Independence, "a war of conquest would still leave its legacy of perpetual hatred, for it was God Himself who placed in every human heart the love of liberty." The course that Republicans had set in the Philippines could hardly have been more dishonorable, Bryan continued. More "wars of conquest" would follow, and America's insatiable quest for empire and future military triumphs would "turn the thoughts of our young men from the arts of peace to the science of war." He concluded with a stinging rejection of Theodore Roosevelt's vision of American world power: America's guiding principle should not be "what we *can* do, but what we *ought* to do," he declared. Rather than conquer benighted lands, America should lead the world through humble and righteous example.[12]

Bryan's speech played especially well with wavering independents. His words convinced a majority of Anti-Imperialist League delegates the following week to reject a third-party challenge and cast their lot with the Democrats.[13] The Republicans suddenly found themselves on the defensive. A sudden surge in unemployment had undermined McKinley's

claims of delivering economic prosperity. Anthracite coal miners in Pennsylvania were threatening to strike, raising the specter of autumn fuel
shortages and election-eve violence. With the Republican victory suddenly in doubt, Mark Hanna fired off an urgent appeal to his wealthy
business friends: Contribute every possible dollar to the Republican
cause, or prepare for defeat in November.[14]

THE OPENING SALVOS OF ROOSEVELT and Bryan sharpened the bitter
political back-and-forth that the war had already unleashed. For months
now, proexpansion Republicans had pounded away with an old line of
attack they had successfully employed against their opponents during and
after the Civil War: They accused the Democrats of causing the deaths
of American soldiers by opposing administration policy. Anti-imperialist
Democrats had responded by accusing the Republicans of trampling the
Constitution and waging a dirty war in the Philippines.

In January senior administration officials had launched a secret
inquiry to prove treasonous behavior by their political opponents. Secretary of War Root had begun the effort in mid-January when he asked
General Otis to forward to Washington any captured documents "showing connections or correspondence with parties here." He had followed
that initial contact by ordering Otis to outline his suspicions about Aguinaldo's secret correspondence with parties in the United States. A third
cable, citing U.S. Senate interest, prodded Otis for "information regarding aid or encouragement received by Aguinaldo and followers from
[persons in the] United States," including any "pamphlets, speeches, or
other documents from United States against its authority and policy"
being circulated among Filipinos or U.S. soldiers. Still another cable
ordered Otis to promptly respond. Although it seems implausible that
the American commander could have ignored such blunt demands from
his superiors, the general's response is nowhere to be found in the War
Department's public record.[15]

Later in the campaign, administration officials revived the search for
a smoking gun that would cripple their political opponents. In July,
rumors swept the American community in Manila that the Democrats

were discussing a formal alliance with the Filipino revolutionaries and that Aguinaldo's junta was raising funds for Bryan's campaign. No supporting evidence ever surfaced, but the gossip was promptly forwarded to Washington by William Howard Taft, head of McKinley's new civilian oversight commission in the Philippines. Later in the fall, Taft passed on the story that Bryan's August speech attacking the administration had convinced Aguinaldo to fight on.[16]

Administration opponents, meanwhile, were busy highlighting abuses by U.S. troops in the Philippines. Since the first weeks of the war, newspapers across the country had printed letters from soldiers that painted a disturbing portrait of the U.S. campaign. The letters, along with news dispatches smuggled past American military censors, described the summary execution of Filipino soldiers and civilians, torture of guerrillas and their sympathizers, and the burning of villages and crops.

"We make everyone get into his house by 7 p.m., and we only tell a man once," Corporal Sam Gillis of the 1st California Volunteers wrote his parents in a letter that found its way into the *San Francisco Call*. "If he refuses we shoot him. We killed over 300 natives the first night."[17]

Even more sensational was a soldier's letter home to Kingston, New York:

> Last night one of our boys was found shot and his stomach cut open. Immediately orders were received from General Wheaton to burn the town and kill every native in sight, which was done to a finish. About 1,000 men, women and children were reported killed. I am probably growing hard-hearted, for I am in my glory when I can sight my gun on some dark skin and pull the trigger.[18]

Independent observers had added to the impression of systematic abuses. "American soldiers are determined to kill every Filipino in sight," reported F. A. Blake, a representative of the International Red Cross, after returning from a fact-finding trip to the Philippines in the late summer of 1899.[19]

Elihu Root had launched a media counterattack after taking control of the War Department the previous summer. Current and retired generals, even Admiral Dewey, had denounced the atrocity allegations as a "pack of lies" and the "rantings" of "sulkers" and "riff-raff."[20] By the summer of 1900, Root's blitz had succeeded in muddying the abuse debate. Opinion journals and newspaper editorial pages reflected the divergent views on the extent of U.S. abuses. The left-leaning *Literary Digest* asserted that most newspaper editors agreed there was "so much smoke there had to be a fire," while the conservative *Public Opinion* concluded that a majority believed that "for every letter describing looting or killing prisoners, ten could be printed which mention nothing of the sort."[21]

The Republican campaign platform flatly asserted that "every step of the progress of our troops has been marked by a humanity which has surprised even the misguided insurgents." But fresh allegations continued to stoke the debate. "Our soldiers here and there resort to horrible measures with the natives . . . ," a *New York World* dispatch from the Philippines reported in July, nine days after Roosevelt kicked off the Republican campaign. "It is now the custom to avenge the death of an American soldier by burning to the ground all the houses, and killing right and left the natives who are only 'suspects.'"[22]

SINCE ASSUMING COMMAND FROM OTIS in May, General Arthur MacArthur had tried to contain the spreading guerrilla war through a carrot-and-stick mix of counterinsurgency operations and civic action. An armistice and amnesty rolled out with great expectations had proved enormously disappointing by the end of August, inducing the surrenders of only 5,022 Filipinos, and only a handful of senior officers among them.[23] On August 31, 1900, as the administration geared up for the fall election campaign, MacArthur briefed War Department adjutant general Henry Corbin by cable on the progress of the American campaign. "Week by week, [the] situation shows little improvement," MacArthur reported. "Month by month, progress [is] slow, but quite apparent."[24]

MacArthur failed to mention the September 1 assumption of legislative powers on behalf of Filipinos by a panel of distinguished Americans (in time for the fall campaign back in the States). President McKinley had dispatched his second Philippine Commission to the islands to soften the war's ragged edges and speed the transition to civilian rule. Arriving in June, the commissioners were chagrined by their reception. "The [native] populace that we had expected to welcome us was not there," wrote commission Chairman Taft, a genial, 320-pound federal judge from Ohio, "and I cannot describe the coldness of the army officers and the army men who received us better than saying that it somewhat exceeded the coldness of the populace."[25]

The turf-conscious MacArthur's frosty reception set the tone, and Taft quickly found himself at odds with other Americans. A large U.S. business, piqued over Taft's announcement that the United States was holding the islands for the primary benefit of Filipinos, took out an ad in a local newspaper with a photograph of Taft and caption that read, "This is the cause of our leaving the Philippines."[26]

Taft defined the American mission as uplifting "our little brown brothers," but MacArthur and his men rejected the benign characterization of the natives who were killing their comrades and terrorizing friendly Filipinos. A marching ditty that soon became popular with troops gave voice to the military's contempt for the natives. "He may be a brother of Big Bill Taft," the soldiers sang, "but he ain't no brother of mine!"[27]

The soldiers had good reason for skepticism. Aguinaldo's strategy of protracted guerrilla warfare had already claimed the lives of 995 Americans during the first seven months of 1900—an average of 4.7 deaths daily. Of that number, 254 had been killed in action or died from battle wounds. Twenty had committed suicide, 40 had drowned and 653 had died from disease.[28]

And by Aguinaldo's careful design, American casualties were about to surge.

For more than a year, the revolutionaries had pointed to the U.S. presidential election as the pivotal moment in their struggle for independence. Throughout the year, guerrilla forces had stockpiled supplies and added recruits in areas beyond the limited reach of occupation forces. As the fall campaign approached, Aguinaldo ordered his forces to "give such hard knocks to the Americans that they will . . . set in motion the fall of the Imperialist party."[29]

During the summer rainy season, U.S. field commanders had detected ominous signs. Aguinaldo's old nemesis, Peyton March, now provincial commander of Abra province in northern Luzon, had been shocked by a July election for a new civil government in the provincial capital of Bangued: Out of a population of thirteen thousand, only twenty-six people registered to vote, and twenty-one actually cast ballots. "Civil government throughout the province," March reported, "is more or less a farce."[30]

As the U.S. political campaign entered the stretch run, guerrilla units struck, ambushing American patrols and attacking garrisons across the archipelago. In a four-day span, U.S. forces suffered two of their worst defeats of the war: On September 13, guerrillas on the central island of Marinduque captured fifty-one soldiers of the 29th Infantry after ambushing their patrol. Four days later, less than fifty miles from Manila, twenty-one Americans were killed and twenty-three wounded in a botched assault in Laguna province. In Ilocos Sur, rated by the Americans as a pacified province, guerrillas cornered an Army patrol in a narrow canyon and killed a lieutenant and four soldiers and wounded fourteen men before the Americans fought their way to safety.[31]

Administration officials scrambled to contain the political fallout. On Secretary Root's instructions, General MacArthur tightened censorship and ordered the word "ambush" deleted from cables. Privately, Root and other administration officials questioned whether MacArthur should be sacked. Among the American commander's harshest critics was Roosevelt's friend General Samuel Young. Tougher measures were required, Young wrote Roosevelt, including the death penalty for Filipinos captured with firearms after taking the allegiance oath, deportation of troublemakers, destruction of agricultural fields used as cover by guerrillas, total press censorship, and "reconcentration" of natives in hostile areas—the Spanish tactic that had outraged Roosevelt and other advocates of intervention in Cuba.[32]

MacArthur, in fact, had already concluded that a stiffer response was needed—but only after the Republicans had won the election.[33]

WILLIAM JENNINGS BRYAN'S CAMPAIGN TO reverse the verdict of 1896 hinged on his ability to make inroads in the vote-rich upper Midwest and urban East, and so it was there he focused his efforts. No one could ever accuse the Great Commoner of taking a desultory approach to campaigning, and he embarked on a frenetic sprint to the finish line, logging more than sixteen thousand miles and delivering six hundred speeches by early November.[34]

But the Republicans had a huge financial advantage and, in Theodore Roosevelt, a crowd-pleasing campaigner who matched Bryan mile for mile. The administration had been outraged by Bryan's August speech attacking its policy in the Philippines, and McKinley and Roosevelt had responded point by point in letters distributed across the country. McKinley's anger was palpable as he denounced the Democratic proposal for a U.S. protectorate in the Philippines as support for "the murderers of our soldiers."

George Frisbie Hoar had urged the president to bolster his letter with a commitment to eventual Philippine independence, a position that the Massachusetts senator asserted would ensure Bryan's defeat. McKinley seriously considered the proposition, but backed off at the last minute, fearing even a hint of concession would strengthen the resolve of Aguinaldo's guerrillas. Instead, he pledged his administration to the more ambiguous goal of "self-government." The following day, convinced he had sealed his defeat, McKinley huddled with senior advisers to discuss how to strengthen the U.S. military position in the islands in the event of a Bryan victory.[35]

But Bryan struggled to recapture the magic of his Indianapolis speech, and his attacks on the administration's conquest of the Philippines fell flat with audiences. Before the month of September was out, he had all but abandoned the issue of imperialism to emphasize regulation of business trusts. Bryan surrogates and sympathetic newspapers followed suit, and imperialism faded from the Democratic campaign.[36] Bryan's abrupt change of course confirmed the nagging doubts of anti-imperialists and Gold Democrats, and the fragile coalition began to crumble.

WHILE BRYAN FADED, THEODORE ROOSEVELT seized control of the campaign. He dazzled audiences as he delivered 673 speeches from one end of the country to the other. "'Tis Tiddy alone that's a-running," observed political humorist Finley Peter Dunne's barroom philosopher, Mr. Dooley, "an' he ain't runnin', he's gallopin'."[37]

In direct and forceful language that resonated with voters, the Republican vice presidential candidate exhorted Americans to stay the course in the Philippines and reject the "communistic and socialistic doctrines" of the Democrats. He shrewdly linked the issues of expansion and prosperity in the minds of voters. "We are for expansion and anything else that will tend to benefit the American laborer and manufacturer," he assured audiences.

Expansion had been a part of the national creed since the days of the thirteen original colonies, Roosevelt maintained. It was how America had conquered a continent and delivered prosperity to its people. "We are making no new departures," he said. "We are not taking a single step which in any way affects our institutions or our traditional policies." He dismissed the Democratic charge that administration policy in the Philippines was leading America down the path of imperialism and militarism. Indeed, he declared, "There is no more danger of its producing evil results at home now than there was of its interfering with freedom under Jefferson or Jackson, or in the days of the Indian wars on the plains."[38]

Only briefly did Roosevelt relinquish the spotlight, when America's most famous writer, Mark Twain, returned from a long European sojourn in October and pronounced himself an anti-imperialist. But newspapers soon wearied of Twain's colorful quotes and trenchant observations on administration policy, and Roosevelt reclaimed his prominence in campaign coverage as he worked his way back across the country to a tumultuous closing rally in New York City.

By the time Americans went to the polls on November 6, Republican spirits had brightened considerably since the dog days of late summer. Mark Hanna had helped settle the Pennsylvania coal strike, and his fundraising appeal had armed Republicans with a $2.5 million war chest that enabled the party to mail twenty-one million postcards to voters and inundate five thousand newspapers with two million copies of campaign literature every week.[39]

But it was Theodore Roosevelt, more than anyone else, who deserved credit for the outcome, as the Republican ticket swept to victory with 7,219,525 votes (51.7 percent) to 6,358,727 (45.5 percent) for Bryan and his running mate, Adlai E. Stevenson. The electoral college margin was even more impressive: 292–155. The only Republican losses had come in the Dixie South and the silver-mining states of Colorado, Idaho, Montana and Nevada.

The political season had begun with both parties proclaiming overseas expansion as the paramount issue, but it was not to be. Even Roosevelt placed greater emphasis on domestic prosperity under Republican stewardship, while raising the specter of socialism and civil unrest should Bryan win. Ultimately, writes historian Richard E. Welch, anti-imperialism was "denied the popular referendum it had seemingly been promised."[40]

In the end, it is impossible to divine the motivations of the more than seven million Americans who cast their ballots for McKinley and Roosevelt. McKinley, for his part, was humble in victory, leaving it to Mark Hanna to claim the election as a "clear mandate" for expansion.[41]

IN THE DAYS FOLLOWING THE election, Vice President–elect Roosevelt frequently turned his thoughts to America's rebellion-racked colony in the Pacific. "By every consideration of honor and humanity we are bound to stay in the Philippines to put down the insurrection, establish order and then give a constantly increasing measure of liberty and self-government, while ruling with wisdom and justice," Roosevelt lectured Harvard President Charles Eliot. To one of his former Rough Rider officers, Roosevelt mused about his unfulfilled ambition to become governor-general of the Philippines, "the one position that I should like to have had."[42]

Armed with another four years of power, the Republican administration was now poised to unleash an even harsher campaign to impose American rule in the islands. Roosevelt longed for a front-row seat. "I only wish," he confessed to his old Rough Rider buddy, "I could run out in the Philippines and look around myself."

PART III

The Bloody Work of Empire

CHAPTER 15

"War Without Limits"

O n Saturday, October 13, 1900, as Theodore Roosevelt pounded away at the Democrats in nine speeches across Kentucky, Major John Henry Parker found time amid his combat duties in the Philippines to scribble another worried letter to the Republican vice presidential candidate. Parker was one of Roosevelt's regular military correspondents in the islands and, like most, a friend from the Cuba campaign. Fifteen months earlier, as the thirty-one-year-old commander of a Gatling gun detachment during the assault on the San Juan Heights, the West Point graduate from Missouri had turned the tide of battle with his devastating fire on the Spanish fortifications—a feat that Roosevelt and his Rough Riders had cheered from atop Kettle Hill.[1]

Parker arrived in the Philippines in time for the "Great Roundup" of 1899, and had seen American forces gradually cede the initiative to Aguinaldo's guerrillas. By the fall of 1900, as the resistance bloodied U.S. forces with their election-season offensive, Parker had become convinced that the administration's conciliatory approach was doomed to fail. General MacArthur and his staff might act as though the war could be fought in "white suits and collars," Parker derisively noted, but it was time for America to get tough with its rebellious colony.[2]

For months, frontline officers like Parker had seethed with frustration over the official policy of kindness toward Filipinos. In reality, the extent of the benevolence varied widely in the field: Some officers had committed themselves wholeheartedly to creating civil governments, building schools and supervising health programs, while others expended minimal effort on such work and showed little mercy toward the locals. Indeed, such highly regarded officers as General Lloyd Wheaton "had not the slightest patience with a policy which looks towards forgiveness and conciliation of the natives," William Howard Taft reported. But four months in the islands had tempered Taft's criticism of military conduct, and he advised Secretary Root in October that once the election was won, "the time will have come to change our lenient policy."[3]

With his back-channel access to Roosevelt, Parker was in a position to shape the administration's new policy, and now, from his vantage point in the war zone, he committed to paper the measures that he and other comrades believed necessary for America to prevail in the Philippines. Parker was sensitive to the harsh resonance of what he was about to propose, especially to someone sitting in America, and so he assured Roosevelt that severe tactics were justified by a strict reading of the U.S. military's guide on the rules of land war, a Civil War–era document known as General Orders 100. Specifically, he wrote, the document authorized the summary execution of murderers, part-time guerrillas, highway robbers, spies, conspirators and other violent elements.

The administration's current strategy of civilized warfare was "the fundamental obstruction to complete pacification," he warned. Constrained as they were, U.S. forces had "applied the methods of the kindergarten where other nations habitually, and successfully, use the most stringent measures." Going forward, officers should be allowed "to make the few punitive examples that will be needed" to break resistance.[4]

By the time that Parker's letter had reached its intended hands in November, Theodore Roosevelt was a heartbeat from the presidency, and a full partner in the administration's war. On November 24, 1900, no longer a powerless outsider submitting unsolicited advice, Vice President–elect Roosevelt forwarded Parker's blueprint for a tough new strategy in the Philippines to Secretary of War Elihu Root.

WITHOUT WAITING FOR GUIDANCE FROM Washington, General Mac-
Arthur had already ordered a postelection offensive throughout the
archipelago. The combined effects of President McKinley's victory and
more aggressive U.S. operations were quickly evident. Offensive actions
by the guerrillas fell by nearly half in November and December, while
surrenders soared from fifty-four in September–October to 2,534 in the
final two months of the year. But MacArthur and other senior officials
in Washington had expected resistance to collapse in the wake of the
Republican victory, and that had not happened.[5]

In fact, American control remained tenuous in thousands of towns
and villages, where guerrilla shadow governments collected taxes and
supplies and punished Filipinos who cooperated with the occupation
forces. From the beginning, the American pacification effort had been
plagued by the inability to provide security to locals under their nominal
control. The Americans simply had too few troops to fight guerrillas and
secure towns and villages scattered across a thousand-mile-long archipelago, a problem given rise by Washington political considerations and
the eager-to-please General Otis. A troop surge initiated by Secretary
Root had been short-circuited by the Boxer Rebellion, and General
MacArthur quickly lost ground to the guerrillas when five thousand U.S.
troops were rushed from the Philippines to China over the summer.

MacArthur had a clear understanding of the difficult task at hand.
When American troops managed to find and engage their elusive enemy,
the guerrillas would simply scatter "and seek safety in the nearest barrio,"
he reported, "a maneuver quickly accomplished by reason of the assistance
of the people." Filipino officials in American-occupied towns and villages
"acted openly in behalf of the Americans and secretly in behalf of the
insurgents," accepting American funds for projects "at the same time they
were exacting and collecting contributions and supplies and recruiting
men for the Filipino forces, and sending all obtainable military information to the Filipino leaders." It was a prudent course for the locals, given
the 350 assassinations and 442 assaults carried out by guerrillas against
fellow Filipinos in American-occupied towns and villages in 1900.[6]

Within his army of seventy thousand, MacArthur presided over an officer corps increasingly torn between the official policy of benevolence and the desire to crush the guerrillas and their supporters. Some officers agonized over the hard choices they now confronted. "It seems that ultimately we shall be driven to the Spanish method of dreadful general punishments on a whole community for the acts of its outlaws which the community systematically shields and hides," one conflicted colonel wrote in August 1900. Others, like Frederick Funston and Lloyd Wheaton, suffered few moral qualms, and they summarily executed guerrillas, burned villages and tortured suspects as a matter of course—part of what Wheaton called the "swift methods of destruction" required for "a speedy termination to all resistance."[7]

As the year drew to a close, MacArthur faced new pressures to end the war. The enlistments of twenty-five volunteer regiments under his command were set to expire on June 30, 1901, and administration officials ordered the American commander to have the situation "well in hand" by that date. He needed no further urging, for MacArthur agreed with hard-liners that Filipinos had mistaken American kindness "as an evidence of weakness." He drew up plans for a severe response.[8]

On December 20, 1900, MacArthur announced tough new measures almost identical to those that Major Parker had recommended to Theodore Roosevelt several weeks earlier. The aim, as MacArthur explained to his commanders, was "to interrupt and, if possible, completely destroy" the resistance infrastructure in towns and villages. Their legal weapons would be martial law and General Orders 100, "the more drastic the application the better," MacArthur instructed, "provided, only, that unnecessary hardships and personal indignities shall not be imposed upon persons arrested and that the laws of war are not violated in any respect touching the treatment of prisoners."[9]

Henceforth, murder charges and possible execution awaited guerrillas captured in civilian clothes. Resistance fighters and sympathizers convicted of lesser crimes would be confined in Manila's notorious prisons, and guerrilla leaders exiled to Guam. Rural populations faced "reconcentration" into camps under American control. Filipinos would have to prove their loyalty by providing information and other assistance to U.S.

forces, with no consideration for guerrilla threats. Newspapers and periodicals that published seditious or objectionable material could be padlocked and their owners prosecuted.

Almost exactly two years after President McKinley had promised Filipinos liberty and "benevolent assimilation," General MacArthur now offered America's colonial subjects a far darker future. His provost marshal in Manila, General J. Franklin Bell, soon to become the star of the American pacification campaign, summed up for his men MacArthur's intent: "Create a reign of fear and anxiety among the disaffected which will become unbearable, in hope that they will thereby be brought to their senses. . . ."[10] In the months ahead, many U.S. soldiers would liberally interpret their new orders. They would wage, in the words of historian Paul Kramer, "a war without limits."

A TEMPLATE FOR THE EXTREME campaign that MacArthur desired already existed in the Philippines, forged by American soldiers on the central island of Panay. U.S. troops under Brigadier General Marcus P. Miller had splashed ashore at Iloilo City, the island's commercial center, on February 11, 1899. By nightfall, much of the city was a blackened ruin—the result of fires set by soldiers on both sides as well as a bombardment by U.S. Navy gunboats. Miller announced that U.S. forces had come to Panay "as friends to protect all Filipinos," and he offered amnesty to all who surrendered their weapons and pledged allegiance to America. The revolutionaries responded by surrounding the city and harassing the American soldiers with sniper fire.

Within weeks, Brigadier General Robert P. Hughes had arrived to take command of U.S. forces on the island. A thin, volatile sixty-year-old Civil War veteran and former Army inspector general, Hughes was perhaps best-known among his fellow officers for penning a posthumous defense of his brother-in-law, General Alfred Terry, in the enduring dispute over Custer's debacle at the Little Bighorn. After decades of desk jobs, he had been reacquainted with combat in the initial fighting around Manila and, as the city's provost marshal, had overseen defeat of the urban uprising.

Hughes arrived at his headquarters on Panay in the late spring of 1899 to find much of the countryside controlled by the enemy. He banned trade from Iloilo City to the interior and deployed gunboats to block food shipments from being landed by native sailboats. To buffer his men from attacks, Hughes established a string of refugee camps along his lines and offered a small daily rice ration to Filipinos who would live there. Later that fall, he began raiding the camps to arrest suspected guerrillas. But other than sporadic probes from small garrisons around the island, the American commander was content to sit back and starve the Panay guerrillas into submission.[11]

By the summer of 1900, that still had not occurred. Six main guerrilla bands operated on the island, with about a thousand rifles between them. They lived openly in small barrios, shielded from the Americans by the local population.

By now, Hughes had become commander of the Army's Department of the Visayas, a vast area encompassing five major islands and more than 2.5 million people. As part of his responsibilities under the policy of attraction, he had pursued civic action projects to attract popular support, with mixed results. One of his pet ideas on Panay was construction of a light railway running through the main agricultural valleys, which he believed would win the support of the island's rice and tobacco farmers. Schools had been opened in a majority of towns, though books and good teachers were hard to come by. The American colonizers had pledged to deliver rule of law and justice to Filipinos, but Hughes had managed to create only two civil courts in his entire department—the result of his inability to find competent lawyers willing to accept a judicial appointment from the Americans.[12]

Hughes found that the island's wealthier citizens were eager for peace, "but the people with the rifles are just as persistent as they were fourteen months ago." Victory remained beyond the reach of the guerrillas, "but 'attrition' is now the announced method, and some of these islands are exceedingly well adapted for just such murderous partisan warfare."[13]

And murderous it was.

Hughes had thirty infantry companies on Panay, roughly six thousand men, but the pervasive reach of the Filipino resistance made for perilous duty. "It is not safe for three men to go out on any road in either Panay or Cebu," Hughes reported. "But as a general thing, ten well-equipped men, by exercise of caution, can go almost anywhere if they do not allow it to be known that they are going, and when they do not return, or, if they do so, that some other route is taken."[14]

As the war stretched into a second year, pitched battles became rarer, and acts of terror and counterterror more common. U.S. soldiers lived in mortal fear of capture by the *insurrectos*, for good reason. Stragglers during military operations often disappeared, sometimes without a trace, at other times turning up as mutilated corpses. Soldiers invited to a barrio to partake of palm wine or a pretty girl might find themselves in guerrilla captivity or worse.[15]

In later testimony before the U.S. Senate, Hughes acknowledged that his tactics against the resistance progressively hardened. In the war's first year, "we adhered strictly to the rules," he said. By the second and third years of war, American troops on Panay "found it necessary to adopt more stringent methods," including burning the houses of Filipinos "caught red-handed" in various offenses. American "severities," as Hughes called them, varied from one detachment to the next. New commanders would arrive on the island "with their ideas of civilized warfare, and they were allowed to get their lesson."[16]

The lessons were punctuated by the terror Panay's guerrillas practiced against collaborators. "The situation of the island is simply hell," Hughes reported in the autumn of the war's second year. A Filipino messenger employed by the Americans in Antique was "prepared for Hamburger steak" by the guerrillas, while an Iloilo resident caught with a U.S.-issued "certificate of allegiance" was "made into hash." Hughes turned away some municipal presidents from allegiance ceremonies because he could not protect them from assassination.[17]

Each blow struck by the resistance provoked swift retribution from U.S. troops, including the burning of houses or entire villages, torture of witnesses or suspects, and, in some cases, summary execution of suspected guerrillas. Gordon's Scouts, an elite 18th Infantry mounted outfit, was widely feared on Panay for its harsh tactics.[18] Its favorite interrogation technique was the "water cure," in which a victim was held down, his mouth pried open with a piece of bamboo or a rifle barrel, and dirty or salty water poured down his throat until the stomach swelled to the bursting point—a painful procedure that typically produced quick results.

By November 1900, the war on Panay had made a mockery of McKinley's pledge of benevolence. Roosevelt and others would later justify the extreme actions of American troops as the result of guerrilla provocations. While that may have been true in some instances on Panay, the overall harshness of the American campaign would prove difficult to defend in the light of later scrutiny.

THE NEW U.S. MILITARY POLICY in the Philippines was still taking shape when MacArthur's orders for a postelection offensive escalated the Panay campaign to new levels of violence—and brought to the fore one of the war's most controversial figures.

Captain Edwin Forbes Glenn had arrived in Iloilo City on April 19, 1900, to take up an assignment as acting judge advocate for the Department of the Visayas. The forty-three-year-old native of Greensboro, North Carolina, married and the father of four daughters, carried an impressive résumé: West Point graduate, college professor, lawyer, amateur historian and, most recently, Alaska soldier-explorer in the mold of John C. Fremont.[19]

Glenn's 1898 search for an overland route through Alaska to the Klondike goldfields had brought him a measure of renown, and with it an invitation from the prestigious National Geographic Society to speak on his experiences. On March 3, 1899, his arrival as an eminent explorer was confirmed when he stood before an audience in the society's Washington, D.C., offices and delivered a lecture on his adventures in America's untamed Arctic territory. Later that spring, Glenn forged even deeper into Alaska's wild interior, further burnishing his reputation at the War Department. By the time he returned to civilization in early 1900, the Army was consumed with a more pressing concern. With new orders in hand, the intrepid captain mothballed his furry Klondike suit and prepared for a tropical deployment in the Philippines.

Glenn arrived in Manila on March 27, 1900, and three weeks later took up his new position as judge advocate under General Hughes in Iloilo City. He quickly came to admire the aggressive mounted infantry units that Hughes had unleashed to kill guerrillas and destroy their civilian base. Just days after Glenn's arrival, the best-known of these, Gordon's Scouts, reported the latest in a string of impressive victories—thirty-five enemy fighters killed without a single American casualty. In Gordon's Scouts, and its twenty-eight-year-old commander, Lieutenant Arthur L. Conger Jr., Glenn had found the ideal partner in his new mission: dismantling the resistance organization on Panay.

Conger was a native of Akron, Ohio, the son of a decorated Civil War officer who had become a prominent Republican while earning a fortune as a corporate executive and Union Pacific Railroad director. He had graduated from Harvard in 1894 and entered the Episcopal Theological Seminary at Cambridge. But two years later, his deepening interest in Asian mysticism and philosophy led him to quit the seminary and move to New York City to volunteer at the national Theosophical Society.[20]

Conger's idyllic world of spiritual self-discovery was shattered in April 1898 when his disapproving father cut him off financially. His sudden penury coincided with America's war with Spain, and young Conger joined an infantry company raised by a New York socialite. After exemplary service on Cuba, Conger decided to make the Army his career and, in September 1898, was commissioned a second lieutenant. Several months later he shipped out to the Philippines with the 4th Infantry Regiment.

By the spring of 1900, Conger worked for General Hughes as a field intelligence operative on Panay. As commander of Gordon's Scouts, he had taken the fight to the elusive enemy, combing coastal mangrove swamps and interior mountains for enemy activity, leaving in his wake a trail of dead guerrillas and charred villages. A photograph taken around that time reveals Conger as a lean young man with soulful eyes and a long, angular face, his hands covered with heavy cavalry gauntlets as he clutched his trademark Mauser "Broomhandle" automatic pistol.[21]

That same spring Conger's adventurous mother arrived on Panay to take up residence, and Emily Conger's recollection of those days captures the fear that consumed American soldiers and civilians. She armed herself with a revolver and a dagger, and lived in "dread of revolt and attack" by the "brutal cowards" and "vermin." Nearly everything about Panay and its native inhabitants shocked her American sensibilities—the wretched poverty, poor sanitation, harsh climate and, in her view, inherently treacherous Filipinos. "Whether I worked or rested," she said, "I was careful to sit or stand close to a wall—to guard against a stab in the back."

In Emily Conger's eyes, the fight in the Philippines pitted "a scrubby lot of hardly human things, stunted, gnarled pigmies [sic], with no hats or shoes, and scarcely a rag of clothing," against the "fine, manly fellows" of Gordon's Scouts and other American units.[22] She cooked holiday feasts for the scouts and lauded their "heroic deeds," "romantic campaigns" and "miraculous escapes." Ever the doting mother, she overlooked the cold-blooded reputation of her son and his men, their wont to shoot first and ask questions later, their torture-aided interrogations and destructive tactics.[23]

As CAPTAIN GLENN BORED DEEPER into the resistance organization, aided by captured documents and interrogation reports provided by Conger's scouts, he formed a detailed picture of the underground network that financed guerrilla operations. Working with Conger and other field commanders, Glenn traced the money back to wealthy landowners and merchants, and some of Panay's most prominent citizens soon found themselves under arrest and interrogation by the relentless American captain.[24] By October, Glenn had broken the resistance in Iloilo City and had joined Lieutenant Conger in the field.

Early on the morning of November 27, 1900, Glenn rode into the town of Igbaras with Conger and a contingent of Gordon's Scouts. As he and his officers ate breakfast, the town president and priest were brought to his temporary headquarters in the Catholic convent. Glenn confronted the municipal chief executive, Joveniano Ealdama, demanding to know the location of the island's most prominent guerrilla commander and his band. When Ealdama pleaded ignorance, Glenn turned the interrogation over to Conger. With a single command—"water detail"—two privates on Conger's team snapped into action, and the Filipino official was stripped to his waist and his hands bound behind his back.[25]

As Glenn and the others looked on, Ealdama was thrown to the floor beneath a water tank, his mouth forced open and the spigot turned. As water gushed down the Filipino's throat and filled his stomach, an interpreter stood over him, ordering in the local dialect: "Answer! Answer!" When Ealdama was filled with water, Conger's men pounded his stomach with their fists. Water spurted from the man's nose and mouth, and the process began anew. Screaming with pain, Ealdama finally agreed to talk.

Other interrogations were under way in the convent. In one, a local schoolteacher was questioned as an Army surgeon pressed two Colt revolvers to his head. In another, an Igbaras police officer was given the water cure.

Glenn now ordered a second round of water cure for Ealdama to determine whether the policeman had spoken truthfully when he told his interrogators that the town president had warned the guerrillas of the arrival of the American troops. One of Conger's men got a syringe from his saddlebags, and, as four or five soldiers pinned the official to the ground, his stomach was filled with water again. The Filipino denied the accusation, so a second syringe was placed in his nose and more water forced into him. When that also failed to yield the desired answer, a handful of salt was thrown into the water can and the briny liquid squirted into Ealdama's mouth and nose. He finally broke. Yes, Ealdama told the Americans, it was true that he had ordered one of his men to warn the guerrillas. What was he to do? He was an officer in the guerrilla army, and all his policemen were part-time guerrillas.[26]

Afterward, Glenn forced Ealdama to lead the Americans into the hills in search of the island's supreme guerrilla commander, General Martin Delgado. When the American detachment arrived back in Igbaras that evening, weary and empty-handed, Glenn ordered the town burned. Torches were lit and, as terrified families fled their houses with the few possessions they could carry, the American soldiers fanned out. By midnight, fewer than twenty of the five hundred structures in Igbaras remained standing.[27]

Their business finished, Glenn and his men rode away the following day.

By the time MacArthur announced his harsh new policy in December 1900, the resistance on Panay was in its death throes. Glenn's intelligence work and months of military operations by Conger's scouts and other units had exhausted the guerrillas. With encouragement from General Hughes, leading citizens of Iloilo City wrote General Delgado in December and urged him to surrender.

Meanwhile, the killing and destruction continued. Shortly after torching Igbaras, Glenn presided over the burning of another Panay town. In early January 1901, General Hughes personally ordered Gordon's Scouts to halt a fiery rampage around the village of Dumangas, fearing it would scuttle negotiations he had opened with the guerrillas. The talks continued, and on February 2, with a crowd of thousands looking on, Delgado surrendered with thirty officers, 140 riflemen, and hundreds of militia. Delgado's zone commanders soon followed suit, and by March, all but one of Panay's guerrilla commanders had laid down their arms.[28]

Aggressive American commanders elsewhere had not waited for MacArthur's permission to abandon the official policy of benevolence. Some, like Funston, had long cited General Orders 100 as justification for summary executions, house burnings and other destructive actions. General Wheaton had shown particular creativity in flouting official policy in Northern Luzon. In November 1900, after General MacArthur had commuted the death sentence of a local guerrilla convicted of three murders, Wheaton had the Filipino tried for three other murders, convicted and hanged—all before MacArthur could intervene.[29]

MacArthur's December proclamation soon filled American military prisons with new arrivals. "There are many arrests made every day now of *insurrecto* emissaries, sympathizers and officers hiding in Manila, and suspected characters and identified insurgents are sent here from all parts of the Islands," Taft reported one week after MacArthur's crackdown began.[30] Captured guerrillas suddenly found themselves imprisoned rather than sent home, and their financial supporters were shipped to

Manila for interrogation and incarceration. On January 26, 1901, an American ship steamed out of Manila Bay carrying thirty-two ranking resistance leaders to exile on Guam. Elsewhere, military courts tried captured guerrillas on charges of murder and lesser crimes. Seventy-nine eventually would be hanged in public executions, and hundreds of others, including Joveniano Ealdama, the Igbaras town president, sentenced to years at hard labor.[31]

In the countryside, U.S. troops now routinely burned houses and crops in response to guerrilla ambushes and assassinations and arrested natives on the slightest pretext. They also encouraged the already severe tendencies of Filipino allies such as the Macabebe Scouts, and native militias like the Guardia de Honor, notorious for its use of torture and summary executions.

But there was more to the new American policy than arrests and executions and killing and burning. Civic action projects continued apace, along with a political carrot for cooperative Filipinos. On December 23, a group of wealthy *americanistas* in Manila announced the formation of the Federal Party. They called for immediate acceptance of American sovereignty and eventual U.S. statehood. Escorted by American soldiers, Federal Party leaders fanned out through the islands to deliver speeches urging an end to armed struggle.[32]

As MacArthur's crackdown and the Federal Party campaign reached full throttle in early 1901, the guerrillas began to falter. Now an even greater blow loomed.

ON WEDNESDAY AFTERNOON, MARCH 6, 1901, ninety men in civilian clothes made their way through the streets of Manila to the Anda Street wharf along the Pasig River. They arrived in small groups, and as the dry-season sun beat down, they passed the anxious minutes in furtive conversation— five Americans, a Spaniard and the rest Filipinos. Horse-drawn wagons rolled to a halt at the wharf, and boxes and crates were unloaded. When everything was ready, a short, bearded American gave a quiet command, and the men filed aboard a steam launch and a barge tied behind.[33]

Smoke puffed and the launch pulled away from the wharf with the barge in tow, slipping into the flow of traffic as it headed down the congested river. The vessels emerged into Manila Bay and turned toward a sleek, three-masted gunboat flying the Stars and Stripes. As the launch eased alongside the steel-hulled ship, the men could make out her name: USS *Vicksburg*.

The bearded American led seven men from the launch aboard the gunboat, and then supervised the boarding of the eighty-odd Filipinos huddled in the barge. At half past seven, the *Vicksburg* weighed anchor, turned its bow to the west and began to move. They passed Cavite, with its Navy yard and Marine base in the distance off the port side, followed by Corregidor Island to the starboard. The gunboat steamed into the South China Sea and disappeared in the gathering darkness, thus beginning the most extraordinary mission of Brigadier General Frederick Funston's storied military career.

Funston's secret expedition had been set in motion more than a month earlier, when a courier dispatched by Emilio Aguinaldo had fallen into American hands in Northern Luzon. Funston took custody of the courier and a worn pouch of encoded dispatches in the Filipino's possession. The little general's heart beat faster when he saw that many of the documents were signed by Colón de Magdalo—a known Aguinaldo alias. Funston's men went to work on the courier, and their interrogation yielded priceless intelligence: Aguinaldo was holed up in the village of Palanan, along the rugged northeast coast of Luzon.[34]

Aided by a handsome Spanish mercenary named Lázaro Segovia, Funston deciphered Aguinaldo's coded dispatches and devised an audacious plan. Army Macabebe Scouts would masquerade as reinforcements requested by Aguinaldo, and Funston and four of his most trusted American officers would pose as prisoners of war captured along the way. The Navy would put the force ashore along Luzon's east coast, within striking distance of Aguinaldo's hideout.

After threading its way through the islands off Luzon's southern coast, the *Vicksburg* emerged into the Pacific Ocean and headed north, up the eastern coast of Luzon. Around two o'clock on the morning of March 14, Funston and his eighty-nine men slipped ashore in Casiguran Sound, nearly a hundred miles south of Aguinaldo's headquarters.

For ten days, the raiders picked their way along jungle trails, waded through mangrove swamps, splashed through the surf and climbed sheer coastal cliffs. Provisions ran short, and the men grew so weak and hungry that Funston feared disaster. The expedition was saved when advance elements of Aguinaldo's security guard, duped by Funston's ruse, arrived with badly needed provisions. Segovia presented the Filipino troops with forged letters of introduction, and Funston's men began the final leg of their march.

On Friday, March 23, the column finally reached the banks of the *1901* Palanan River. In his palm-thatched headquarters on the opposite shore, Aguinaldo tracked the approach of his long-awaited reinforcements. Segovia and the Macabebe Scouts were ferried across the river in small boats, and were greeted by cheers as they marched into the heart of Aguinaldo's lair. Segovia and his two Filipino officers were ushered into the headquarters and struck up a conversation with Aguinaldo and his aides. Suddenly, the Spaniard sprang the trap. "Now, Macabebes, go for them!" he shouted, and the raiders opened fire. A few minutes later, Funston stood before the stunned Aguinaldo and announced, "You are a prisoner of war of the Army of the United States of America."[35]

At dawn on Thursday, March 28, 1901, the *Vicksburg* delivered Funston and his prize captive to Manila. They boarded a steam launch for the short ride up the Pasig River to Malacañang Palace, where General MacArthur greeted his triumphant protégé in his bathrobe. "Well," Funston coolly announced, "I have brought you Don Emilio."

In America, screaming front-page headlines trumpeted Funston's feat. President McKinley promoted the Kansan to a brigadier general's rank in the Regular Army, while Vice President Theodore Roosevelt applauded the "crowning exploit of a career filled with cool courage." Anti-imperialists denounced Funston's ruse as further proof of America's dishonorable path in the Philippines.

Magnanimous in victory, MacArthur installed Aguinaldo in a spacious house near his palace and reunited him with his family. The revolutionary leader repaid the American commander's kindnesses on April 19, issuing a proclamation that urged his supporters to end the armed struggle and accept U.S. sovereignty. "The country has declared unmistakably for peace," Aguinaldo declared. "So be it."[36]

AGUINALDO'S CAPTURE WAS ANOTHER DEVASTATING blow for Filipino
resistance fighters, now facing the heaviest military pressure the Americans had brought to bear during two years of war. In Northern Luzon,
MacArthur had replaced the aging General Samuel Young with an
aggressive forty-five-year-old cavalryman, Brigadier General J. Franklin
Bell. In mid-March 1901, two weeks after taking command, Bell ordered
his new provincial commander in guerrilla-infested Abra province to end
the war. Major William C. H. Bowen responded by banning travel and
trade, and the provincial guerrilla organization collapsed within weeks.

Punitive campaigns across Luzon achieved similar results. One resistance leader after another fell, culminating with the capitulation of three
top commanders—Juan Villamor, Manuel Tinio and Gregorio Aglipay—
in a four-day span in late April. On May 1 MacArthur declared a truce
to give the remaining guerrillas time to turn themselves in. Before the
month was out, twelve thousand had surrendered with six thousand rifles.
By late summer, only two major commanders remained at large: General
Miguel Malvar, in the Luzon province of Batangas, and General Vicente
Lukbán, on Samar Island.[37]

After more than two years of war against the Americans, Filipino resistance had reached its breaking point in the spring of 1901. More than the
psychological blows of McKinley's reelection and Aguinaldo's capture,
the decision of many to accept American rule may best be explained by the
destruction unleashed by MacArthur's punitive military campaign.
"Property had been destroyed right and left," wrote Major Bowen in Abra,
"whole villages had been burned, storehouses and crops had been
destroyed, and the entire province was as devoid of food products as was
the valley of the Shenandoah after Sheridan's raid during the civil war."[38]

A Republican congressman returned from a tour of Northern Luzon
in 1901 with a similarly apocalyptic view of the American campaign.
"The good Lord in Heaven only knows the number of Filipinos that were

put under the ground," the congressman declared. "Our soldiers took no
prisoners, they kept no records; they simply swept the country, and wherever and whenever they could get hold of a Filipino they killed him."[39]

CHAPTER 16

The Massacre at Balangiga

On Saturday, September 28, 1901, the seventy-four soldiers of Company C, 9th U.S. Infantry, awoke to a momentous event: After forty-eight days of enervating duty in the Samar Island town of Balangiga, the men had finally received their first mail from home. In the Catholic convent along the river, the company's officers—Captain Thomas Connell of New York City, a twenty-eight-year-old West Pointer; First Lieutenant Edward A. Bumpus, twenty-seven, a Harvard graduate from Quincy, Massachusetts; and Major Richard S. Griswold, a surgeon from Hartford, Connecticut—had yet to emerge from their quarters. They had received their mail the previous evening and stayed up late discussing the shocking news in the Manila papers: William McKinley had died from an assassin's bullet fourteen days earlier, and Theodore Roosevelt was now president of the United States. Fifty yards to the east, across the town plaza, enlisted men lined up for breakfast or perused their mail as they ate. Scores of Filipino men stood around the plaza, clutching their ubiquitous long bolo knives as they awaited orders for the day's work of clearing jungle and collecting garbage.

The 9th Infantry had been the last U.S. troops to leave China, and they had returned to the Philippines in June to find the war winding down. Company C had performed honor guard duties for the July 4 transfer of power from General Arthur MacArthur to a civilian administration headed by William Howard Taft. Shortly afterward, the unit had been ordered to Samar. Connell and his men had splashed ashore on August 11 to a friendly greeting by Balangiga President Pedro Abayan and the cheers of local residents.[1]

America's newest outpost in the Philippines was a town of about three thousand people on the east bank of the Balangiga River as it rushed from the jungle into Leyte Gulf. About five hundred people, mostly fishermen and small farmers, lived along the dozen-odd dirt streets of the *población*, the urban center that surrounded the Catholic church, convent and town hall. The rest scratched out livings in scattered jungle barrios connected by footpaths. Most of the houses were simple one- or two-story structures of bamboo and woven nipa palm fronds. The sea was Balangiga's sole link to the outside world.[2]

Connell's first official act was to gather the citizens of Balangiga for a mass oath-taking ceremony as the Stars and Stripes was hoisted over the plaza. His second was to order the local men to clean up garbage and sewage dumped beneath their houses and cut away the encroaching jungle.[3]

The captain's patience with the locals quickly frayed. He was already piqued by their defiance of his sanitation directive when a pair of soldiers quarreled with a Filipina wine vendor and wound up in a fistfight with her two brothers. Connell ordered all local men detained for twelve-hour work details, and scores were crammed into two suffocating tents. His men compounded that indignity by seizing or destroying food supplies and crops in outlying barrios, and showing disrespect to local women. By late September, Balangiga residents seethed with resentment toward the American soldiers in their midst.[4]

As September 28 dawned, the men of Company C sensed the tensions. Some had noted unusual activities over the past day or two—unexplained comings and goings by the town's women, some wearing veils not seen before; late-night funeral processions and church gatherings; and the sudden absence of the local priest, Father Donato Guimbaolibot, who no

longer turned up for nightly chess contests with Major Griswold and Lieutenant Bumpus.

At six thirty a.m., American soldiers sat around their open-air mess
halls, rifles racked in their barracks. Only four sentries posted around the
plaza were armed. One of them, Private Adolph Gamlin, a twenty-one-
year-old farm boy from Hamburg, Iowa, was headed back to his post after
returning his mess kit to the main barracks when he saw a familiar face
approaching. As Balangiga Police Chief Valeriano Abanador came
abreast, he suddenly ripped the rifle from Gamlin's grasp, smashed the
butt into the soldier's head and shouted something in the local Waray
dialect. On cue, church bells clanged and the men around the plaza
sprang into action. Hundreds of other bolo-wielding Filipinos burst from
the church and nearby jungle.

At the long mess table along the east side of the plaza, Sergeant
John D. Closson heard the shout and frantic bells and looked out to see
scores of natives rushing toward him. A few feet away, Sergeant George
F. Markley had just held his plate out to the company cook when he heard
the commotion. Instinctively he yelled, "Get your rifles, boys!"

It was too late.

"They're in on us!" a soldier screamed. "Run for your lives!"[5]

ON THE OTHER SIDE OF the world, a half day behind the Philippines,
Theodore Roosevelt was nearing the end of his fourteenth day as president of the United States. It had been a dizzying two weeks since McKinley's death, crammed with Cabinet meetings, briefings, appointment
considerations and other matters. Roosevelt had promptly served notice
that he had no intention of being a caretaker president. After the mad
dash from a cabin in the Adirondacks to Buffalo, New York, he had overruled the recommendation of his predecessor's Cabinet that he take his
oath in the black-swathed mansion where McKinley had died a few hours
earlier. At Roosevelt's insistence, the brief ceremony took place a mile
away in the ivy-cloaked residence of a good friend. Sunlight streamed
through a stained-glass window, shading the library in green hues, as

Roosevelt swore his oath and pledged to "continue absolutely unbroken the policy of President McKinley for the peace, the prosperity, and the honor of our beloved country."[6] In Roosevelt's thinking, America's control over the Philippines was vital to all three.

The new president loftily described America's mission as "the salvation of the Philippines." But the problems of civilizing and democratizing the unruly islands were just beginning, and, as Roosevelt's friend Will Taft had recently informed him, this phase of America's imperial crusade promised to be as challenging as the military conquest.

A majority of Americans shared Roosevelt's commitment to the Philippines in September 1901, but a vocal minority rejected the Republican assertion that the last election had settled the expansion debate. New England anti-imperialists and allies like Indian rights activist Herbert Welsh had continued to publish books and pamphlets attacking administration policy in the islands. Antiexpansion Democrats also continued with their criticisms, accusing the administration of suppressing a sovereign people's right to self-determination in the Philippines.[7]

Mark Twain had taken up the cause too late to block a Republican victory, but he was determined to deny McKinley the moral high ground in the islands. In February, *The North American Review* had published his stinging condemnation of America's conduct, "To the Person Sitting in Darkness." Twain had accused the United States of duplicity in the Philippines, and savaged Republican colonial policy with trenchant irony. "There have been lies, yes, but they were told in a good cause," he wrote. "We have been treacherous, but that was only in order that real good might come out of apparent evil. . . . We have debauched America's honor and blacked her face before the world; but each detail was for the best. . . ."

With Twain's caustic words still reverberating, McKinley was sworn in for his second term on March 4, 1901. Light rain misted the crowd around the Capitol's east portico as McKinley concluded his address with a stout defense of his actions in the Philippines.[8] Afterward, he embarked on a national tour "to heal the sharp divisions" created by the war. He embraced his anti-imperialist critic, Senator George Frisbie Hoar, during a visit to the revolutionary shrines at Lexington and Concord, and in a Harvard speech asked his countrymen to come together to remake the

Philippines in America's image. In May, he traveled to San Francisco to personally thank soldiers returning from the war and to claim the vast Pacific in the name of American freedom.[9]

As McKinley attempted to silence debate over the nation's presence in the Philippines, American civilians poured into the islands to teach, preach and make money. Among the many commercial ventures explored by Taft's colonial administration was the production of rubber, an increasingly important commodity needed for undersea communication cables and tires for bicycles and newly popular automobiles. Initial experiments showed promise, but production of cheap rubber was one of countless dreams American colonizers never realized in the Philippines.[10]

After three years of U.S. control, Manila had taken on the patina of a big American city. Military bands unleashed the strains of Sousa marches over the metropolis in evening concerts. The English Hotel Café on Escolta Street, in a sign of the times, billed itself as "the meeting place of Manila's Best Citizens—thoroughly American." Grocery stores and restaurants sold Fairbanks Fairy Soap, Heinz pork and beans, Armour sliced ham, Pabst Milwaukee beer, Tennessee handmade sour mash and ten-year-old Kentucky whiskey. The crack of baseball bats was fast replacing the swish of Spanish jai alai racquets around the city, along with the thwack of golf balls driven and chipped by Will Taft and other Americans at a new country club.

On July 4, General MacArthur had handed executive power to Taft and military command to Major General Adna Chaffee, an old Ohio cavalryman who had recently led U.S. expeditionary forces in China. Though popularly known as the smiling, bighearted friend of Filipinos, Taft harbored deeply conflicted sentiments toward his colonial subjects. In public, he invited upper-class natives into his Manila social circle and condemned the discrimination they had suffered at the hands of U.S. Army socialites. Privately, he disparaged Filipinos as "magnificent liars" who were "deceptive, venal, [and] corrupt," and utterly incapable of self-rule.[11]

McKinley's death, eight days after anarchist Leon Czolgosz had fired two bullets into his midsection at point-blank range, had stunned Taft and his colonial administration. Roosevelt's reputation for "impulsiveness and lack of deliberation," as Taft delicately put it, raised fears in Manila that the transition to civilian rule might be scuttled.[12] But the concerns proved unfounded, and the new president quickly endorsed McKinley's colonial policies. Writing his governor in Puerto Rico, Roosevelt pledged to give his colonial administrators "the largest liberty of action possible, and the heartiest support on my part."[13] His thoughts had already turned to the new Holy Grail of the expansionist agenda: construction of a canal across the Central American isthmus.

On September 28, as America's "little brown brothers" in Balangiga were plotting the violent demise of their new colonial masters, Roosevelt contemplated further possibilities for projecting U.S. power around the world. Alas, he teased Secretary Root, "The Isthmian canal will not be ready for several months yet."[14]

EMILIO AGUINALDO'S PEACE PROCLAMATION AND the resulting surrenders had convinced administration officials in Washington that the war was finally over, and with it the congressional blank checks for military spending. Enjoined to reduce the financial strain of America's imperial ventures, Secretary Root assigned his penny-pinching Adjutant General Henry C. Corbin to scrutinize Army expenditures in the Philippines.

Troop reductions were high on Corbin's agenda, but first he took aim at Army communication costs.[15] Undersea cable expenses at the end of the nineteenth century were comparable to modern satellite phone fees, and with the guerrilla threat waning, Corbin saw no need to pay such a premium for speedy communications. He ordered MacArthur to mail enlisted casualty and sick lists rather than cable them. An exception would be made for the deaths of officers, but only to the extent of a one-word code to designate the deceased officer's name, rank and regiment.[16]

The ambitious General Chaffee settled into his new Manila headquarters on July 5 and immediately embraced the cost-cutting campaign. His second cable to Corbin recommended closing the Cavite commissary used by Navy and Marine personnel, since Manila depots were "accessible" (albeit twenty miles across Manila Bay). He suggested other savings and revenue-generating ideas, including the sale of surplus Army horses, mules and shotguns to Taft's civilian administration.

Chaffee was more diplomatic than MacArthur, but he shared his predecessor's disdain for what they both viewed as Taft's ill-advised rush to civil government in the islands. Under the guise of economy, Chaffee challenged Taft in a dispute over Army subsidies for expatriate civil servants. He urged the War Department to reject Taft's request to continue commissary privileges for his civilian employees, and risked the ire of Root and Corbin by running up hefty cable expenses to argue his case.[17]

Corbin arrived in Manila in mid-July to personally inspect operations and share his plan for a 60 percent reduction in Army expenditures. That target would be reached in part by reducing the size of the occupation force, abandoning minor posts, and handing off police responsibilities to Taft's new constabulary force. Other cost savings would be achieved by steps such as consolidating Manila's seven military hospitals into one, selling off the fleet of government launches and steamers, and, much to Chaffee's satisfaction, barring U.S. civilians from buying commissary goods at Army rates.[18]

As Chaffee concerned himself with cost accounting, the work of mopping up resistance proceeded apace. Militarily, Chaffee had three problem areas: the Luzon province of Batangas; the Visayan island of Samar; and the Muslim areas of Mindanao and Jolo islands in the far south. The Muslim trouble was six hundred miles distant and unrelated to the independence movement, so it was assigned a lower priority. Batangas was a concern because of its proximity to the capital, but that very fact simplified logistics and increased the likelihood of success for U.S. forces. Samar posed the most difficult challenge.

Three hundred miles from Manila, Samar was the third-largest of the Philippine Islands, yet one of the most primitive and inaccessible. It was covered by mountains, jungles and swamps, and had only a few miles of roads. American troops had occupied a handful of coastal towns in western and northern Samar during the early 1900 expedition to open hemp trading ports, but had done little since. The Army's inactivity had allowed the island's guerrilla chief to recruit, raise funds, stockpile supplies and strengthen defenses. General Vicente Lukbán was one of Aguinaldo's last two senior commanders in the field, and he was in no hurry to surrender.

VICENTE RILLES LUKBÁN WAS FORTY-ONE years old in the summer of 1901, a moonfaced, mustachioed, Manila-educated lawyer who had spurned a comfortable life under Spanish rule for the dream of an independent Philippines. In September 1896, Lukbán had been arrested and tortured by Spanish authorities. After his release from Manila's notorious Bilibid Prison the following May, he promptly joined General Aguinaldo's staff, and later that year accompanied Aguinaldo into exile in Hong Kong.

In 1898, after the Americans had transported Aguinaldo and his commanders back to the Philippines to fight the Spaniards, Lukbán was given command of revolutionary forces in his native Bicol region of southeastern Luzon. On December 21, 1898, as Spanish authorities prepared to transfer power to the Americans, Aguinaldo appointed Lukbán commander over Samar and Leyte islands in the Visayas. A few weeks later, Lukbán arrived on Samar with a hundred soldiers to claim the island for the fledgling Republic of the Philippines.[19]

Lukbán spent the next year preparing for the arrival of the Americans. A widower, he took a Samar woman as his wife and familiarized himself with the island's customs and history. He established his headquarters in the mountains above the west coast town of Catbalogan and raised a guerrilla army of a few thousand fighters. His workshops manufactured crude bamboo cannon, cartridges, spears and other weapons, and he organized militia units armed with the machetelike bolo knives popular with the island's fishermen and farmers. Jungle camps and trails were secured from attack with snares, trip-wired weapons and mantraps lined with poison-dipped stakes.[20]

From the hills above Catbalogan, Lukbán tracked the arrival of American troops in January 1900. As the Americans settled into their new garrisons, Lukbán and his forces watched and waited. They harassed outposts and patrols, but avoided pitched battles. And then, with the guerrilla war gathering force across the archipelago, Lukbán struck.

On Sunday morning, April 15, 1900, hundreds of guerrillas armed with bolos, spears, pistols and a few Spanish Mausers attacked a 43rd Infantry outpost in the northern Samar town of Catubig. Barricaded inside the town convent, thirty-one Americans held off the attackers for two days. When the guerrillas set the building ablaze, fifteen Americans were killed as they tried to reach boats along the river. The others huddled behind the building in trenches dug with their bayonets. For two more days, Corporal Anthony J. Carson of Malden, Massachusetts, held the survivors together until a relief party arrived from the coast. Eighteen Americans died during the four days of fighting. Carson was awarded the Medal of Honor for his heroism.[21]

For the next year, American forces on Samar hunkered down while MacArthur pacified Luzon and other islands. In the spring of 1901, when MacArthur finally ordered aggressive action on Samar, General Robert Hughes arrived from Panay to find the seven U.S. infantry companies on the island virtually incapable of offensive operations. Eleven coastal towns were little more than burned-out shells, affording "little or no shelter for troops." Further hindering operations was the absence of "a single road or *carabao* [water buffalo] trail leading into the interior." The few miles of roads that existed along the coast were of little use because of the destruction or decay of every last bridge. Even maps of Samar proved problematic, showing rivers running in the wrong direction and towns and villages miles from their actual location.[22]

Assisted by his aggressive aide-de-camp, Lieutenant Arthur L. Conger of Gordon's Scouts and water-cure fame, Hughes formulated a pacification plan that hinged on starving the island into submission. He would send his troops into the inland valleys and lower slopes to destroy rice fields and other crops that sustained the guerrillas. Four Navy gunboats would end the smuggling of supplies from neighboring islands.

Operating around the northern town of Cervantes in the summer of 1901, 1st Infantry troops under Lieutenant W. K. McCue got a crash course in the savage nature of the war on Samar. Soldiers suffered wounds from spring-loaded spear traps and stake-lined pits as they slogged along jungle trails. As one of McCue's scouts pursued four guerrillas through the forest, he fell into a pit and ran spears through both feet.[23]

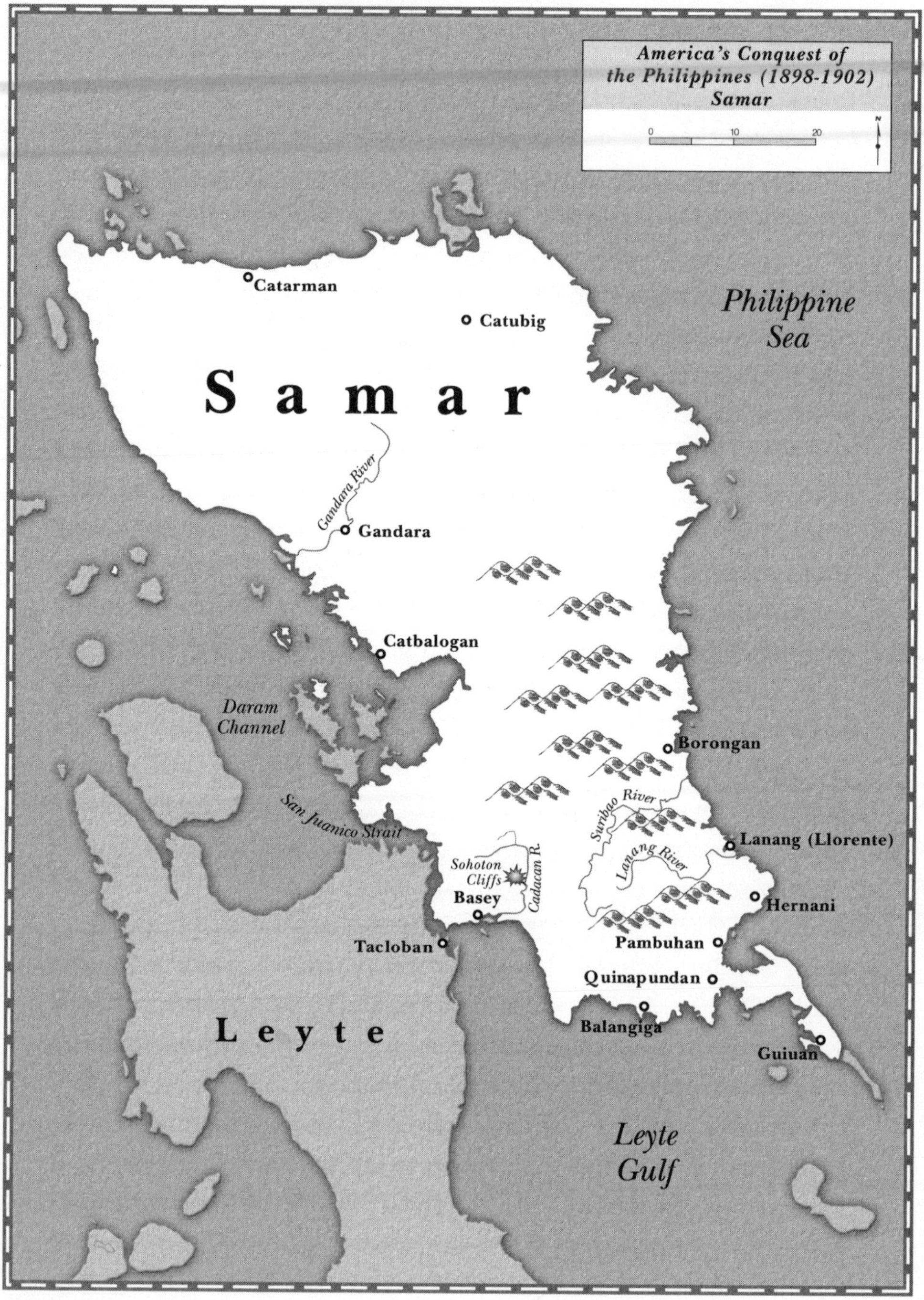

America's Conquest of the Philippines (1898-1902)
Samar
0
10
20
N
Catarman
Catubig
Philippine Sea
Samar
Gandara River
Gandara
Catbalogan
Daram Channel
Borongan
San Juanico Strait
Suribao River
Lanang (Llorente)
Lanang River
Sohoton Cliffs
Cadacan R.
Basey
Hernani
Tacloban
Pambuhan
Quinapundan
Balangiga
Guiuan
Leyte
Leyte Gulf

The harsh tactics that U.S. forces would employ on Samar later in 1901 have earned the criticism of many scholars over the years, but the summer campaign directed by Hughes was every bit as devastating. U.S. soldiers killed guerrillas and civilians alike, burned villages, destroyed crops and slaughtered water buffalo and other livestock as they swept inland. Thousands of hungry and frightened natives poured into U.S. garrisons to take the oath of allegiance, while others starved in the mountains.

In late August, an Army detachment hiking through the mountains of northern Samar stumbled onto Lukbán's hideout. The U.S. soldiers killed three men in Lukbán's group and captured two others, along with Mrs. Lukbán, their infant child and a cache of documents.[24] The papers revealed Catbalogan's role as the financial and logistical nerve center of Lukbán's organization on Samar, despite twenty months of U.S. occupation. Town officials and other prominent citizens played vital roles in sustaining resistance, as did the representatives of two British trading firms. On September 13, Hughes ordered the British traders to leave Samar, and the following day he arrested several town officials and prominent citizens and hustled them off to Iloilo. There, Hughes's crack intelligence operative, now Major Edwin Glenn, went to work with his interrogation teams. Within days, Glenn had begun dismantling Lukbán's underground network.[25]

By late September, three months of sustained American operations had ravaged Samar and depopulated the interior. Tens of thousands of refugees huddled in squalid camps on the outskirts of occupied towns. Victory was at hand on Samar, Hughes assured his superiors. "In due course of nature and after a few more funerals," he boasted, "I think that island will have had sufficient experience in the discomforts of war to be willing to accept peace on any sort of terms."[26]

IN SAMAR'S UNRULY SOUTH, THE pacification campaign of 1901 got off to a shaky start. On June 19, 1st Infantry Lieutenant Edward E. Downes set off from the southeastern town of Guiuan with a twenty-six-man patrol. The soldiers destroyed food supplies, burned crops and villages and slaughtered water buffalo, but saw little sign of guerrillas. Three days out, two soldiers were wounded in a brief skirmish. The following day, with the patrol now lost and low on food and water, Downes led his men into an ambush. Bolomen sprang from the undergrowth, stabbing and slashing the soldiers. Downes fell, mortally wounded by knife thrusts to his groin and chest. The terrified soldiers scattered, abandoning the bodies of their commander and other comrades. The survivors stumbled through the jungle for three days before reaching their base.[27]

Hughes responded with punitive operations aimed at "cleaning up" the area. In one typical foray, a 1st Infantry detachment spent an entire day destroying rice fields around Quinapundan before torching the village.[28] Some weeks later, 1st Infantry Lieutenant Campbell King found the surrounding countryside "in a most pronounced condition of insurrection." Men, women and children lived in jungle hovels near their destroyed homes and tracked the approach of American troops by blowing conch shells. They were "sullen and defiant," King reported, their resolve steeled by the occasional casualties they inflicted on his troops. He recommended placing an Army outpost in their midst "as a constant menace to their lives."[29]

General Chaffee had similar ideas, and in August he had dispatched seven companies of the 9th Infantry to take up garrison duties on Samar. Among the new units was Captain Connell's Company C. Within days, the soldiers of Company G, based forty miles up the coast at Basey, learned a hard lesson about the perils that lurked in the Samar jungle. On September 2, twelve soldiers had ventured into the bush to make repairs to a telephone line that ran to the coast when a band of bolomen set upon them. The attack was over quickly and the guerrillas driven off with heavy casualties, but two soldiers had been killed and two others wounded.[30]

Connell and his men found Balangiga Mayor Pedro Abayan friendly enough in their early dealings. But, like many municipal officials the Americans had installed across the archipelago, he was leading a double life. In late May, as word spread of the imminent arrival of more American troops, Abayan had written a letter to General Lukbán pledging to "observe a deceptive policy with them [Americans] doing whatever they may like, and when a favorable opportunity arises, the people will strategically rise against them."[31] About six weeks after contacting Lukbán,

Abayan had written a letter to Army headquarters in Manila, requesting a detachment of U.S. troops to protect his people "against the *insurrectos* and the Moro pirates." Not long afterward, Connell had arrived with his men to officially claim Balangiga as U.S. territory.

After a month of Connell's cleanup campaign, crop-destruction operations and other incidents, Abayan and his town council had seen enough.[32] A meeting was arranged with the chiefs of Balangiga's outlying barrios and Lukbán's southern district commander, Captain Eugenio Daza, and plans for a surprise attack were drawn up. Seven units of seventy fighters, nearly five hundred in all, would compose the assault force. Barrio blacksmiths set to work hammering out more bolos, spears and stilettos.[33]

IN THEIR SIX WEEKS IN Balangiga, the soldiers of Company C had not reported a single encounter with the guerrillas. They remained wary of the locals, but their letters suggested growing confidence. "We keep constantly on the alert with bayonets fixed, magazines loaded, and Indian file, so that in case any bolomen try to surprise us from the long grass or impenetrable thickets, we will be instantly ready for them," Lieutenant Edward Bumpus, Connell's second in command, wrote home in late August. Nine days later, he seemed less concerned with the guerrilla threat. "We have scouted over all the country within a radius of several miles of this post, and have not been troubled by any *ladrones* with bolo or gun," he wrote. "As we never go without arms, and hardly ever alone, no native is liable to bother an American soldier if he values his health."[34]

The guerrillas had yet to harm the men of Company C, but the isolated duty and tropical climate had begun to take a toll. "One of the men in the company shot himself the other day and died," Bumpus wrote on September 6, "and one man deserted while crazed with *tuba*, the native drink, and has probably died in the woods." Another private named Scheetherly had come unhinged while on sentry duty and tried to shoot a comrade before he ran howling into the jungle. Three men caught him and held him down until Major Griswold arrived. On the surgeon's instructions, Scheetherly was rolled tightly in a canvas pup tent and hauled off to a hospital bed. There, Scheetherly sat on the edge of his cot, talking and laughing to himself, convinced that he was back in snowy New York at Christmastime. When Bumpus set out for Basey in an outrigger canoe to fetch supplies on September 25, Scheetherly was sent along for treatment.[35]

Lieutenant Bumpus returned to Balangiga late Friday evening, September 27, with the long-awaited mail in hand. As the officers read letters from home and discussed President McKinley's death late into the night, the men of Balangiga made their final preparations. Women and children had been sent away, along with Father Guimbaolibot. Fighters armed with bolos, spears, clubs, arrows and daggers took up positions in the jungle, within a few feet of the American barracks.

In the gray predawn of Saturday, September 28, a company of guerrillas disguised as female religious devotees slipped into the church. Their assignment was to attack the officers in their quarters in the adjoining convent. An hour later, more fighters posing as veiled women entered the town carrying bamboo tubes packed with bolos. A bugler sounded reveille, and enlisted men stirred from their barracks. Mess tables soon filled with soldiers eating breakfast and reading mail. Around the plaza, inside the church, and at the jungle's edge, hundreds of Filipinos waited. Suddenly, the shout of Police Chief Abanador shattered the morning calm: "Attack, men of Balangiga!"[36]

As church bells pealed furiously, fighters ripped off disguises, brandished weapons and charged their assigned targets. Units fanned out to attack the mess hall and kitchen, main barracks and two smaller barracks. Those concealed in the church poured into the convent in search of the three American officers.

Most of the Americans were seated at the long mess table sheltered by tents along the eastern side of the plaza, and it was there that the scores of native prisoners and laborers standing around the square converged behind Abanador. First Sergeant James M. Randles was among the first to fall, his skull split with an ax. Another soldier's head was severed from his shoulders by a bolo and fell into his plate. The Americans fought back with anything they could grab—chairs, clubs, knives and forks, pots and pans. Cook Melvin D. Walls, a pitcher on the company baseball team, threw a pot of boiling water at the attackers, then continued to hold them at bay by hurling canned goods.

Sergeant John D. Closson, a tall and muscular man, had been seated at the south end of the mess table when the attack began. He ran to the back stairs of the main barracks, about twenty paces west of the mess tents, arriving simultaneously with the assailants. He bulled his way through a throng of Filipinos, but was dragged to the floor by unseen hands. As he threw wild punches, natives slashed him with their bolos. Blood streaming from half a dozen wounds, Closson managed to grab a rifle and jump out a window. As he hit the ground, two bolomen started for him. Closson smashed one in the head with his rifle butt and shot the other. He worked his way around to the front of the barracks, blasting away at his adversaries, until he saw three other soldiers trying to force their way into the hall. Closson fired through the door, and the Filipinos on the other side fled upstairs. The Americans followed and found three more rifles, which they used to clear the building room by room, gunning down nearly a score of Filipinos.[37]

Private Adolph Gamlin, the sentry who had been knocked senseless by Abanador's blow to his head, had staggered to his feet and followed the throng of Filipinos swarming toward the main barracks. He dashed to a bamboo ladder that served as a rear entrance, where he saw several Americans desperately trying to climb inside to get their rifles. The ladder suddenly snapped and several soldiers fell to the ground, where they were hacked to death by bolomen.[38]

When the attack began, Sergeant George F. Markley had dashed out of the mess tent and sprinted for his barracks, a nipa hut about thirty paces north of the main quarters. He dodged a local policeman who tried to club him and fought off a boloman standing on the porch of his barracks. Grabbing his rifle, he shot a Filipino who was stabbing Private Frank Vobayda across the room and drove off several natives who were clubbing and slashing Corporal Arnold Irish. When they had cleared the room of attackers, Markley, Irish and Private Carl E. Swanson turned their fire on the scores of bolomen milling about the plaza, and the Filipinos began to scatter. Hurrying toward the sound of shots near the mess tents, the three Americans were relieved to find Sergeant Frank Betron and several other soldiers firing at natives as they fled into the jungle east of the kitchen.

Betron and his men had been eating under their shack when the bells began ringing, and they found themselves in a desperate hand-to-hand struggle with a swarm of enemy fighters. Corporal Burke forced his way into the hut and fell to the floor with one of the Filipinos, rolling over and over until he was able to grab a revolver and shoot the man. Betron and others overwhelmed their assailants and grabbed their rifles.

At the convent, the bolomen had quickly overrun the sentries and poured into the rooms of the three American officers. Bumpus was sitting in a chair, a pile of mail in his lap, when a Filipino swung his bolo and sheared away the American's face from the bridge of his nose to his throat. Griswold was hacked to death in his quarters. Connell jumped out a second-story window and ran about twenty feet toward the main barracks before three Filipinos cut him down in the street.[39]

While Markley and Betron rallied their men east of the plaza, other survivors banded together in desperate fights. Private George Allen scrambled atop a pile of broken concrete that anchored a cross that stood in front of the church. He was joined there by Private Elbert B. DeGraffen-reid, and they stayed alive by hurling chunks of concrete at their would-be killers until other soldiers cleared the plaza with rifle fire.

Hearing a call for help that sounded like Captain Connell, Corporal Irish and Sergeant Markley now set out for the officers' quarters. They found the captain's blood-soaked body in the street and discovered the cry had come from Corporal Taylor Hickman, sole survivor of the convent guard post. Hickman had slipped outside to join the officers' cook, Private Walter J. Bertholf, in a stand against the bolomen.[40]

By seven thirty a.m., the Americans had driven the attackers from the town. Markley and other soldiers stood at the river's edge, sniping at Filipinos who were trying to swim to the far bank. Sergeant Betron, now in command of what remained of Company C, decided to abandon Balangiga before the natives learned how to operate the bolt-action rifles and returned to finish them off. Five outrigger canoes were readied and the wounded gently laid inside. The canoes were about to pull away when somebody noticed the Stars and Stripes still fluttering over the town. Private Claude C. Wingo ran back to the plaza, hauled down the flag and hurried back to the boats. Paddles churned and the forlorn flotilla pulled away from Balangiga and headed west along the coast.

Throughout the day and into the night, the canoes thrashed through heavy seas. The first two boats reached Basey about three thirty a.m. on September 29, twenty hours after leaving Balangiga. Nine of the wounded aboard had died along the way. Sergeant Markley and Private Swanson, who had been forced to abandon their leaky canoe and put ashore to find another boat, reached the island of Leyte at five a.m.

More horrors awaited the occupants of the two remaining canoes. Four soldiers, including the badly wounded privates Litto Armani and John D. Buhrer, had been forced ashore around midnight. They hid along the beach until daylight, when the two stronger men set off in search of another boat. They had gone about a hundred yards when they came upon the body of Private Charles Powers, his head split open with a fresh wound. The men heard screams and turned to see thirty Filipinos swarming around their two wounded comrades. Running for their lives, the two able-bodied soldiers found another canoe and again put to sea, where they were rescued later that morning by a military transport rushing reinforcements to Balangiga. Private Wingo and another soldier who had shared a canoe with the unfortunate Powers were never seen again.[41]

BACK DOWN THE COAST, THE men of Balangiga emerged from the jungle to reclaim the town and tend to their fallen. The victory had come at the cost of twenty-eight comrades, including Mayor Abayan and Police Chief Abanador. But the magnitude of their triumph rivaled any achieved by Filipinos during three years of war against the Americans. Forty-eight U.S. soldiers were dead or dying, and another twenty-one wounded. The survivors had fled in terror, lowering the Stars and Stripes after only forty-eight days. The victory was made even more momentous by the fact that the Americans had left behind fifty-seven Krag-Jørgensen rifles and twenty-five thousand rounds of ammunition—a haul like nothing the lightly armed Samar resistance had ever seen.

General Hughes had boasted that the people of Samar would plead for peace "after a few more funerals." He would have his funerals, but no peace.[42]

CHAPTER 17

Hell-roaring Jake

The slaughter of Company C at Balangiga unleashed shock waves up the military chain of command, and presented Theodore Roosevelt with his first crisis as president. After being told for more than a year that the war in the Philippines was over, Americans now read hysterical headlines proclaiming the "Balangiga Massacre" as the nation's worst military defeat since Custer's debacle at the Little Bighorn twenty-five years earlier. Commentators denounced America's treacherous colonial subjects in the Philippines and demanded punishment, while U.S. soldiers in the islands plotted their revenge.

General Adna Chaffee rushed two infantry battalions to Samar as Washington demanded an explanation as to how such a disaster could have occurred. Chaffee laid the blame on Governor William Howard Taft and his lenient policies toward Filipinos. Too many of Taft's men—even Army officers—believed that Filipinos "are more friendly than they really are, and that they are satisfied with our presence among them," Chaffee fumed. "As a rule I would not trust 50 percent of the male population. . . ."[1]

Taft believed the hard-line general had overreacted to an isolated incident. He had put Manila on edge with nightly mounted patrols galloping through city streets, Taft sniped to Secretary of War Elihu Root, and he had rashly proclaimed that the Americans were "standing on a volcano" in the Philippines. "This feeling seems to have been communicated to all of his subordinates," Taft complained, "and the Army and Navy Club is filled with rumors of insurrection in the most peaceful provinces."[2]

Overreaction or not, Roosevelt was not prepared to risk his presidency in an endless overseas war. He ordered Chaffee to crush resistance.

Chaffee was only too happy to oblige. Orders went out to his soldiers to punish every hostile act "quickly and severely" and instill a "wholesome fear" of the Army. He reassured Washington that the men he had dispatched to Samar would "start a few cemeteries for *hombres*" and get the savage island under control.[3]

Samar would be punished, and Chaffee had just the man to do it.

IN THE ANNALS OF THE U.S. Army, Jacob Hurd Smith ranks as one of the most colorful scoundrels ever to wear the uniform. His forty-one years in the service were punctuated with frequent scandals and occasional battlefield bravery. Civil War comrades and political patrons intervened repeatedly to save his career. In between ethical and legal scrapes, "Hell-roaring Jake" appeared on some of the Army's biggest stages.

Smith was born January 29, 1840, in Jackson County, Ohio, about thirty miles from the Ohio River. He was educated in public schools and later attended the Collegiate and Commercial Institute in New Haven, Connecticut, where he excelled at copperplate penmanship, a skill highly valued before the advent of typewriters.[4]

In May 1861, in the patriotism-charged early days of the Civil War, Smith enlisted in the 2nd Kentucky Volunteers and was commissioned a second lieutenant. He saw action in the mountains of western Virginia and took a saber slash to the head at Barboursville. The following spring, on April 7, 1862, twenty-two-year-old Captain Jake Smith fell with a minié ball in his hip on the second day of the battle of Shiloh.[5]

After a painful convalescence, Smith spent the remainder of the war as an army recruiter in Louisville, Kentucky. The city was the most important Union base and logistical center in the western theater, and a hub for illicit wartime trade between North and South. As a recruiter, Smith specialized in providing freed slaves to bounty brokers hired by Northern states and municipalities to fulfill their recruitment quotas. Before the war was out, Smith had parlayed a $92,000 payment from several unscrupulous brokers into a small fortune by investing in black-market gold, diamonds, whiskey and other commodities. When the war ended in 1865, Smith mustered out of the Army and used some of his ill-gotten wealth to buy a farm in Illinois. He and his wife, Emma, daughter of an infamous wartime black marketeer, settled in Chicago.[6]

Out of boredom or financial necessity, Smith resumed his Army career in March 1867 as a brevet major with the 13th U.S. Infantry. Two years later, he was poised to secure a coveted appointment as an Army judge advocate when a lawsuit accusing Smith and his father-in-law of fraud and other wartime transgressions landed on the desk of Secretary of War William W. Belknap. In his panicked attempt to clear his name, Smith admitted that he had lied under oath during an earlier deposition. President Ulysses Grant promptly withdrew Smith's name from the judge advocate's list.[7]

A pattern had been established in Smith's career, a continuous loop of ethical breaches, misconduct and poor judgment. Over the next two decades, while other men were winning glory and promotions in the Indian wars, Smith was in and out of civil and military courts, fighting to save his career. During a Texas posting in the 1880s, a general court-martial convicted him of conduct unbecoming an officer and a gentleman for failing to pay a poker debt. Smith's courtroom misbehavior and outright lies in an appeal to the Army adjutant general resulted in another court-martial, and in 1886 he was ordered dismissed from the service. Powerful Ohio friends persuaded President Grover Cleveland to intervene, and Smith escaped with a presidential reprimand.

In 1898, Smith was fifty-eight years old—four years from mandatory Army retirement—when the *Maine* blew up in Havana Harbor. Despite his checkered past, Jake Smith was given command of a 2nd Infantry battalion and sent to Cuba. The afternoon of July 1, 1898, found Smith in the thick of the fight before Santiago. In a stroke of good fortune, it fell

Assistant Secretary of the Navy Theodore Roosevelt at his desk in Washington, D.C., promoting his agenda for war with Spain and America's overseas expansion.

The wreckage of the USS *Maine* rests in the mud of Havana Harbor.

An obscure Navy commodore named George Dewey became a national hero after destroying Spain's fleet at Manila Bay on May 1, 1898.

Major General William Shafter in Florida, 1898, overseeing preparations for the invasion of Cuba.

Roosevelt and his Rough Riders atop San Juan Hill, overlooking Santiago, Cuba.

Spanish Admiral Pascual Cervera y Topete led his ships single file through the narrow mouth of Santiago Bay on July 3, 1898.

The death throes of the Spanish warship *Vizcaya*, at left, are captured in this photograph taken during the battle of Santiago Bay.

U.S. soldiers pose on the walls of Manila's old city.

Emilio Aguinaldo, leader of a Philippine independence movement fighting to end Spanish rule.

President William McKinley.

Massachusetts Senator Henry Cabot Lodge.

Soldiers from the Oregon Volunteer Infantry fire on Philippine forces, March 1899.

Indiana Senator Albert Beveridge.

Massachusetts Senator George Frisbie Hoar.

U.S. troops in action, 1899.

An American soldier poses before the corpses of three Filipino soldiers.

U.S. soldiers transport their dead and wounded, Luzon, 1899.

One of the most storied American soldiers of his era, Major General Henry Ware Lawton stood six feet four and sported a British-style helmet and yellow rain slicker. Lawton is seen here in March 1899, eight months before he was killed in a minor engagement with guerrillas north of Manila.

Colonel Frederick Funston (seen here late in his career), commander of the 20th Kansas Volunteers.

Funston's Kansans in action on Luzon, March 1899. Filipino entrenchments lie just beyond the firing line.

914. Approach to the Bridge of Spain in the New Town, Manila.

Copyright, 1899, by J. D. Cress.

As war devastated the countryside, U.S. military administrators worked to transform Manila into a modern city with electricity and automobiles.

Major General Elwell Otis (*seated center*) with his staff in Manila.

U.S. soldiers watch over Filipino prisoners in Manila's old walled city in 1899.

Riflemen of the Washington Volunteer Infantry open fire on Luzon.

Filipino fighters lie dead in a trench, Luzon, 1899.

American artillery rolls into the Philippine Republic's abandoned capital at Malolos after Aguinaldo's retreat on April 1, 1899.

Brigadier General Samuel B. M. Young led a column of a thousand Americans on a 120-mile march in a bold attempt to cut off Aguinaldo's escape.

Aguinaldo's youngest general, twenty-two-year-old Manuel Tinio, delayed advancing American forces in a valiant effort at San Jacinto.

General Gregorio del Pilar led sixty soldiers in a heroic rearguard action at Luzon's Tirad Pass. Del Pilar died in the battle, along with fifty-one of his men.

U.S. soldiers skirmish with Filipino fighters in Central Luzon, September 1899.

Marine Corps Major Littleton Waller, 1900.

Waller's Marines, who won high praise during the fighting against Chinese rebels known as Boxers, are shown here during their first days in China in the summer of 1900.

A 1900 presidential campaign cartoon shows GOP President McKinley raising the American flag abroad while his Democratic opponent, William Jennings Bryan, tries to chop it down.

Major General Arthur MacArthur ordered U.S. forces to use extreme measures against Filipino guerrillas in late 1900.

Lieutenant General Adna Chaffee (*left*) with Brigadier General Jacob H. Smith.

Captain Edwin Forbes Glenn gained fame as an Alaska explorer in 1898 before becoming a crack intelligence operative in the Philippines.

Lieutenant Arthur L. Conger commanded Gordon's Scouts in the brutal fight against guerrillas on Panay Island.

U.S. soldiers are seen administering the "water cure" in these three photographs taken during the war in the Philippines.

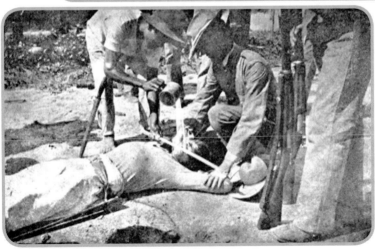

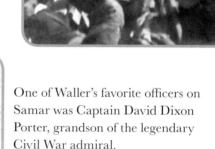

Major Waller's Marines launch a cutter with a Colt machine gun on the bow and push up the Cadacan River in search of guerrillas, Samar, 1901.

One of Waller's favorite officers on Samar was Captain David Dixon Porter, grandson of the legendary Civil War admiral.

Smoke rises from a Samar village torched by Waller's Marines during the 1901–2 campaign.

Lieutenant General Nelson Miles documented torture, summary executions, and other extreme actions by U.S. soldiers in the Philippines.

Filipino schoolgirls pose with their American teacher, 1901.

William Howard Taft (*left*), America's first civilian governor in the Philippines, with Secretary of War Elihu Root, Roosevelt's most trusted adviser.

A 1902 cartoon depicts GOP Senator George Frisbie Hoar and other opponents of expansion as aiding the Philippine resistance.

President Roosevelt broke his silence on the Philippine military abuse scandal in a provocative Memorial Day address at Arlington National Cemetery in May 1902.

to Smith to secure the American left flank atop the San Juan Heights, and he did so boldly by seizing a prominent wooded hill about eight hundred yards from Spanish lines. Around four p.m., Smith was inspecting his line when a Spanish bullet struck him in the chest. The bullet caused only minor damage, but his refusal to leave his post earned him high praise from his superiors. He was promoted to brevet lieutenant colonel and given command of the 12th U.S. Infantry regiment.[8]

IN MID-MARCH 1899, SIX WEEKS after war broke out in the Philippines, Lieutenant Colonel Jake Smith led the 12th Infantry ashore at Manila. He was thrown into the fight against Aguinaldo's retreating forces in Central Luzon, and quickly earned a reputation as a hard fighter and big talker. Smith made headlines when he ordered his soldiers to shoot Filipino men who returned to occupied towns, and subsequently advocated the summary execution of captured guerrillas.[9]

In October 1899, Smith was promoted to colonel and given command of the 17th Infantry regiment. With the booming battlefield voice that had earned him the sobriquet "Hell-roaring Jake," he personally led his men in operations against the guerrillas. He burnished his no-nonsense reputation by building an open-air prison fashioned from steel rails, and within weeks "Smith's Cage" had sixty inmates. Turnover was rapid as Smith's military courts cranked out a flurry of capital murder convictions against captured guerrillas.[10] In late April, after capturing General Antonio Montenegro along with hundreds of guerrillas, Smith was promoted to brigadier general of volunteers.[11]

By the fall of 1900, Smith had assumed considerable powers as military governor of the Luzon provinces of Pangasinan, Tarlac and Zambales. Although no advocate of benevolence toward Filipinos, Smith shrewdly lavished attention on William Howard Taft and his Philippine Commission during a visit to his headquarters that December.[12] Smith made a favorable impression on his fellow Ohioan, and in February 1901 Taft lobbied on Hell-roaring Jake's behalf in military promotion discussions with Secretary Root. Smith, according to Taft, "has reached a time when a Brigadier Generalship would worthily end his services, for I believe it is his intention to retire upon promotion."[13] On March 30, 1901, in a rise of remarkable improbability, Jacob Hurd Smith received the star of a brigadier general in the Regular Army.

ON OCTOBER 8, 1901, AS the shock waves of Balangiga continued to shake the Roosevelt administration, General Chaffee ordered Jake Smith to Samar. He had just taken up his post when news of yet another disaster broke. Forty-six soldiers of Company E, 9th Infantry, had been overrun on Samar by hundreds of bolomen, who killed ten Americans and wounding six.[14] Soldiers and correspondents buzzed with anticipation at the "awful retribution" that General Chaffee's new commander on Samar had in store. The *Manila Times*, an unabashed Smith admirer, offered a prediction: "Samar will soon have the unenviable distinction of being the bloodiest island in the annals of the insurrection."[15]

CHAPTER 18

"Kill and Burn!"

On the morning of October 23, 1901, a steam launch pulled along-side the armored cruiser USS *New York* as she rode at anchor off the west coast of Samar, and a wiry little man with a bushy mustache and brigadier general's star climbed aboard. General Jacob Smith had arrived on the island a few days earlier, after a private meeting with General Chaffee in Manila. Much later, after the conduct of American soldiers on Samar had prompted questions about Chaffee's orders, the commander would insist that he had merely told Smith that he must recover the rifles and ammunition seized at Balangiga. "Capture the arms if you can, buy them if you must," Chaffee would recall saying. "Whichever course you adopt, get them back."[1] Now, spurred by those words (and any others Chaffee neglected to recall), Hell-roaring Jake had come aboard the *New York* to brief his newly arrived field commander for southern Samar, Major Tony Waller of the U.S. Marine Corps.

Waller had leaped at the assignment. In the year since his triumphant return from China, he had become embroiled in bickering within the Cavite officer corps, and found himself relegated to command of the Marine detachment at remote Subic Bay. He had lapsed into months of liquor-sodden self-pity, culminating a few weeks earlier with a surprise inspection by Rear Admiral George Remey that found Waller too drunk to get out of bed. Waller was relieved of command and suspended from duty for ten days.[2] And then the Balangiga attack had occurred. As General Chaffee rounded up reinforcements, Rear Admiral Fred Rodgers had presented Waller with command of a Marine battalion—and a shot at redemption in the climactic campaign of the Philippine War.

Smith briskly laid out the duties that awaited Waller and his men. The Marines would be responsible for the southernmost reaches of the island, a swath that stretched from the town of Basey in the southwest to Hernani in the southeast, roughly six hundred square miles of coastal plain, swamps and upland jungle. The area was "one of the hardest problems in the whole command," Smith warned. The natives could not be trusted, and must not be shown mercy. Any unfriendly act should be punished summarily, and no prisoners taken. Paraphrasing General Sherman, Smith assured Waller that a short and severe campaign would be more humane than a drawn-out affair.[3]

If Smith had stopped there, he would have passed into history with scarcely a second thought. But Hell-roaring Jake had not been hand-picked to manage the Samar campaign because of his benevolence toward the enemy, and, with characteristic bluntness, he made sure that Waller fully understood the severity expected.

Kill all persons capable of bearing arms, Smith commanded.

Waller was stunned. From what he knew of Samar, even children carried bolo knives. Were they to be killed? "I would like to know the limit of age," he pressed.

Ten years of age, came the cold reply. "I wish you to kill and burn," Smith said. "The more you kill and the more you burn, the better you will please me."[4]

WITH SMITH'S WORDS IN HIS head, Waller retired to his quarters and drew up orders for his men. Their mission, he wrote, would be to stem the flow of food into the Samar interior and starve, capture or kill the guerrillas and their supporters. Any males who did not present themselves to the Marines by October 25 were to be "regarded and treated as enemies." Remain vigilant and never be unarmed, even at meals or the latrine. "Place no confidence in the natives," he continued, "and punish treachery immediately with death." Expect no quarter from the guerrillas, and give none in return. Remember the fate of the Americans at Balangiga. "Avenge our late comrades in North China," he exhorted, "the murdered men of the 9th United States Infantry."[5]

At first light on October 24, the collier *Zafiro* transported the Marines to the port of Basey, along the southern Samar coast, and two companies along with Waller's headquarters staff went ashore. After a brief inspection by General Smith and Admiral Rodgers, Waller and the remaining Marines continued down the coast to Balangiga. A Navy patrol boat and gunboat shelled a line of enemy trenches overlooking the town, and Captain David Dixon Porter, fearless grandson of the famed Civil War admiral and decorated veteran of the fighting on Luzon and China, splashed ashore with two companies of Marines.

The Army had retaken Balangiga the day after the attack, and the horrified relief party had buried Captain Connell and his men in the town plaza. Now a company of 11th Infantry troops huddled nervously behind a sandbagged fortress on the beach, a Gatling gun pointed toward the jungle.

Waller, Porter, General Smith and Admiral Rodgers made their way into Balangiga, past the burned shells of buildings. At the plaza the Americans made a ghastly discovery: wild hogs had torn up the graves of the men of Company C. Smith ordered a fence built around the cemetery, and then flew into a rage.

"Kill and burn!" he shouted to the Marines. "Kill and burn!"[6]

SMITH'S BLOODLUST WAS NO SECRET, for as American troops poured into Samar, the *Manila Times* had proclaimed the day of "awful retribution" at hand. "The reports from Samar say that the natives there are aware of the dire punishment which will soon overtake them, and the dark and bloody days in store, and are fleeing from the island by hundreds . . . ," the *Times* reported. At the White House, where the surge in violence in the Philippines was being anxiously monitored, President Roosevelt could pick up his copy of the *Washington Post* on October 28, 1901, and, under the headline "Repression in Samar," read of General Smith's activities. "Dispatches from Catbalogan, Samar, say that stringent and energetic measures are being taken to suppress the insurrection in that island," the paper reported.[7]

Among those measures was a roundup of suspected resistance supporters by Major Edwin Glenn. A Navy gunboat ferried Glenn up and down the narrow strait separating Samar from Leyte, stopping periodically so he could go ashore to arrest and carry away municipal officials and other citizens suspected of supporting guerrilla activities. "His work was thorough," General Robert Hughes would drily report, "and had a widely spread effect."[8] Father Donato Guimbaolibot, the Balangiga parish priest, had already felt those effects. He had been arrested on Leyte on suspicion of involvement in the attack on Company C and was undergoing interrogation and torture on Samar by one of Glenn's young intelligence operatives, First Lieutenant Julien Gaujot.[9]

Smith now issued a flurry of coercive decrees. He gave Samar municipal executives until November 6 to surrender all arms and anyone involved in the Balangiga attack or face destruction of their town, deportation to Guam and confiscation of personal property. To curtail the flow of food and supplies to the guerrillas, he ordered boat owners to paint their vessels red and obtain permission before leaving Samar's shores. Residents of towns and villages near signal lights or fires used to guide smugglers were warned they would be fired on by gunboats and troops.[10] Glenn's intelligence work had revealed Leyte's importance in sustaining the Samar guerrillas, and so Smith decreed that "all natives found passing between these two islands, or afloat on either shore, will be fired upon and killed." He also asked Chaffee to suspend civil government on Leyte until resistance on Samar ceased.[11]

Meanwhile, U.S. troops across Samar fulfilled Smith's punitive desires. Suspected guerrillas and their supporters were shot on sight in their fields and homes, their villages burned, food supplies destroyed and livestock slaughtered. Andrew Pohlman, a soldier with a 1st Infantry detachment at Borongan on Samar's east coast, later wrote that U.S. troops killed more than two thousand guerrillas in the first two months of Smith's campaign. "Each ruthless act committed by the insurgents was the cause of harsher methods being adopted by the Americans," he wrote. "After the massacre at Balangiga there were no more prisoners taken on either side. . . ."[12] At Sulat, twenty-five miles up the coast from Borongan, Captain M. S. Jarvis of the 1st Infantry reported successful hunting in the first month of Smith's campaign. In addition to burning about ninety houses and killing twenty water buffalo, Jarvis reported two engagements in which he killed thirty guerrillas, wounded two and captured three—all without suffering a single casualty.[13]

The resistance was on the defensive, but still capable of wreaking terrible vengeance on *americanistas* in the towns and barrios. On October 23, guerrillas in northern Samar captured five native policemen in an area where U.S. troops had conducted aggressive operations. American soldiers caught up with the band of about twenty guerrillas the following morning. Three of the native policemen were rescued alive, although one had been severely beaten and hanged by the neck "until only his toes touched the ground." Two policemen had been killed—one beaten to death, and the other beaten, hanged by the neck, and stabbed three times in the abdomen. Before returning to their camp, the soldiers burned the nearby village of Pipa.[14]

Waller and his Marines were just settling into their new outposts in Basey and Balangiga in late October when a tragic incident involving a popular Navy cadet named Loveman Noa underscored the perils that surrounded them. The twenty-three-year-old Noa had grown up in Chattanooga, Tennessee, the son of Hungarian Jewish immigrants, and had graduated from the Naval Academy in 1900. Late that year he was ordered to the Philippines.[15] Assigned to the gunboat *Mariveles*, Noa was introduced to Samar in June 1901 during the offensive launched by General Hughes, and returned to the island's waters in September to help sever the guerrilla supply line. Noa burned houses, destroyed boats and killed water buffalo as part of his antismuggling duties, but he also gave food and showed other kindnesses to Filipinos.

On the morning of October 26, 1901, Noa and a crew of six armed sailors set off from the *Mariveles* in a small boat on a smuggling patrol near Basey. Late in the afternoon, with their boat taking on water, Noa put in to shore near the village of Nipa Nipa. His crew had gone off to scout the surrounding jungle when several Filipinos rushed from hiding and attacked Noa with clubs and bolos. Mortally wounded, the young American bled to death on the beach.

As GENERAL SMITH AND ADMIRAL Rodgers stood in a driving rain at Catbalogan for Cadet Noa's funeral, the Marines had begun putting their imprimatur on the island. "We are not making war against women and children," Waller had instructed Captain Porter before leaving his young company commander in Balangiga. "We are making war against men capable of bearing arms." Waller's definition of combatants may have been only slightly more generous than General Smith's. "We were to shoot on sight anyone over twelve years old, armed or not, to burn everything and to make the island of Samar a howling wilderness," one Marine later recalled.[16]

From Basey and Balangiga, the Marines swept through coastal villages and pushed into the swamps and jungles of southern Samar in search of guerrillas. Shafts of smoke from burning nipa huts marked the progress of their patrols. Fleeing natives were invariably identified in Marine reports as enemy "bolomen." While the Marines probed at will during the day, they retired to their camps before nightfall. An informant warned Waller during his first week on the island that a large force of Lukbán's guerrillas had crept to the outskirts of Basey during the night but had called off their attack at the last minute. On Waller's second night in Basey, guerrillas cut his telephone line to Smith's headquarters in Tacloban. Waller retaliated immediately, and by nightfall the line had been repaired and the village of Hibasen burned to the ground.

As the Marines expanded their operations, the guerrillas avoided contact when possible. Despite their victory at Balangiga, Lukbán's forces in the south remained badly outmanned and outgunned. A typical thirty-guerrilla unit bivouacked in the village cemetery at Lipata fought with one Krag-Jørgensen rifle captured from a 9th Infantry soldier the previous August, two revolvers, and twenty-seven bolos. The unit's primary activity was collecting food and cash from locals to keep starvation at bay.[17]

In their weakened condition, the guerrillas waited for Samar's climate and terrain to wear down the Marines. Oppressive heat and humidity and daily rains made search-and-destroy "scouts" through head-high grass and dense jungle even more arduous. Waller's men had yet to suffer any casualties from enemy fire, but such tropical torments as "dhobie itch" and "weeping eczema" had begun to take a toll.

Recapturing his old swagger, Waller reveled in the duty. He was once again the can-do hero of China, leading patrols and raids, inspiring his men by tireless example. On October 30, the forty-five-year-old Marine headed to Balangiga on a gunboat, stopping along the way to destroy two villages, kill one native and capture a guerrilla lookout. He led another foray to the barrio of Quinapundan and came ashore under brisk fire from three snipers. Waller led still another probe from Balangiga in search of a guerrilla gunpowder factory. Finding nothing, he marched three miles farther west, where his Marines came under fire and destroyed twenty-three houses in the village of Bulasao.[18]

Meanwhile, Porter and his Marines were leaving their mark around Balangiga. He awoke from his first night in the deserted town and led a sixty-man patrol into the jungle to scout their surroundings. The Marines returned in the afternoon after marching twelve miles through swamps and soggy jungle, leaving behind three dead Filipinos, numerous burned houses and three thousand pounds of destroyed rice.

Each morning thereafter, Porter's men ranged through the jungle, killing Filipinos they came across and burning crops and houses. On October 31, the Marines happened on a nipa hut where they found uniforms, photographs and other equipment and personal effects that had belonged to soldiers of Company C. The Marines killed two unarmed inhabitants under circumstances that Porter did not describe. "It was understood that everybody in Samar was *insurrecto*," he would later testify, "except those who had come in and taken the oath of allegiance."[19]

AFTER DESTROYING EVERY TOWN AND village for a twenty-five-mile stretch down the coast from Basey, Waller turned to a larger prize. A Filipino named Francisco Taguilla had appeared at Waller's headquarters in late

October with an intriguing story. Two months earlier, Taguilla related, guerrillas had taken him into the Sohoton Mountains northeast of Basey to help construct a fortress carved into sheer limestone cliffs. The jungle bastion was defended by about two hundred men armed with bolos, two rifles and many bamboo cannon, Taguilla said. In the days that followed, Waller heard similar stories from other informants. Some estimated the size of Lukbán's force at the Sohoton cliffs at between four hundred and seven hundred men. They described the fortress as nearly impregnable, perched hundreds of feet above the river, accessible only by jungle trails studded with deadly pits, snares and other mantraps. Tony Waller was determined to capture the stronghold.

At dawn on November 6, Waller led a flotilla of light-draft boats and dugout canoes up the Cadacan River in the gauzy light. Bobbing along behind Waller's cutter was a gun platform he had personally designed—a bamboo raft with a three-inch light artillery piece lashed to the deck. About three hours upriver, the jungle on both banks erupted with rifle fire and bamboo cannon blasts from hidden guerrillas. Waller's one hundred Marines sprayed the brush with Colt machine guns and Krag-Jørgensen rifles, and the enemy broke off contact. Farther upstream, the guerrillas sprang another ambush, killing two Marines, Waller's first casualties in the Samar campaign. After pushing several more miles upstream with no sight of the enemy fortress, Waller ordered his men to turn back. It was too risky to remain in the jungle after dark. The return trip was uneventful, save for the Marines and sailors strafing the jungle to preempt enemy ambushes.

Back in Basey that evening, Waller received disturbing information from his spies. The guerrillas at Sohoton had upgraded their defenses with fifty-five rifles captured at Balangiga, and they were now lying in wait for the Americans.[20]

BEFORE LAUNCHING ANOTHER EXPEDITION AGAINST the Sohoton fortress, Waller turned his men loose in a final round of destructive operations closer to the coast. On November 10, Waller reported the results of his first two weeks on the island: 39 Filipinos killed, 18 captured, 255 houses burned, 30 canoes destroyed and 13 water buffalo slaughtered.[21]

With Smith's Christmas deadline for ending Samar operations six weeks away, Waller was now ready to conquer the island's forbidding interior. His plan called for three columns of Marines to advance into the jungle by land and water, converging on the enemy stronghold at the Sohoton cliffs. Waller would lead one of the columns and Porter a second. The third would be commanded by Captain Hiram I. Bearss.

The twenty-six-year-old Bearss was a native of Peru, Indiana, with handsomely chiseled features, a cleft chin and a lantern jaw. He was only five feet, seven inches tall, but what the muscular Bearss lacked in height he more than made up for in courage and resolve. His blazing speed on the football field had earned him the nickname "Jack Rabbit" at DePauw University, but it was another attribute that made a lasting impression. "His real merit was his heart and no small body ever carried one as big," Coach Arthur N. Sager later recalled. After leaving DePauw, Bearss attended Norwich University, an acclaimed military academy in Northfield, Vermont. There he gained renown as a star football halfback and inveterate practical joker who racked up demerits at a prodigious rate.[22]

Bearss was back in Indiana, studying law under a family friend, when war with Spain broke out in 1898. He entered the Marines with a temporary commission in May, too late to see action, and in February 1899 was mustered out of the service. Three months later, with America now at war in the Philippines, he reentered the Marines as a first lieutenant. That fall, Bearss shipped out for the islands.

While his comrades claimed glory against the Boxer rebels in China in the summer of 1900, Bearss was being schooled in the new style of warfare that confronted the Americans in the Philippines, leading counterinsurgency patrols through the hills and jungles around Subic Bay. He was reunited with Waller there the following summer, and when the Marines were ordered to Samar after Balangiga, Waller made sure the tough Hoosier was assigned to his command. Within days of his arrival on the island, the tireless Bearss earned the sobriquet that he would carry to his grave: Hiking Hiram.

On November 14, Waller began his thrust into the Samar interior by
setting in motion from Balangiga a column commanded by Porter. The
following day, Bearss led his contingent of fifty Marines from Basey, and
on November 16 Waller set out by boat up the Cadacan River. Bearss left
a trail of destruction on his march, destroying 165 houses along the way.
On the afternoon of the sixteenth, Bearss and Porter joined forces, and
by evening the Marines were within sight of the guerrilla stronghold.

Lukbán's commander in the area, Juan Colinares, had spent three
years preparing the Sohoton fortress as a last bastion against the Americans. Camps and workshops sprawled along opposing limestone cliffs that
towered two hundred feet above the Cadacan River. Caves and grottoes
honeycombed the porous rock. The guerrillas had enlarged some of the
passages and hacked out bunkers and footholds connected by a lattice-
work of bamboo ladders. Woven baskets packed with rocks dangled from
vine ropes, ready to be dropped on attackers attempting to scale the cliffs
from the river. Overland trails to the cliffs bristled with stake-lined pits,
spring-loaded spears and other lethal snares. Forty bamboo cannon were
positioned to scythe an enemy assault force with shrapnel.

As the moon rose over the cliffs, Porter and Bearss waited in the
jungle with their Marines. Waller was just downstream with another fifty
men and the three-inch artillery piece, ready to provide fire support for
Porter's assault. But the rocks suspended above the river concerned
Waller, and a garbled exchange of messages left Porter and Bearss with
the understanding that the major had decided to hold his force in reserve
rather than risk his boats in the initial assault. The young lions would
attack without Waller.[23]

Early on the morning of November 17, Porter and Bearss led their men
along a trap-studded trail toward the enemy camps on the left bank of the
river. The Americans suddenly stopped, their pathway blocked by a battery of bamboo cannon. Corporal Harry Glenn rushed up the trail and
yanked a burning fuse from one of the guns before it could blast the column at point-blank range. With Porter in the lead, the Marines charged
over the crest of the cliffs and found themselves in a camp that had been
abandoned in such haste that rice pots were still cooking over open fires.

A Marine spotted two guerrilla camps across the river, and Porter ordered his men to bring up the Colt machine gun and take up combat positions. The Americans opened fire on the unsuspecting Filipinos, and began to make their way down the cliff to search for a way across the river. Two dugout canoes and a raft were found, and the Marines paddled across under fire and quickly established a beachhead on the opposite bank.

As their comrades atop the opposite precipice kept the guerrillas pinned down, Marines clawed their way up the sheer cliffs on the right bank. Some shredded their shoes on the jagged limestone, and many were barefoot and bleeding by the time they reached the top. A thin line of Marines formed along the crest and charged toward the enemy positions. After firing two volleys the guerrillas fled through the jungle. Another camp was discovered, and the Americans quickly routed its occupants. After a few more minutes of scattered fighting, the battle was over. Thirty guerrillas lay dead and forty bamboo cannon had been destroyed, along with stores of rice and other food and supplies. The Marines had taken the vaunted Sohoton fortress without a single casualty.[24]

THOUGH DISAPPOINTED TO FIND THE battle over by the time he arrived, Waller could not have been more generous in his praise of Porter and Bearss. "These officers carried out their instructions in the face of hardships, dangers, and incredible obstacles," he wrote. "Not only was personal courage of a high order displayed, but intelligence, discrimination, and zeal."[25] Porter and Bearss lauded Sergeant John Quick of Cuba fame for covering the second cliff-top assault with his devastating machine gun fire, and Corporal Glenn for saving his comrades from death or serious injury by defusing a bamboo cannon that was about to fire into their ranks.

Waller's report to General Smith cast the Sohoton triumph as "the most important of the whole campaign as far as [its] effect on the insurgents were concerned. We have proved to them that their impregnable places can be taken." In a separate letter to Smith, Waller waxed poetic in praise of his Marines, who had achieved everything men could accomplish "without wings."

Smith managed to surpass Waller's rhetoric. "There is nothing impossible for the American fighting men," he wrote, "and your work in the

Sohoton Province is an additional proof of that fact. Success by bare-footed Americans began at Valley Forge, and I am proud to know that the same indomitable spirit that won in spite of obstacles over one hundred years ago has shown itself in Samar."

The Navy and Marine brass added their accolades, and even the cranky General Chaffee was moved to soaring prose as he saluted the "manly heart and soldierly spirit" of Waller's Marines, "which makes light of obstacles and is never daunted or satisfied while service can be rendered to our country."

WITH THEIR RATIONS EXHAUSTED AND shoes and uniforms in tatters, the Marines withdrew to the coast to rest and recuperate. But Waller was just getting started. He talked of following the Cadacan River even deeper into the heart of Samar, then "striking a trail that I know to exist and which will lead me out to the east coast near Hernani."

On November 27, Waller led his men back up the Cadacan River in search of guerrillas and the cross-island trail that increasingly dominated his thoughts. The Marines established a supply camp about two miles above the Sohoton fortress and began to explore their surroundings. A patrol led by Captain Robert H. Dunlap, a future brigadier general, stumbled onto the hastily abandoned camp of guerrilla commander Juan Colinares and captured a small brass cannon, powder mills, twenty-seven bamboo guns, tools, bolos, spearheads and scrap-iron projectiles.

Meanwhile, Porter led a column that hacked its way deeper into the jungle before turning back at the base of a formidable mountain. On the return march, Porter's men had come across a well-worn trail to the northeast. Waller was convinced that it was a fabled Spanish route to Samar's east coast—a discovery that he believed would allow the Americans to divide guerrilla forces and bring the island to heel. Waller could barely contain his excitement at the prospect of a cross-island march in the spirit of history's great soldier-explorers. In his mind's eye, clouded as it was with an insatiable thirst for glory, he could not have imagined the terrible fate that awaited his Marines in the Samar jungle.

CHAPTER 19

Death in the Jungle

C hristmas Eve, 1901, found Major Tony Waller on the move again as he prepared to launch his expedition across Samar. In the weeks since their last foray into the island's interior, the Marines had kept busy with daily patrols and search-and-destroy operations, "killing all we come across," observed Private Harold Kinman.[1] The 350 guerrillas operating in southwestern Samar had been "so punished by the repeated hammerings and by the capture of their stronghold that they have scattered and fled" into the swamps and jungles, Waller reported to General Jake Smith.[2]

Smith had not ended the war on Samar by Christmas, as he had promised General Chaffee, but it was not for lack of effort. The sixty-one-year-old brigadier general had conducted the campaign with the zeal of a young company commander, spending days on end personally overseeing field operations. As the year drew to a close, his belief that Lukbán's guerrillas owed their survival to Samar's affluent merchants, landowners and Catholic clergy became the impetus for even harsher policy. On Christmas Eve, Smith issued a sixteen-hundred-word circular that laid out the treachery of the island's ruling class—and the severe consequences they would now suffer to "create in all the minds of all the people a burning desire for the war to cease. . . ." Henceforth, the island's rich and powerful would have to prove their loyalty through concrete acts. They would be compelled to reveal guerrilla hiding places and weapons caches, and even guide American patrols through the jungle. Once again, Smith invoked the spirit of General Sherman to justify his latest escalation. "Short, severe wars are the most humane in the end," he declared. "No civilized war, however civilized, can be carried on on a humanitarian basis."[3]

Waller, meanwhile, had continued to bask in the glory of his Sohoton victory. So pleased had Smith been with Waller's performance that he had recommended the Marine for a brevet colonelcy. With Smith's blessing, Waller headed east with a hundred Marines on December 8 to mount operations in the southeastern corner of his territory before continuing on to the east coast to begin his cross-island expedition. Heavy monsoon rains had rolled in off the Pacific, turning campsites into mud holes, streams into raging torrents, and the jungle into one vast swamp. After a grueling ten-day march, the Marines finally arrived at the southeastern town of Pambuhan. They had killed eight guerrillas along the way, but resistance had been so scarce as to convince Waller that his work was complete. "Of course there will be bands of *ladrones* to encounter," he wrote Smith, "but this condition has existed several hundred years and, in my humble opinion, will continue until by education and prosperity these people are taught where their interests lie."[4]

WALLER'S DECLARATION OF VICTORY SET the stage for his cross-island expedition. He had first pitched the idea to Smith in late October, proposing the creation of a chain of outposts stretching from coast to coast, allowing the Marines to interdict the flow of supplies to Lukbán in the north and isolating the remaining guerrillas in the south. Smith was receptive. He believed that Waller's expedition could identify the best route for a telephone line that could connect his isolated east coast outposts with his headquarters on Leyte. It was agreed that Waller would launch his expedition from the east coast, blazing a trail through the island's interior to Basey, on Samar's southwest coast.[5]

It was a daunting proposition, but not unprecedented. In June 1901, two companies of the 1st U.S. Infantry had hiked from Borongan on the east coast to Catbalogan in five days. The men suffered from thirst and fatigue as they scaled cliffs and mountains, but conditions were dry and conducive to hiking. The march had proven that the island could be traversed—at least during Samar's drier months.[6]

Waller, on the other hand, would be setting out at the height of the Samar monsoon season, through an area that averages more than three inches of rain a *week*—and far more during the months of November through January. The Sohoton campaign had given him a taste of the travails lurking in the Samar jungle, but little experience with the sort of mountainous terrain that lay in his path. Some of the ridgelines approached two thousand feet, with slopes exceeding 50 percent grade, and the heavy jungle teemed with leeches, poisonous snakes and a legion of biting and stinging insects.

Equally problematic was the fact that Waller had done little research for his trek. His request for maps and reconnaissance reports had been returned with apologies by Smith's headquarters. "Sorry to say," explained Smith's adjutant, "we have no maps at all of the kind you ask for." The extent of Waller's logistical preparations consisted of setting up a supply camp near the Sohoton cliffs, past the halfway point of his passage. He had concluded that his trek would take less than a week, a calculation based on the straight-line distance from Lanang to Basey, about forty miles.[7] Undaunted, Waller boarded a gunboat in Pambuhan on Christmas Eve for the short voyage up the coast to Lanang.

Perched along the Pacific coast at the point where the Lanang River emptied into the ocean, the town (now known as Llorente) was garrisoned by a company of the Army's 1st Infantry. It was so far off the beaten path that food and medical supplies ran chronically low and months passed without mail from home.[8] Waller was briefing the garrison commander, Captain James Pickering, on his plans when the garrison's second in command, Lieutenant Kenneth Williams, stumbled in after a fruitless twelve-day search for the Spanish trail. Williams described the hardships of the trek through mountainous jungle, a debilitating journey even with prepositioned supplies and shelters. He and his commander urged Waller to postpone his expedition.[9]

At dinner, the Army officers again tried to convince their guest to cancel his expedition. Waller refused, even after revealing that the Marines had exhausted most of their supplies during the march to the east coast. He asked for six days' rations for fifty men and thirty Filipino bearers, but Captain Pickering was in no position to help—he barely had enough food to sustain his own men until January 5, when the next supply ship was due. Pickering offered Waller a four-day supply of bacon, hard-tack and coffee.[10] If everything went right, it would sustain the Marines through the treacherous jungle. Unfortunately for Waller and his men, almost nothing would go right.

ON THE MORNING OF SATURDAY, December 28, 1901, fifty-five U.S. Marines armed with Krag-Jørgenson rifles made their way down the steep banks of the Lanang River, just upstream from the crashing swells of the Pacific Ocean. Dark-skinned Filipino bearers loaded packs and bedrolls into dugout canoes, and Waller and his men took their places in the low-riding craft. As the canoes turned into the surging current with a rhythmic flurry of paddles, the sun broke through the clouds for the first time in days.[11] With this good omen, Waller and his Marines disappeared into the Samar jungle.

Waller had handpicked his best men for the journey, beginning with his choice of deputy commander, twenty-four-year-old Captain David Dixon Porter. Completing the command group were "Hiking Hiram" Bearss, twenty-four-year-old First Lieutenant Alexander S. Williams of New York City, and twenty-one-year-old First Lieutenant Frank Halford of Indianapolis, Indiana. Sergeant John Quick would ride herd on fifty enlisted Marines, veterans of China and the Samar campaign. A pair of Filipino scouts would guide the expedition, and thirty-three native por-ters would paddle the canoes and carry supplies.

The expedition forged upstream under sunny skies, past spindly coco-nut palms and magnificent stands of vine-cloaked Philippine mahogany and other towering hardwoods. From the comfort of a dry canoe, the jungle presented a magnificent sight: Trumpet-shaped orchids and other epiphytes dangled from the canopy; lush clumps of nipa palms swayed along the water's edge; occasional waterfalls cascaded over sheer cliffs.[12] The outrigger-equipped canoes moved easily through the water, and by the time Waller ordered the men ashore to make camp, the expedition had logged seventeen miles.

The men got under way again at first light, following the north branch of the Lanang River as it twisted through the jungle. Ahead lay misty mountains concealed by a thick canopy that appeared more benign and gently contoured than it was in fact. Down on the ground, the terrain revealed its true nature—plunging ravines, tortuously winding streams and rivers and sharply rising ridgelines, all cloaked in steamy jungle.

A few miles upstream, Waller and his men encountered the first in a series of rapids and waterfalls. The Marines and bearers expended much time and energy getting the boats past the treacherous obstacles, but soon the canoes could go no farther. Waller ordered the expedition to proceed on foot. Torrential rains began to fall, and the men spent the remainder of the day crossing and recrossing the raging river as it tumbled down the steep mountainside. Nightfall found the Marines exhausted from the hard hiking, and water sores and raw patches had begun to form on their skin. Their misery was compounded by their failure to start a fire. The men sat shivering in the rain, eating a meager dinner of raw bacon and soggy hardtack.

By the third day, the incessant rains had transformed small brooks into raging torrents, forcing the men to slash their way through the jungle to avoid the rising waters. "The knowledge that we had made 4 or 5 miles in direction for each 12 miles of march was depressing," Waller wrote. "Day after day followed, with the same arduous and dangerous crossing and recrossing of the river."[13] Worried by the increasingly slow pace, Waller had already reduced rations when one of the Marines took it upon himself to discard the wet hardtack. The blunder now made hunger a constant companion of the Marines.

As they slogged through the dungeonlike world beneath the triple-canopy jungle, the Americans were surrounded by an endless sea of green that grew more monotonous with each passing hour. Starvation was only one of a growing number of threats. Cobras and pythons inhabited the Samar rain forest, along with monkeys, birds and other creatures, but they remained unseen, practicing the survivor's arts of camouflage and

concealment. The men became miserably acquainted with the most vora-
cious of the jungle predators: mosquitoes, ants and leeches. Thirteen years
later, after surviving his own near-death experience in the Amazon rain
forest, Theodore Roosevelt would pay tribute to the deadly perils of the
jungle's smallest creatures. "These insects, and the fevers they cause, and
dysentery and starvation and wearing hardship and accidents in rapids
are what the pioneer explorers have to fear."[14]

Thrashing through the heavy undergrowth, the Marines struggled to
catch their breath in the saunalike air. Vines and thorny bushes ripped
their soggy uniforms, and sharp rocks tore their shoes. "We had seen no
signs of human beings, except once in a while a lonely temporary fishing
shack," Waller wrote. "The banks of the river were high and mountainous, covered with massive timbers and a network of vines and undergrowth. There were not even birds to break the monotony."[15] Aside from
the river, rain or occasional falling tree, the only sounds were the swish
of bolos slashing the undergrowth and the curses and labored steps as
men slipped and stumbled through the muck.

Waller and his men spent their third night in the jungle on a "wretched
little sand and shingle bar" along the river. They managed to start a fire,
then huddled together as they sipped coffee and ate two slices of bacon
each. They awoke to more rain, and spent the last day of 1901 slashing
a trail up a steep ridgeline. By now, blisters and water sores made walking difficult for many of the men. With the pace of the march slowing
even more, Waller further reduced rations by half, and cut meals to two a
day.

The men reached the narrow crest of a hogback ridge in the waning
light of December 31. Waller's map showed the Spanish trail passing this
point, but it was heartbreakingly clear to all that it did not exist. As night
fell, the Marines hacked a small bivouac from the underbrush. Shivering
in their wet and torn uniforms as a cold wind howled, Waller and his men
settled in for a miserable New Year's Eve.[16]

The Marines began the first day of 1902 hungry and tired, and their
condition quickly deteriorated as they hacked their way down the steep
back slope. Some suffered fevers from prolonged exposure to the elements
and infected water sores, cuts and leech bites. Some could barely hobble

on raw and bloody feet. They moved by compass to the west-southwest, hopeful they were nearing the familiar territory of the Sohoton River. They came upon a westward-flowing river, and with each step expectations rose that the ordeal was about to end. But in the late afternoon the river suddenly began to turn north, not south as the men had hoped, and then, with cruel abruptness, it merged into a large river that flowed due east—back through the jungle they had traversed for six brutal days.

That evening, Waller gathered his officers for a grim council. Some of the men were nearly too sick and weak to take another step. Rations had been reduced again to one-third of the normal daily allotment, and dinner consisted of a single slice of raw bacon per man. The paramount question before the Marines was whether they should turn back. Waller believed the waterway before them was the Suribao River, which emptied into the Pacific a few miles up the coast from Lanang. But, loath to admit defeat, he recommended they press forward. A vote was taken, and Waller was overruled. They would build rafts and float down the Suribao to the east coast.[17]

In the gray light of morning, the men gathered logs, lashed them together with vines and launched the vessel with one man aboard. It promptly sank. With many of the Marines now barely able to walk, Waller laid out his emergency plan. He would take Lieutenant Halford and thirteen of the strongest men and strike out for Basey to the southwest. The main column, under the command of Captain Porter, would follow as fast as the weakest could move. Gathering his group, Waller set off through the jungle.

AFTER STUMBLING ALONG WALLER'S TRAIL for a day, Porter sent word ahead that his disheartened men were begging to build another raft. Waller put his group to work, and a bamboo craft was launched into the river with one man aboard, but it, too, promptly sank. Waller instructed Porter to make one final attempt to launch a raft. If successful, Waller would turn back and oversee their escape by river.

While awaiting further word from Porter, Waller led his men ahead through the jungle. After two hours they came to a clearing planted with banana trees, young coconut palms (prized by the natives for their edible heart), sweet potatoes and greens. They collected all the food they could carry, and continued on until they found another clearing planted with well-tended sweet potatoes and greens. The sun broke through the overcast for the first time in days and, using the lenses from Waller's field glasses, the Marines built a fire and cooked enough sweet potatoes to last two days.

As Waller and his men ate and rested in the clearing, Captain Bearss arrived from Porter's contingent with another Marine and Waller's messenger. Bearss reported that the raft built by the main group had also sunk. Waller scribbled another note to Porter, ordering his deputy to bring his men forward to the clearings, where they could rest and eat before continuing on. In the meantime, Waller would press ahead to the supply camp near the Sohoton cliffs and bring back food, clothing and shoes as fast as possible.

An hour passed with no sign of Porter's column, and Waller ordered his men to move out. They picked up a trail and followed it until nightfall, making camp on a gravel bar along the river. As the Marines sat around a campfire, feasting on sweet potatoes, Waller's messenger arrived. He told Waller that he had been too afraid of running into guerrillas to find Porter, and so he had turned back. Reassured by Bearss that their comrades would continue to follow their trail, Waller decided to press ahead.[18]

For three more days, Waller led his men through the forest. Many were barefoot, their shoes having disintegrated. At times the Marines soared across swift-flowing rivers on swinging vines, and they climbed and descended one ridgeline after another, working west-southwest as best as they could with a broken compass. Finally, they came upon another clearing and seized five Filipinos they found living there. Awaking early the next morning, they set off through the jungle with one of their captives, a dark-skinned boy, as a guide.

At daylight on January 6, their tenth day in the jungle, Waller and his ragged band awoke and each man ate a slice of raw bacon before resuming the march. They reached the Cadacan River, their route inland during the Sohoton cliffs assault, and were preparing to set off downstream in a large dugout canoe they found when a cutter carrying Captain Dunlap and his resupply party chugged into sight. Joy swept over Waller and his men as they dragged themselves aboard. Some of the Marines wept quietly. Others laughed hysterically. They were gaunt and shoeless, their clothes shredded, their bodies covered with cuts and sores and the bloody bites of leeches and insects. But a far worse fate awaited their comrades left behind in the jungle.

CAPTAIN PORTER HAD FOLLOWED WALLER'S trail with the thirty-seven Marines in his charge until the morning of January 3, when he was handed Waller's message ordering a final attempt to build rafts. Porter understood the note to say that Waller would rejoin the main column shortly. When he never appeared, Porter decided to lead his men back to the east coast. He ordered their few remaining cans of bacon distributed for a final meal before breaking camp. From here on, Porter and his men would eat only what they could forage in the forest.

Porter set off first with a fast-moving vanguard that would attempt to alert the Army garrison at Lanang to the unfolding disaster. Williams would hold in place for a while to see whether Waller appeared, then follow with the remaining men. Porter laid out his plan in a note that he placed in a small tin can tied to a tree along their trail. And then, with Sergeant Quick, six Marines and six Filipino bearers, Porter headed east through the jungle toward Lanang.[19]

UPON REACHING BASEY ON THE afternoon of January 6, Waller ordered a relief party readied. It departed the following morning on the Marine cutter, heading up the Cadacan River with orders to establish a camp near the forest shack where Waller had seized his young guide. There they were to await Waller's arrival with more men and supplies.

Waller, meanwhile, steamed over to Tacloban to pick up a new uniform and publicize his latest feat. He briefed General Smith's adjutant on the march ("the most difficult ever made in the Philippine Islands," Waller called it) and filed a self-aggrandizing report to Rear Admiral

Rodgers that soon hit the *New York Times* and other U.S. papers.[20] The *Times* article, headlined "Major Waller's Feat," made no mention of the unfolding disaster that Waller had left behind in the jungle.

On January 8, nearly forty-eight hours after his rescue, Waller headed back up the Cadacan River to direct the search for his men. For eight days, he and his rescue party stumbled through the jungle. Finally, with his rations exhausted and his men sick and physically spent, Waller called off the search and headed back to the coast. After briefing General Smith on the latest developments, he returned to his headquarters in Basey. Feverish and suffering from an injured ankle, Waller collapsed into bed.

AFTER LEAVING LIEUTENANT WILLIAMS WITH the sickest Marines, Porter had expected to reach Lanang in four days. It took him twice that long. "Words are inadequate to describe the suffering and hardships endured, resulting from the lack of food, constant downpour of rain, floods, and sore feet," Porter wrote afterward. On the eighth day, four of Porter's men could go no farther, and they were left beside a jungle potato patch. Later that morning, Porter found the expedition's canoes, and he and his men set off down the raging Lanang River. Darkness had fallen when Porter and his men reached the coast. Captain Pickering readied a relief party of ten soldiers, an Army surgeon and thirty Filipino porters to head into the jungle to rescue the lost Marines.

For two days, Lieutenant Kenneth Williams tried to launch the relief expedition, but the raging river nearly swept his seven canoes out to sea. In the predawn darkness of January 14, Williams and his men managed to fight their way upstream from Lanang, and for several exhausting hours, they dodged uprooted trees, coconuts and other debris as they struggled upriver. They made camp on a slope above the river, and huddled there for the next thirty-six hours before they were able to launch their canoes again in the rising floodwaters. After another grueling day on the river, the weary soldiers reached the barrio where the Marines had first set out on foot. They found the four Marines whom Porter had left beside the jungle potato patch and put them in a canoe for the journey back to the coast, then headed deeper into the forest.[21]

NOTHING IN HIS YOUNG LIFE could have prepared First Lieutenant Alexander Shives Williams Jr. for the ordeal of leading thirty sick and dying Marines through the Samar jungle. The son of a corrupt New York City police inspector forced into retirement by Commissioner Theodore Roosevelt, Williams graduated from Columbia University and entered the Marine Corps as a second lieutenant in 1899. The blue-eyed, ruddy-cheeked Marine had performed ably after arriving in the Philippines in June 1900, but now he faced a crisis that would have overwhelmed even the most experienced officer.

Williams had attempted to lead his sick and exhausted band in Porter's footsteps after they separated on January 3, but the worsening rains and failing strength of his men made progress difficult. Rising floodwaters had submerged the trails the Marines had blazed on their outbound trek, and Williams and his men struggled for two and a half days to scale the slippery mountainside that the Marines had descended in several hours on their outbound journey. After finally reaching the mountaintop bivouac where the Marines had spent their bleak New Year's Eve, Williams and his men endured an equally grueling descent before collapsing in a clearing. There the strongest of the group scoured the forest, finding enough wild tubers and edible greens for two paltry meals.

In their weakened state, Williams and his Marines became convinced their Filipino bearers were withholding food and plotting to kill them. On January 9, their thirteenth day in the jungle, Williams commanded his starving men to move out. But twenty-six-year-old Private Joseph Baroni of Bangor, Maine, was too sick to move, and he was left behind. From this point on, "my recollection of time and events is very hazy," Williams wrote. "By day we stumbled painfully forward and by night lay in a stupor, tormented by the most vivid dreams of food and comforts." Some of the Marines were so "despairing in mind and so nearly dead from starvation and exposure that they could not crawl, and, most cases, move." Hard-drinking Private Timothy Murray, a thirty-four-year-old immigrant from Athlone, Ireland, became the second Marine to sit down in the jungle to await death. Eight more would do likewise in the days ahead.

As the situation became more desperate, unlikely heroes emerged. Three privates became a source of "constant hopefulness and expressed determination" for the group, bucking up the spirits of Williams and their disconsolate comrades. One of them was twenty-three-year-old Richard Kittle, who had grown up on a farm in New York's Catskills and worked as a coachman in New York City before joining the Marines.

On January 17, after twenty-one days in the forest, Williams and the surviving members of his band stumbled into the high clearing about a mile above the Lanang River. They found a few tubers to eat, and, in their semilucid state, began setting up camp. When Williams ordered three Filipino bearers to search for firewood, the men refused. One struck Williams with a bolo, "inflicting several small wounds," he reported afterward. A sergeant named McCaffery staggered to the lieutenant's aid, rifle raised, but he was too weak to work the bolt. The three Filipinos ran into the jungle.

THE FOLLOWING MORNING, A FEW miles away, the Army rescuers led by Lieutenant Kenneth Williams struggled up the Lanang River against the swift current. As they fought their way through the rapids, their canoes capsized repeatedly, dumping soldiers and supplies into the frothing waters. Each time the canoes were retrieved and the push upstream resumed.[22] About nine thirty a.m., as the rescuers struggled through a particularly difficult stretch of river, eleven gunshots rang out from the slope above them. The attackers quickly broke off contact, but now it became a competition between the soldiers and the guerrillas as to who would reach the missing Marines first.

The race ended in shocking fashion a few minutes later when the Army team arrived at a riverside clearing to find ten Marines sprawled in the mud and driving rain. They had been sent ahead by Alex Williams to make contact with any rescue party that might be searching for them, and had survived by killing two dogs and devouring them raw. Now they lay about "without shoes, shirts, or trousers enough to cover their privates." Only two were able to stand. The others were "delirious with fevers" and unable to rise.[23]

The Army team rushed to their aide, feeding those who could eat and providing medical attention to the others. They pitched tents and made the men as comfortable as possible, then set off up the mountainside to find the remaining Marines. The rescuers hacked and clawed their way up the slope, wading and swimming across swollen streams as they worked their way higher. More than a mile above the river, they found Alex Williams and nine enlisted Marines scattered around a clearing, semiconscious, nearly naked and "on the verge of starvation and death."

The soldiers and Filipino bearers tenderly carried Williams and his men back down the mountainside and launched the canoes. The boats shot downstream like logs in a flume, careening through rapids that flipped some of the boats and dumped their occupants into the churning waters. Miraculously, not a man was lost. Just before nightfall the boats reached Lanang.

Captain Porter and Sergeant Quick were at the water's edge as the Marines were carried ashore, and they escorted the ghastly procession to the post hospital. For the first time in three weeks, Alex Williams and his men savored the pleasure of a bed, clean sheets and pillows, shielded from the incessant rain and swarming insects. As an Army surgeon attended to the Americans, the delirious Williams told a chilling tale of death and betrayal in the jungle.

ON THE MORNING OF JANUARY 20, the Navy gunboat USS *Arayat* arrived at Tacloban with Porter, Alex Williams, Sergeant Quick and the other twenty-two Marines who had reached Lanang. Two would die in the following days, including the heroic Private Kittle. Also aboard the gunboat, clapped in irons belowdecks, were the expedition's Filipino bearers. They had freely returned to the Army garrison at Lanang, only to face the murderous rage of the survivors. Among the purported evidence of treachery was the fact that several bearers and a scout known as Slim had watched the assault on Alex Williams and had done nothing.

In Tacloban, Porter had an officer telephone Waller in Basey with the news that he would be sending several mutinous Filipinos to him. Sergeant Quick accompanied the men across the San Juanico Strait that afternoon and found Waller lying on a cot, feverish and swathed in bandages from head to foot. Shocked by the news that ten Marines had been left in the jungle, Waller listened quietly as Quick accused the Filipino porters of attempting to murder his men. Porter and Alex Williams recommended that the natives be shot, Quick reported. Waller asked the sergeant's opinion. "I would shoot them all down like mad dogs," Quick replied.[24]

In his muddled state, Waller became convinced that the actions of the Filipino scouts and porters were part of a larger plot by guerrillas hidden in their midst. That afternoon, without trial or investigation, eleven Filipinos who had served Waller's expedition were led into Basey's central plaza by armed Marines. The crack of Krag-Jørgensen rifles shattered the air, and the accused men fell dead.

Two days later, Waller's fever broke and he composed a telegram to General Smith. "It became necessary to expend eleven prisoners," Waller reported without elaboration. "Ten who were implicated in the attack on Lieutenant Williams and one who plotted against me."

THREE DAYS AFTER THE KILLINGS, General Adna Chaffee arrived in Tacloban for an inspection tour. A rumor had reached the general that the Marines had executed some prisoners. Now, riding in a horse-drawn Army ambulance to the 6th Separate Brigade headquarters, Chaffee suddenly turned to Jake Smith. "Smith," he demanded, "have you been having any promiscuous killing in Samar for fun?"

Smith would later testify that he had yet to see Waller's telegram and was baffled by Chaffee's question. "No, sir," he replied.

"Well," Chaffee continued, "I understand that at Basey they have been killing some people over there."[25]

Chaffee's sudden interest in summary executions and other unsavory deeds by U.S. soldiers on Samar was no coincidence. Ten thousand miles away, news reports on the extreme nature of Hell-roaring Jake Smith's campaign had triggered fresh questions and debate over the conduct of American troops in the Philippines. A political tempest was about to engulf President Roosevelt.

PART IV

Questions of Honor

CHAPTER 20

"Deeds of Hideous Cruelty"

A t the stroke of nine o'clock on Thursday evening, January 30, 1902, a trio of buglers sounded a regal call, and President Theodore Roosevelt and his wife, Edith, stepped onto the landing above the White House Grand Foyer. Several hundred guests applauded as the elegantly attired first couple glided down the carpeted stairway, accompanied by representatives of the armed services and members of the Cabinet, led by Secretary of War and Mrs. Elihu Root. The dignitaries paused as the Marine Corps band played "The Star-Spangled Banner," and then swept into the Blue Room to greet the guests gathered for the annual Army and Navy reception.[1]

In his first four months in office, the forty-three-year-old Roosevelt had lived up to his reputation for bold action. He had outraged Southern whites by dining at the White House with black educator Booker T. Washington and provoked big business by calling for congressional regulation of trusts. He had also delighted expansionists (and infuriated anti-imperialists) by vowing to build more battleships, construct a canal across Central America and colonize the Philippines.

The grand old Executive Mansion that Roosevelt had officially christened the "White House" looked magnificent this evening swathed in

American flags and blazing azaleas. Brilliant flag and floral arrangements were matched by the colorful sight of the nation's military luminaries, medals and ribbons arrayed against crisp dress uniforms. Among the storied American soldiers present were the Army commander General Nelson Miles, Marine Corps Commandant Charles Heywood and Rear Admiral Robley Evans.

It was fitting that Roosevelt should conclude his first White House social season by honoring the armed forces, for America's men in uniform had secured the nation's rise as a global power over the previous four years. And now the most controversial episode in America's emergence—the conquest of the Philippines—was nearly complete as harsh campaigns sanctioned by Roosevelt extinguished the last embers of rebellion. "Terrible Reprisals in Samar," the *Washington Post* had reported a few weeks earlier. "American Troops Engaged in a Campaign of Extermination and Devastation." In the Luzon province of Batangas, Brigadier General J. Franklin Bell had broken resistance by forcing civilians into resettlement camps—the very policy condemned by Roosevelt and others when employed by Spain against Cuban guerrillas a few years earlier.

The Filipino guerrillas were all but finished, but not U.S. opponents of the war. The grim news reports from Samar (along with General Jacob Smith's provocative pronouncements) had revived calls in the United States for a review of the military's conduct in the Philippines. The usual suspects at the Anti-Imperialist League, along with bestselling author Mark Twain, continued to crank out pamphlets and books denouncing America's actions in the islands.

On Capitol Hill, the Philippines still stirred passions like no other issue. An ongoing Senate debate over a tariff bill for the islands had become the latest pretext for Democrats and Republicans to reprise their arguments over duty and national honor. The prospect of an even more riveting drama now loomed, for Republican Senator George Frisbie Hoar had goaded the president and Senator Henry Cabot Lodge into holding hearings that would examine alleged U.S. abuses in the islands. Now, as they prepared to receive the nation's military officers in the White House Blue Room, Roosevelt and Root could only hope that any damaging revelations could be contained behind the closed doors of the Senate committee hearings set to get under way the following morning.[2]

For two hours Roosevelt and the first lady, her hair glittering with diamond side combs and blue ostrich tips, exchanged pleasantries with the long line of diplomats and soldiers that stretched through the Blue Room. As the procession filed past the president, General Miles commanded his own crowd of well-wishers. Tall and handsome, the vain veteran of Civil War and Indian campaigns was popular within the Army, and a recent public scolding by Roosevelt had not sat well with many Americans. Miles and his wife took their places in line and soon stood before the president. As countless eyes looked on, the recent antagonists smiled and exchanged cordial greetings.

It was all for show. The contempt that Roosevelt and his Army commander held for each other was deep and unbridled, and it was about to explode into open conflict over the issue of U.S. military abuses in the Philippines.[3]

At ten thirty the following morning, Senator Henry Cabot Lodge gaveled his Committee on the Philippines to order, and the long-awaited examination of American conduct in the distant islands got under way in a richly paneled Capitol committee room. From the outset the hearings played out as political theater, with the minority Democrats intent on bloodying the administration and the Republican majority determined to highlight America's good deeds in the islands.

Lodge summoned the committee's first witness, and William Howard Taft, the administration's portly governor in the Philippines, stepped forward. Carefully prompted by friendly senators, Taft characterized the transition to civilian rule in the islands as proceeding smoothly, interspersing his comments with rambling discourses on climate and geography, native hospitality, and other banal topics.[4] The authoritative Albert Beveridge of Indiana did his part to keep the hearings on script, frequently reminding his colleagues that only he among them had actually spent time in the islands. But after three years of brutal war, Democrats were in no mood for a seminar on Philippine trivia.

The bitterness that now seethed behind the closed committee doors had been foreshadowed on the Senate floor in the preceding days. "You have butchered three times as many people in the Philippines as the Spanish did in the course of three centuries," Democrat Benjamin Tillman of South Carolina had railed earlier in the week. "To kill men with arms in their hands is another thing from burning men at the stake," riposted John C. Spooner, the powerful Wisconsin Republican, referring to a particularly gruesome lynching in Tennessee that had recently come to light. When Henry M. Teller, a Colorado Republican who had turned against the administration's expansionist policies, charged GOP colleagues with concealing the truth about the Philippines, Lodge rushed across the chamber to confront his accuser.[5]

The Massachusetts senator did not strike his colleague, as some feared, but it was a preview of the unpleasantness to come. Despite his best efforts, Lodge briefly lost control of the hearings on February 4, when Taft came under questioning about the severe nature of the war in the islands. American "retaliatory measures," Taft patiently explained, had been provoked by Filipino actions. "Under those circumstances, it is not to be wondered at that similar small bodies of American soldiers . . . with the lack of strength of character incident to lack of experience, should possibly at times have yielded in their outraged feelings against the Filipinos and have resorted to methods which under the circumstances they regarded as more or less justified."[6]

What sorts of cruelty had been committed by American troops? Democrat Charles A. Culberson of Texas drawled.

"I have heard charges of whippings and charges of what has been alluded to as the water cure," Taft blithely responded. "They were rife in Manila."

Had Taft heard of a particular case involving the executions of two Filipino prisoners by General Frederick Funston's 20th Kansas? Culberson pressed.

The flustered Taft stunned the senators with his response:

> What I am trying to do is to state what seemed to us to be the expla-
> nation of these cruelties—that cruelties have been inflicted; that
> people have been shot when they ought not to have been; that there

have been in individual instances of water cure, that torture which I believe involves pouring water down the throat so that the man swells and gets the impression that he is going to be suffocated and then tells what he knows, which was a frequent treatment under the Spaniards, I am told—all these things are true.

Catching himself, Taft awkwardly tried to make light of the use of the water cure on America's colonial subjects. "There are some rather amusing instances of Filipinos who came in and said they would not say anything until they were tortured," he said.

When the loquacious governor finally stopped talking, Lodge tried to limit the damage. Surely our soldiers had been provoked by the mistreatment of their colleagues? he suggested. But Taft missed his cue. "There was usually very little to criticize" when it came to "treatment of American prisoners by the insurgent officers high in command," Taft replied. Hastily, he assured the committee that the overall conduct of U.S. soldiers had been exemplary. In fact, he declared, "It is my deliberate judgment that there never was a war conducted, whether against inferior races or not, in which there were more compassion and restraint and more generosity, assuming that there was a war at all, than there have been in the Philippine Islands." Lodge finally spared Taft further embarrassment by gaveling the session to an end.

Taft's last day before the committee, February 20, was anticlimactic. He fielded queries from like-minded senators about health in the islands, the drinking habits of Filipinos and the moral condition of Manila ("as good as that of any American city I know of," Taft pronounced). As the session drew to a close, Taft was gently asked whether America should quit the islands.

The governor reminded his audience that he had opposed annexation of the Philippines, but his nearly two years there had filled him with "the missionary spirit" to fulfill America's civilizing and democratizing duties. "When a nation has before it a task like this, I think it is honorable on its part to carry it out." Indeed, he declared, when the political debate calmed, Americans would realize "that there was no other course for us to pursue than the one we have pursued."[7]

[handwritten margin note: Congressional committee investigates The Culprts]

As the investigation unfolded, President Roosevelt and senior administration officials projected a mood of insouciance. But their public posture concealed growing concerns. General Miles was now threatening to publicly air the Army's dirty laundry if Roosevelt did not give him a greater role in the island's military affairs. On February 17, during a White House meeting, Miles showed the president the draft of a letter he had written to Root, alleging systematic brutality by U.S. soldiers in the Philippines. He vowed to end the abuses if Roosevelt would send him to the islands.[8]

Roosevelt was incensed by the threat, and he set in motion an administration counterattack. Root dispatched a letter to the Lodge committee that defended the behavior of U.S. troops in the Philippines, and echoed the argument of military field commanders and Taft that occasional brutal acts by U.S. soldiers were a natural reaction to terrible provocations. Any misdeeds had not been "sanctioned or permitted" by senior commanders or administration officials. To the contrary, misbehavior had been promptly investigated and punished, Root declared. He cited forty-four cases of cruelty that had been prosecuted in military courts, resulting in thirty-nine convictions (although he failed to note that he had reduced the punishment in many of the cases). "The war in the Philippines has been conducted by the American Army with scrupulous regard for the rules of civilized warfare," Root wrote, "with careful and genuine consideration for the prisoner and the non-combatant, with self-restraint, and with humanity never surpassed."

The following day, Roosevelt began to prepare a paper trail that put the administration in the most favorable light. He wrote a "confidential" letter to Root recounting his meeting with Miles and the draft letter presented by the general. The facts assembled by Root and Taft showed that "the accusation that there had been anything resembling systematic or widespread cruelty by our troops was false," Roosevelt wrote. He contrasted the humane actions of U.S. troops in the Philippines with those of soldiers commanded by General Miles at Wounded Knee, South Dakota, in 1890. Miles's men had carried out a massacre "in which squaws, children, unarmed Indians, and armed Indians who had surrendered were killed, sometimes cold-bloodedly and with circumstances of marked brutality," and yet the Army commander had made no attempt "to investigate the matter [at Wounded Knee] or punish the perpetrators." In the Philippines, "nothing had occurred as bad as this massacre," Roosevelt wrote.[9]

Meanwhile, Root broadened his own inquiry into U.S. military abuses. He had Army case files from the Philippines carted to his mansion near Dupont Circle for a more careful review, and he read late into the evening. The files raised further concerns. Root noted that during the first two years of war U.S. commanders had issued periodic reminders to their troops to treat the natives humanely. But the directives and communications had stopped in the fall of 1900, around the time that pressure for a take-no-prisoners campaign had boiled up through the officer corps. The implication was troubling—had the Army declared open season on Filipinos once the Republicans won the election? Even as he assured the Senate that the behavior of U.S. troops had been above reproach, Root pressed the military high command for answers. Among his questions: "How does it happen that we have no orders on the treatment of natives since 1900, a year and a half ago?"[10]

THEODORE ROOSEVELT HAD BEEN RESPONSIBLE for the war in the Philippines for only five months in February 1902, but he had given thought to the actions of U.S. troops in the islands for the past three years. In April 1899, after only two months of fighting, he had suggested that the abuses already being reported should be seen in a larger context:

> In a fight with savages, where the savages themselves perform deeds of hideous cruelty, a certain proportion of whites are sure to do the same thing. This happened in the warfare with the Indians, with the Kaffirs of the Cape [in South Africa] and with the aborigines of Australia. In each individual instance where the act is it should be punished with merciless severity; but to withdraw from the contest for civilization because of the fact that there are attendant cruelties, is, in my opinion, utterly unworthy of a great people.[11]

Roosevelt's prescription for addressing "deeds of hideous cruelty," if scrupulously followed, likely would have curtailed such acts. But the typical response of U.S. commanders had been weak and inconsistent. Historian Stuart Miller contends that the War Department, both before and after Root's arrival in July 1899, pressed General Otis to investigate cases of alleged atrocities only if the accounts had been too widely publicized to ignore. Invariably, Otis would "forward the press clipping to the author's commanding officer, who in turn would typically ask the soldier to write a retraction." And that would be the end of it.[12]

By the time Root assumed management of the war, the allegations of U.S. abuses had become a political embarrassment for Republicans. His first instinct was damage control rather than fact-finding, and he set in motion a public relations campaign aimed at countering criticism of Army conduct. In the two-plus years that followed, Root had seen ample evidence of abusive behavior by American troops in the Philippines—certainly enough to warrant a closer look, had he been so inclined.

The problem for Root and the U.S. military high command was that the abuse allegations touched some of the most celebrated American soldiers in the islands, including the iconic Frederick Funston. Private Charles Brenner of the 20th Kansas had accused Funston of ordering his men to shoot all prisoners during the early days of the war, and he singled out two officers who had carried out the command. When General Otis ordered Funston's immediate superior, General Arthur MacArthur, to investigate, Brenner produced a corroborating witness, a fellow private, who confessed to killing two prisoners when ordered by one of the officers. After receiving MacArthur's investigative report with this information, Otis took no action against Funston or the officers who oversaw the executions, but ordered Private Brenner court-martialed for leveling a "false charge" against a superior officer. When the Army judge advocate in Manila advised Otis that a trial could implicate "many others," the American commander advised his superiors in Washington to drop the matter.[13]

After Taft arrived in Manila in mid-1900, Root was given even clearer warnings as to the brutal—and possibly illegal—nature of U.S. military actions in some areas. In August 1900, Taft reported that General

MacArthur was "strongly in favor of punishing military officers and men who have been guilty of cruelty to the natives," but the military justice system had broken down. Courts-martial had been undermined by "the natural resentment against the natives' method of warfare, which is really nothing but ambush and murder, and which seems in the minds of ordinary military officers to justify unusual methods of recrimination."[14]

As he toured the countryside, Taft continued to gather evidence of the harsh measures employed by an increasing number of U.S. units. After a trip through Northern Luzon in early 1901, he unloaded on Roosevelt's friend General Samuel B. M. Young. "He knows no method but fear, and the sword and blood," Taft reported to Root, "and wherever he has been the work of pacification has been long delayed." Taft found similar abuses on the island of Marinduque, off the coast of southern Luzon. "The severity with which the inhabitants have been dealt with would not look well if a complete history of it were written out," he warned.[15]

Given all the information about torture and other abuses that came across Root's desk at the War Department, virtually all of it from friendly sources, the conclusion of Root's authorized biographer, Philip C. Jessup, that the secretary of war "must have had some indication that there were cases of torture and cruelty" is an understatement. Jessup surmises that Root's lack of action stemmed from the fact that he "was surrounded by military men and must have been influenced by their point of view which tended to excuse brother officers and to dwell upon the provocations which the Filipinos undoubtedly supplied."[16] A more likely explanation is that the superlawyer Root felt an obligation to protect his client—the president of the United States.

Exactly what Root told President Roosevelt about the reports of torture and other abuses in the Philippines has been lost to history. Nothing in their personal papers sheds meaningful light on the subject (which was typical of Roosevelt, a fastidious manager of potentially embarrassing documents).[17] What we do know is that by early February Roosevelt was aware of a brewing scandal involving military abuses in the Philippines, for on February 7 Taft had given Root a secret report on the subject.

The author of the explosive report was Major Cornelius Gardener, a West Pointer who had been named military governor of the southern

Luzon province of Tayabas in March 1901. In Gardener's area, as else-where, the replacement of U.S. volunteers with Army regulars had been accompanied by an increase in torture and other harsh tactics.[18] By late in the year, Gardener had seen enough, and on December 16 he addressed a five-page report to Governor Taft in Manila. Gardener accused U.S. troops of burning villages to deprive the guerrillas of shelter, torturing Filipinos to obtain information, and generally treating all natives as though they were "an *insurrecto* at heart. . . ." Additionally, outrages by American troops were going unpunished by higher military authorities. As a result, Gardener warned, goodwill with Filipinos was "being fast destroyed and a deep hatred toward us engendered."[19]

Taft was handed a copy of Gardener's report as he sailed from the Philippines on December 24, and he read it during his Pacific passage. Upon arriving in Washington, he discussed the report with Root and gave the secretary of war a copy. Inexplicably, Root waited another twelve days before taking action. On Root's instructions, Army Adjutant General Henry Corbin ordered General Chaffee to conduct a "careful inquiry" regarding Gardener's allegations. But rather than flash the command by cable to get the investigation under way immediately, Root ordered it sent by boat—ensuring that Chaffee would not receive it until mid-March. Root had bought the White House another month.[20]

ROOSEVELT, MEANWHILE, PREPARED TO SEIZE national headlines with a stroke so bold as to divert public attention from the issue of military "cru-elties" in the Philippines, at least temporarily. On the same day that Root waylaid the Gardener report—February 19, 1902—Roosevelt's attorney general, Philander Knox, announced that the administration had decided to file an antitrust lawsuit to break up the Northern Securities Company. Formed by New York tycoon J. P. Morgan and other principals, the hold-ing company brought together the leading railroads that carried grain, cattle and other cargo throughout the Northwestern United States. It had been hatched after Roosevelt took office, almost as a dare to the new president. And so now, Roosevelt made Northern Securities his vehicle for attacking the anticompetitive machinations of big business.[21]

Roosevelt's deliberations on the case had been so secretive that he blindsided Secretary Root, his closest adviser, fearing that the former Wall Street lawyer might try to talk him out of the confrontation. That may have proved true, but Root also would have underscored the political risks Roosevelt courted by taking on the men whose money gave Republicans a huge edge in national political campaigns. Roosevelt had struck a blow for the common man, but in the process he had alienated the very men he needed to win the White House in his own right in 1904. Conservative Republican power brokers now confidently predicted that they had the votes to dump the reform-minded upstart and nominate business-friendly Senator Mark Hanna on the first ballot. And that was before taking into consideration the impact of a military abuse scandal in the Philippines.[22]

WASHINGTON WAS STILL ABSORBING Roosevelt's Northern Securities bombshell when the Lodge committee hearings on the Philippines produced more grist for administration critics. On February 25, Brigadier General Robert P. Hughes, who had overseen harsh campaigns on Panay and Samar, took the stand. In his second day of testimony, Hughes talked about the island that had become synonymous with Filipino treachery in the eyes of many Americans. He painted the natives of Samar as an especially duplicitous people, walking about with guns hidden in bamboo containers and beneath palm fronds draped over their shoulders. He blamed the guerrillas for the mass relocation of Filipinos from the island's interior to tumbledown camps controlled by American troops, and depicted the refugees as "perfectly contented" with their choice.[23]

On Monday, March 3, Hughes conceded that his campaigns became tougher over time, "as it naturally would in any operations with that people." Democrat Joseph Rawlins of Utah, a lawyer and former college professor of classics, had Hughes describe how his troops would burn a village if they took gunfire from it. "The destruction was as a punishment," Hughes explained, since the residents had allowed guerrillas "to come in there and conceal themselves and they gave no sign." Hughes conceded that the punishment would fall on noncombatants left in the village, mainly women and little children, but "you can punish the man probably worse in that way than in any other."

"But is that within the ordinary rules of civilized warfare?" Rawlins probed. "Of course, you could exterminate the family, which would be still worse punishment."

"These people," Hughes retorted, "are not civilized."[24]

On March 5, Hughes was back on the stand when Democrat Thomas M. Patterson of Colorado asked about the interrogation of Filipinos using the torture known as the water cure. Hughes at first denied knowing what that meant, but under further questioning said he had heard of only one case where the torture had been used in the islands.[25]

As the tension rose, Hughes tried to make light of Patterson's tough cross-examination. "The water cure with us out there may mean a great many things," he said. "As one of my friends remarked to me the other day, 'You are getting the water cure down there.'"

Senator Patterson was not amused.

"The only knowledge we have here," he curtly replied, "is that it is used in the way of torture."[26]

Hughes became indignant.

"I have read a paper since I came home, emanating from Boston, describing it, and I can assure you, Mr. Senator, that the thing was not practiced under my command, or at least I think I am sufficiently well advised as to what was being done to say that never was practiced in the Department of the Visayas."[27]

GENERAL HUGHES HAD SOMEHOW FORGOTTEN the water cure exploits of his counterinsurgency stalwarts on Panay, Major Edwin Glenn and Lieutenant Arthur Conger, but not for long. The probing questions of unfriendly senators and fresh allegations of torture on newspaper front pages had finally awakened Root to the seriousness of the "cruelty" problem. Publicly, Root continued to insist that the war in the Philippines had been a model of "humanity and magnanimity," and he reiterated that contention in an angry letter to General Miles on March 5. Privately, he had begun to press General Chaffee for answers and action.[28]

On March 4, Root had sent a sharp cable ordering Chaffee to end the arrest-and-torture spree that Major Glenn had unleashed along the coasts of Samar and Leyte. He directed that Glenn and one of his subordinates, Captain James A. Ryan, be relieved and ordered to Manila pending an investigation. In case Chaffee had missed the point, Root added: "Disciplinary measures . . . seem necessary to produce obedience."[29]

Root's recent barrage of queries and commands had impressed on Chaffee the gravity of the situation, and after receiving the secretary of war's March 4 cable, the old cavalryman had fired off a pointed telegram to General Smith: "Do you know whether or not troops under your command practice water cure on natives? If any such action [exists] forbid it."

Secretary Root and General Chaffee had good reason to worry about unpleasant surprises emerging from Jake Smith's command. Several weeks earlier Chaffee had quietly ordered an investigation into the "promiscuous killings" attributed to the Marines on Samar, and the general now informed his superiors in Washington of the troubling results of his inquiry: Major Tony Waller, America's storied Marine, had been arrested and ordered before a court-martial on charges of murdering Filipino prisoners.

CHAPTER 21

The Trial of Major Waller

Major Tony Waller would later say that he departed Samar "without the faintest suspicion of anything wrong." Certainly General Jake Smith gave no indication of what was to come. As the Marines prepared to board an Army transport for their return to Luzon on February 26, 1902, Smith had stood on the Tacloban docks and proclaimed Waller and his men "as fine a group of soldiers as have ever served under my command. . . ."[1]

Three days later, Waller and his Marines lined the railings of the Army transport *Lawton* as it steamed into Manila Bay and turned toward Cavite. The band on the cruiser *New York* struck up "Home, Sweet Home," and the warship's crew erupted in cheers for the survivors of the Samar campaign. Some of the Marines burst into tears. Cheering crowds awaited them on the Cavite docks, and Colonel James Forney, the new commander of the Marine Brigade, presented Waller and his men with the best quarters available, a month's pay, and five days' leave.[2]

Waller left his exhausted Marines to reacquaint themselves with the saloons and bawdy houses of Cavite and headed across the bay to Manila to brief General Chaffee on his Samar tour. Arriving at Army headquarters in the old walled city, he was escorted into the general's office. At the very least, Waller had expected congratulations for a job well-done. He was puzzled by Chaffee's stiff greeting. And then, making no attempt to cushion the blow, the dour American commander curtly informed Waller that he was under arrest and would face a court-martial on charges of murdering prisoners.

Waller's arrest shocked Americans. Emboldened war opponents cited it as proof that the Republican venture in the Philippines had gone terribly wrong, while the major's defenders suggested the allegations had been trumped up by jealous rivals, or, if true, resulted from temporary insanity after the jungle ordeal. Once celebrated as the gallant face of America's global power, Waller now found himself reviled as the symbol of shameful conquest. He was the "Butcher of Samar" in scurrilous newspaper stories that put a sadistic spin on the executions. One luridly (and falsely) described how Waller had a Filipino tied to a tree and shot in a different part of his body over three days until the coup de grâce was finally delivered.[3]

General Chaffee and the Army had quickly disavowed Waller, but the major still commanded support in Washington, particularly at the Navy Department and Marine Corps headquarters, where Waller was touted as a future general officer and Corps commandant. But even sympathetic observers puzzled over the major's actions in shocked disbelief.

Along with the speculation of Waller's fate, Washington pondered the fallout for President Roosevelt. The handicapping of Roosevelt's political future only intensified when General Miles, touted as a likely presidential contender in 1904, leaked the news that the president and Secretary of War Root had denied his request to conduct an inquiry into the Army's conduct of the war. Miles implied that the administration was hiding dark secrets in the Philippines.[4]

"It is certain that if half the stories told of the atrocities of Major Waller in Samar are proved true, and are cabled to the United States, we may look for an explosion beside which the former outbursts will seem but the faintest of mutterings," the American-owned *Manila Times* opined. "It would not be too much to say that on the conduct of Major Waller in Samar may hang the fate of the next presidential election."[5]

On Monday morning, March 17, 1902, Major Littleton Waller Tazewell Waller slipped into his heavy dress uniform (minus his sword, which was surrendered upon arrest) and made his way to the barracks on the Army headquarters post in Manila where his court-martial was to get under way. As ceiling fans stirred the sticky air, Waller and his legal team took their seats at a small table on the north side of the room.

The team's three members were Army Major Edwin Glenn, Navy Commander Adolph Marix, and civilian attorney Oscar Sutro. Glenn, who held a law degree from the University of Minnesota, was still awaiting the outcome of the investigation that Secretary Root had ordered into his Samar activities. The fifty-three-year-old Marix, bald and thickening around the midsection, was a German-born Jew who had served as recorder for the *Maine* court of inquiry in 1898. He had been overseeing the corruption-ridden port of Manila when his old friend Tony Waller had enlisted his services. The British Columbia–born Sutro had arrived in Manila the previous year to set up a law practice for a major San Francisco firm, and he counted among his many friends the U.S. governor in the islands, William Howard Taft.

A few feet away from Waller and his counsel sat the judge advocate assigned to prosecute the case, Major Henry P. Kingsbury. A thirty-year Army veteran, the fifty-one-year-old Kingsbury had grown up in North Carolina, only about 120 miles from Waller's Virginia home. After graduating from West Point in 1871, he had served with the 6th Cavalry in Kansas, Texas and Oklahoma, and fought against the Apaches in the early 1880s. Handsome and ambitious, Kingsbury married Florence Elizabeth Slocum, daughter of Union Civil War General Henry W. Slocum, in an 1889 wedding that had been a prominent New York City social event.[6] Now, with the president of the United States and the secretary of war suddenly eager to show the American people they were serious about curbing military abuses in the Philippines, Kingsbury found himself in a position to win fame and promotion—if only he could convict his high-profile defendant.

Waller's guilt or innocence would be decided in a simple majority vote by thirteen men—seven Army officers and six Marines—who sat across from the opposing legal teams.[7] Presiding over the panel was sixty-two-year-old Army Brigadier General William Henry Bisbee, a former Central Luzon field commander who was sympathetic to the use of harsh tactics against the guerrillas.[8] On his right sat the ranking Marine on the panel, Colonel James Forney, a bearded Civil War veteran, six feet, seven inches in height.

After Bisbee swore in the court and the judge advocate, Waller stood at attention alongside Major Kingsbury as he introduced the members of his defense team. Kingsbury commenced with the reading of charges, which accused Waller of murdering eleven men at Basey, Samar, on January 20, 1902. It was a violation of the fifty-eighth article of war, punishable by death.

The court quickly adjourned when Waller's defense team contested the Army's jurisdiction in a case involving a Marine. Bisbee initially ruled in Waller's favor, but consultations with General Chaffee and Secretary Root convinced the old general otherwise. For months the administration had downplayed the atrocity allegations, but the high-profile trial of a military hero now served the political ends of President Roosevelt and his men as they tried to project toughness on the issue. Given that the hero happened to be a Marine, Chaffee had no objections to moving forward. And so, when the parties returned to the courtroom on March 21, Bisbee ordered the trial to proceed.

Directed to enter a plea, Waller admitted that he had ordered the execution of the eleven prisoners. But this was not a case of murder, he declared.

"Not guilty," the Marine announced in a firm voice.

AFTER A SHORT RECESS, the prosecution began its case by attempting to establish the facts surrounding the executions. This proved no easy task. There was contradictory testimony over whether eleven or twelve Filipinos were shot, and whether the executions had occurred over one or two days. First on the stand for Kingsbury was Captain Robert H. Dunlap, who had been on duty at Waller's headquarters in Basey on January 20 when Lieutenant John Gridley, son of the deceased *Olympia* skipper, had telephoned from Tacloban with the news that some Marines and native prisoners would be arriving by boat. Gridley had described the terrible condition of some of Captain Porter's men and reported that the Filipino bearers had withheld food and attacked Lieutenant Williams. He also told Dunlap that Captain Porter and Sergeant Quick both recommended that the captives be shot.

Later that morning, Dunlap testified, Quick arrived and briefed Waller, who was confined to a cot with a raging fever. The sergeant described the condition of the surviving Marines and recommended that the native prisoners be shot for betraying the expedition. Afterward, Dunlap heard Waller order his adjutant, Lieutenant John Day, to take the newly arrived prisoners out "and shoot them." Under cross-examination by Waller, Dunlap testified that he supported the decision to shoot the captives, and had urged the major to do so.[9]

Kingsbury asked a few more questions to fix the timetable of the January 20 events, and then General Bisbee weighed in with a few questions for Dunlap. Had Major Waller questioned the prisoners about their alleged treachery? Had the major conducted any investigation prior to ordering the executions?

"I don't know of any investigation, sir," Dunlap replied uneasily, "but I believe that [Lieutenant] Day talked to some of the prisoners before they were shot."

Did any of the Marines protest the order to execute the prisoners?

"Mr. Day and I were the only ones present," Dunlap said, "and neither of us protested the order."

As the heavy midday heat blanketed the room, Bisbee gaveled the trial's first day of testimony to a close.

THE COURT CONVENED THE FOLLOWING MORNING at fifteen minutes after ten. Kingsbury called to the stand Waller's adjutant, twenty-six-year-old Lieutenant John Horace Arthur Day.[10] On January 20, Waller had entrusted Day with the execution of the eleven prisoners. On his own volition, the lieutenant had spared a Filipino named Slim whom he had grown to like. After executing the other ten men, Day returned to Waller and asked that Slim be allowed to live. But Waller would not relent, and this man, too, was shot.

On the witness stand, Day quickly complicated matters for Waller when he testified that the major had ordered him to shoot a prisoner the day before the group execution. But Kingsbury was more interested in highlighting the fact that Waller had not granted the prisoners a trial, and he let Day's statement pass.

After a prosaic cross-examination by Waller, General Bisbee attempted to sort through Day's muddled time line. The lieutenant again asserted that the prisoners had been shot over two days—first one, and then ten more the following day. Three enlisted Marines who had been members of the firing squad followed with even more contradictory testimony on the timing and number of executions.[11]

Tony Waller now had the blood of at least twelve prisoners on his hands.

WALLER BEGAN HIS DEFENSE with the aim of proving that the executions were not only lawful, but necessary, given the inherent treachery of the inhabitants of southern Samar. Captain David Porter testified that Waller had fully complied with the orders of General Smith. Indeed, Porter testified, Waller's written order did not "go as far" as Smith's directive, which was left unstated for the time being.

In his cross-examination on Monday morning, March 24, Kingsbury asked Porter whether Smith had given Waller the "power of life and death over unarmed and defenseless prisoners."

"That was the impression I received," Porter replied. But, he conceded, Smith did not explicitly state this.

Did you actually see the natives commit any act punishable by death? Kingsbury continued.

"I did not," Porter replied.

Porter conceded that Sergeant Quick's recommendation that the Filipino bearers and scouts be shot was based on his conversations with Alex Williams and the last group of Marines to emerge from the jungle.

"You did not believe that Lieutenant Williams and his men were in any physical danger from the carriers," Kingsbury said. "If you had you would not have abandoned them, would you?"

Marix leaped to his feet with an objection. Kingsbury rephrased the question: "Did you believe that Lieutenant Williams and his party were in danger?"

"No," Porter conceded.

JUST BEFORE NOON, WALLER'S TEAM called Lieutenant Alexander Williams to the stand. The Marine was still weak from his ordeal, and his hand bore the teeth marks of one of the executed Filipinos. In slow and dramatic fashion, Williams recalled the agony of his men as they fell in the jungle from starvation and exhaustion. At times stroking his campaign hat and knitting his brow as he considered his words, Williams was adamant: The lives of his men could have been spared, if only the Filipinos had shared their food and jungle expertise. Instead the natives hid food while watching the Americans slowly starve, he asserted. Only when the Army rescue team arrived did the Filipinos suddenly pull sweet potatoes from their packs and offer them to the Marines, he testified.

The lieutenant's testimony built to the jungle confrontation with the bearers. The column of Marines had halted for the night, Williams recalled, and several of the sick and exhausted men had crawled under a piece of canvas they had strung up as a shelter while he searched for firewood. He made his way to the river, and ordered three Filipino bearers to assist him. When one approached with a bolo in his hands, Williams became frightened and drew his pistol. "Instantly he seized the barrel of my pistol in his right hand and my right hand with his teeth," Williams testified. The Filipino dropped his bolo and one of his comrades grabbed it and "began hacking at my ribs," Williams continued. "I thought every moment that the next blow would go through me, so I let go the pistol and got my hand free; seized the bolo and succeeded in wrenching it away from the native." When other Marines responded to the lieutenant's cries, the Filipinos ran away.

Williams's testimony generated sensational headlines in Manila and the United States. "Graphic Details of His Single-Handed Combat

Against Three Ferocious Savages," trumpeted one paper.[12] "All present listened with bated breath to the story of how the human wild-cats leaped upon him, one seeking to tear him with his teeth, and another to pierce his heart with a bolo." The young lieutenant had "proved to be the star witness of the whole trial thus far," the paper proclaimed.

CAPTAIN BEARSS WAS NEXT on the stand and testified that the Filipino known as Victor had made an attempt on Waller's life on the night of January 5. But the story that Bearss proceeded to tell seemed less than conclusive: Waller's bolo had gone missing during the night, and it had been found on the ground near Victor, who was "lying behind a tree, some distance from where he should have been."[13] But no attack ever occurred.

Other Marines now supported Waller's contention that the duplicity of Samar's natives had justified the summary executions. "The natives were very treacherous," testified Private Charles S. Morgan, "and they wouldn't obey orders."

That was not the case with a wiry Filipino scout known as Smoke, who took the stand in Waller's defense on Thursday, March 27. Clad in a well-worn khaki uniform and speaking in the Visayan dialect through an interpreter, Smoke testified that he had remained in the jungle with the last group under Lieutenant Williams. As their situation grew more desperate, Williams had sent him ahead to Lanang to get help. Along the trail, Smoke said, he found the four men left in a clearing by Captain Porter, and he gathered sweet potatoes and other edible plants for the Marines before moving on. Finally reaching Lanang, Smoke asked Captain Pickering to rush food and medicine to the dying Americans. After the Marines had been rescued, Smoke testified, a bearer named Juan had told him that Victor had planned to kill Waller in the jungle. Smoke said he reported the conversation to Waller later that day.

Smoke's testimony concluded on a dramatic note after Major Glenn asked the scout whether the Filipino bearers had plotted to harm Lieutenant Williams and his men. The scout and the interpreter engaged in a sharp discussion in Visayan for several seconds before the interpreter finally addressed the court. Smoke had answered in the affirmative, according to the interpreter: Some of the Filipinos had indeed planned to kill Williams and his men because they didn't want to share their food.[14]

The parade of defense witnesses testifying to the treachery of the Filipinos on the Marine expedition continued on Good Friday, March 28, 1902. "How would you class them, then: as civilized, semi-civilized, barbarous or savage?" Glenn asked one witness, Army Lieutenant George Peters of the 19th Infantry, which had replaced the Marines in southern Samar.

"As savages," Peters said.

Another survivor of Waller's expedition claimed to have understood the Filipinos to use the Visayan word for "kill" or "dead" and talk about a gun and fleeing to the hills. "They were all thieves," the Marine private testified, "and if I'd had my say they'd all have been hung."[15]

As the trial passed the midway point, Waller's disastrous expedition claimed yet another victim. Marine Private John J. Sullivan of Boston, Massachusetts, had shown signs of depression and "mental aberration" on his return from Samar, and had been placed under observation at the Cavite naval hospital. He seemed to be improving after a few days of care, and on Sunday morning, March 30, returned to duty. That evening, when the mess call sounded for supper, Sullivan lingered in the barracks. After his comrades had gone, he placed a rifle muzzle in his mouth and pulled the trigger.[16]

The day after Sullivan's suicide, Tony Waller took the stand in his own defense. At times speaking in a voice that faded to a whisper, at other moments projecting in clear and emphatic tones, Waller defended his actions as not only justified by the native treachery but sanctioned by his superior's instructions. Waller described how General Smith's briefing aboard the *New York* had led to his written orders directing his Marines to "punish treachery with death."

"Was that order in accordance with instructions given you by General Smith?" Commander Marix asked.

"It was absolutely inspired, sir," Waller replied.

The courtroom listened in hushed silence as Waller described the incident on the night of January 5, when he claimed that Victor stole his bolo as a prelude to an attack. Victor was "the infamous captain of *insurrectos* who led the detachment from Basey in the Balangiga massacre," Waller told the court, citing information provided by loyal Filipinos. Smiling grimly, he added, "Had I known that beforehand, he would not have gone along on the expedition."[17]

Waller emphatically rejected suggestions that he was under mental duress when he ordered the executions. He admitted that he was running a high fever, but his judgment was not impaired, he assured the court.

On April 1, Waller concluded his defense.

As THE TRIAL MOVED TOWARD its conclusion, a new drama gripped Manila. Cholera had broken out in late March, and had spread from the city's poorer quarters to the affluent enclaves inhabited by foreigners and wealthy Filipinos. American authorities had imposed emergency measures to halt the advance of the disease, and anyone desiring to enter or leave Manila was now required to obtain a permit. Two hundred constabulary troopers manned checkpoints and patrolled the city outskirts. Still, the death toll had continued to rise, reaching ninety-three by April 2.

In an effort to isolate new cases, special teams had begun making house-to-house inspections in poorer neighborhoods. When the authorities burned infected barrios to the ground, desperate Filipinos took to concealing cases. So fearful were some that they turned sick family members out into the streets and buried their dead under the cover of darkness.[18]

RUMORS HAD CIRCULATED FOR SEVERAL DAYS that the defense planned to put General Jacob Smith on the stand at some point. On April 1, Major Kingsbury stole Waller's thunder when he casually announced that Smith would be a rebuttal witness for the prosecution. With General Lukbán now in custody and his successor negotiating surrender terms, Smith was due in Manila in a matter of days, as soon as he handed off command of the 6th Separate Brigade.

The court-martial marked time while awaiting the arrival of its surprise witness, and on the morning of Monday, April 7, 1902, General
Jacob Hurd Smith strode into the court. The little general quickly crossed
the room, sword clinking at his side, took his oath and prepared to begin
his testimony. After recounting his first conversation with Waller aboard
the *New York* on October 23, 1901, Smith testified that he had ordered all
his commanders to summarily punish treachery under the guidelines of
General Orders 100. But he most certainly had not directed his subordinates to summarily execute offenders, as Waller had told the court.

Smith now walked a fine line, repudiating the executions while praising the Marines. "The Marines did good work, magnificent work, equal
to that of any soldiers that ever fought anywhere," he enthused. Waller,
too, "had been doing extraordinarily fine work, had acted with vigor and
had proved a fine officer."[19]

But in the end, Smith buried the Marine commander.

A question by Kingsbury yielded the coup de grâce: Did you ever
indicate to Major Waller that "he held the power of life and death" over
prisoners?

"No, sir," Smith replied. "I had no such authority myself and could
not delegate any authority I did not have."[20]

Incensed by Smith's disavowal, Waller debated how to proceed. The
general had failed to mention his verbal orders to "kill and burn" and
"take no prisoners." But what if Smith denied giving such a command?
Should he dare challenge a brigadier general in open court? Waller
decided to hold his fire until his rebuttal.

The next day, with his life and career on the line, Waller began his
testimony by challenging Smith's account. The general had left no doubt
as to the severity of the campaign he expected on Samar, Waller asserted.
"His actual language was: 'I want no prisoners,'" Waller testified.

The courtroom stirred as Waller's counsel asked the Marine what he
understood Smith to mean.

"That there would be no quarter," Waller responded.

Waller's counsel set up the major's next bombshell. "Had you any
order from General Smith to kill and burn? If so, state what they were."

"He said," Waller continued, "'I wish you to kill and burn. The more you kill and burn, the better you will please me.' Not once only, but several times. I think every officer there heard him."

As the weight of Waller's words settled over the room, the Marine forged ahead. Smith had gone even further, Waller asserted. He "wanted all persons killed who were capable of bearing arms." He had been very specific when asked for clarification: "All over ten years of age were to be killed."

Waller described how he had briefed Captain Porter about Smith's order and told his deputy to ignore it—"we do not make war on women and children," Waller recalled saying. And then, several weeks later, General Smith had sent him another message calling for further depredations. "The interior of Samar must be made a howling wilderness," the message read.

His stunning rebuttal delivered, Waller stepped down from the stand.

On Friday, April 11, 1902, Waller rose before the court to deliver his final plea for acquittal. "I am called upon to defend myself against the most serious charge which can be brought against a person whether in military or civil life," he began. "I do not beg for mercy or plead extenuation—I was either right or wrong. If I was wrong, give me the whole, full complete sentence required by the law. If I was right then I am entitled to most honorable acquittal."[21]

Waller again admitted that he had ordered the execution of the eleven prisoners. But he maintained that he had acted within his rights as the ranking commander on the ground in southern Samar, especially given the nature of the enemy. His twenty-two years in the Marine Corps showed a pattern of just and lawful actions toward prisoners, Waller maintained. He had rescued survivors of the shattered Spanish fleet at Santiago, Cuba, in 1898, he reminded the court. Just recently he had received a letter from the widow of one of Admiral Cervera's staff officers, thanking him for his chivalrous efforts.

In any event, the summary execution of prisoners was hardly a rarity in war, he declared. During his service with the British army in Egypt in 1882, Arab forces had executed captured British colonial troops and mounted their heads on lances. "The Arab cavalry was never spared after that," Waller said. "If prisoners were captured, even foot troops, and it was found out after capture that they were or had been cavalry, they were executed without referring the matter to the commanding general before execution; yet these acts were approved by him afterwards." Similar incidents had occurred during the China campaign, Waller said. "Whenever a 'boxer' or fanatic was captured either in the European concessions or outside he was brought in and executed without referring the matter to the commander in chief. This was true with every nation represented in the Allied Forces."

General Smith's briefing had inspired his instructions to his officers to distrust the people of Samar, but his own experiences had hardened those views, Waller said. The island's residents "were treacherous in every way. When one was trying to befriend and benefit them they would attempt to murder. They seldom took prisoners; they set traps and dug pits and did everything that savage, treacherous minds could conceive."

The massacre of American troops at Balangiga had increased the ferocity of their campaign, Waller admitted. He and his men had served alongside the 9th Infantry in China, and they had felt a bond with the soldiers slaughtered in the surprise attack. "Picture to yourselves, if you please, the butchered men, picture to yourselves the bodies of the officers where in one case in pure revelry of blood appetite, in wanton sacrilege of the human body, they cut open and poured in jam and jelly. For weeks as we drove these devils from point to point we picked up little tokens of the 9th Infantry—photographs, cards, everything that a soldier cares for."

Anger flashed as Waller spoke of the personal betrayals of the Filipinos accompanying his jungle expedition. The scout named Slim "had been cared for, his family cared for, but he turned on my people and tried by every means in his power to destroy them by starvation."

He ended on a defiant note.

"As the representative officer responsible for the safety and welfare of my men, after investigation and from the information I had, considering the situation from all points, I ordered the eleven men shot," Waller said. "I honestly thought I was right then. I believe now that I was right. Whatever may happen to me, I have the sure knowledge that my people knew, and I believe the world knows, that I am not a murderer."

He bowed to the court and took his seat.

AT ELEVEN THIRTY A.M. the following morning, Major Kingsbury took the floor to deliver his closing. He began by drawing a distinction between military law and martial law, and noted that martial law was not in effect on Samar. Waller had been governed by military law, and under those conventions, the Marine had no grounds to execute prisoners. Indeed, Kingsbury argued, a proper military court would have concluded that the Filipinos had done nothing to deserve their fate.

There was no evidence against the natives, Kingsbury continued, but merely the fears of impaired men who had been abandoned in the jungle by their commander, an officer who had "listened to the whispers of ambition instead of duty." Indeed, if the natives had wanted to kill Williams and his men, why hadn't they acted when they were ordered to carry the rifles of the exhausted Marines?

The horror that befell the Marines in the Samar jungle was not the result of Filipino treachery, he asserted, but the "foolhardiness" of Major Waller. "Who was it who brought disaster to the Marine Corps? Who was it that brought upon them hunger, hardship and death? Who was it that abandoned ten of his helpless comrades, who were left to die slowly of hunger and want and whose very bones are now bleaching in the sun on the banks of the Lanang?"

Render justice to the dead Filipinos, Kingsbury exhorted the court.

"When these natives stood up for the raffle of death, to be condemned or snatched from execution . . . they also stood beneath the flag of the United States, beneath the laws of the United States, and in the charge of an officer of that government, whose duty it was to see that they received the protection of the laws of that government."[22]

General Bisbee and his panel retired behind closed doors to consider their decision. In less than half an hour, they had reached their verdict. By an eleven-to-two vote, Major Tony Waller was acquitted of all charges. He strapped on his sword, and walked from the courtroom a free man.

CHAPTER 22

"The President Desires All the Facts"

Through a long and snowy Washington winter, General Nelson Miles had held his fire as the clouds of scandal gathered over the White House. Finally, as the Waller court-martial was about to get under way, the aggrieved Army chief took his revenge. In a mid-March interview with journalist and Democratic political pundit Henry Watterson, Miles revealed that President Roosevelt had blocked his request to personally investigate America's war in the Philippines. Watterson allowed his readers to imagine the dark secrets that the general might have uncovered. Miles was a battle-tested warrior who "has coaxed submission many times of the aborigines, when to subdue them by force of arms would have cost too much. He could, and would, bring order out of chaos if sent to Manila," but, alas, his request "sleeps in some pigeonhole."[1]

Roosevelt fired back immediately. In an anonymous interview the president gave the *Boston Herald*, he denounced General Miles as a self-aggrandizing "intriguer" whose "whole effort is to discredit the administration." Furthermore, "there is absolutely no truth in the statement that the President and Secretary Root fear General Miles," the *Herald* declared, "or are personally uneasy because of anything he may do."[2]

The dispute escalated. A Democratic congressman from Texas called for Roosevelt to release all his correspondence relating to Miles's request to visit the Philippines. A day later, the general appeared before the Senate Committee on Military Affairs to testify against an Army reform bill that Roosevelt and Root had made a top priority. The administration's proposal to replace the office of commanding general with an armed forces chief of staff would lead to a dangerous leadership vacuum in time of crisis, Miles asserted. He threatened to resign rather than implement the plan.[3]

Speculation swirled that Miles would be sacked first. He had turned sixty-two the previous August and could be retired at the president's pleasure. The *Evening Times* of Washington reported on March 22 that Roosevelt had made up his mind to rid himself of his scheming Army chief.[4] The president's decision to release his correspondence with Miles over the issue only stoked the speculation. The documents would prove to all "the wisdom of denying General Miles' request" to go to the Philippines, Roosevelt sniped.[5] Miles, in turn, leaked a March 24 letter he had written hinting at an administration cover-up. The Army commander further revealed that his denunciation of the "marked severity" of the U.S. war was based on internal administration documents, including a February 7 letter from Governor Taft to Secretary Root.

Root was furious that Miles had disclosed the contents of confidential War Department documents, especially those containing allegations against U.S. troops. "In the interest of good discipline and effective service such a course is much to be regretted," Root scolded the general. "Such charges ought not to be published against our countrymen whom we have sent to labor and fight under our flag on the other side of the world before they can be heard in their own defense."

The Democrats could only rub their hands with glee. On issues domestic and foreign, Roosevelt was at odds with a good number of his fellow Republicans. He had angered party conservatives (and given rise to talk of a Mark Hanna challenge) with his Northern Securities lawsuit and attack on trusts. And he was alienating independents and Republican moderates by denying U.S. excesses in the Philippines.

"Chaos! Everywhere!" Watterson chortled. "For the first time these thirty years, it is the Republicans who are at sea."[6]

———

AT LEAST HENRY CABOT LODGE HAD MANAGED to shield the president in the plodding Senate investigation of U.S. conduct in the Philippines. In more than two months of hearings, Lodge had limited the witness list to senior military commanders and administration officials. On March 17, as Major Waller's trial got under way in Manila, the latest member of this reliable circle strode into the hearing room in his crisp white Army dress uniform. His bushy, muttonchopped visage was instantly recognizable, even before he stepped to the witness table and stated his name: E. S. Otis, major general, United States Army.

Elwell Otis was only days from retirement, but he had welcomed a return to the spotlight that had turned elsewhere since his victory tour during the fall presidential campaign of 1900. With Albert Beveridge as his gentle guide, the former U.S. commander in Manila restated the administration's brief: American troops had achieved the occupation of the Philippines with kindness and benevolence, despite the inherent cruelty and duplicity of the Filipinos.

What was the truth of the abuse allegations? Had American soldiers practiced cruelty or kindness toward Filipinos?

"The greatest kindness," Otis declared. "I investigated myself, and through inspectors appointed by me, every statement of harsh treatment that I heard of while in the islands." Further prompted by Beveridge, Otis went on to describe the care given to sick and wounded native troops, including segregated wards established in American military hospitals. "We were laughed at by the Spaniards and by Europeans for the humanity we exercised."[7]

Otis assured the panel that Filipinos "are not fitted for self-government." Furthermore, a U.S. withdrawal would result in "anarchy or despotism, and they all understand it."[8] Day after day, Otis expounded on the administration's talking points. The war had been triggered by Aguinaldo and his radical nationalists, he asserted, but the Americans had responded with humanity. As for his personal actions, "no man ever worked harder in the interests of peace than I did."[9]

———————

IN EARLY APRIL, AS THE Waller court-martial headed into its final week and Democratic attacks over military abuses intensified, Roosevelt took to the road. He had accepted an invitation to address a trade exposition in Charleston, South Carolina, in the heart of a region where Roosevelt's standing had suffered since his White House dinner with Booker T. Washington the previous October. Now Roosevelt aimed to mend some political fences.

Roosevelt and his entourage left Washington on a special train on April 7, and headed south through the spring-dappled Virginia countryside. Elihu Root had remained behind in Washington to keep an eye on the Senate hearings on the Philippines and developments in the Waller trial. "President deeply concerned over progress Waller court and other cases," Root had wired Chaffee. "Press forcefully. Submit daily cable." Leaving management of the worsening scandal in Root's able hands, Roosevelt was heartened by the warm crowds that greeted his train as it passed through Virginia and North Carolina. An even more enthusiastic reception awaited him in Charleston.

On his second day in the city, April 9, the thirty-seventh anniversary of Lee's surrender at Appomattox, Roosevelt kicked off the festivities by leading a military procession through city streets lined with cheering admirers. The president was escorted by a detachment of Marines commanded by Captain Henry Leonard, who had lost an arm in the fighting at Tientsin, China. Afterward, Roosevelt proceeded to the Charleston exposition, where a crowd of ten thousand awaited his keynote address.[10]

Roosevelt's theme was national reunification, but he dwelled at length on the importance of America's presence in the Philippines. He heralded the wars in Cuba and the Philippines as milestones in America's rise above the sectional divisions of the Civil War. He reminded his audience that he had served under ex–Confederate General Joe Wheeler on Cuba, and had selected another former Confederate general, Luke Wright of Tennessee, as his vice governor in the Philippines, "one of the most important places in our Government at this time."

America had shown the world its power by planting the Stars and Stripes in the Philippines, and now it was "bringing order and peace out of the bloody chaos in which we found the islands." Despite what they might have been hearing and reading, America's progress in the Philippines "has been indeed marvelous." Indeed, he continued, General Wright had observed in a letter a few days earlier that "there was far more warfare about the Philippines in *this* country than there was warfare in the Philippines themselves!"[11] The South Carolinians roared with approval.

The following day, with the spring air perfumed by the sweet scent of piney woods, Roosevelt headed north through the Carolinas to Washington. He had been energized by the adoring crowds. Alas, he could expect no such reception back in the capital. Dramatic events had transpired in his absence, and the stench of scandal now permeated the city.

ON THE SAME DAY ROOSEVELT EMBARKED on his southern tour, the Lodge Committee's agenda called for another former American military commander in the Philippines to begin his testimony. But before Major General Arthur MacArthur made it to the stand, the Democrats threw the hearings into an uproar.

Senator Charles A. Culberson, a forty-seven-year-old lawyer and first-term Democrat from Texas, announced that it had come to his attention that Governor Taft had withheld from the committee a critical report from one of his provincial governors. Culberson mentioned no names, but he referred to the report of Major Cornelius Gardener, alleging abuses by U.S. soldiers in the province under his control. The Texan noted that Taft had provided numerous other provincial reports favorable to the administration. He demanded that the unfavorable account be given to the committee for its review.

Lodge leaped to Taft's defense. The report had been withheld at the War Department's request because it "made most sweeping attacks on the officers of the Army and the Army in that province."[12] The document had been promptly dispatched to General Chaffee for comment, Lodge said (failing to note it had been sent by boat rather than by cable). It would be released as soon as the War Department had General Chaffee's response in hand, he assured his colleagues.

But Culberson would not be mollified. How was it that the dean of Senate Republicans, Orville H. Platt of Connecticut, had been quoting provincial reports claiming rosy conditions in the islands, while a document that contradicted the administration's assertions of honorable victory was being withheld?[13]

Fairness had dictated the decision of the president and Secretary Root, Lodge retorted.

The Democrats scoffed. Where was this concern when the government's witnesses had accused General Aguinaldo of murder and other crimes? Indeed, if this argument were applied uniformly, then critical testimony would not be aired in committee hearings until a rebuttal witness was on hand.[14]

Joseph Rawlins of Utah now accused Root of another serious omission in his February report to the committee. Root had presented the torture allegation of a former Massachusetts sergeant as a fabrication, when, in fact, the Army had botched the investigation. This raised serious questions as to whether the administration was "attempting to repress evidence of misdeeds," Rawlins thundered. He demanded accountability for soldiers guilty of misconduct.[15]

The Republicans could hardly disagree. By unanimous vote, the committee asked Secretary Root to deliver the Gardener report, along with any rebuttal from General Chaffee.[16]

ROOSEVELT RETURNED TO WASHINGTON EARLY in the morning of Friday, April 11, to find the capital in an uproar over the mounting evidence of military misconduct. Front-page headlines across the country earlier in the week had revealed General Smith's shocking orders to Major Waller to "kill and burn!" and "make Samar a howling wilderness!" The War Department had tried to limit the damage by releasing a February order from Hell-roaring Jake that urged kind treatment of the natives, so the public might know "the actual attitude of General Smith toward the people of Samar."[17] But the furor over Smith's commands was still simmering on the eve of Roosevelt's arrival when Lodge released the Gardener report, with still more allegations of abusive behavior by U.S. soldiers.

Lodge also released a second report that Taft (or, more probably, Root) had withheld from the committee. This one, from a colonial administration official in Batangas province, where thousands of civilians languished in U.S. resettlement camps, revealed that about one-third of the population—a hundred thousand people—had died from military operations and disease. Farms were in ruins and work animals dead, the report said. "I foresee the coming of famine with all its horrible consequences," the official warned.[18]

Fresh shock and outrage swept the country. "Extermination Of Natives In Philippine Provinces," howled the front-page headline in the Republican *San Francisco Call*. General Miles stirred the pot, pronouncing Waller's testimony as vindication of his charges of Army brutality. He even resurrected the anti-imperialist criticism of the Army's highly suspicious kill ratio against the guerrillas.[19] Against that backdrop, General MacArthur appeared before the Lodge Committee and blithely assured the senators that U.S. troops in the Philippines had waged "the most humane war ever fought."[20]

As news of the scandal flashed around the world, European commentators reveled at the sight of the upstart Americans, so quick to judge others, dishonored by their own dirty colonial war. "We have no doubt American honor will be vindicated in the same manner as the British has recently been by an award of swift, uncompromising justice to the guilty parties," wrote one English observer, referring to British military abuses against Boer guerrillas in South Africa.[21]

Across the country, Americans searched their souls. Before a gathering in New York City, Professor Felix Adler posed the question on the minds of many: Was it unpatriotic to criticize a war while America's soldiers were still fighting and dying? Adler, for one, argued that criticism of a conflict that was not defensive in nature, as was the case in the Philippines, was acceptable. "You will ask if it is possible that torture has been used," the professor continued. "I am as loath to believe it as you. I could not and would not believe it. But evidences multiply and certain facts stand out now with such emphasis that it is impossible any longer to escape such a conviction."[22]

The arrival of a new week and the radiant glories of a Washington spring brought little relief for Roosevelt. News of Major Waller's acquittal in Manila was splashed across the morning papers of Monday, April 14, along with the rising cries of whitewash from anti-imperialist quarters. The day quickly turned darker for Roosevelt when the Philippine hearings were gaveled to order in the Senate and Charles S. Riley, the former Army sergeant recently cited by Senator Rawlins, took his seat at the witness table.

A plumbing and heating store clerk from Northampton, Massachusetts, Riley had been a first sergeant in the 26th U.S. Volunteer Infantry, assigned to the Philippines from October 1899 until March 1901. He had spent much of his time on Panay, and on November 27, 1900, had been posted in the town of Igbaras when Edwin Glenn and a contingent of Army scouts had ridden into town to interrogate the town president and other officials. By midnight, much of the town was in ashes—burned on Glenn's orders—and Riley and his comrades had become acquainted with the brutal interrogation methods of American counterinsurgency experts in the islands.

The sergeant had written home about what he had witnessed, and his letter had found its way into a local newspaper. After a feeble Army investigation had concluded the charges were unfounded, and Secretary Root had cited the case as an example of falsified allegations, Riley had come to the attention of Senate Democrats. The sergeant had been discovered by Herbert Welsh, a former Indian rights activist from Philadelphia who had devoted himself to exposing U.S. military misconduct in the Philippines. Welsh had dispatched two hired agents to track down returning soldiers who had witnessed torture, and had personally traveled to New England to take depositions and persuade Riley and other soldiers to tell their stories before the Lodge Committee.[23] Now, to the administration's horror, Riley began to describe in vivid detail the water-cure interrogation of the Igbaras president, carried out at the direction of Edwin Glenn.

When Riley was finished, Lodge and Beveridge gamely tried to blunt the impact of the disturbing testimony. Lodge recited a list of alleged guerrilla atrocities, and both senators suggested the sergeant had merely witnessed an isolated incident.

Beveridge went even further, dismissing the water cure as though it were a college fraternity prank. He chided Riley for not writing home about "any of the outrages committed by the natives upon the Americans?"

"I was not comparing the case at all," said Riley. "I simply stated the facts as an event of the day and did not say whether it was inhuman [sic] or not."

"But it did not occur to you to make any statement about the outrages that were committed on Americans by natives?"

"Those I believe I stated at other times," Riley said.

"And those letters were not published?" Beveridge retorted.

"No, sir."[24]

Next on the witness stand was a comrade of Riley's from the 26th Volunteer Infantry, former Private William Lewis Smith. The machinist from Athol, Massachusetts, corroborated Riley's account and also testified that the American scouts had given the water cure to two native policemen that day. He recalled the matter-of-fact way that the Panay scout commander, Lieutenant Arthur Conger, had ordered the torture, with a simple command: water detail.

"That is all I heard him say," said Smith. "The men went on then and did the rest of it."[25]

When Riley and Smith proved unshakable, Lodge and his fellow Republicans again tried to minimize the severity of the torture. ("The chief effect is fright, is it not?" Beveridge interjected.) They also continued to suggest that Filipino atrocities had provoked the American actions. ("American soldiers had been murdered in many ways?" asked Charles H. Dietrich, Republican of Nebraska. "We never had a soldier injured in our district," Smith replied.[26])

Dietrich ended the extraordinary session by again suggesting that two rounds of water cure had not visibly harmed the Igbaras town president.

"I do not know that it injured him, and I don't know that he suffered any ill effects from it afterward," Smith said. "I don't know anything about that."[27]

THE EVIDENCE OF AMERICAN MISCONDUCT had converged from multiple sources, and now it spun into critical mass. No longer could President Roosevelt and administration supporters dismiss the allegations as the fabrications of anti-imperialist zealots and opportunistic Democrats. Even loyal Republicans like Senator George Frisbie Hoar and former House Speaker Thomas Reed had become convinced of the depravity of America's war in the Philippines.

The Democrats had certainly exploited the abuse scandal, and they could be counted on to do so in the coming congressional and presidential campaigns. Roosevelt's bête noire, General Miles, was already positioning himself as a contender for the Democratic nomination, raising the specter of the dashing general reminding Americans of the dishonorable acts that Roosevelt had allowed to go unpunished. The military misconduct issue had reenergized the anti-imperialists as well, and they, too, would certainly pillory the president's complacence. With his political future at stake, Roosevelt sprang into action.

The morning after Sergeant Riley's testimony, Roosevelt convened an emergency Cabinet meeting to discuss military brutality in the Philippines. In the wake of the Gardener report, the Waller trial and the latest Lodge Committee testimony, it was no longer prudent to ignore the problem—that much was clear to the master politician Roosevelt and the lawyerly Root. What was to be done about General Jake "Howling Wilderness" Smith and his alleged orders to kill everyone on Samar over the age of ten? And Major Edwin Glenn, whose abuses in Leyte and Samar had now been eclipsed by revelations of his water-cure sessions on Panay?

Decisive action was demanded, the president and his advisers agreed.

The Cabinet meeting broke up, and Roosevelt and Root moved to reclaim control of the public debate. The president had "expressed himself very strongly against the use of unnecessary harsh measures by Army officers in dealing with Filipinos," reporters were told. He and Root agreed there should be a "rigid investigation of all charges of cruelty of any kind by the Army in the Philippines."[28]

Late that afternoon, Root wired a lengthy cable to General Chaffee in Manila. He ordered the hard-line general to prepare a report on all the various abuse allegations and to conduct "an inquiry into all charges," including those made in newspapers and by former soldiers who had testified before the Lodge Committee. The American commander was also instructed to conclude his investigation of the Gardener allegations, prosecute General Smith should Waller's testimony be confirmed, and prepare charges against Major Glenn, Lieutenant Conger and any other officers involved in the alleged Panay atrocities. "As the two years allowed for the prosecution by the statute of limitations is nearly at an end," Root wrote with sudden urgency, "no time is to be lost."[29]

Roosevelt would demand honorable conduct in the Philippines, and "see that the most vigorous care is exercised to detect and prevent any cruelty or brutality, and that men guilty thereof are punished," Root directed. "Great as the provocation has been in dealing with foes who habitually resort to treachery, murder, and torture against our men, nothing can justify or will be held to justify the use of torture or inhuman conduct of any kind on the part of the American Army." At the same time, the president offered assurances that he would not abandon his soldiers. "It is believed," Root wrote, "that the violations of law and humanity . . . will prove to be few and occasional and not to characterize the conduct of the Army generally in the Philippines."

Above all, Roosevelt wanted no more surprises. "The president desires to know in the fullest and most circumstantial manner all the facts," Root ordered, "nothing concealed and no man being for any reason favored or shielded."

PRESIDENT ROOSEVELT'S SUDDEN ATTENTION to war crimes in the Philippines reverberated across America. "Cruelty and Barbarity Will Be Investigated," thundered front-page headlines in the *Atlanta Constitution*. "Barbaric War To Be Stopped." The president, it was said, was even considering a special commission to prosecute the "water cure crowd."[30]

As more former soldiers prepared to testify before the Lodge Committee about the water cure, shame and anguish piqued consciences around the country. Among the outraged was former Republican House Speaker Thomas Reed, whom, only six years earlier, Roosevelt and Lodge had supported over McKinley as their party's presidential nominee. The expansionists had waved the banner of exceptionalism and claimed divine guidance in their quest for empire. Now the knowledge that America's soldiers had behaved no differently from the brutal Europeans devastated righteous men like Tom Reed and George Frisbie Hoar.

"They were—these Filipinos—only a short time ago our wards to whom we owed sacred duties, duties we could not abandon in the face of a censorious world without soiling our Christian faith," a heartbroken Reed wrote a friend. "Now they are 'niggers' who must be punished for defending themselves. This is the history of the world with perhaps a stronger dash of hypocrisy than usual to soothe our feelings."[31]

CHAPTER 23

"Blood Grown Hot"

General Adna Chaffee was already devoting more time than he cared to the "cruelty" issue when Secretary Root's urgent command to accelerate punishment of misconduct arrived on April 17, 1902. Cables from the War Department about some new allegation had become an almost daily occurrence in recent weeks. Root had become particularly concerned with the public outcry over reports that a 28th Infantry private had choked on his own vomit after being bound and gagged on an officer's orders. The case seemed to confirm the growing perception back home that the war in the Philippines had stripped America's soldiers of their decency and honor, even toward their own.[1]

Embracing President Roosevelt's sudden spirit of full disclosure, Chaffee fired off a cable alerting Secretary Root to more Samar war crimes. The most sensational offense was the apparent murder of the acting town president of Basey and two other Filipino prisoners, shot "through [the] influence, direction or knowledge of Major [Edwin] Glenn and Lieutenant [Norman] Cook, Philippine Scouts," Chaffee wrote. Additionally, the parish priest of Basey had been abused "by direction or knowledge of Major Glenn." The general advised that murder charges be filed against Cook, while another of Glenn's operatives, Lieutenant Julien E. Gaujot, should face trial for giving the water cure to three priests (including Father Donato Guimbaolibot of Balangiga). He further recommended that Glenn be court-martialed for torturing the Igbaras town president. Finally, he informed Root that he would detain General Smith, who was about to depart for the United States.[2]

On Saturday, April 19, Chaffee steamed out to the Army transport *Buford* to inform Smith that he would not be leaving the islands just yet. The following day, Hell-roaring Jake headed ashore to find the news of his impending court-martial splashed across the front page of the *Manila Times*. Sympathetic to the Army, and especially to Smith, the newspaper sourly asked: "Where Will It Stop?"[3]

Military officers wondered the same. "Each day's news of the contemplated trials of other officers strengthens the determination to ignore the demand for convictions coming down from the Secretary of War," the *Times* reported on April 22. "Many officers believe it is a case of sink or swim together."[4] The American Chamber of Commerce cabled Roosevelt, warning that U.S. business interests in the islands were being "seriously threatened" by the trials and investigations.[5]

Chaffee, meanwhile, had other pressing problems. No sooner had he accepted Roosevelt's congratulations for ending the war on Luzon with the surrender of the Batangas guerrilla chief than a crisis erupted in the far south. Two U.S. soldiers had been killed by Muslim guerrillas in central Mindanao, and local clan leaders had refused to turn over the culprits. An enraged Chaffee had ordered a force of twelve hundred men to find and arrest the killers and punish their protectors.[6] Roosevelt was appalled, and his patience with his commander was wearing thin.

Chaffee had irritated administration officials with a pointed cable to Secretary Root in which he strongly backed General Smith and blamed military misconduct on the tropical climate and treacherous opponents. He also had implied that Roosevelt did not "fully comprehend" the war's difficulties. He even defended the use of torture, asserting that victory would not have been achieved "had not serious measures been used [to] force disclosure [of] information." Only in passing did Chaffee concede that some officers had committed excesses because of "blood grown hot in their dealings with deceit and lying. . . ."[7]

From Roosevelt's perspective, Chaffee had little appreciation for the political maelstrom unleashed by the abuse scandal. And now, just as one Philippine war of the Army's making was winding down, Chaffee wanted to start another, against a fanatical minority that had resisted four centuries of Spanish rule. Roosevelt ordered Chaffee to pull his troops back and negotiate with the Muslims. The American commander protested vigorously, but the president would not be swayed. Roosevelt then roiled the waters even further by rejecting Chaffee's panel to hear the Smith case and informing the general that he would exercise his right as commander in chief to appoint a new court.[8]

As tense cables rocketed back and forth across the Pacific, outrage boiled through Army ranks. Channeling the military's anger, the *Manila Times* accused Roosevelt of triggering perhaps "the most profound crisis in the history of the United States Regular Army." Roosevelt had given "a vote of no confidence in General Chaffee and his conduct of military affairs in the Philippine Islands" by calling off the Mindanao campaign, while the president's extraordinary intervention in the Smith court-martial was "another direct slap in the face" to Chaffee and an insult to the officers entrusted to hear the case.[9]

Insubordinate talk swept the ranks. Roosevelt aimed to sacrifice Smith and other officers to save his political skin, soldiers fumed. Some even blamed Roosevelt for the burgeoning war crimes scandal—in his eagerness to end the war by the close of 1901, the new president had led field commanders to conclude that "any methods they pursued, if successful, would be tolerated, and even approved," the embittered officers asserted. They vowed to expose "secret and confidential instructions" that would lay responsibility for the excesses at Roosevelt's doorstep.[10]

The rebellious talk tripped alarms at the War Department, and on the evening of April 22 Roosevelt convened an emergency White House meeting with Adjutant General Henry Corbin and Assistant Secretary of War William Sanger. (Root had sailed to Cuba to escape mounting calls for his resignation, while General Miles was persona non grata with the president.) In the end, Roosevelt backed down. Chaffee would be free to attack the Muslims if they did not comply with his demands. As for the

Smith court-martial, Chaffee's panel would hear the case, while the president would review the verdict.

It was all a misunderstanding, Roosevelt's spokesman announced.[11]

THE MURDER TRIAL OF TONY Waller's adjutant, Lieutenant John Day, had begun in Manila on April 16 before the same panel that had acquitted the major. Day took the stand in his defense, and again demonstrated his flair for the dramatic when he casually mentioned other unreported military killings in Basey. (He was referring to the murders of the acting town president and two other Filipinos at the direction of Major Glenn.)

In his summation, Day's attorney argued that the Marine had carried out a legitimate order to execute prisoners. Major Kingsbury countered that Day should have known Waller's order was illegal, as no trial had been held. Day had drenched "United States soil with the black blood of eleven of its . . . unarmed and defenseless prisoners."

Once again, Kingsbury's florid pleas failed to move the court. Lieutenant Day was acquitted on all charges.

THE SPOTLIGHT NOW TURNED TO Brigadier General Jacob Hurd Smith. Political pressure from Washington made it impossible for General Chaffee to shield his comrade from a court-martial, but he cushioned the blow. Unlike his Marine subordinates, Smith was charged with a much less serious offense: conduct prejudicial to good order and military discipline.

Chaffee could hardly have picked a more sympathetic panel to sit in judgment of the architect of Samar's "howling wilderness" campaign. The president was General Lloyd Wheaton, who had pioneered the Army's harsh counterinsurgency tactics in the Philippines. At Wheaton's side would be Brigadier General J. Franklin Bell, now under scrutiny over his use of resettlement camps, crop destruction and other tactics in Batangas; and Brigadier General William Bisbee of Waller trial fame, who had sanctioned torture and would later boast of hanging captured guerrillas in Central Luzon. Rounding out the panel were General Samuel S. Sumner and five colonels.

As the opposing legal teams prepared their cases, speculation raged over the identity of the next officer to face a court-martial. Would it be General Hughes, the pacifier of Panay and patron of Major Glenn? Or General Bell, whose Batangas campaign had shared "the same general vigorous tone" of Smith's work in Samar? Perhaps even General Chaffee, who bore command responsibility for both campaigns? "More of the stars in the Philippine constellation may be dimmed . . . ," warned the *Manila Times*, "unless Secretary Root awakes to the grave condition of affairs his sudden activity has brought about, and calls a halt."[12]

THE COURT-MARTIAL OF JAKE SMITH got under way on April 25 in a rented Spanish mansion south of the old walled city. As expected, Smith pleaded not guilty to the charge of conduct prejudicial to good order and military discipline, which arose from the orders he had issued to Major Waller. Smith's counsel, Colonel Charles Woodruff, then jolted the court with his next move.

Smith wished to expedite the proceedings, Woodruff announced, and would stipulate certain facts. First of all, the general had indeed instructed Waller "not to burden himself with prisoners." Furthermore, he admitted telling Waller "to kill and burn" and to make Samar "a howling wilderness." Additionally, Smith had instructed Waller to kill all persons capable of bearing arms, designating "the age limit of ten years."

Astonished by the admissions, the chief prosecutor, Major Harvey C. Carbaugh, a skilled Army judge advocate from Chicago, asked Smith to acknowledge the statements.

"I do," Smith calmly replied. "I admit that."[13]

CARBAUGH BEGAN HIS CASE by calling Captain David D. Porter to the stand. Waller's understudy recalled Smith's instructions on the day the Marines went ashore on Samar, including his command to exact retribution from the natives for the Balangiga massacre. Smith's exact words, Porter testified, were: "We must bring this thing home to these people." Porter recalled other comments uttered by Smith as they surveyed the burned ruins of Balangiga, including "kill and burn" and "we want no prisoners." Lieutenant John Day followed with additional testimony about Smith's desire for a harsh campaign.

Tony Waller was scheduled as the third and final prosecution witness. But late in the day, Carbaugh informed the court that the major was reportedly ill, and court was adjourned. On April 28, after a mysterious two-day absence that was never fully explained, Waller took the stand and for the final time recounted Smith's now infamous instructions. Under cross-examination, Waller appeared eager to help Smith's case. He understood the general's orders to apply only "to those in active hostilities," he testified. He readily agreed with Colonel Woodruff that "drastic measures and strenuous measures were necessary to accomplish the pacification of Samar."

At every turn, Woodruff attempted to show that Smith's commands had not been literally interpreted by Waller and his Marines as license to violate the laws of war. Waller acknowledged as much.

Did you permit "any killing or burning that was not demanded by the circumstances and authorized by the laws of war?" Woodruff asked.

"I did not, sir," Waller said.

"Did you on your expeditions ever kill women or children?"

"No, sir."

"In any of these conversations that you had with General Smith did you gather the idea that he wanted you to kill women or children?"

"No, I did not."

Beginning Smith's defense, Woodruff cast the trial as a referendum on the U.S. military campaign in the Philippines, and an extension of the domestic debate over America's conquest of the islands. "The Army has been held up to the scorn and contempt of the world, and of our own people, in particular, for being vindictive, cruel and oppressive in dealing with a conquered, helpless, simpleminded, misguided people," Woodruff told the court. The judgment was based on the "occasional acts of individuals" that had been "magnified, dilated upon, and gloated over" to discredit the Roosevelt administration and the Army.[14]

The evidence would show that the people of Samar had provoked Smith's robust but legitimate campaign, Woodruff continued. "We will prove that the natives by their methods placed themselves outside the pale of civilized warfare, ignored every rule of civilized warfare, were in fact outlaws, savages. We will show most magnificent results with minimum expenditure of blood due to the sharp, relentless plan adopted by General Smith, as executed by the magnificent body of men who pushed his really humane campaign to a successful issue."[15]

OVER THREE DAYS, A PARADE of enlisted men and officers who had served on Samar testified to the treachery of the island's people—their feigned friendship toward the Americans, secret scheming and sudden ambushes. Balangiga survivors described in horrific detail the mutilation of their dead comrades and other offensive acts. "Paper and other materials had been placed over the officers' heads and set fire to, so that their heads and shoulders were burned," testified Sergeant Clifford M. Mumby. "Some of the men had been cut across the body, and the cuts filled with jam taken from the issue commissary. The bodies had all been stripped of their clothing."

Other soldiers described surviving encounters in which their attackers included boys as young as twelve, and they recalled finding children hidden along jungle trails, waiting to unleash spring-loaded spears and other booby traps on American patrols. Fifteen-year-old Pedro Villanueva, who had been Captain Thomas Connell's servant at Balangiga, testified that the American officer had been killed by another fifteen-year-old. One of Major Glenn's water-cure specialists, First Lieutenant Julien A. Gaujot, buttressed the defense claim that the guerrillas used child soldiers against the Americans. "Colonel Guevara told me, himself," Gaujot testified, "that there was not a boy of eight years of age on the Gandara River that could not handle a bolo and make a cartridge."[16]

In his closing argument on Monday, May 3, Judge Advocate Carbaugh accused General Smith of issuing a sheaf of circulars and orders as legal cover for the illegal campaign he set in motion through verbal and secret written orders. It was true that the Marines did not carry out the full extent of Smith's commands, but that was a credit to the good judgment of Waller and his officers, Carbaugh argued, not Jake Smith. The general had brought dishonor upon himself, the Army and, indeed, the nation by issuing orders so harsh that, if carried out, would "remove the United States as standard bearer from the front rank of civilized nations standing for humanity in warfare."

Woodruff began his closing by decrying the home-front attacks on the armed forces in the Philippines. "I regret to say that our people at home appear to have forgotten the magnificent services of the men here; of the sacrifices which they have made for America's honor and glory. Through good and evil report, through sun and rain, through mud and dust, across rivers, over mountains, through tangled underbrush, in sickness and in health, they have reflected nothing but honor and glory on the flag of their country."

General Smith never intended that his "take no prisoners" command be interpreted as license for wanton slaughter, and that, in fact, had not occurred. Major Waller and Captain Porter had testified that they had taken prisoners and shown mercy to natives. Smith's plan "was to make the interior of Samar such a 'howling wilderness' that the natives would be forced to come into the coast towns for their own protection," Woodruff said. The campaign was modeled on the severe Union campaigns waged by such great generals as Sherman and Sheridan during the Civil War. "You, who marched with Sherman from Atlanta to the sea, know how your routes were marked by clouds of smoke by day and [pillars] of fire by night. And that was war."

The court-martial of Jake Smith was an injustice against a fine soldier who had been poised to return to his family after three years of gallant service in the Philippines, "covered, as he and all those who knew him thought, with honor and glory," Woodruff declared. The charges were politically motivated, spurred by "noisy public sentiment in the United States, based upon rumors fostered for some unknown, and I believe, ignoble purposes. . . ." General Smith, he concluded, "can face his conscience, this court and the American people, with full knowledge and belief that he did his duty, his full duty as an honorable American soldier."

Woodruff's stirring summation led many spectators to believe that Smith, like his Marine subordinates, would be acquitted.[17] But with the eyes of the nation upon them, the court found Smith guilty as charged. The true sentiments of General Wheaton and his comrades, however, may have been expressed in the sentence they levied: Jake Smith should be admonished for his behavior, they concluded, but face no further punishment.

BACK IN WASHINGTON, PRESIDENT ROOSEVELT's vow to investigate and punish military misconduct in the Philippines had done little to calm the rising storm. Anti-Imperialist League stalwarts cranked out new pamphlets highlighting military abuses in the islands. Congressional floor debates on unrelated topics suddenly became forums for denouncing misconduct in the Philippines. Much to the concern of Roosevelt and other Republicans, some of the voices now raised against American policy in the islands were those of loyal expansionists, outraged by the mounting evidence of abuses.

Meanwhile, embarrassing testimony about the Army's use of the water cure continued to flow from the Lodge Committee. Grover Flint of Cambridge, Massachusetts, a former lieutenant in the 35th Volunteer Infantry, testified that he had witnessed about twenty cases of the torture administered by American soldiers and native scouts on Luzon.[18] Senator Lodge attempted to counter the latest revelation with a report from a Women's Christian Temperance Union chapter in Wisconsin, asserting that the moral condition of the Philippines had improved under American occupation.

Uneasiness within Republican ranks had been rising since the initial reports on General Bell's use of resettlement camps earlier in the year. Several Republican newspapers had denounced the tactics as criminal. "We have actually come to do the thing we went to war to banish," declared the pro-administration *Baltimore American*.[19] The Lodge Committee testimony and Waller court-martial revelations had ratcheted up criticism of Roosevelt and his men. The *Indianapolis News*, hometown newspaper of Senator Albert Beveridge, pronounced Smith's campaign as proof that the administration's failed policy in the Philippines had caused American troops to adopt "the methods of barbarism."[20]

Behind the scenes, Roosevelt and his circle faced anxious questions from powerful Republicans. George H. Lyman, the influential collector of the Port of Boston, asked Lodge for reassurances that there was no truth to the stories of American soldiers torturing Filipinos. New England merchant financier Henry Lee Higginson, a deep-pocketed party donor, warned that the revelations had shaken his faith in the administration's venture in the Philippines. In fact, Higginson wrote, "A very considerable number of staunch [R]epublicans . . . who have never looked at any other ticket, would like to get out of these islands."[21]

Democratic outrage had been sharpened by a recent speech given by General Frederick Funston, who mockingly suggested that American critics of the war ought to be strung up like the *insurrectos* he and his men had executed.[22] In a scathing response that stretched over two days, Democratic Senator Edward Carmack of Tennessee excoriated Funston as a "licensed swaggerer and braggart" who needed schooling in the principles of American democracy. But Carmack saved his most severe remarks for Roosevelt and his conquest of the Philippines. The administration's military campaign had strewn the archipelago "with the ashes of its homes and drenched it with the blood of its people," Carmack charged. It had crushed dissent by denying the very liberties that Roosevelt had promised to bestow. "Spain has had her revenge," Carmack declared, "for we have become the imitators of her most famous iniquities."[23]

The pressure on Roosevelt mounted in the last week of April as the Smith court-martial played out in Manila. Another round of hysterical headlines about Hell-roaring Jake's reign of terror on Samar provoked howls of outrage in Congress and across the country. "In the records of all the great wars since the Middle Ages, you cannot find such a disgraceful and wicked order as that issued by General Smith," declared Senator Henry M. Teller, the Colorado Republican. In the House of Representatives, Republican Joseph C. Sibley of Pennsylvania likened General Smith to King Herod for issuing orders to kill children. "He is a disgrace . . . to every man who ever wore the uniform of the United States, and he is a blot and a disgrace to our present civilization," said Sibley, an expansionist who had steadfastly supported administration policy in the Philippines. Two House resolutions called on Secretary Root to reveal whether Smith's order had been issued with the department's knowledge or approval. (Root denied both.) Even Henry Cabot Lodge was moved to concede, "General Smith's order is one which every American should regret."[24]

Pro-administration institutions such as the *New York Times* were conflicted by the obvious need to address the abuse allegations and their fear of weakening the administration. Americans "have been shocked by Gen. Jacob H. Smith's admission that he issued the order to burn and kill," the *Times* conceded, and warned of more revelations to come. But the paper dismissed demands for an independent investigation. President Roosevelt's pledge to investigate abuses and the prompt courts-martial of Major Waller and General Smith "leave no doubt in most minds that the national character is safe in the keeping of those who are officially accountable."

In the Senate, however, Lodge was less certain whether the backlash could be contained. He managed to block a Democratic attempt to expand the investigation by summoning Major Cornelius Gardener and Filipino revolutionary leaders as witnesses. But as a concession to the growing outrage, he hinted that he was willing to dispatch an investigative committee to the Philippines. "The Republicans of the Senate," the *Atlanta Constitution* crowed, "are beginning to weaken under the fire of the minority. . . ."[25]

As LODGE AND OTHER CONGRESSIONAL Republicans wavered, Theodore Roosevelt calmly pondered his next move. With clenched-teeth fury, he had suffered the condemnation of his policies and calls for Root's resignation. He had choked back his contempt for Southern white supremacists like Edward Carmack, who attacked the military's treatment of Filipinos while acquiescing to violence against black Americans. His disdain for the anti-imperialists was just as intense. (Moorfield Storey had just coauthored a provocative new pamphlet, "Secretary Root's Record: Marked Severities in Philippine Warfare.") They were all traitors, selling out America's soldiers and besmirching the national honor.

Roosevelt was ready to return fire.

The opening salvo was launched on May 1, in a leaked *Washington Post* story in which the War Department distanced itself from General Smith and deflected blame to General Chaffee.[26] The following day, the *New York Times* urged Americans to reconsider their outrage over the revelations from the Pacific. "It is not so certain that we at home can afford to shudder at the water cure, unless we disdain the whole job," the *Times* editorialized. "The army has obeyed orders. It was sent to subdue Filipinos. Having the devil to fight, it has sometimes used fire." Now Roosevelt called on his old friend Henry Cabot Lodge to deliver the coup de grâce to the enemies of expansion.[27]

At two o'clock on Monday, May 5, a dazzling spring day in Washington, Lodge rose on the Senate floor to deliver one of the most important speeches of his career. Over the previous decade, the fifty-one-year-old Lodge had been at the forefront of every fight in the cause of American expansion: construction of a blue-water navy, annexation of Hawaii, intervention in Cuba, and retention of the Philippines. He had saved the Treaty of Paris in 1899, and defended the administration's dirty war in the Philippines. At every turn, he had remained true to his friend Theodore—securing his position as McKinley's assistant secretary of the Navy, his nomination as vice president. Now, as he gazed around at the galleries packed with administration supporters, Lodge held the immediate fortunes of Roosevelt's presidency in his hands.

Lodge began by expressing "deep regret" that American soldiers had resorted to torture and other brutalities in the Philippines. However, he patiently continued, as though he were back at Harvard teaching freshman history, there was a reason American boys had committed these deeds. He recited a list of murders and assaults "of the most flagrant character" carried out by the Filipinos against American soldiers, acts of torture and treachery, mutilation and savagery. "Only last night I heard of three of our men having been captured and carried to a neighboring town," he said. His chilling tale ended with the murder of all three Americans, one by stoning and the other two by bolos. "Do you wonder that the American soldiers after that went into battle with cries for vengeance?" Lodge demanded. "I am not here to excuse torture or cruelty, but I cannot condemn human nature in an American soldier under such circumstances as those."[28]

Lodge recalled other murders committed by the guerrillas, including the assassination of hundreds of loyal Filipinos. "I say that whatever else may be true or false, if we go out of those islands and leave these friendly Filipinos to a fate like that we are unworthy of the name of a great nation, and it would be a greater infamy than any cruelty ever practiced." The attacks that Democrats and anti-imperialists had hurled against the Army—"not a Republican army, not a Democratic army, but the Army of the United States"—were beyond the pale, he declared. "If Army men have done wrong, let them be punished. But let us, oh, let us be just, at least to our own. Let us remember not only their sufferings but their temptations, their provocations, their trials." The critics had tarnished the Army's glory, the nation's glory, in the eyes of the world. But, he concluded, "When the whole story shall be made up I believe that, notwithstanding all that has been said, all the denunciations heaped upon our troops and officers, the record of that army, clean and victorious from Trenton to Manila, will shine brightly in the annals of the Republic. . . ."[29]

IN THE WAKE OF LODGE'S SPEECH, a drumbeat of voices weighed in to defend both the Army and the Republican administration—current generals like Frederick Funston, Civil War heroes, Cabinet officers and dozens of Republican newspapers across the country. Most of the pro-administration commentary took the tone of the *Providence Sunday Journal,* which accepted "the wisdom of fighting fire with fire" and assured its readers that the water cure "does not necessarily have serious after effects."[30]

Roosevelt remained above the debate, but behind the scenes he put his prolific pen to good use, reassuring troubled citizens that he was serious about curbing abuses. "I hope it is unnecessary to say that no one in the country can be more anxious than I am—save perhaps Secretary Root—to discover and punish every instance of barbarity by our troops in the Philippines," Roosevelt wrote a Massachusetts bishop on May 9. "No provocation, however great, can be accepted as an excuse for misuse of the necessary severity of war, and above all not for torture of any kind or shape."[31]

The administration's aggressive counterattack had staggered the critics, but did not silence them. The Senate's daily affairs were now dominated by a vitriolic debate over Roosevelt's civil government legislation for the Philippines. Senator Beveridge attacked the motives of Democrats for opposing administration policy in the islands and pressing the investigation of military abuses. Carmack slyly coined a new slogan for administration policy in the Philippines: "Malevolent Dissimulation." Lodge, meanwhile, attempted to suspend his hearings on the Philippines, but the Democrats would not hear of it. And so the spectacle of former soldiers testifying to the use of the water cure and other brutal measures served as a prelude to each afternoon's Senate debate over America's policy in the islands.[32]

On Thursday, May 22, old George Frisbie Hoar placed his imprimatur on the military misconduct debate with a three-hour speech on the Senate floor. It would be his last great address on the Philippines, and a powerful finale it would be. Two days earlier Roosevelt had fulfilled America's promise of Cuban independence, and the transfer of power had unfolded in Havana amid flag-waving pomp. Now Hoar called for Roosevelt to do the same in the Philippines. His harshly poetic critique of the administration's record in the islands echoed for weeks afterward:

> You have wasted six hundred millions of treasure. You have sacrificed nearly ten thousand American lives—the flower of our youth. You have devastated provinces. You have slain uncounted thousands of people you desire to benefit. You have established reconcentration camps. . . . You make the American flag in the eyes of a numerous people the emblem of sacrilege in Christian churches, and of the burning of human dwellings, and of the horror of the water torture. . . . Your practical statesmanship has succeeded in converting a people who three years ago were ready to kiss the hem of the garment of the American and to welcome him as liberator, who thronged after your men when they landed on those islands with benediction and gratitude, into sullen and irreconcilable enemies, possessed of a hatred which centuries cannot eradicate.[33]

STUNG BY HOAR'S REBUKE, Theodore Roosevelt now resolved to charge into the fray in defense of the Army and administration policy in the

Philippines. He chose as his stage Memorial Day ceremonies at Arlington National Cemetery.[34]

At noon on Friday, May 30, 1902, Roosevelt left the White House in a horse-drawn carriage escorted by mounted military officers. Seated alongside the president were Secretary of War Root (just back from Cuba), presidential secretary George Cortelyou and a naval aide. The carriage clattered through the streets of Washington under a warm spring sun and crossed the Potomac River into Virginia. It wound its way up the slopes lined with the bone white headstones of the nation's fallen soldiers, now adorned with flowers and small flags fluttering in the breeze, and rolled past the mansion that Robert E. Lee had left forever on a fateful spring day forty-one years earlier. Behind the old plantation house, the Marine Band began to play Chopin's funeral march, and a procession of grizzled Civil War veterans fell in for the short hike to the pavilion where Roosevelt was to speak. The presidential carriage arrived a little after one p.m., and as the gathered crowd applauded, a twenty-one-gun salute crackled over the Arlington hills.[35]

Roosevelt began by paying homage to the old warriors before him and the sacrifices they had made on behalf of the nation, before seamlessly proceeding to the topic that had become a threat to his young presidency. The conflict in the Philippines was drawing to an end, he declared, "a small but peculiarly trying and difficult war in which is involved not only the honor of the flag but the triumph of civilization over forces which stand for the black chaos of savages and barbarism." The achievements of America's soldiers in the islands may have paled in comparison to the great victories won by the bemedaled heroes before him, Roosevelt allowed, but "they have shown themselves not unworthy of you, and they are entitled to the support of all men who are proud of what you did."

Moving now to the issue of military misconduct, Roosevelt reminded his audience that "these younger comrades of yours have fought under terrible difficulties and have received terrible provocations from a very cruel and very treacherous enemy." Some had committed "acts of cruelty," he conceded. He had launched a "determined and unswerving effort . . . to find out every instance of barbarity on the part of our troops," and to punish the guilty and prevent future abuses.[36]

Roosevelt could have ended on that lofty note, but his anger toward his critics would not allow him. The fury he felt toward the Southern Democrats who had criticized the missteps of America's soldiers in the Philippines while ignoring their own cruelty toward black Americans now boiled over. "From time to time there occur in our country, to the deep and lasting shame of our people, lynchings carried on under circumstances of inhuman cruelty and barbarity," Roosevelt shouted, "cruelty infinitely worse than any that has ever been committed by our troops in the Philippines; worse to the victims, and far more brutalizing to those guilty of it."

More knife thrusts to his tormentors followed before Roosevelt changed direction again, launching into yet another attempt to minimize the extent of American misconduct in the islands. "We would have been justified by Abraham Lincoln's rules of war in infinitely greater severity than has been shown," Roosevelt asserted. In fact, "our warfare in the Philippines has been carried on with singular humanity. For every act of cruelty by our men there have been innumerable acts of forbearance, magnanimity, and generous kindness."

He closed with a tribute to the soldiers who had propelled America to global greatness, yet now found themselves under attack at home. "Here and there black sheep are to be found among them; but taken as a whole they represent as high a standard of public service as this country has ever seen," he thundered. "They are doing a great work for civilization, a great work for the honor and the interest of this nation, and above all for the welfare of the inhabitants of the Philippine Islands. All honor to them; and shame, thrice shame, to us if we fail to uphold their hands!"[37]

Roosevelt stepped back from the podium, basking in the triumph and satisfaction of the moment as applause rolled over the hallowed hills.

IN THE AFTERMATH OF ROOSEVELT'S ADDRESS, public opinion swung firmly back in the Republican camp (except in the South, where his comments on lynchings provoked further anger and denunciations). A majority of Americans accepted the president's assurances that the extent of the abuses had been overstated and that erring soldiers had acted out of extreme provocation. They also took Roosevelt at his word that the few legitimate cases of abuse would be punished.[38]

Roosevelt now claimed victories in quick succession. On June 3, the Senate approved his Philippine civil government legislation on a strict party-line vote. Only one Republican broke with the president and voted with the Democrats: George Frisbie Hoar.

The following day, the Senate symbolically turned the page by taking up another item high on the president's agenda: construction of a canal connecting the Atlantic and Pacific oceans. On June 19, the Senate bowed to Roosevelt's will once again and voted sixty-seven to six to build the strategic passageway through the Colombian province of Panama.

Although public outrage and press coverage of the atrocity issue began to fade, the president could not completely escape the taint of scandal. Headlines from the Philippines brought news of more trials and investigations, including the court-martial of Major Edwin Glenn and his intelligence operatives on Samar.

But the arrival of summer—and the annual congressional scramble to escape the sweltering capital—finally presented Senator Lodge with a pretext to suspend the hearings on the Philippines, and he gaveled the committee to adjournment on June 28. The water-cure testimony had scandalized the Army, damaged the administration and shocked the nation, but Lodge had blocked the more exhaustive investigation sought by Democrats and anti-imperialists.

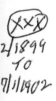

Congress adjourned on July 1, and with his Democratic tormentors taking their leave, Theodore Roosevelt prepared to follow. But first, he had one important piece of unfinished business: In a presidential proclamation, he declared an end to the war in the Philippines.

As he scribbled his signature on the document, Roosevelt ignored resistance in the Muslim south that would flare for years. He also glossed over the fact that the American soldiers he extolled as liberators had shattered the dream of Philippine independence. Instead, with a calculated stroke of his pen, Roosevelt postdated his declaration to imply fulfillment of Filipino aspirations: "July Fourth, 1902," he wrote.[39]

CHAPTER 24

------ •·•·• ------

Homecoming

As the war in the Philippines sputtered to a close, Secretary of War Root intensified his drive to slash the cost of America's imperial duties. A drawdown in troop levels offered the most impressive savings, and so a fleet of transport ships was kept in constant motion, returning soldiers by the thousands. The unlucky ones made the journey in government-issue coffins, and Root had managed to wring savings even from the return of America's dead. When the body of Marine Corporal Wallace A. Sullivan of Bristol, West Virginia, reached San Francisco on April 15, the War Department wired his parents, offering a choice as to the disposition of their son's remains: The Marines would ship the body home, "at your own expense," or bury young Sullivan at San Francisco National Cemetery, nearly three thousand miles away from family and friends, on the government's dime.[1]

Major Tony Waller and his Marines prepared to make the Pacific crossing under happier circumstances as their tour of duty in the islands drew to an end in the spring of 1902. Waller's acquittal had prompted a flurry of congratulatory letters from fellow Marines and foreign officers he had met in China, as well as friends and complete strangers. In Yokohama Harbor, Japan, where the news was flashed to ships of the U.S.

Navy's Asiatic Squadron, a lunch party of officers aboard the USS *York-town* had raised their glasses in Waller's honor.[2]

As the date of his departure approached, Waller maintained a high profile on the military social circuit. He hosted a ten-course dinner and dance in Cavite that was rated by the *Manila Times* as "one of the most brilliant affairs since the American occupation." Fellow Marines presented Waller with a silver loving cup and flagon. Afterward, the revelers danced into the night as the all-Filipino Navy yard band belted out popular American tunes. "This battalion of Marines will be greatly missed," a correspondent observed, "as they have entertained a great deal and in a manner that few can attain."[3]

On May 2, Waller led his 1st Battalion of Marines, twelve officers and 450 men, aboard the Army transport *Warren* in Manila Bay. Among the thousand-plus passengers packed onto the transport was Company I of the Army's 9th Infantry. (The remainder of the battle-scarred regiment would follow on the transport *Hancock* a few days later.) In addition to their military kit and souvenirs, the soldiers had smuggled pet monkeys, parrots, snakes and other tropical creatures aboard the ship.[4]

With its consignment of soldiers and contraband safely aboard, the *Warren* made its way to the mouth of Manila Bay and dropped anchor off the fishing village of Mariveles. Since the cholera outbreak in March, departing ships had been required to pass a five-day quarantine here to prevent spread of the disease beyond the islands. As the *Warren* rode at anchor, a discharged soldier of the 25th Infantry suddenly fell ill and died. Waller and the other passengers were ordered ashore to a crude quarantine camp surrounded by barbed-wire fences and armed guards. Twelve days passed without further illness, and late in the afternoon of May 15, the *Warren* weighed anchor and steamed into the South China Sea. Though his name would be forever associated with the islands, Tony Waller would never set foot in the Philippines again.[5]

THE AFTERNOON OF WALLER'S DEPARTURE, the Army cable ship *Burnside* headed south from Manila Bay carrying the players who would take the stage in the next act of America's war crimes drama. Among the passengers were the bearded West Pointer Major Edwin Glenn, and the thirteen-member Army panel that would sit in judgment of his actions at Igbaras, Panay. Also aboard were several American and Filipino soldiers who would testify on Glenn's behalf, along with the prosecution's star witness: Joveniano Ealdama, the former president of Igbaras. Glenn's water-cure-aided confession had led to Ealdama's conviction as a "war traitor," and he was currently serving a ten-year sentence of hard labor at Manila's Bilibid Prison.[6]

Glenn had fought hard to avoid a court-martial in America, arguing that the "high state of excitement in the United States" over the water cure would preclude a fair trial. When General Chaffee warned the War Department that the trials of Glenn and two junior officers would feature some sordid testimony of "inhuman treatment," Secretary Root ordered the trials moved to Samar.[7]

The *Burnside* dropped anchor off Catbalogan on the west coast of Samar, and Glenn's trial got under way in a courtroom arranged on the ship's canopied deck. Glenn admitted that he had ordered the water cure administered to Ealdama, but argued that it was a legitimate act necessary to break guerrilla resistance on Panay.

Ealdama took the witness stand and recalled his harrowing encounter with Glenn on November 27, 1900. He testified that he feared he would die during his two rounds of water cure at the hands of Glenn's men. The interpreter for the Americans "told me to say yes, that I was in communication with the *insurrectos*" to stop the torture, and so he did. Afterward, he experienced "shortness of breath and pain in the stomach. My throat also hurt me on account of so much water coming out through it."[8]

The crux of Glenn's defense was his contention that the water cure was necessary to elicit information from Filipinos, and caused no harm to the victim. Five defense witnesses—including two former guerrillas tortured in American custody—testified that they had undergone the water cure without ill effect. Quartermaster Sergeant Martin Geary of the 26th U.S. Volunteers said that after undergoing the water cure out of curiosity, he felt so good that he "ate a very hearty dinner." Colonel Nicholas Roces of the Native Constabulary testified that several former guerrillas in his command were convinced that the water cure literally had cured their dengue fever.[9]

Glenn testified that he, too, had undergone the water cure several months before the incident at Igbaras to weigh its effects. It was the mildest punishment that could force guerrillas to give information, he said. "I am convinced that my action resulted in hastening the termination of hostilities and directly resulted in saving many human lives, and directly injured no one."[10]

After a week's testimony, the court found Glenn guilty of violating the laws of war. It suspended him from duty for one month and fined him $50. Lieutenant Julien Gaujot was convicted of war crimes for giving the water cure to three Filipino priests, including Father Donato Guimbao-libot of Balangiga. He was sentenced to three months' suspension and forfeited $150 in pay. Lieutenant Norman Cook was acquitted of ordering the murders of the acting president of Basey and two other Filipinos.[11]

THE FADING SPOTLIGHT NOW TURNED to Major Cornelius Gardener and his allegations of systematic Army brutality in Tayabas province.

At Secretary Root's direction, General Chaffee in April had appointed a board to hear evidence and weigh the veracity of Gardener's allegations of physical abuse, torture and other misdeeds committed by American troops. From the outset, Chaffee and his panelists scarcely hid their contempt for the Army whistleblower.

Through press leaks and public attacks, the board undermined Gardener's claims and suggested that he, too, had engaged in the water cure and "other drastic measures." The *Manila Times* suggested that a smoking-gun telegram from Gardener would reveal the major's dark secrets, but the document was never produced (nor any other especially damaging revelations about Gardener).[12] The Army did provide evidence that Tayabas was not as peaceful as the major had suggested in his communications to superiors. The implication was that Gardener's soft approach toward Filipinos had allowed the guerrillas to run rampant in his province.[13]

Gardener took the stand on June 26 and testified that he had attempted to fulfill McKinley's benevolent policy when he arrived in Tayabas in January 1900. He found the towns "entirely depopulated" and Filipinos living in far-flung barrios, fearful of the Americans. Gardener said he had built confidence with peaceful citizens by treating them fairly while pursuing aggressive operations against the remaining guerrillas. Subsequent Army abuses had seriously undermined trust in the Americans, he said.[14]

He went on to describe unpunished outrages committed by officers and soldiers—deeds he had begun reporting as early as July 1901. One of the offenders, Lieutenant George Catlin, had a habit of choking and punching any native who failed to doff his hat as a show of respect.[15] Instead of being cashiered or at least removed from field command by Army superiors, Catlin was transferred to another Tayabas town, where his behavior toward Filipinos became even more outrageous. He would strike natives in the face with his whip or cane, or kick them whenever they failed to show proper deference. Some Filipinos were so terrified of the American that they fled to the hills. When the Army still did nothing, Gardener said, he filed his report with Governor Taft.[16]

The rancorous hearings dragged on for more than six weeks. A procession of Army officers testified that, contrary to Gardener's assertions, they had conducted a humane and honorable war. On July 12, after hearing scores of witnesses and amassing more than eight hundred pages of evidence, the board announced it had completed its work and would forward its findings to Washington. The case quietly faded away, without any soldier ever being punished as a result of Gardener's report or testimony.[17]

ABOARD THE ARMY TRANSPORT *WARREN,* Tony Waller passed the first nine days of his monthlong voyage poring over after-action reports and official communications as he prepared the final account of his Samar tour for Marine Corps headquarters. The *Warren* sailed past the island of Formosa, then on to Nagasaki, Japan, where it took on coal for the Pacific crossing. As the ship sailed northward, the men savored the cool, temperate climate after years in the tropics. Soon they shivered in fog and cold drizzle, prompting inevitable complaints from some that the muggy Philippines had made their blood thin.[18]

On Thursday, June 12, after twenty-eight days at sea, the *Warren* steamed into San Francisco Bay. The arrival of troop-laden transports from the Philippines had become old news in the city, but word had spread that the famed (and now infamous) Major Waller was arriving with his battle-scarred Marines. As he stepped ashore, a scrum of reporters jostled for an interview.

A wire service reporter soon claimed to have scooped the competition, and newspapers across America printed Waller's pithy pronouncements on Saturday, June 14. "Hades is a winter resort compared to Samar," Waller was quoted as saying. He boasted of leaving the island "a howling wilderness," supported the use of "the severest measures" against the guerrillas, and endorsed General Smith's harsh orders as "the only thing that could be done."[19] It was sensational stuff from the Marine whose actions had unleashed the war crimes trials. But so many of the statements attributed to Waller were either embellished or demonstrably false as to raise questions whether the entire encounter had been concocted by the reporter.

A furious White House and War Department did not wait for verification, and ordered Waller to explain himself. He promptly denied giving the interview. As Waller and his men boarded a train bound for New York City, furious anti-imperialist newspapers demanded punishment of the unrepentant "Butcher of Samar."[20]

CONTROVERSY OVER WALLER'S PURPORTED COMMENTS simmered throughout the week. It was reported that President Roosevelt was considering hauling the Marine before another court-martial.[21] The furor awaited Waller and his men on Friday morning, June 20, when their train rolled into Jersey City, New Jersey. The Marines marched to the waterfront and boarded a pair of Navy tugs for the short trip to the Brooklyn Navy Yard.

Three companies of Marines waited at the Brooklyn docks under sunny skies, and Waller and his men marched ashore as a Navy band struck up "Home, Sweet Home." "With flags flying and bands playing, it seemed like a picturesque repetition of the stirring days of the Spanish-American War," observed a reporter for the *Brooklyn Eagle*. Tears streaked the sun-crisped cheeks of the Samar survivors.

On the dock, Waller formed his men behind a tattered flag from the Samar campaign. On his command, the Marines stepped off smartly to the cheers of their comrades. At the Marine barracks, Colonel Robert Meade assured Waller and his men that their countrymen appreciated their service in China and the Philippines.

Afterward, reporters mobbed Waller.

"I have absolutely no statement to give out," the Marine protested.

"Nothing about the 'water cure,' sir?" a reported pressed.

"As to 'water cure,' we don't know anything about that," Waller said.

"Will you say whether or not the statements concerning cruelty to the Filipinos are true?"

"I will say that so far as I am concerned much that has been written about me is the product of over-fertile imaginations."

As Waller made his escape, the reporters sought out his men. A few Marines agreed to talk about their experiences in the Philippines.[22]

"Oh, they are all lies, them things that's been published about cruelty to the Filipinos," one khaki-clad private was quoted as saying. "You couldn't be cruel enough to the damn little pests."[23]

Waller and his long-suffering wife, Clara, departed from Brooklyn the following morning. He yearned to return home to Norfolk, Virginia, to see his sons for the first time in nearly three years. But duty demanded that he first report to his superiors in Washington. There, newsmen again shadowed him as he called on Brigadier General Charles Heywood at Marine Corps headquarters.

Afterward, the Marine commandant accompanied Waller to an audience with Roosevelt's newest Cabinet member, Navy Secretary William H. Moody. Officially, the conversation "did not touch on business matters," but Moody and Heywood both praised the performance of Waller and his men in the Philippines. That evening, after dodging reporters again, Waller and his wife boarded a boat for Norfolk. A hero's welcome awaited him there.[24]

WHILE WALLER REACQUAINTED HIMSELF with family life in Virginia, President Roosevelt declared an end to the war in the Philippines and headed to his Long Island estate. On the afternoon of July 5, he arrived in the sleepy fishing village of Oyster Bay amid trilling steam whistles, cheers and shouts of "Teddy!" Three of his younger children smothered him in hugs and kisses, and they set off in an open surrey for Sagamore Hill, the forty-acre Roosevelt family estate, three miles beyond the village.[25]

Summers at Sagamore Hill propelled Roosevelt to new heights of manic activity, and he spent hours each day entertaining the youngest members of his clan. They played tennis, rode horses, hiked the woods and fields, rowed the nooks and crannies of Oyster Bay, watched birds, caught tadpoles. A cordon of bodyguards, ubiquitous in the months since McKinley's assassination, kept unwanted visitors at bay. That included reporters, who complained about soaring prices in the village as they filled their empty notebooks with fanciful rubbish. The president occasionally cantered into the village on horseback, invariably trailed by a parade of young Roosevelts that included little Archie, decked out in Rough Rider garb.[26]

At eight thirty a.m. each weekday morning, Roosevelt reported to his Sagamore Hill library to read mail and conduct the nation's business under the efficient direction of his personal secretary, George Cortelyou. A tranquil mood settled over the shores of Oyster Bay and wafted across much of the country. The war in the Philippines was over and the soldiers were returning home, with America's new standing as a world power secure. The sordid tales of military misconduct had fallen off newspaper front pages, and Americans were singing "In the Good Old Summertime."[27]

On July 12, Roosevelt's bliss was interrupted by the arrival of Elihu Root. Worn down by the strain of the abuse scandal, the secretary of war was scheduled to sail away on a European holiday in ten days' time. But first, a delicate matter demanded the president's immediate attention. Root handed Roosevelt the transcript of Jake Smith's court-martial, just arrived from the Philippines. For the president, a critical moment of truth was at hand: He had promised to punish American "cruelties" in the islands, but was a reprimand sufficient penalty for a senior officer who had ordered his subordinates to kill everyone over the age of ten?[28]

Over the past months of criticism and debate, Roosevelt had reached

firm conclusions about the military misconduct. That American troops
had been provoked by a savage and treacherous enemy he did not doubt.
He also accepted that American soldiers had rather extensively used the
water cure, a "mild torture" in which "nobody was seriously damaged."
But the Smith case wasn't about the water cure, and the president was
troubled by the issues it raised.

Roosevelt did not have a problem with the overall harshness of the
Samar campaign—he had made it clear to the Army "that I thoroughly
believe in severe measures when necessary, and am not in the least sensitive about killing any number of men if there is adequate reason." General Smith's language to Waller on Samar was rough, but, in reality, "not
much worse than that General Sherman used on one occasion in refer-
ence to the Sioux Indians." The difference, in Roosevelt's mind, was that
Smith had used such language in an order—a dangerous thing for a commanding officer, and, as Roosevelt had heard from a number of sources,
an old habit with Smith. Equally disturbing to the president was the rac-
ism underpinning Smith's harsh language, including his characterization
of his work in the Philippines as "shooting niggers."[29]

There were political considerations as well: The administration's
attempt to make an example of Waller had been thwarted by his acquittal. The Smith court had delivered a conviction, but had sentenced the
general to a slap on the wrist—a mockery of justice that might provoke a
backlash in the fall political campaign. But should Roosevelt overrule the
court and impose too harsh a sentence, he risked angering conservatives
and alienating the military.

Root now offered a pitch-perfect solution: Retire Hell-roaring Jake.

Roosevelt enthusiastically embraced the recommendation. Four days
later, while Smith was at sea on a U.S.-bound Army transport, the War
Department announced that the president had ended the career of the
controversial general.[30]

Bipartisan praise greeted Roosevelt's action. But it was still not enough
to satisfy his toughest critics.

On July 27, five leaders of the Anti-Imperialist League issued another
open letter to Roosevelt alleging abuses "far more general" than admitted
by the administration and calling for a systematic investigation. The

authors—Charles Francis Adams, Carl Schurz, Edwin Burritt Smith, Moorfield Storey and Herbert Welsh—praised the president's intervention in the Smith case, but labeled it a mere first step "toward the reestablishment of the National prestige and the restoration of the morale of the army."[31]

U.S. troops had been guilty of torture, kidnapping, murder, robbery and rape, the anti-imperialists charged—crimes the authors said had been concealed through the coordinated efforts of the Army, Secretary of War Root and Senator Lodge. "Much, we have reason to assert and stand ready to prove, has been and still remains concealed, while many wrongdoers, for various 'reasons,' have been, and still are, favored or shielded." The anti-imperialists offered to prove their allegations before military tribunals or another body of Roosevelt's choosing.

As he had done from the beginning, Roosevelt simply ignored the anti-imperialists. He sensed that the public was tired of the Philippines. If American misconduct demanded justice, the retirement of General Smith was enough for many.

"I think he has been very adroit," Adams grudgingly conceded. "He has conciliated almost everyone."[32]

ON AUGUST 1, THE BLACK knight of America's war in the Philippines arrived in San Francisco Bay aboard the Army transport *Thomas*. Since the spring General Jacob Hurd Smith had been pilloried on the floor of Congress and vilified in newspapers across America. Among the scores of cartoons spawned by the general's infamous Samar orders was one in the *Denver Post*, purporting to show the new Filipino dollar. On one side of the coin was the head of General Smith, flanked by a bolo knife and a lighted torch. Above his likeness were the words "Kill and Burn All Over Ten" while below was "Herod II." The reverse showed an American soldier injecting water into a Filipino through a syringe, along with the motto: "Empire of the United States, In Water Cure We Trust."[33]

In the weeks following his trial, Smith had been the subject of high-level discussions that had frayed nerves on both sides of the Pacific. General Chaffee and senior administration officials feared that Smith might blame higher-ups for his actions, and so they prepared to contain the damage. Privately, Chaffee declared Smith mentally unstable—a charge that, if leaked to the press, would allow Chaffee and administration officials to discredit anything that Smith uttered.[34] When Root ordered Chaffee to convene a medical board to confirm Smith's insanity, the commanding general suddenly balked. Smith was guilty of "erratic and egotistical statements," wrote Chaffee, but he was in "good physical condition" and would be found "fit for duty." Root dispensed with the medical board and ordered Smith to proceed to the United States.[35]

As the *Thomas* eased alongside the San Francisco waterfront, shouting reporters informed Jake Smith of the news that all of America had known for two weeks: President Roosevelt had ended his military career. As soldiers stood on the dock and cheered the conqueror of Samar, Smith hurried ashore without a word to the press.

For two days, he cloistered himself in a room at the Occidental Hotel before emerging to face reporters. Chaffee and Root need not have worried about being thrown to the wolves. Smith made no attempt to shift the blame. His campaign on Samar was tough, he conceded, but harsh methods were required against such a savage enemy. As for his retirement, it had come as a shock, he admitted, but "I am a soldier and take what is coming to me."[36]

A tumultuous welcome awaited Smith on August 11, when he reached his hometown of Portsmouth, Ohio. Bands played and cannon boomed. In the evening, a local National Guard company marched to the hilltop home where Smith was staying and fired a salute. There was talk among the general's supporters of challenging his retirement in court. All the while Smith's elderly mother assured reporters her son was an American hero, not a villain.[37] Eight days later, Smith was guest of honor at a public reception hosted by Portsmouth's leading citizens. He had merely done his duty "in bringing into subjection the tribes of Samar," he declared. He would let the nation decide whether he had "acted the part of a soldier or not."[38]

For all the condemnation Hell-roaring Jake had endured, many Americans were quick to forgive his conduct on Samar. Republican newspapers now offered praise for "the splendid example" he had set in stoically accepting his fate. As Americans turned away from the unpleasantries of the Philippines, Smith's rehabilitation was already under way. "Every American should ponder well the words spoken by Gen. Jacob H. Smith at the dinner given in his honor by his fellow-townsmen of Portsmouth, Ohio," the Republican *Inter-Ocean* of Chicago proclaimed. "They give a definition of the soldier's attitude whose noble simplicity and rectitude have seldom been equaled."[39]

CHAPTER 25

"Where Is the Line to Be Drawn?"

Jake Smith's rousing homecoming no doubt eased President Roosevelt's concerns that the military brutality issue would damage Republican prospects in the fall midterm elections. Unfortunately, in all the thousands of letters that he penned during his years of public service, Roosevelt said little about the scandal. But one letter from the summer of 1902 provides an extraordinary glimpse inside the president's mind.

On July 19, Roosevelt had taken time out from his summer activities at Sagamore Hill to explain the tempest to his old friend the German diplomat Hermann Speck von Sternberg. Roosevelt may have been embarrassed by the barrage of editorials and cartoons mocking America for its criticism of European conduct in various colonial wars while engaging in many of the same brutal practices in the Philippines. Whatever his reasons, Roosevelt ruminated at length on the unpleasant subject.

As he had done in his address at Arlington National Cemetery, Roosevelt minimized the extent of the abuses by American soldiers. "In the Philippines our men have done well, and on the whole have been exceedingly merciful," he wrote. "But there have been some blots on the record."[1]

He went on to talk about the Waller and Smith trials, and his assessments of both men (Waller's gallantry impressed him, while Smith's coarse rhetoric did not). Roosevelt had accepted the Army's assurances that its preferred technique for loosening Filipino tongues was harmless, but he did concede far greater use of torture than the Army or administration had ever admitted. "Not a few of the officers, especially those of the natives [under U.S. command] and not a few of the enlisted men, began to use the old Filipino method of mild torture, the water cure," he wrote. But, he insisted, "Nobody was seriously damaged, whereas the Filipinos had inflicted incredible tortures upon our own people."

At no point in his letter did Roosevelt ponder the larger questions raised by the scandal: What were the ethical implications of the U.S. Army's use of the water cure and other extralegal methods in its operations in the Philippines? And how did this square with the image, promoted by Roosevelt and other expansionists, of a righteous America leading the world to justice and liberty? Only in passing did Roosevelt even hint at the moral stakes for America, and only after justifying the actions of U.S. troops and depicting the water cure as harmless. "Nevertheless," he wrote, "torture is not a thing that we can tolerate."[2]

ROOSEVELT DECIDED TO GET an early start on the fall campaign with a New England swing aimed at promoting Republican candidates and fine-tuning the party's message. In later stops he would emphasize the regulation of trusts, enforcement of the Monroe Doctrine and other issues, but Roosevelt began the tour in Hartford, Connecticut, with yet another defense of America's overseas expansion under Republican rule.

He touched on the triumphs in Cuba and Puerto Rico before turning to the subject that had vexed his first year in office, the war in the Philippines. America had been tested mightily in those distant islands, he conceded, but wasn't that true of any great work? If the Republicans had listened to the arguments of "lazy and selfish men," we would have left those benighted islands in "wild chaos." Now, instead of national humiliation, America was poised to reap the benefits of its fortitude. For a moment, Roosevelt might have been confused with Lodge as he recited the commercial rewards that awaited America in the Philippines. "The awakening of the Orient means very much to all the nations of Christendom, commercially no less than politically," he said. "And it would be short-sighted statesmanship on our part to refuse to take the necessary steps for securing a proper share for our people of this commercial venture." In the end, he declared, Republican policy had been vindicated.[3]

Roosevelt made the military abuse scandal the centerpiece of a speech in Weirs, New Hampshire, on August 28. He praised the Army for having "done its work so well in the Philippine Islands," and castigated the critics who had "cruelly maligned" America's soldiers. "The temptation to retaliate for the fearful cruelties of a savage foe is very great; and now and then it has been yielded to." However, he insisted, "There have been a few, and only a few, such instances in the Philippines; and punishment has been meted out with unflinching justice to the offenders."[4]

Perhaps the continuing attacks from Democrats and anti-imperialists had convinced Roosevelt he still needed to address the issue. But most Americans had moved on. Many, in fact, had come to view the water-cure stories with apathy or even humor. In that vein, the *Washington Times* had made light of an incident three days earlier in which Roosevelt's military guard had administered "the water cure, in proper Philippine style" to a drunk who had tried to serenade the president during an overnight stop in Nahant, Massachusetts. Roosevelt's guards had finally seized the interloper, pinned him to the ground beneath a faucet and opened the spigot. "All the song he ever had was washed down his throat," the paper smugly observed. Mocking the protests of administration critics, the *Times* concluded, "The news of the latest 'water cure or outrage,' has thus far been kept from the President."[5]

ROOSEVELT'S CAMPAIGN SWING NEARLY ENDED in tragedy on September 3 when a trolley car rammed his carriage at his last stop in Pittsfield, Massachusetts. A Secret Service agent sitting in front of the president was killed, and Roosevelt was thrown from the vehicle. He suffered cuts and bruises, and a leg injury required surgery a few weeks later. But, as it had so many times before, fortune smiled on Roosevelt.

Three days later, the Anti-Imperialist League committee headed by Charles Francis Adams wrote Roosevelt once more to complain about his silence to its July petition on the atrocity issue. The committee again offered to provide witnesses for any formal inquiry. And again, Roosevelt ignored the proposal.

During the fall campaign, Roosevelt, Root and Lodge mounted a coordinated defense of Army conduct and administration policy in the Philippines. The hopes of Democrats and anti-imperialists—and fears of Republicans—that the issue would finally galvanize voters proved groundless. On Election Day, November 4, the Republicans more than held their own outside the Deep South. Democrats picked up twenty-six seats in the House of Representatives, but the GOP maintained a comfortable margin of thirty. The Senate remained solidly Republican. Roosevelt would head into the 1904 presidential campaign with a compliant Congress.[6]

ON NOVEMBER 11, GENERAL ADNA CHAFFEE returned from the Philippines to take up a new assignment as commander of the Army's Department of the East. In his monthlong passage across the Pacific, his ship had survived a harrowing typhoon, and now he was pleased to discover that the storm clouds whipped up by the war crimes scandal earlier in the year had dissipated.

Chaffee's culpability for the harsh campaigns of the Philippine war's final year had been a subject of much discussion in the United States as the debate had reached its peak the previous spring. Secretary Root had exposed Chaffee to even more intense scrutiny in May, when he had declared that operational orders for the campaigns in Samar and Batangas had not originated with the War Department. But Chaffee had been spared the indignity of testifying before the Lodge Committee to explain the severe campaigns that unfolded on his watch. His 1902 annual report to the War Department would be his most extensive comment on the issue.

As he headed east by train to Washington, the War Department released Chaffee's account. Far from repudiating what had occurred, Chaffee had mounted a vigorous defense of his subordinates, including the retired Jake Smith and General J. Franklin Bell.[7] His version was most notable for its omissions. Chaffee had revealed nothing about the verbal instructions he had given General Smith as he departed for Samar. Instead, he denied responsibility for Smith's excesses while suggesting that he had no inkling of the severity of the campaign under way on Samar.[8]

Chaffee's orders to General Smith remained a mystery until his retirement in 1906, when Hell-roaring Jake authorized their release by his nephew, Congressman Henry T. Bannon of Ohio. According to Smith, Chaffee had defined his mission thusly: "I do not propose to hamper you at all, but on the contrary, give you all the assistance you need to crush the insurrection in Samar. . . . The interior must be made a wilderness if that is the only remedy."[9]

THE CONVICTIONS OF JAKE SMITH, Major Edwin Glenn and Lieutenant Julien Gaujot had allowed the administration to assert that justice had been served, but a handful of trials continued to play out in the Philippines. In one, Captain James Ryan of the 15th U.S. Cavalry went before a general court-martial in Manila on the same charge that Smith had faced: conduct prejudicial to good order and military discipline. Ryan was accused of giving the water cure to Filipino prisoners on Mindanao, and repeatedly dunking a town vice president headfirst in a bucket of water to elicit information. The court concluded that Ryan's actions were lawful, and acquitted him of all charges.[10]

Just before Christmas, Major Glenn went on trial in Manila on murder charges. Glenn immediately went on the attack, declaring that all his actions had been sanctioned by higher-ups. He requested that generals Chaffee and Smith be compelled to return to the islands so he might question them under oath. Glenn argued that a telegram that Chaffee had sent to his Batangas commander in the closing months of the war had been widely interpreted by U.S. field officers as authorization for the use of the water cure and other extreme measures.[11]

Chaffee found himself in a very awkward position. After promoting Jake Smith to command the punitive campaign on Samar in the fall of 1901, Chaffee had highly recommended Glenn and personally assigned him to Smith's staff. "Glenn has an excellent nose for smelling out *insurrectos*," Chaffee had written, "and once he gets on his trail, he is not liable to escape him." Left unsaid was Glenn's well-known reputation for using extreme methods to get his results.[12]

Now, from his new command in New York, Chaffee disavowed Glenn. His Luzon order was never intended to sanction torture and other atrocities, Chaffee told reporters. In fact, officers who received it "did not use it as an excuse to apply any water cures."[13]

Glenn was on his own now, charged with murdering seven Filipino civilians whom he had impressed as guides in a fruitless search for guerrillas. The crux of his defense was that extreme measures were not only justified by guerrilla tactics, but they were sanctioned by higher military authorities. He further argued that General Orders 100 sanctioned the summary execution of guides. (Some of his witnesses claimed the guides had been shot while attempting to escape.) In the end, Glenn was acquitted. He would never face further action for his conduct in the Philippines.[14]

Chaffee's replacement, Major General George W. Davis, expressed puzzlement over the court's verdict. At the very least, the trial record left no doubt as to Glenn's "reckless disregard for human life." Such conduct personally offended his "sense of right and justice," Davis wrote, as well as his "conception of law and duty."[15]

Privately, Glenn complained bitterly about the betrayal of higher officers who "did not protect us in doing that which they sent us to do. . . ."[16]

General Davis forwarded Glenn's trial record to Washington with a warning to his superiors: Army officers were fed up with the investigations and courts-martial. He expressed his personal hope that Glenn's trial would be the last.[17]

In Washington, meanwhile, administration critics were making a push to restart the hearings before Senator Henry Cabot Lodge's Committee on the Philippines. When Senate Democrats asked Secretary Root to release transcripts of the courts-martial in the islands, Lodge had balked, citing the cost of printing such "voluminous" proceedings. The Democrats made the water-cure-related death of a Filipino priest, a Father Augustine de la Pena, a new focal point, and the partisan sparring had quickly exceeded the acrimony of the previous spring. Senator Albert Beveridge suggested the case was the latest in a series of canards perpetrated by the Democrats and called for an end to the "policy of insinuation and badger about American soldiers" in the Philippines. Senator Edward Carmack of Tennessee accused the Republicans of a cover-up.[18]

And so it went in early 1903. When Lodge and his committee voted to hear no further testimony on military misconduct, administration opponents announced they would hold their own rump sessions. On February 26, Senator Carmack called to order an open meeting in his Capitol office. Witnesses who had been prepared to testify before the Lodge Committee instead presented their accounts before the gathering of administration critics. Senator Lodge and Republican members of his committee had been invited to attend and cross-examine witnesses. They never appeared.[19]

IN LATE MARCH 1903, NEW ENGLAND anti-imperialists rented Boston's Faneuil Hall for a pair of public rallies aimed at galvanizing outrage over the administration's mishandling of atrocity cases. Moorfield Storey, Herbert Welsh and other stalwarts of the movement fired up a crowd with impassioned speeches. They accused Root and Lodge of suppressing the terrible secrets of America's conquest. The gray-haired mother of the U.S. soldier who had been gagged and choked on his own vomit in Army custody sat on the stage behind the speakers as several hundred spectators cheered the demands for a fuller accounting by Roosevelt.[20]

On April 2, 1903, the president dispatched Lodge to deliver the administration's final word on the matter. Nearly a full year had passed since Roosevelt had convened his emergency Cabinet meeting and vowed to exhaustively investigate the allegations of wrongdoing and punish the perpetrators. Scores of cases of torture, summary executions and other questionable military actions had been brought to light in Senate hearings, courts-martial, boards of inquiry and independent probes. Yet Roosevelt's pledge to deliver justice had proven hollow. Only three officers had been punished: One of them, General Jake Smith, had been retired; Major Edwin Glenn and Lieutenant Julien Gaujot had been briefly suspended and fined.

Lodge conceded nothing as he rose to address the annual Home Market Club banquet in Boston. "We Republicans deeply deplore the fact that any cruelties were ever committed by any American officer or any American soldier upon anyone in the Philippines," he said. But justice had been served. "We do not forget, as the other side forgets, the cruelties that our men endured." He recited yet again the gruesome deaths suffered by U.S. soldiers in the archipelago. Enough, Lodge declared. "The Republican Party has passed, in both sessions of the Congress, wise, far-reaching legislation for the benefit of the Philippines. They will pass more in the years to come. But there is one thing that the Republican Party will not do: It will not further seek to hound down officers and men of the Army of the United States for everything which happened two years ago, and which have been tried by the courts and before the country."[21]

ONE FINAL LOOSE END DEMANDED ATTENTION before President Roosevelt could declare the abuse scandal dead and buried.

The fear of a political backlash had prevented Roosevelt from firing General Nelson Miles the previous spring. In the fall, the president had decided that it might be better to get Miles out of the country rather than have him within earshot of voters, and so he had dropped his objections to a Philippines fact-finding trip. The Army chief had spent several weeks in the islands interviewing witnesses and collecting atrocity stories before returning to Washington in January. On February 19, he had completed his damning report.[22] Secretary Root had hoped to keep the document under wraps, but Miles's reputation for news leaks had ruled that out. For Roosevelt and Root, the salient questions were when to publish the report, and how to minimize its damage.

On April 27, 1903, Root finally released the general's opus. Much of what Miles had found had been previously reported, but there were a number of revelations. Among the most disturbing concerned the Batangas campaign waged by General Bell. Miles had been struck by the utter devastation of the countryside as he traveled from Laguna province to Batangas in

November 1902. At the town of Lipa, Filipinos had unburdened themselves to Miles with stories of harsh treatment by American soldiers. They told of being forced to abandon their villages and crowd into towns under U.S. military control. Six hundred Filipinos had been crammed into one small building; some had died of suffocation, a doctor recalled. Fifteen people told Miles they had been given the water cure. One sixty-five-year-old man, a prominent citizen named Vicente Luna, had passed out while undergoing the torture. He had been dragged back to his home while unconscious, and died there when soldiers burned the dwelling, Miles wrote.

General Miles reported a litany of other atrocities, including the summary execution of prisoners and torture of town officials and priests. One priest showed Miles "long, deep scars on his arm, which he said were caused by the cords with which he was bound cutting into his flesh." Another cleric, Father José Diaznes, one of the three Samar priests tortured by Lieutenant Gaujot under Major Glenn's direction, had his front teeth knocked out by his interrogators and $300 stolen. The three priests had been moments from summary execution when a 1st Infantry major intervened to save them, Miles reported.

The activities of Major Glenn and Lieutenant Arthur Conger came under special scrutiny in the general's report. "It appears that Maj. Glenn and Lt. Conger and a party of assistants and native scouts were moved from place to place for the purpose of extorting statements by means of torture," Miles wrote, "and it became so notorious that this party was called 'Glenn's Brigade.'"

Miles raised the explosive issue that Roosevelt and Secretary Root had carefully avoided: the knowledge, or at least acquiescence, of higher authorities. He noted that Glenn and Conger had been assigned to the staff of Brigadier General Robert Hughes while committing their illicit acts, and left no doubt as to his belief that it would not have been "possible for officers to be engaged in such acts without the personal knowledge of the General upon whose staff they were serving at the time. . . ." Indeed, Miles wrote, "It was common talk at the places where officers congregated that such transactions had been carried on either with the connivance or approval of certain commanding officers."

One of the most chilling passages in the report was an account of the incident that had led to Major Glenn's court-martial (and recent acquittal) on murder charges. Glenn had dispatched an American-led patrol of Filipino scouts into the Leyte countryside with instructions that eight civilian captives acting as guides were to be killed if the local guerrilla hideout was not located. When the patrol failed to find the enemy fighters, the guides "were separated into two parties, numbering three or four respectively, and while tied together were all murdered by being shot or bayoneted to death, some in a kneeling position. . . ." One guide whose son was a scout employed by the Americans was spared.

Miles singled out the resettlement policies of General Bell in Batangas as yet another violation of the laws of war, as was Bell's practice of selling rice at a profit to Filipinos who had been forced into towns and confined as prisoners of war. Taking aim at the pillar of the Roosevelt administration's defense, Miles concluded: "The excuse that the unusual conditions justify the measures herein condemned are without foundation."[23]

If ever the American people were going to rise up in outrage over the acts committed in their name in the Philippines, the release of a damning report by the commander of the United States Army should have been the moment. Miles was something less than a neutral observer, but he was a respected war hero with forty-one years of service to the nation, and his account was buttressed with facts and details.

It made no difference.

A measure of the apathy that greeted the Miles report was the coverage of the nation's leading newspapers. The *New York Times* ran its story on page three. In Massachusetts, the bastion of anti-imperialist sentiment, the *Boston Daily Globe* buried the report on page fourteen.

A few more allegations were investigated, with little vigor. The most prominent case involved Colonel Robert Howze. Miles had initiated an investigation that had confirmed allegations that Howze had ordered the whipping deaths of two Filipinos in Northern Luzon. Secretary Root ordered a board of inquiry to review the case, but did not wait for the outcome: He publicly expressed his belief in Howze's innocence, and even wrote a letter to the *New York Evening Post* in the colonel's defense. It surprised no one when Root's review cleared Howze of all charges.[24]

For many Americans, the allegations of torture and other excesses had ceased to be a serious matter. "What's that sound of running water out there, Willie?" a mother asked her son in a *Cleveland Plain-Dealer* cartoon. "It's only us boys, Ma," Willie replied. "We've been trying the Filipino water-cure on Bobbie Snow, an' now we're pouring him out."[25]

The *New York World* had foreseen the indifference that now led Americans to ignore the documented cases of military misconduct. On April 16, 1902, the *World* had conjured a breakfast-table conversation as the "American Public" pored over a newspaper filled with accounts of Philippine atrocities:

> It sips its coffee and reads of its soldiers administering the "water cure" to rebels; of how water with handfuls of salt thrown in to make it more efficacious, is forced down the throats of the patients until their bodies become distended to the point of bursting; of how our soldiers then jump on the distended bodies to force the water out quickly so that the "treatment" can begin all over again. The American Public takes another sip of its coffee and remarks, "How very unpleasant!"
>
> But where is that vast national outburst of astounded horror which an old-fashioned America would have predicted at the reading of such news? Is it lost somewhere in the 8,000 miles that divided us from the scenes of these abominations? Is it led astray by the darker skins of the alien race among which these abominations are perpetrated? Or is it rotted away by that inevitable demoralization which the wrong-doing of a great nation must inflict on the consciences of the least of its citizens?[26]

Not every prominent Republican agreed with Roosevelt and his men that the demands for a full accounting of U.S. conduct in the Philippines was the cynical work of political enemies. That view was not even universal among senior military officers.

In Washington, Army Judge Advocate General George B. Davis (not to be confused with Major General George W. Davis) had penned a powerful memorandum to Secretary Root that he passed along with the records of Major Glenn's first trial. The general was shocked by the light sentence given Glenn for what he considered the serious offense of torture, and the larger implications of the case for the Army and the nation. Military law did not permit "the infliction of suffering for the sake of suffering or for revenge, nor of maiming or wounding except in fight, nor of torture to extort confessions," Davis wrote. Yet Glenn had admitted the water cure had been "the habitual method of obtaining information from individual insurgents"—a blatant violation of the rules of war, in Davis's legal opinion.[27]

America had started down a dangerous road by claiming that military necessity trumped rule of law, Davis warned.

"No modern state, which is a party to international law, can sanction, either expressly or by a silence which imports consent, a resort to torture with a view of obtaining confessions, as an incident to its military operations," he wrote. "If it does, where is the line to be drawn? If the 'water cure' is ineffective, what shall be the next step? Shall the victim be suspended, head down, over the smoke of a smouldering fire; shall he be tightly bound and dropped from a distance of several feet; shall he be beaten with rods; shall his shins be rubbed with a broomstick until they bleed?"[28]

For Davis, haunted by the Army's Faustian bargain in the Philippines, the answer was unambiguous: The United States "cannot afford to sanction the addition of torture to the several forms of force which may be legitimately employed in war."[29]

POLITICAL PRESSURE HAD FORCED Theodore Roosevelt to acknowledge the seriousness of the war crimes scandal in April 1902 and pledge vigorous action. But he never made good on his Memorial Day pledge to make a "determined and unswerving effort . . . to find out every instance of barbarity on the part of our troops" and "punish those guilty of it." Roosevelt had pressured a few convictions out of the military courts, which he and his allies held up as proof that justice had been served and American honor upheld. But the punishments were light, and Roosevelt never made any attempt to demand accountability up the chain of command.[30]

By the spring of 1903, Roosevelt had survived the scandal without lasting injury. Try as they might, the Democrats and anti-imperialists had failed to persuade a majority of Americans that the administration had betrayed the public trust by concealing and minimizing the harsh tactics used to win the war in the Philippines.

Interest in the Philippines faded quickly, and with it memories of the water cure and other extreme methods American soldiers had employed to end Filipino resistance. Historian Stuart Creighton Miller argues that the anti-imperialists inadvertently contributed to the national amnesia by blaming the war and its excesses on a high-level conspiracy in which powerful politicians had "carried out, through deceit and subterfuge, the policy and means of expansion overseas against the will of the majority of their countrymen."[31] The reality is that a majority of Americans enthusiastically welcomed the nation's emergence as a world power, and the pride and prosperity that followed. Given the opportunity to repudiate the expansionist agenda at the polls in 1900 and again in 1902, a decisive majority of Americans had cast their lot with the Republicans.

An exhilarated Roosevelt in early 1903 boasted to the French ambassador in Washington that the United States would soon dominate "foes more formidable than Spain ever was."[32] When his grand plan for a canal through the Colombian province of Panama was rejected by that country's senate later that summer, a furious Roosevelt privately encouraged talk of Panama's secession from "these contemptible little creatures in Bogota." In October, Roosevelt met with an agent for the Panamanian revolutionaries. Shortly afterward, he positioned troops and ships within striking distance of Panama.[33]

On November 3, 1903, the Panamanian plotters acted. An independent republic was declared and consolidated power as four hundred U.S. Marines went ashore at Colón. The United States was one of the first countries to recognize the new government. A canal treaty was quickly signed as American gunboats patrolled the coast, blocking the arrival of Colombian troops. The United States was granted sovereignty "in perpetuity" over a ten-mile-wide canal zone across the heart of the new nation.

Roosevelt's critics responded with a fury not seen since the height of the war crimes scandal a year earlier. "A rough-riding assault upon another republic over the shattered wreckage of international law and diplomatic usage," thundered William Randolph Hearst's *Chicago American*.[34] On December 21, sensing a backlash in Congress over rising troop deployments,

Roosevelt put strict limits on American military activities in Panama. "If there should come a brush with Colombia," he commanded, "I want to be dead sure that Colombia fires first."[35] Memories of the Philippines remained painfully fresh, and Roosevelt was determined not to blunder into another war.

To friends and enemies alike, Roosevelt professed his innocence in the Panamanian affair. "I did not foment the revolution on the Isthmus," he protested. He had merely acted in America's "interest and honor."[36]

In private, Roosevelt endured the playful jibes of his closest advisers. Attorney General Knox, when asked by Roosevelt to lay out the legal basis for the administration's actions in Panama, quipped: "No, Mr. President, if I were you I would not have any taint of legality about it." But have I defended myself? Roosevelt persisted. The sharp-witted Elihu Root could not resist. "You certainly have, Mr. President. You have shown that you were accused of seduction and you have conclusively proved that you were guilty of rape."[37]

FLIPPANCY ASIDE, ROOSEVELT HAD SENSED the growing doubts of Americans toward expansion and military conquest after the sordid events in the Philippines, and he had proceeded carefully in Panama. He had gotten his way with the deployment of small numbers of U.S. troops and ships and the implied threat of military force—a decisive break with America's approach to the Philippines, and a cost-effective blueprint that Roosevelt would employ elsewhere in the Caribbean in the years ahead.

By then, America's dreams of empire had passed, buried forever beneath the fertile rice plains and forested peaks of the Philippines.

"Many Americans had been willing to go along with annexing territory overseas as long as annexation was cheap and easy," writes historian H. W. Brands. "The war of resistance in the Philippines demonstrated that it could be expensive and hard. In doing so, the war poisoned the well of American public opinion for similar ventures elsewhere."[38]

For many Americans, even those who supported the conquest of the Philippines and stood by Roosevelt through the military misconduct disgrace, the cost had been too high—in human lives, in treasure, and, most of all, in national honor.

Epilogue

As the war crimes scandal engulfed the Roosevelt administration in the spring of 1902, pundit Henry Watterson had predicted "the paramount issue, the issue of issues, in 1904 will be the Philippines." In reality, by the time Americans went to the polls that November, the islands had faded from the national consciousness.

America's Asian colony had regained the national spotlight for a brief period that summer. August 13 had been designated as Philippines Day at the St. Louis World's Fair, and a grand military parade was planned to commemorate the sixth anniversary of the American occupation of Manila. William Howard Taft, Roosevelt's new secretary of war, and General Adna Chaffee led three divisions in an hour-long parade through the fairgrounds. The procession included General Frederick Funston and other officers who had helped conquer the islands.

Taft had envisioned the exposition as an opportunity to showcase America's civilizing and democratizing influence in the Philippines, as well as to attract U.S. investment and tariff concessions for the islands. The Philippine exhibit was the largest at the fair, forty-seven acres of gleaming replicas of Manila's government buildings, the capital's old walled city and nipa-hut villages inhabited by imported ethnic minorities.

HONOR IN THE DUST

A handpicked battalion of 1,369 Philippine Scouts under the command of fifty-nine American officers performed daily drills for admiring audiences. The *St. Louis Post-Dispatch* marveled at the native troops' "soldierly bearing, intelligent countenances and obliging ways," and the fact that "many speak English and are all uniformed in Khaki like the soldiers of Uncle Sam."

But when American women became smitten with the dark-skinned soldiers, the warm feelings quickly dissipated. The *Post-Dispatch* warned of the breach of racial taboos. "The problem is how and where to draw the color line on the Filipinos who have been brought to the Fair," the paper fretted. "To what extent, if any, shall the tanned tribesmen of the tropics be permitted to associate with their white assimilators?"[1]

Very little, as it turned out.

Threats directed at the scouts escalated to violence in early July, when members of a U.S. Marine detachment assigned to the fair attacked several Filipino soldiers. A week later, fair police prevented several scouts from leaving the grounds with white women. Bystanders cheered.[2]

That same month, Democrats nominated an unabashed anti-imperialist, Judge Alton B. Parker of New York, to challenge Theodore Roosevelt in the fall presidential election. Parker made one final attempt to transform the Philippines into a winning issue for the Democrats. Like so many others, he failed miserably.

On November 8, 1904, Roosevelt was reelected in a landslide. He won 56.4 percent of the popular vote and thirty-three of the forty-five states.

ONLY FORTY-SIX YEARS OLD as he began his second term, Roosevelt mustered all his manic energy and vision in a crusade to transform America. He reined in the power of big business, safeguarded food and drugs, created national parks and monuments and promoted conservation of America's natural resources. But his deepest passion lay in foreign policy, and it was there that Roosevelt left his most enduring marks.

Roosevelt was fond of quoting an African proverb, "Speak softly and carry a big stick," but his extension of America's global power was anything but subtle. In 1905, he issued the Roosevelt Corollary to the Monroe Doctrine, staking America's right to exercise international police power in the Caribbean and Latin America. He secretly blessed Japan's annexation of Korea, thereby casting America's lot with the Rising Sun as a counterweight to European influence in Asia. He capped his presidency with a portentous display of American power, dispatching sixteen Navy battleships, the "Great White Fleet," on a forty-three-thousand-mile cruise that touched the shores of six continents.

Although Roosevelt did not hesitate to intervene in the affairs of other countries, he did not attempt another Philippines-style military conquest.

In September 1906, when Cuban President Tomás Estrada Palma invited U.S. assistance to put down a revolt, Senator Albert Beveridge rushed to Sagamore Hill to urge Roosevelt to seize the island. Beveridge dreamed of a "Continental Republic" that would stretch from Canada through the Caribbean and Central America and across the Pacific, and he appealed to the American people to support the annexation of Cuba.[3] But Roosevelt realized that America's dream of empire had passed. When he finally ordered U.S. Marines to Cuba, he pledged to withdraw the force as soon as peace was restored. Privately, the president described Beveridge and his desire to acquire Cuba in language that critics had once used in describing Roosevelt's fixation with the Philippines. The Indiana senator, Roosevelt wrote, was "perfectly rabid" on the subject.[4]

ALTHOUGH ARMED RESISTANCE TO AMERICAN rule in the Philippines had effectively ended by the summer of 1902, sporadic violence continued in the Muslim south. In late February 1906, on the island of Sulu, one thousand Muslim tribesmen revolted against the local leadership installed by the Americans and fled to a natural fortress in an extinct volcano known as Bud Dajo. In Manila, U.S. Governor Leonard Wood, Roosevelt's old friend and Rough Rider comrade, ordered eight hundred soldiers to crush the rebellion. In four days of operations, U.S. soldiers killed every last one of the Muslims—men, women and children. Twenty soldiers died in the fighting. Wood assured Secretary of War Taft that "no man, woman, or child was wantonly killed." Native women had charged the

American troops along with the men, Wood said, while children "had been used by the men as shields."[5]

A photograph showing U.S. troops standing casually over the bodies of dead Muslims at Bud Dajo made its way back to the United States and was published by several newspapers. It briefly sparked public indignation that recalled the war crimes scandal of 1902, but the furor faded quickly.

Roosevelt was unmoved by the controversy. In a telegram, he congratulated Governor Wood and his soldiers for "the brave feat of arms wherein you and they so well upheld the honor of the American flag."[6]

The Stars and Stripes would fly over the islands for another forty years.

As AMERICANS PURGED THEIR MEMORIES of the Philippines, the men who conquered the islands and wrapped their names in glory (and infamy) forged ahead with their lives.

General Jacob H. Smith became a popular figure in Civil War and Spanish-American War veterans' organizations. Former comrades hailed him as a hero who had been sacrificed on Roosevelt's altar of political expediency. After the United States entered the First World War in the spring of 1917, the seventy-seven-year-old Smith wrote the War Department asking to be reinstated to duty. The department praised his patriotism, but politely declined. Smith died in San Diego, California, on March 1, 1918.

General Adna Chaffee was promoted to lieutenant general and named Army chief of staff by President Roosevelt in January 1904. Chaffee held the position for two years and then retired. He moved to Los Angeles, where he became president of the Board of Public Works. He died on November 1, 1914.

Upon Chaffee's retirement, Roosevelt named General J. Franklin Bell, the architect of the controversial Batangas campaign, as Army chief of staff. He held the position until 1910. Bell was an active-duty major general when he died on January 8, 1919, at the age of sixty-two.

General Frederick Funston was on duty in San Francisco, California, in April 1906 when a massive earthquake devastated the city. He declared martial law and organized rescue and relief efforts. Later that year, President Roosevelt dispatched Funston to Cuba to help quell an insurrection. Funston returned to the Philippines from 1911 to 1913, and governed the port of Veracruz, Mexico, during the six-month occupation by U.S. forces in 1914. He subsequently commanded U.S. forces along the troublesome border with Mexico. On the evening of February 19, 1917, General Funston was in the lobby of a San Antonio, Texas, hotel, listening to an orchestra play "The Blue Danube Waltz," when he collapsed and died of a heart attack.

Major Edwin Glenn resumed his rise through the Army ranks after his two Philippine trials. Shortly after the United States entered the First World War in 1917, Glenn received his brigadier general's star. A promotion to major general soon followed, and he commanded U.S. troops in France before retiring in 1919. He died on August 5, 1926. Today, the Glenn Highway in Alaska is named for him.

Glenn's young water-cure expert, Lieutenant Arthur L. Conger, never faced trial for his actions in the Philippines. During the First World War he served as chief of the combat intelligence branch on General John J. Pershing's American Expeditionary Force staff. Conger was promoted to colonel and later served as U.S. military attaché to Germany and Switzerland before retiring in 1928. While still in the Army, Conger had gained renown as a military historian, and in 1931 published his most acclaimed book, *The Rise of U. S. Grant*. He devoted the final decades of his life to promoting the practice of theosophy. He died in Pasadena, California, in 1952 at the age of seventy-nine.

Major Cornelius Gardener, whose report on U.S. misconduct stoked the war crimes scandal in the spring of 1902, never advanced beyond the rank of colonel. He finished his career as commander of the 16th U.S. Infantry in Alaska and died in 1913, shortly after retiring from the Army.

In his memoirs, published late in his long life, General William H. Bisbee recounted his experiences as a Civil War soldier, Indian fighter and regimental commander during the war against Spain and the conquest of the Philippines. He made no mention of presiding over the Waller court-martial in 1902 or serving on the Smith and Glenn trials. He died in 1942 at the age of 103.

The Samar campaign introduced the United States Marine Corps to jungle warfare, and its survivors became icons of Marine sacrifice and heroism. For years afterward, Waller's Marines would walk into mess halls and be greeted with the toast "Stand, gentlemen! This man served on Samar!"

David Dixon Porter served in Panama, Haiti and the Dominican Republic before returning to the Philippines in 1911. After more than a decade of tropical duty, his health failed and he was bedridden. He also battled alcoholism, depression and anorexia, and spent the better part of a year in Navy hospitals before returning to duty.[7] He would continue to trade on his Samar service for the remainder of his career, and waged a fifteen-year campaign to secure recognition for his heroics at the Sohoton cliffs. On April 25, 1934, President Franklin D. Roosevelt presented the Medal of Honor to Porter and Hiram Bearss in a White House ceremony. Porter retired as a major general three years later. He died in Philadelphia in 1944, at the age of seventy-seven.

"Hiking Hiram" Bearss earned the Distinguished Service Cross during the First World War while commanding the 102nd Infantry at Marcheville in 1918. A year later he retired as a colonel for medical reasons. In 1938, four years after receiving the Medal of Honor with Porter, Bearss died in a car crash on an Indiana highway. He was sixty-three.[8]

Alexander S. Williams, the young lieutenant left in command of the sickest Marines in the Samar jungle, went on to serve in Cuba, Mexico, Panama, Haiti and the Dominican Republic. In March 1926, while commanding the 4th Marine regiment in San Diego, Colonel Williams was found guilty of public intoxication in a controversial court-martial instigated by Brigadier General Smedley D. Butler. Williams was demoted four numbers in grade and transferred to San Francisco. On the evening of October 1, 1926, after attending a dinner theater with friends, Williams drove off the Embarcadero into San Francisco Bay and drowned. His death was ruled an accident, and he was buried with full military honors at Arlington National Cemetery.[9]

Lieutenant John H. A. Day, Waller's adjutant on Samar, was a marked man in the Marines after his boasts unleashed the war crimes trials of 1902. A decade later, after he'd amassed a checkered disciplinary record, a review board recommended his retirement due to mental illness. President William Howard Taft disapproved the finding, but the reprieve was only temporary. In 1915 a court-martial found Day guilty of drunkenness, absence from duty, conduct prejudicial to good order and discipline, and conduct unbecoming an officer and a gentleman, and he was dismissed from the Marines. Day returned to the country of his birth, Belgium, and was wounded in action and decorated for bravery while serving with the Belgian army in the First World War. Returning to the United States, he was pardoned by President Woodrow Wilson in March 1919, but his petition for reinstatement in the Marines was rejected.[10]

Sergeant John H. Quick was a Marine Corps legend by the time he left the Philippines in 1902, and his star continued to rise in the years that followed. In 1914, Sergeant Major Quick raised the Stars and Stripes over Veracruz, Mexico, and was commended for his "coolness, bravery and judgment" under fire in the fighting against Mexican revolutionary forces. Quick served with the 6th Marine regiment in France in 1917 and 1918, and was awarded the Distinguished Service Cross and Navy Cross for bravery during the battle of Belleau Wood. He retired from the Marines when the war ended, and died in St. Louis on September 9, 1922, at the age of fifty-two. Today, John Quick Road is named for him at the Marine Corps base at Quantico, Virginia.[11]

Tony Waller kept a low profile as the war crimes controversy faded, and soon reclaimed his place as the preeminent Marine field officer in U.S. interventions in Panama, Mexico, Haiti and Cuba. Waller continued to reflect on his ordeal in the Philippines with self-pity rather than regret. In a 1909 letter to U.S. soldiers in the Philippines who had named their camp after him, he wrote: "Please express to your comrades the deep gratitude I feel in the implied approval of my actions during the Philippine Campaign. So many knocks and blows have come to me that I feel deeply touched by this token of your confidence."[12]

As a senior colonel in 1910, Waller was a favorite to be named Marine Corps commandant. But President Taft instead appointed Colonel William P. Biddle, Waller's longtime rival. In denying him the coveted position, Taft recalled President Roosevelt's rebuke following Waller's 1902 court-martial: "The shooting of the native bearers by the orders of Major Waller was an act which sullied the American name. . . ."

When Biddle retired in 1914, Waller was again in line to command the Marine Corps. Once more the Samar executions came back to haunt him. Among those writing to oppose Waller's promotion was Moorfield Storey, the old Boston anti-imperialist. Passed over again, Waller retired in 1920 as a major general. He died on July 13, 1926, at the age of seventy.

Waller's three sons followed him into military service. His oldest, Littleton Jr., fought in both world wars and was promoted to major general in the Marine Corps; his second, John, was a Navy admiral; and his third, Tazewell, finished his career as a Marine brigadier general. In 1942, the Navy commissioned the USS *Waller*, a Fletcher-class destroyer named for Tony Waller. The warship saw extensive duty in the Pacific island-hopping campaign, including the liberation of the Philippines in 1945.

THE ANTI-IMPERIALIST LEAGUE REMAINED in existence until 1921, when it disbanded in the belief that Filipino politicians no longer desired independence. Mark Twain continued to write on U.S. actions in the Philippines, including a biting 1902 satire he titled "A Defense of General Funston." But Twain's publisher, Harper and Brothers, eventually bowed to criticism and refused to publish some of his more provocative writings on imperialism.[13] In his essay on Funston, Twain delivered perhaps the most scathing indictment of the use of the water cure by U.S. troops in the Philippines. "Funston's example," Twain wrote, "has bred many imitators, and many ghastly additions to our history: the torturing of Filipinos by the awful 'water-cure,' for instance, to make them confess—what? Truth? Or lies? How can one know which it is they are telling? For under unendurable pain a man confesses anything that is required of him, true or false, and his evidence is worthless."[14]

By 1903, Senator George Frisbie Hoar had abandoned his efforts to alter U.S. policy in the Philippines. But late that year, when Roosevelt intervened in Panama, Hoar subjected the president to one final reproach.

On September 30, 1904, as Roosevelt campaigned for reelection, church and fire bells tolled across Worcester, Massachusetts, announcing the death of the man once hailed as the conscience of the Republican Party.

SENATOR ALBERT J. BEVERIDGE HAD PLANNED to ride the expansion cause all the way to the White House, but America's infatuation with the issue proved fleeting. Beveridge won reelection to the Senate in 1905, and reinvented himself as an advocate of Roosevelt's domestic reform agenda. After losing his bid for reelection in 1910, Beveridge cast his lot with the breakaway Progressive Party in 1912 and delivered the keynote speech at the convention that nominated Roosevelt for president. His political career ended with losing Progressive candidacies for governor of Indiana in 1912 and the Senate in 1914. Beveridge reinvented himself yet again as a writer of historical literature. His four-volume life of Supreme Court justice John Marshall was awarded the Pulitzer Prize for biography in 1920. He died in April 1927 at the age of sixty-four.

William Howard Taft was elected president with Roosevelt's support in 1908, but his tepid support of his predecessor's reforms split the Republican Party in 1912. As a third-party candidate, Roosevelt outpolled Taft by more than six hundred thousand votes, but Democrat Woodrow Wilson won an electoral landslide of 435 votes to Roosevelt's 88 and Taft's 8. After leaving the White House, Taft remained active in Philippine affairs and lobbied against an early grant of independence to the islands. In 1921, Republican President Warren G. Harding appointed him as chief justice of the U.S. Supreme Court, a position Taft held until his death in 1930.

Henry Cabot Lodge had said the Senate would never witness a harder fight than that over the Treaty of Paris in 1899, but he was wrong. In 1919, at the age of sixty-nine, Lodge led the bitter Senate brawl that ended with the rejection of the Treaty of Versailles and U.S. membership in the League of Nations. As a result, Lodge has been described as abandoning his expansionist beliefs in favor of isolation. In fact, he never wavered in his support of a globally powerful America. Rather, he was a strident unilateralist who "did not wish to see that power ceded to an organization with amorphous mandates and possibly inimical members," writes former U.S. diplomat Warren Zimmerman.[15]

Unfortunately for Lodge and like-minded Republicans, the party fell into the hands of isolationists in the 1920s. By the 1930s, the vision of an exceptional America as a force for global good had been embraced by the Democrats. Lodge did not live to see the abandonment of his cherished ideals. He died in 1924, at the age of seventy-four.[16]

After handing the reins of the War Department to William Howard Taft and returning to Wall Street for a year, Elihu Root rejoined Roosevelt's Cabinet as secretary of state in 1905. His tenure at Foggy Bottom coincided with the emergence of an international movement dedicated to ending atrocities by King Leopold's colonial regime in the Belgian Congo. Root was never comfortable with human rights as a pillar of American foreign policy, and this particular movement discomfited him because it included some of the same political activists who had condemned U.S. atrocities in the Philippines.[17] But growing pressure from a broad coalition that included even Wall Street titans such as J. P. Morgan convinced Root to pay heed to the Congo issue. Eventually, after Belgian efforts to buy support in Congress were exposed, Root backed the British in their efforts to pressure King Leopold's withdrawal from the Congo.[18]

In 1908, Root was elected to the U.S. Senate from New York. He was diligent in his duties and surprised his critics by breaking with his Wall Street friends to support legislation establishing a corporation tax. In foreign affairs, he tried to rein in U.S. intervention in various Latin American countries. But he refused to support independence for the Philippines. Root's work in creating a system of compulsory arbitration to settle international disputes won him the Nobel Peace Prize in 1912—seven years after Roosevelt was awarded the prize for mediating the Russo-Japanese War.

As Roosevelt's displeasure with Taft plunged the Republican Party into crisis, Root counseled his friend to bide his time and make another bid for the White House in 1916. When Roosevelt refused, Root remained loyal to the party and supported Taft. But his love for his fellow New Yorker remained steadfast. "I care more for one button on Theodore Roosevelt's waistcoat than for Taft's whole body," he told a friend.[19]

In a concluding irony for the man who managed America's controversial war in the Philippines, Root devoted the final years of his life to
the pursuit of peace and humane warfare. His efforts contributed to the
enactment of laws of war, the creation of a Central American Court of
Justice, and the World Disarmament Conference that convened in
Geneva in 1927. In 1935, on the eve of a key Senate vote, the eighty-nine-
year-old Root publicly called for American participation in a world court.
The Senate rejected his advice in a close vote. Root died two years later.[20]

THEODORE ROOSEVELT NEVER REALIZED his dream of becoming America's colonial overlord in the Philippines. Despite travels that would take
him into the heart of Africa and the remote reaches of the Amazon rain
forest, he never even set foot on the islands.

Roosevelt soon had second thoughts about America's dominion over
the Philippines. He mused whether early independence might not be in
U.S. interests after all. His qualms were not moral or constitutional, but
strategic. With Japan on the rise, "the Philippines form our heel of Achil-
les," he fretted. Thirty-five years later, Japan's invasion of the archipelago
proved him prescient. Still, he never regretted America's conquest. To
Roosevelt, it had been "a piece of duty that ought to be done."[21]

Historians and biographers have devoted little space to the military
misconduct storm that buffeted the first year of Theodore Roosevelt's
presidency. Perhaps it is understandable, given all the great achievements
in the six years that followed. But Roosevelt helped create the void in
American memories. The Philippines constantly occupied his thoughts
from 1898 until 1902, as his private letters and public speeches reveal. Yet
Roosevelt mentions the islands only nine times in his six-hundred-page
autobiography. The war crimes scandal of 1902 does not rate a single word.

A NOTE ON THE SOURCES

—————•—•——————

For a writer attempting to breathe life into events long past, there is no greater thrill than the hours spent poring over the words penned by people who were there. This narrative is primarily drawn from such firsthand sources: War Department reports and cables, personal correspondence, diaries, court-martial transcripts, congressional testimony, military personnel files, newspaper articles, and other contemporaneous documents and accounts. Specifics may be found in the chapter notes.

Historian Rick Atkinson has observed, "The ground itself has a great deal to say," and I heartily agree. During my two stints in Asia as a newspaper correspondent, including five years based in Manila, I immersed myself not only in the history of the Philippines but also in its geography. I visited sixty provinces (out of eighty, as of this writing) and walked the rice paddies and jungles of Luzon and Samar, where many of the key events in this story unfolded. These experiences proved invaluable as I transformed piles of notes and documents into a book.

Beyond the primary documents lies a trove of secondary sources that helped shape this narrative: journal articles, dissertations, monographs, and books produced by first-rate historians. At the top of the list is Dr. Brian McAllister Linn of Texas A&M University. His body of work on the U.S. war in the Philippines is unparalleled, and his two books on the conflict—*The U.S. Army and Counterinsurgency in the Philippine War, 1899–1902* and *The Philippine War: 1899–1902*—became my indispensable references on America's military struggle in the islands. Two other books on the war that I found especially informative are *Schoolbooks and Krags: The United States Army in the Philippines, 1898–1902*, by John M. Gates, and *Battle for Batangas: A Philippine Province at War*, by Glenn Anthony May. Of more recent vintage, *The Blood of Government: Race, Empire, the United States, & the Philippines*, by Paul A. Kramer, offers a fresh and provocative take on America's experience in the islands. For a view of the war from the Filipino perspective, I recommend *The Tinio Brigade: Anti-American Resistance in the Ilocos Provinces 1899–1901*, by Orlino A. Ochosa.

My understanding of America's domestic political debate over the Philippines was broadened to a large extent by three books: *Response to Imperialism: The United States and the Philippine–American War, 1899–1902*, by Richard E. Welch Jr.; *Twelve Against Empire: The Anti-Imperialists, 1898–1900*, by Robert L. Beisner; and *"Benevolent Assimilation": The American Conquest of the Philippines, 1899–1903*, by Stuart Creighton Miller. Welch's superb scholarship also yielded *George Frisbie Hoar and the Half-Breed Republicans*, the definitive biography of the great Republican anti-imperialist.

Two books that I thoroughly enjoyed and frequently consulted were *In Our Image: America's Empire in the Philippines*, Stanley Karnow's Pulitzer Prize–winning history of America's involvement in the islands, and *Sitting in Darkness: Americans in the Philippines*, by David Haward Bain.

The actions of the U.S. military on Samar in 1901–02 have been scrutinized by a number of scholars in recent decades, but it was a 1964 book written by a Washington, D.C.–based FBI agent that first piqued my interest in this story. I read Joseph L. Schott's *The Ordeal of Samar* while living in the Philippines in the late 1980s, and found myself wanting to go beyond his account of the bloody Samar campaign and its aftermath to learn more about the bitter Senate hearings on the war and the courts-martial of celebrated U.S. military officers accused of murdering and torturing Filipinos. Schott's engaging book lacks source notes and suffers from other shortcomings, but he deserves credit for salvaging this forgotten story from the dustbin of American history. I, for one, am grateful.

The Spanish-American War vaulted the United States to world power and precipitated its annexation of the Philippines, and my knowledge of this conflict was broadened by several books. *The War Lovers: Roosevelt, Lodge, Hearst, and the Rush to Empire*, by Evan Thomas, skillfully chronicles the campaign by Roosevelt and others to pressure President McKinley into the war against Spain. *The Spanish War: An American Epic 1898*, by G.J.A. O'Toole recounts the hostilities with novelistic flair, while Ivan Musicant's *Empire by Default* is a sweeping blow-by-blow account. The Washington backdrop is brilliantly sketched in a gem that I discovered on the bargain table of a Dallas used-book shop. After reading *In the Days of McKinley* by Margaret Leech, I was not surprised to discover that it had won the Pulitzer Prize for history in 1960.

When I began work on this book, I knew that Theodore Roosevelt was central to my story. Just how much so I realized only after completing my research. As Roosevelt's prodigious correspondence reveals, the Philippines were prominent in his thoughts from 1898 until he declared America's conquest of the islands complete in 1902. My understanding of Roosevelt the Expansionist—the driving force behind America's war with Spain and conquest of the Philippines—was aided by the work of such eminent Roosevelt biographers as H. W. Brands and Nathan Miller. But my debt to Roosevelt scholar Edmund Morris goes much deeper. As I wrote, I found myself returning again and again to the first two volumes of Morris's splendid trilogy—*The Rise of Theodore Roosevelt* and *Theodore Rex*. These books helped me understand the man who led America onto the world stage. On a deeper level, they served as a constant reminder of the transcendent power of beautifully drawn American history.

BIBLIOGRAPHY

Archival Materials

LIBRARY OF CONGRESS (WASHINGTON, D.C.)
Henry C. Corbin Papers
Theodore Roosevelt Papers
Elihu Root Papers
William H. Taft Papers

NATIONAL ARCHIVES (WASHINGTON, D.C.)
Record Group 94, Records of the Adjutant General's Office, 1780–1917
Record Group 127, Records of the United States Marine Corps
Record Group 153, Records of the Judge Advocate General's Office
Record Group 395, Records of U.S. Army Overseas Operations and Commands, 1898–1942

NATIONAL PERSONNEL RECORDS CENTER (ST. LOUIS)
Hiram I. Bearss Records
William P. Biddle Records
John H. A. Day Records
James Forney Records
Mancil C. Goodrell Records
Henry P. Kingsbury Records
John H. Quick Records
Littleton W. T. Waller Records

UNITED STATES MARINE CORPS ARCHIVES (QUANTICO, VIRGINIA)
Hiram I. Bearss Papers
William P. Biddle Papers
Smedley D. Butler Papers
Henry C. Cochrane Papers
David Dixon Porter Papers
James Forney Papers
Ben H. Fuller Papers
Mancil C. Goodrell Papers
Robert W. Huntington Papers
Harold Kinman Papers
Littleton W. T. Waller Sr. Papers

Government Publications

U.S. Army, Adjutant General's Office. *Correspondence Relating to the War with Spain and Conditions Growing Out of the Same Including the Insurrection in the Philippine Islands and the China Relief Expedition, Between the Adjutant-General of the Army and Military Commanders in the United States, Cuba, Porto Rico, China, and the Philippine Islands from April 15, 1898, to July 30, 1902.* Washington, D.C.: Government Printing Office, 1902.
U.S. Congress. *Congressional Record* (56th Congress and 57th Congress).
U.S. Congress. Senate. *Affairs in the Philippine Islands. Hearing Before the Committee on the Philippines of the United States Senate.* Senate Document 331 (3 pts.), 57th Congress, 1st Session, 1902.
U.S. Congress. Senate. *Charges of Cruelty, Etc. to the Natives of the Philippines.* Senate Document 205, 57th Congress, 1st Session, 1902.
U.S. Congress. Senate. *Trials or Courts-martial in the Philippine Islands in Consequence of Certain Instructions.* Senate Document 213, 57th Congress, 2nd Session.
War Department. Annual Reports of the War Department (1898–1903).
Navy Department. Annual Reports of the Navy Department (1898–1903).

Newspapers

Army and Navy Journal
Atlanta Constitution
Boston Daily Globe
Brooklyn Daily Eagle
Chicago Daily Tribune
Dallas Morning News
Los Angeles Times

Manila Times
New York Herald
New York Sun
New York Times
New York World
Norfolk Virginian
Norfolk Ledger-Star
San Francisco Call
Washington Post
Washington Times

Periodicals

Atlantic Monthly
Century
Collier's Weekly
Frank Leslie's Illustrated
Harper's Weekly
Literary Digest
McClure's
Scribner's

Books

Abbot, Willis John. *Blue Jackets of '98: A History of the Spanish-American War*. New York: Dodd, Mead and Co., 1899.

Adams, William Llewellyn. *Exploits and Adventures of a Soldier Ashore and Afloat*. Philadelphia: J. B. Lippincott Co., 1911.

Agoncillo, Teodoro. A *A Short History of the Philippines*. New York: New American Library Inc., 1969.

Aguinaldo, Emilio. *True Version of the Philippine Revolution*. Tarlac, Philippines: publisher unknown, 1899.

———, and Vicente Albano Pacis. *A Second Look at America*. New York: Robert Speller & Sons, Publishers, Inc., 1957.

Alger, R. A. *The Spanish-American War*. New York: Harper & Brothers, 1901.

Ayers, Edward L., and John C. Willis, eds. *The Edge of the South: Life in Nineteenth-Century Virginia*. Charlottesville and London: University Press of Virginia, 1991.

Bain, David Haward. *Sitting in Darkness: Americans in the Philippines*. Boston: Houghton Mifflin Co., 1984.

Beale, Howard. *Theodore Roosevelt and the Rise of America to World Power*. Baltimore: Johns Hopkins University Press, 1956.

Beede, Benjamin, ed. *The War of 1898 and U.S. Interventions, 1898–1934: An Encyclopedia.* New York: Garland Publishing Inc., 1994.

Beer, Thomas. *Hanna.* New York: Alfred A. Knopf, 1929.

Beisner, Robert L. *Twelve Against Empire: The Anti-Imperialists, 1898–1900.* New York: McGraw-Hill Book Co., 1968.

Biggs, Chester M. Jr. *The United States Marines in North China, 1894–1942.* Jefferson, NC: McFarland & Company, Inc., 2003.

Bisbee, William Henry. *Through Four American Wars: The Impressions and Experiences of Brigadier General William Henry Bisbee.* Boston: Meador Publishing Co., 1931.

Bishop, Joseph Bucklin. *Theodore Roosevelt and His Time: Shown in His Own Letters,* Vol. 1. New York: Charles Scribner's Sons, 1920.

Blount, James H. *The American Occupation of the Philippines: 1898–1912.* New York: G. P. Putnam's Sons, 1912.

Bonsal, Stephen. *The Fight for Santiago.* New York: Doubleday & McClure Co., 1899.

Bowers, Claude G. *Beveridge and the Progressive Era.* Boston: Houghton Mifflin Co., 1932.

Bowring, John. *A Visit to the Philippine Islands.* London: Smith, Elder and Co., 1859.

Bradford, James C., ed. *Crucible of Empire: The Spanish-American War and Its Aftermath.* Annapolis, MD: Naval Institute Press, 1993.

Bradley, James. *The Imperial Cruise: A Secret History of Empire and War.* New York: Little, Brown and Co., 2009.

Braeman, John. *Albert J. Beveridge: American Nationalist.* Chicago: The University of Chicago Press, 1971.

Brands, H. W. *Bound to Empire: The United States and the Philippines.* New York: Oxford University Press, 1992.

———. *The Reckless Decade: America in the 1890s.* New York: St. Martin's Press, 1995.

———. *The Selected Letters of Theodore Roosevelt.* New York: Cooper Square Press, 2001.

———. *TR: The Last Romantic.* New York: Basic Books, 1997.

Brown, Charles H. *The Correspondents' War: Journalists in the Spanish-American War.* New York: Charles Scribner's Sons, 1967.

Brown, Fred R. *History of the Ninth U.S. Infantry, 1799–1909.* Chicago: RR Donnelley and Sons, 1909.

Bryan, William Jennings. *Republic or Empire: The Philippine Question.* Chicago: Conkey, 1900.

Bumpus, Everitt C. *In Memoriam.* Norwood MA: Norwood Press, 1902.

Burton, H. W. *The History of Norfolk, Virginia.* Norfolk: Norfolk Virginian Printing, 1877.

Butler, Nicholas Murray. *Across the Busy Years: Recollections and Reflections,* 2 vols. New York: Charles Scribner's Sons, 1939–40.

Carter, William H. *The Life of Lt. General Chaffee.* Chicago: University of Chicago Press, 1917.

Clark, George B. *His Road to Glory: The Life and Times of "Hiking Hiram" Bearss, Hoosier Marine.* Pike, NH: The Brass Hat, 2000.

Clifford, John H. *History of the Pioneer Marine Battalion at Guam, L.I., 1899, and the Campaign in Samar, P.I., 1901*. Portsmouth, NH: Chronicle Job Print, 1914.

Collum, Richard S. *History of the United States Marine Corps*. Philadelphia: L. R. Hamersly & Co., 1890.

Conger, Emily Bronson. *An Ohio Woman in the Philippines*. Akron, OH: Press of Richard H. Leighton, 1904.

Constantino, Renato. *The Philippines: A Past Revisited*. Manila, Philippines: Renato Constantino, 1975.

Cosmas, Graham. *An Army for Empire: The United States Army and the Spanish-American War*. Columbia, MO: University of Missouri Press, 1971.

Crane, Stephen. *Prose and Poetry*. New York: Literary Classics of the U.S., 1984.

———. *Wounds in the Rain: War Stories*. New York: Frederick A. Stokes Company, 1900.

Cruikshank, Bruce. *Samar: 1768–1898*. Manila: Historical Conservation Society, 1985.

Dabney, Virginius. *Virginia: The New Dominion*. Garden City, NY: Doubleday & Company, Inc., 1971.

Davis, Charles Belmont, ed. *Adventures and Letters of Richard Harding Davis*. New York: Charles Scribner's Sons, 1917.

Davis, Richard Harding. *The Cuban and Porto Rican Campaigns*. New York: Charles Scribner's Sons, 1898.

Dewey, Adelbert M. *The Life and Letters of Admiral Dewey*. Akron, OH: The Werner Co., 1899.

Dewey, George. *Autobiography of George Dewey*. New York: Charles Scribner's Sons, 1913.

DiNunzio, Mario R., ed. *Theodore Roosevelt: An American Mind*. New York: St. Martin's Press, 1994.

Donant, Alan E. *Colonel Arthur L. Conger*. Pasadena, CA: Theosophical University Press, 1999. Accessed April 3, 2010, http://www.theosociety.org/pasadena/conger/alconger.htm.

Donnelly, Mark P., and Daniel Diehl. *The Big Book of Pain: Torture and Punishment Through History*. Stroud, United Kingdom: History Press, 2008.

Dowdey, Clifford. *The Great Plantation: A Profile of Berkeley Plantation and Plantation Virginia from Jamestown to Appomattox*. New York: Rinehart, 1957.

Dunn, Susan. *Dominion of Memories: Jefferson, Madison, and the Decline of Virginia*. New York: Basic Books, 2007.

Dyal, Donald H., et al. *Historical Dictionary of the Spanish-American War*. Westport, CT: Greenwood Press, 1996.

Fleming, Peter Fleming. *The Siege at Peking: The Boxer Rebellion*. 1959. Reprint, New York: Dorset Press, 1990.

Forbes, W. Cameron. *The Philippine Islands*. Cambridge, MA: Harvard University Press, 1945 (revised edition of 1928 book).

Ford, John D. *An American Cruiser in the East*. New York: A. S. Barnes and Co., 1905.

Foreman, John. *The Philippine Islands: A Political, Geographical, Ethnographical, Social and Commercial History of the Philippine Archipelago and Its Political Dependencies Embracing the Whole Period of Spanish Rule*. New York: Charles Scribner's Sons, 1899.

Funston, Frederick. *Memories of Two Wars: Cuban and Philippine Experiences*. New York: Charles Scribner's Sons, 1911.

Gates, John M. *Schoolbooks and Krags: The United States Army in the Philippines, 1898–1902*. Westport, CT: Greenwood Press, Inc., 1973.

Goldstein, Donald M. *The Spanish-American War: The Story and Photographs*. Washington, D.C.: Brassey's, 1998.

Gould, Lewis L. *The Presidency of William McKinley*. Lawrence, KS: The Regents Press of Kansas, 1980.

Graff, Henry F., ed. *American Imperialism and the Philippine Insurrection*. Boston: Little, Brown and Co., 1969.

Grigsby, Hugh Blair. *Discourse on the Life and Character of the Hon. Littleton Waller Tazewell*. Norfolk, VA: J. D. Ghiselin, 1860.

Hagedorn, Hermann. *Leonard Wood: A Biography*. New York: Harper & Brothers, 1931.

Halberstam, David. *The Coldest Winter: America and the Korean War*. New York: Hyperion, 2007.

Hamersly, Lewis Randolph. *The Records of Living Officers of the U.S. Navy and Marine Corps*, 6th edition. New York: L. R. Hamersly and Co., 1898.

Healy, Laurin Hall, and Luis Kutner. *The Admiral*. New York: Ziff-Davis, 1944.

Heinl, Robert D. *Soldiers of the Sea: The U.S. Marine Corps, 1775–1962*. Annapolis, MD: United States Naval Institute, 1962.

Hoar, George Frisbie. *Autobiography of Seventy Years*, 2 vols. New York: Scribner's, 1903.

Hochschild, Adam. *King Leopold's Ghost: A Story of Greed, Terror and Heroism in Colonial Africa*. Boston: Houghton Mifflin Co., 1998.

Hurley, Vic. *Jungle Patrol: The Story of the Philippine Constabulary*. New York: E. P. Dutton and Co., Inc., 1938.

James, D. Clayton. *The Years of MacArthur, Vol. 1, 1880–1941*. Boston: Houghton Mifflin, 1970.

Jessup, Philip C. *Elihu Root*, 2 vols. New York: Dodd, Mead & Co., 1938.

Johnson, Willis Fletcher. *The History of Cuba*. New York: B. F. Buck and Company, Inc., 1920.

Jones, Harry W. *A Chaplain's Experience Ashore and Afloat*. New York: A. G. Sherwood & Co., 1901.

Karnow, Stanley. *In Our Image: America's Empire in the Philippines*. New York: Random House, 1989.

Kazin, Michael. *A Godly Hero: The Life of William Jennings Bryan*. New York: Alfred A. Knopf, 2006.

Kinzer, Stephen. *Overthrow: America's Century of Regime Change from Hawaii to Iraq*. New York: Times Books, 2006.

Knapp, Betting L. *Stephen Crane*. New York: Continuum Publishing, 1987.

Kramer, Paul A. *The Blood of Government: Race, Empire, the United States, and the Philippines*. Chapel Hill, NC: The University of North Carolina Press, 2006.

Lancaster, Robert A. *Historic Virginia Homes and Churches*. Philadelphia: J. B. Lippincott Company, 1915.

Leech, Margaret. *In the Days of McKinley*. New York: Harper & Brothers, 1959.

Lejeune, Major General John A. *The Reminiscences of a Marine*. Philadelphia: Dorrance and Co., 1930.

LeRoy, James A. *The Americans in the Philippines: A History of the Conquest and First Years of Occupation*. Boston: Houghton Mifflin Co., 1914.

Levenson, J. C., ed. *Stephen Crane: Prose and Poetry*. New York: The Library of America, 1984.

Lewis, Alfred Henry, ed. *A Compilation of the Messages and Speeches of Theodore Roosevelt 1901–1905*. Washington, D.C.: Bureau of National Literature and Art, 1906.

Linn, Brian McAllister. *Guardians of Empire: The U.S. Army and the Pacific, 1902–1940*. Chapel Hill, NC: University of North Carolina Press, 1997.

———. *The Philippine War: 1899–1902*. Lawrence, KS: The University Press of Kansas, 2000.

———. *The U.S. Army and Counterinsurgency in the Philippine War, 1899–1902*. Chapel Hill, NC: University of North Carolina Press, 1989.

Lithgow, William. *Rare Adventures and Painful Peregrinations*. 1632. Reprint, Glasgow: James MacLehose and Sons, 1906.

Lodge, Henry Cabot, ed. *Selections from the Correspondence of Theodore Roosevelt and Henry Cabot Lodge, 1884–1918*. New York: Scribner's, 1925.

Lord, Walter. *The Good Years: From 1900 to the First World War*. New York: Bantam Books, 1962.

Lubow, Arthur. *The Reporter Who Would Be King: A Biography of Richard Harding Davis*. New York: Macmillan Publishing Co., 1992.

Marolda, Edward J., ed. *Theodore Roosevelt, the U.S. Navy, and the Spanish-American War*. New York: Palgrave Macmillan, 2001.

May, Ernest R. *Imperial Democracy: The Emergence of America as a Great Power*. New York: Harper & Row, 1980.

May, Glenn Anthony. *Battle for Batangas: A Philippine Province at War*. New Haven and London: Yale University Press, 1991.

McCullough, David. *The Great Bridge: The Epic Story of the Building of the Brooklyn Bridge*. New York: Simon and Schuster, 1972.

———. *The Path Between the Seas: The Creation of the Panama Canal, 1870–1914*. New York: Simon and Schuster, 1977.

McKinley, William. *Speeches and Addresses of William McKinley*. New York: Doubleday & McLure Co., 1900.

Millard, Candice. *The River of Doubt: Theodore Roosevelt's Darkest Journey*. New York: Doubleday, 2005.

Miller, Nathan. *Theodore Roosevelt: A Life*. New York: William Morrow and Co., 1992.

Miller, Stuart Creighton. *"Benevolent Assimilation": The American Conquest of the Philippines, 1899–1903*. New Haven, CT: Yale University Press, 1982.

Millett, Allan. *Semper Fidelis: History of the United States Marine Corps*. New York: The Free Press, 1980.

————, and Jack Shulimson, eds. *Commandants of the Marine Corps*. Annapolis, MD: Naval Institute Press, 2004.

Moeller, Martin Jr. *AIA Guide to the Architecture of Washington* (Part 3). Baltimore: Johns Hopkins University Press, 2006.

Morgan, H. Wayne. *America's Road to Empire: The War with Spain and Overseas Expansion*. New York: John Wiley and Sons, Inc., 1967.

Morison, Elting E., ed. *The Letters of Theodore Roosevelt*, 8 vols. Cambridge, MA: Harvard University Press, 1951–54.

Morris, Edmund. *The Rise of Theodore Roosevelt*. New York: Ballantine Books, 1979.

————. *Theodore Rex*. New York: Random House, 2001.

Musicant, Ivan. *Empire by Default: The Spanish-American War and the Dawn of the American Century*. New York: Henry Holt and Co., 1998.

Nasaw, David. *The Chief: The Life of William Randolph Hearst*. New York: Houghton Mifflin Co., 2000.

The National Cyclopedia of American Biography. New York: James T. White & Co., 1910.

Ochosa, Orlino A. *The Tinio Brigade: Anti-American Resistance in the Ilocos Provinces, 1899–1901*. Quezon City, Philippines: New Day Publishers, 1989.

Olcott, Charles S. *The Life of William McKinley*, 2 vols. Boston: Houghton Mifflin, 1916.

O'Toole, George. *The Spanish War*. New York: W. W. Norton & Co., 1984.

Paine, Ralph D. *Roads of Adventure*. Boston: Houghton Mifflin Co., 1922.

Palmer, Frederick. *With My Own Eyes: A Personal Story of Battle Years*. Indianapolis: The Bobbs-Merrill Co., 1932.

Parramore, Thomas C., with Peter C. Stewart and Tommy L. Bogger. *Norfolk: The First Four Centuries*. Charlottesville: University Press of Virginia, 1994.

Peterson, Norma Lois. *Littleton Waller Tazewell*. Charlottesville: University Press of Virginia, 1983.

Pohlman, Andrew. *My Army Experiences*. New York: Broadway Publishing Co., 1906.

Preston, Diana. *The Boxer Rebellion: The Dramatic Story of China's War on Foreigners That Shook the World in the Summer of 1900*. New York: Walker & Company, 2000.

Pringle, Henry F. *The Life and Times of William Howard Taft*, 2 vols. New York: Farrar & Rinehart, 1939.

————. *Theodore Roosevelt: A Biography*. New York: Harcourt, Brace, 1956.

Rejali, Darius. *Torture and Democracy*. Princeton, NJ: Princeton University Press, 2007.

Roberts, J. A. G. *A Concise History of China*. Cambridge, MA: Harvard University Press, 1999.

Roberts, William R., and Jack Sweetman, eds. *New Interpretations in Naval History: Selected Papers from the Ninth Naval History Symposium*. Annapolis, MD: Naval Institute Press, 1991.

Robertson, Michael. *Stephen Crane, Journalism, and the Making of Modern American Literature*. New York: Columbia University Press, 1997.

Roosevelt, Theodore. *An Autobiography*. New York: The Macmillan Company, 1913.

————. *Presidential Addresses and State Papers*, Vol. 1. New York: The Review of Reviews Co., 1910.

———. *The Rough Riders*. New York: Charles Scribner's Sons, 1899.

———. *The Strenuous Life: Essays and Addresses*. New York: Charles Scribner's Sons, 1906.

Roth, Russell. *Muddy Glory: America's "Indian Wars" in the Philippines, 1899–1935*. West Hanover, MA: Christopher Publishing House, 1981.

Royle, Charles. *The Egyptian Campaigns, 1882 to 1885*. London: Hurst and Blackett Ltd., 1900.

Ruffin, Edmund. *The Diary of Edmund Ruffin*. Baton Rouge, LA: Louisiana State University Press, 1972.

Russell, Henry B. *The Story of Two Wars*. Hartford, CT: The Hartford Publishing Co., 1899.

Sauers, Richard A. *Pennsylvania in the Spanish American War: A Commemorative Look Back*. Harrisburg, PA: Capitol Preservation Committee, Commonwealth of Pennsylvania, 1998.

Sawyer, Frederic H. *The Inhabitants of the Philippines*. New York: Charles Scribner's Sons, 1900.

Schirmer, Daniel B. *Republic or Empire*. Cambridge, MA: Schenkman, 1972.

Schmidt, Hans. *Maverick Marine: General Smedley D. Butler and the Contradictions of American Military History*. Lexington, KY: The University Press of Kentucky, 1987.

Schott, Joseph L. *The Ordeal of Samar*. New York: Bobbs-Merrill, 1964.

Schriftgiesser, Karl. *The Gentleman from Massachusetts*. Boston: Little, Brown and Co., 1944.

Schumacher, Father John. *Revolutionary Clergy: The Filipino Clergy and the Nationalist Movement, 1850–1903*. Quezon City, Philippines: Ateneo, 1981.

Sexton, William Thaddeus. *Soldiers in the Sun: An Adventure in Imperialism*. Harrisburg, PA: Military Service Publishing Co., 1939.

Shaw, Angel Velasco, and Luis H. Francia, eds. *Vestiges of War: The Philippine-American War and the Aftermath of an Imperial Dream, 1899–1999*. New York: New York University Press, 2002.

Shulimson, Jack, et al., eds. *Marines in the Spanish-American War: Anthology and Annotated Bibliography*. Washington, D.C.: History and Museums Division, Headquarters, U.S. Marine Corps, 1998.

Silbey, David. *A War of Frontier and Empire: The Philippine-American War, 1899–1902*. New York: Hill and Wang, 2007.

Spector, Ronald. *Admiral of the New Empire: The Life and Career of George Dewey*. Baton Rouge, LA: Louisiana State University Press, 1974.

Spence, Jonathan D. *The Chan's Great Continent: China in Western Minds*. New York: W. W. Norton & Co., 1998.

———. *The Search for Modern China*. New York: W. W. Norton & Co., 1990.

Stallman, R. W., and E. R. Hagemann, eds. *The War Dispatches of Stephen Crane*. Westport, CT: Greenwood Press Publishers, 1977.

Stickney, Joseph L. *Admiral Dewey at Manila*. Chicago: Imperial Publishing Co., 1899.

Storey, Moorfield, and Julian Codman. *Secretary Root's Record: "Marked Severities" in Philippine Warfare*. Boston: George H. Ellis Co., 1902.

————, and Marcial Lichauco. *The Conquest of the Philippines, 1898–1925.* 1926. Reprint, Mandaluyong, Philippines: Cacho Hermanos, Inc., 1985.

Taylor, James O., ed. *The Massacre of Balangiga.* Joplin, MO: McCarn Printing Co., 1931.

Taylor, John R. M. *The Philippine Insurrection Against the United States,* 5 vols. Pasay City, Philippines: Eugenio Lopez Foundation, 1971.

Tazewell, C. W., ed. *Waller Scrapbook: Hero or Butcher of Samar?* Virginia Beach, VA: W. S. Dawson Co., 1990.

Thayer, William Roscoe. *The Life and Letters of John Hay.* Boston: Houghton Mifflin Co., 1915.

————. *Theodore Roosevelt: An Intimate Biography.* Boston: Houghton Mifflin Co., 1919.

Thomas, Evan. *The War Lovers: Roosevelt, Lodge, Hearst and the Rush to Empire, 1898.* New York: Little, Brown and Co., 2010.

Thomas, Lowell. *Old Gimlet Eye: The Adventures of Smedley D. Butler as Told to Lowell Thomas.* 1933. Reprint, Quantico, VA: Marine Corps Association, 1981.

Traxel, David. *1898.* New York: Alfred A. Knopf, 1998.

Tuchman, Barbara. *The Proud Tower: A Portrait of the World before the War, 1890–1914.* New York: Macmillan Co., 1966.

Tyler, Lyon Gardiner, ed. *Encyclopedia of Virginia Biography,* Vol. 4. New York: Lewis Historical Publishing Company, 1915.

Urwin, Gregory J. W. *The United States Infantry: An Illustrated History, 1775–1918.* Norman, OK: University of Oklahoma Press, 1988.

Vivian, Thomas J. *With Dewey at Manila.* New York: R. F. Fenno & Company, 1898.

Vogel, Steve. *The Pentagon: A History.* New York: Random House, 2007.

Warshaw, Leon J. *Malaria: The Biography of a Killer.* New York: Rinehart & Co., 1949.

Welch, Richard E. Jr. *George Frisbie Hoar and the Half-Breed Republicans.* Cambridge, MA: Harvard University Press, 1971.

————. *Response to Imperialism: The United States and the Philippine-American War, 1899–1902.* Chapel Hill, NC: The University of North Carolina Press, 1979.

Wertenbaker, Thomas Jefferson. *Norfolk: Historic Southern Port.* Durham, NC: Duke University Press, 1962.

White, Trumbull. *United States in War with Spain and the History of Cuba.* Chicago: International Publishing Co., 1898.

White, William Allen. *Autobiography.* New York: Macmillan, 1946.

Wilcox, Marrion, ed. *Harper's History of the War in the Philippines.* New York: Harper & Brothers, 1900.

Wilson, H. W. *The Downfall of Spain: Naval History of the Spanish-American War.* London: Sampson Low, Marston and Co., 1900.

Wilstach, Paul. *Tidewater Virginia.* New York: Tudor Publishing Co., 1964.

Wolff, Leon. *Little Brown Brother: How the United States Purchased and Pacified the Philippine Islands at the Century's Turn.* Garden City, NY: Doubleday, 1961.

Worcester, Dean C. *A History of Asiatic Cholera in the Philippine Islands.* Manila, Philippines: Bureau of Printing, 1909.

————. *The Philippine Islands and Their People: A record of personal observation and experiences, with a short summary of the more important facts in the history of the archipelago.* New York: Macmillan, 1899.

———. *The Philippines Past and Present,* 2 vols. New York: Macmillan, 1914.

Yarsinske, Amy Waters. *The Elizabeth River.* Charleston, SC: The History Press, 2007.

Zimmerman, Warren. *First Great Triumph: How Five Americans Made Their Country a World Power.* New York: Farrar, Straus and Giroux, 2002.

Articles and Papers

Amano, Dominador V. "The Balangiga Encounter." *Sunday Inquirer Magazine* (September 26, 1993): 3–5.

Arens, Fr. Richard Arens, SVD. "The Early Pulahan Movement in Samar." *Leyte-Samar Studies* 11 (1977): 57–113.

Berge, William H. "Voices for Imperialism: Josiah Strong and the Protestant Clergy." *Border States: Journal of the Kentucky-Tennessee American Studies Association* (1973). Accessed December 20, 2009, http://spider.georgetowncollege.edu/htallant/border/bs1/berge.htm.

Borch, Frederic L. "From Frontier Cavalryman to the World Stage: The Career of Army Judge Advocate General George B. Davis." *Army History* (Winter 2010): 6–19.

Borrinaga, Rolando O. "100 Years of Balangiga Literature: A Review." *ICHTHUS* 2 (2001): 59–81.

Cassard, William G., Chaplain. "Rescuing the Enemy," from "The Story of the Captains: Personal Narratives of the Battle off Santiago by Officers of the American Fleet." *The Century Magazine* 58 (May 1899): 116–118.

Chaput, Donald. "The American Press and General Vicente Lukbàn, Hero of Samar." *Leyte-Samar Studies* 8 (1974): 21–32.

———. "Leyte Leadership in the Revolution: The Moxica-Lukbàn Issue." *Leyte-Samar Studies* 9 (1975): 3–12.

Colina, Adelaida B., and Junonia A. Jumalon. "Report on the Flora of Basey Region, Southwestern Samar, Philippines." *Leyte-Samar Studies* 7 (1973): 38–68.

Crane, Stephen. "Marines Signaling Under Fire at Guantánamo." *McClure's Magazine* 12 (February 1899): 332–36.

Davis, Richard Harding. "The Rough Riders Fight at Guásimas." *Scribner's* 24 (September 1898): 259–73.

Daza, Eugenio Daza. "Some Documents of the Philippine-American War in Samar." *Leyte-Samar Studies* 17 (1983): 173–79.

Evans, Captain Robley D. "The 'Iowa' at Santiago," from "The Story of the Captains: Personal Narratives of the Battle off Santiago by Officers of the American Fleet." *The Century Magazine* 58 (May 1899): 50–62.

Fritz, David L. "Before the 'Howling Wilderness': The Military Career of Jacob Hurd Smith." *Military Affairs* 43 (December 1979): 186–90.

Ganley, Eugene F. "Mountain Chase." *Military Affairs* 24 (February 1961): 203–21.

Haydock, Michael. "Marine Scapegoat in the Philippine Insurrection." *Military History* (February 2002): 47–52.

Heinl, Col. Robert D. Jr. "How We Got Guantánamo." *American Heritage* 13 (February 1962): 18–21, 94–97.

Holden-Rhodes, James. "Crucible of the Corps." In *Marines in the Spanish-American War: Anthology and Annotated Bibliography.* Compiled and edited by Jack Shulimson, et al., 67–78. Washington, D.C.: History and Museums Division, Headquarters, U.S. Marine Corps, 1998.

Imperial, Reynaldo H. "Balangiga and After." Paper presented at the Balangiga Roundtable Conference, Tacloban, Philippines, November 27–28, 1998.

Kramer, Paul. "The Water Cure." *The New Yorker* (February 25, 2008): 38–43.

Linn, Brian M. "Guerrilla Fighter: Frederick Funston in the Philippines, 1900–1901." *Kansas History* 10 (Spring 1987): 2–16.

———. "Pacification in Northwestern Luzon: An American Regiment in the Philippine-American War, 1899–1901." *Pilipinas* 3 (December 1982): 14–25.

———. "Provincial Pacification in the Philippines, 1900–1901: The First District, Department of Northern Luzon." *Military Affairs* 51 (April 1987): 62–66.

———. "The Struggle for Samar." In *Crucible of Empire: The Spanish-American War and Its Aftermath*, edited by James C. Bradford, 158–82. Annapolis, MD: Naval Institute Press, 1993.

———. "We Will Go Heavily Armed: The Marines' Small War on Samar, 1901–1902." In *New Interpretations in Naval History: Selected Papers from the Ninth Naval History Symposium*, edited by William R. Roberts and Jack Sweetman, 273–92. Annapolis, MD: Naval Institute Press, 1991.

Lukacs, John. "The Meaning of '98." *American Heritage Magazine* 49 (May/June 1998). Accessed September 4, 2009, http://www.americanheritage.com/articles/magazine/ah/1998/3/1998_3_72.shtml.

Marshall, Edward. "How It Feels to Be Shot." *Cosmopolitan* 25 (September 1898): 557–58.

May, Glenn A. "Filipino Resistance to American Occupation: Batangas, 1899–1902." *Pacific Historical Review* 48 (November 1979): 531–56.

———. "Why the United States Won the Philippine-American War, 1899–1902." *Pacific Historical Review* 52 (November 1982): 353–77.

Millett, Allan R. "The Spanish-American War." In *Marines in the Spanish-American War: Anthology and Annotated Bibliography.* Compiled and edited by Jack Shulimson, et al., 31–37. Washington, D.C.: History and Museums Division, Headquarters, U.S. Marine Corps, 1998.

Oswald, Mark G. "The 'Howling Wilderness' Courts-Martial of 1902." U.S. Army War College, Carlisle Barracks, Pennsylvania, 2001.

Plante, Trevor K. "'New Glory to Its Already Gallant Record': The First Marine Battalion in the Spanish-American War." *Prologue* 30 (Spring 1998): 21–31.

Shafter, USA Major General William R. "The Capture of Santiago de Cuba." *The Century Magazine* 57 (February 1899): 612–30.

Taylor, Captain Henry C. "The 'Indiana' at Santiago," from "The Story of the Captains: Personal Narratives of the Battle off Santiago by Officers of the American Fleet." *The Century Magazine* 58 (May 1899): 62–75.

Twain, Mark. "In Defence of General Funston." *North American Review* 174 (May 1902): 613–24.

———. "To a Person Sitting in Darkness." *North American Review* 172 (February 1901): 161–76.

Tyson, Carolyn A., ed. "The Journal of Frank Keeler, 1898." *Marine Corps Letter Series* 1 (1967).

Wainwright, Richard, Commander, U.S.N. "The 'Gloucester' at Santiago," from "The Story of the Captains: Personal Narratives of the Battle off Santiago by Officers of the American Fleet." *The Century Magazine* 58 (May 1899): 77–86.

Wall, Gerald J. Jr. "What's Left of Company C." *Saga Magazine* (November 1953): 34–37, 66–67.

Wallach, Evan. "Drop by Drop: Forgetting the History of Water Torture in U.S. Courts." *The Columbia Journal of Transnational Law* 45 (2007).

———. "Waterboarding Used to Be a Crime." *Washington Post* (November 4, 2007).

Young, Kenneth Ray. "Atrocities and War Crimes: The Cases of Major Waller and General Smith." *Leyte-Samar Studies* 12 (1978): 64–77.

———. "Guerrilla Warfare: Balangiga Revisited." *Leyte-Samar Studies* 11 (1977): 21–31.

Zwick, Jim. "Mark Twain's Anti-Imperialist Writings in the 'American Century.'" In *Vestiges of War: The Philippine-American War and the Aftermath of an Imperial Dream, 1899–1999*, edited by Angel Velasco Shaw and Luis H. Francia., eds. 28–56. New York: New York University Press, 2002.

NOTES

———•◦•———

The following abbreviations are used in the notes. These and other sources are listed in the bibliography.

ANJ ....*Army and Navy Journal*
BDE ....*Brooklyn Daily Eagle*
CR ....*Congressional Record*
Correspondence ..........................U.S. Army, Adjutant General's Office, *Correspondence Relating to the War with Spain . . . from April 15, 1898, to July 30, 1902*, Washington, D.C.: Government Printing Office, 1902
Glenn GCM 34401 ....Transcript of Edwin F. Glenn Court-martial (1902), Record Group (RG) 153, National Archives and Records Administration
LC ....Library of Congress, Washington, D.C.
NARA....................................National Archives and Records Administration, Washington, D.C.
NPRC ....National Personnel Records Center, St. Louis, Missouri
NYT..*New York Times*
Root Papers ....Papers of Elihu Root, Library of Congress
Senate, *Affairs*........................Transcript of Senate Committee on the Philippines hearings, published as *Affairs in the Philippine Islands. Hearing Before the Committee on the Philippines of the United*

States Senate, Senate Document 331, 57th Congress, 1st
Session, 1902

Smith GCM 30739...............Transcript of Jacob H. Smith Court-martial (1902),
Record Group (RG) 153, National Archives and Records
Administration

Taft Papers...........................Papers of William Howard Taft, Library of Congress

TR Letters ....*The Letters of Theodore Roosevelt*, 8 vols., edited by Elting
Morison

TR Papers............................Papers of Theodore Roosevelt, Library of Congress

USMCA................................U.S. Marine Corps Archives, Quantico, Virginia

Waller GCM 30313 ....Transcript of Littleton W. T. Waller Court-martial
(1902), Record Group (RG) 153, National Archives and
Records Administration

Waller Papers........................Papers of Littleton W. T. Waller Sr., U.S. Marine Corps
Archives, Quantico, Virginia

Waller Report.......................Report of Major Littleton W. T. Waller on Marine Corps
operations on Samar Island, Philippines, 1901–1902,
dated May 24, 1902, in Waller Papers, United States
Marine Corps Archives, Quantico, Virginia

WD.......................................*Annual Reports of the War Department* (1898–1903), cited by
volume, part and page

Prologue

1   The interrogation of Joveniano Ealdama is reconstructed from two primary sources:
Ealdama's testimony in the 1902 court-martial of Major Edwin F. Glenn (GCM
34401, Edwin F. Glenn, Record Group 153, NARA), and the eyewitness accounts
of three U.S. soldiers—Charles S. Riley, William L. Smith and Edward J. Davis—
who testified before the U.S. Senate Committee on the Philippines in 1902. Their
testimony is reprinted in Senate, *Affairs,* 1527–29, 1538–40 and 1726–35; also see
"Told of 'Water Cure' Given to Filipinos," *NYT,* April 15, 1902, and "Saw the
'Water Cure' Given," *NYT,* April 18, 1902.

2   Ealdama's given name is misspelled as "Tobeniano" in some official U.S. documents.

3   The history of water torture is drawn from several sources. Two books were particularly useful: Darius Rejali, *Torture and Democracy* (Princeton: Princeton University
Press, 2007), 279–80; and Mark P. Donnelly and Daniel Diehl, *The Big Book of Pain:
Torture and Punishment Through History* (Stroud: History Press, 2008), 88–89. Scottish
traveler William Lithgow described "the strangling torments" of the water torture
he suffered in Spain in 1620 in his remarkable memoir, *Rare Adventures and Painful
Peregrinations* (1632; reprint, Glasgow: James MacLehose and Sons, 1906), 404 and
413.

Chapter 1—Call to Arms

1 Charles Hamilton to "Dear Father," February 5, 1898, Spanish-American War Centennial Web site, www.spanamwar.com/mainehamiltonlet.htm (accessed November 13, 2009).

2 Ibid.

3 "Navy Auxiliary Board," *BDE*, April 21, 1898; "Fleet Boats for the Navy," *NYT*, March 18, 1898; "A Dozen Vessels Bought," *NYT*, March 26, 1898; "Work at the Navy Yard," *NYT*, April 22, 1898; Donald H. Dyal, et al., *Historical Dictionary of the Spanish-American War* (Westport, CT: Greenwood Press, 1996), 141 and 355–56.

4 The Edison cameramen and Hearst's *New York Journal* produced seventeen such "Edison-Journal Views" that played in packed New York vaudeville halls. In early June, Hearst loaned the *Buccaneer* to the Navy for use off Cuba. See David Nasaw, *The Chief: The Life of William Randolph Hearst* (New York: Houghton Mifflin Co., 2000), 33.

5 "New York's Defenses Are Now Complete," *BDE*, April 22, 1898; "To Block Sound Traffic," *BDE*, April 22, 1898.

6 "Marine Battalion Increased in Size," *BDE*, April 21, 1898.

7 Margaret Leech, *In the Days of McKinley* (New York: Harper & Brothers, 1959), 118.

8 Hermann Hagedorn, *Leonard Wood: A Biography* (New York: Harper & Brothers, 1931), 1:141.

9 William McKinley, *Speeches and Addresses of William McKinley* (New York: Doubleday & McLure Co., 1900), 67–78.

10 TR cablegram to Commodore George Dewey, February 25, 1898, H. W. Brands, *The Selected Letters of Theodore Roosevelt* (New York: Cooper Square Press, 2001), 170–71.

11 *CR*, 55th Congress, 2nd Session, 2916–19.

12 Leech, *McKinley*, 181; Ivan Musicant, *Empire by Default: The Spanish-American War and the Dawn of the American Century* (New York: Henry Holt and Co., 1998), 178.

13 Leech, *McKinley*, 181–82.

14 Ibid., 190–91.

15 "Effigy of Weyler," *BDE*, April 18, 1898.

16 "Patriotism Grows Rampant," *BDE*, April 22, 1898.

17 "He Objected to War," *BDE*, April 22, 1898.

18 "Marines Start Tonight," *BDE*, April 22, 1898; "Patrol for This Harbor," *BDE*, April 23, 1898.

19 "*State of Texas* Loading," *BDE*, April 21, 1898.

20 "Marine Landing Parties," *BDE*, April 19, 1898; "Marine Battalions Increased in Size," *BDE*, April 21, 1898.

21 "Marines Signaling Under Fire at Guantánamo," J. C. Levenson, ed., *Stephen Crane: Prose and Poetry* (New York: The Library of America, 1984), 1054; "Marines Start Tonight," *BDE*, April 22, 1898; "Marines Off for the War," *NYT*, April 23, 1898.

22 "Marines Off for the War," *NYT*, April 23, 1898.

23 Allan R. Millett and Jack Shulimson, eds., *Commandants of the Marine Corps* (Annapolis, MD: Naval Institute Press, 2004), 129.

24 Jack Shulimson, et al., *Marines in the Spanish-American War: Anthology and Annotated Bibliography* (Washington, D.C.: History and Museums Division, Headquarters, U.S. Marine Corps, 1998), 45.

25 "For the Auxiliary Fleet," *NYT,* April 15, 1898; also see Edward J. Marolda, ed., *Theodore Roosevelt, the U.S. Navy, and the Spanish-American War* (New York: Palgrave Macmillan, 2001), 82.

26 "Marines Off for the War," *NYT,* April 23, 1898.

Chapter 2—"He Is No Tender Chicken"

1   "Theodore Roosevelt Is in Town," *NYT,* April 22, 1898.

2   Martin Moeller Jr., *AIA Guide to the Architecture of Washington*, pt. 3 (Baltimore: Johns Hopkins University Press, 2006), 170; Steve Vogel, *The Pentagon: A History* (New York: Random House, 2007), 30.

3   Ibid. For additional history and background on the State, War, and Navy Building, see www.whitehouse.gov/about/eeob.

4   Edmund Morris, *The Rise of Theodore Roosevelt* (New York: Ballantine Books, 1979), 555.

5   Nathan Miller, *Theodore Roosevelt: A Life* (New York: William Morrow and Co., 1992), 36.

6   William Roscoe Thayer, *Theodore Roosevelt: An Intimate Biography* (Boston: Houghton Mifflin Co., 1919), 8.

7   William H. Berge, "Voices for Imperialism: Josiah Strong and the Protestant Clergy," *Border States: Journal of the Kentucky-Tennessee American Studies Association* 1 (1973), accessed December 20, 2009, http://spider.georgetowncollege.edu/htallant/border/bs1/berge.htm; and Lukacs, "The Meaning of '98," *American Heritage* 49 (May/June 1998), accessed September 4, 2009, http://www.americanheritage.com/articles/magazine/ah/1998/3/1998_3_72.shtml.

8   Elting E. Morison, ed., TR Letters, 1:599.

9   Miller, *Theodore Roosevelt*, 117.

10 Allan R. Millet, *Semper Fidelis: The History of the United States Marine Corps* (New York: The Free Press, 1980), 116.

11 "The Launch of the *Maine*," *NYT,* November 19, 1890.

12 Ibid.

13 Stephen Kinzer, *Overthrow: America's Century of Regime Change from Hawaii to Iraq* (New York: Times Books, 2006), 17–29.

14 TR to James S. Clarkson, April 22, 1893, Brands, *Letters*, 84.

15 "For an Honest Election," *NYT,* October 24, 1895.

16 TR to Lodge, December 27, 1895; TR to William Cowles, December 22, 1895, Brands, *Letters*, 112.

17   "Mr. Roosevelt in Chicago," *NYT*, October 16, 1896.

18   "Roosevelt on His Ranches," *NYT*, September 20, 1896.

19   TR to Alfred Thayer Mahan, May 3, 1897, TR Letters, 1:607–08.

20   TR to Alfred Thayer Mahan, June 9, 1897, TR Letters, 1:622.

21   "Naval War College Opened, Assistant Secretary of the Navy Roosevelt Appeals for a Great Navy," *NYT*, May 3, 1897; TR Letters, 1:621; also see Morris, *The Rise of Theodore Roosevelt*, 569–70.

22   William Allen White, *Autobiography* (New York: Macmillan, 1946), 297–98.

23   TR to Bellamy Storer, August 19, 1897, TR Letters, 1:655.

24   *New York Sun*, August 23, 1897.

25   TR to Charles Addison Boutelle, September 16, 1897, TR Letters, 1:680.

26   H. W. Brands, *TR: The Last Romantic* (New York: Basic Books, 1997), 329.

27   TR to Brooks Adams, March 21, 1898, TR Letters, 1:797–98.

28   Roosevelt's meeting with Alger is described in Morris, *Rise*, 613.

Chapter 3—America's Marine

1   Reliable biographical material on Littleton W. T. Waller Sr. is surprisingly sparse for a public figure of such controversy and acclaim. No full-length biography exists, and he did not write his memoirs. He rarely granted on-the-record interviews, and only a few dozen personal letters survive. In my effort to draw as full and accurate a portrait of Waller as possible, I have tapped a wide array of primary sources. Waller's Marine Corps papers, which are preserved at the U.S. Marine Corps Archives in Quantico, Virginia, yielded valuable insights into his upbringing and personality as well as his military exploits. Among the gems was a handwritten field report Waller filed from China in July 1900, in which, in his fine cursive, he drew on his knowledge of Shakespeare to describe his battle-worn battalion as "like Falstaff's army in appearance, but with brave hearts and bright weapons." Waller's military personnel file, archived at the National Personnel Records Center in St. Louis, provided a useful time line of his movements, disciplinary files and medical records (which included several accidents related to his drinking). At the National Archives in Washington, D.C., I gleaned additional information on Waller from Marine Corps operational records from the Philippines and the China Relief Expedition of 1900. My starting point for reconstructing Waller's family history and childhood was C. W. Tazewell's *Waller Scrapbook: Hero or Butcher of Samar?* (Virginia Beach, VA: W. S. Dawson Co., 1990), a collection of genealogical information, newspaper articles and other information published in 1990 by one of Tony Waller's nephews. Other primary and secondary sources I consulted include U.S. census records for 1850–1920; various Tidewater Virginia property, probate and tax records; microfilmed copies of four Norfolk, Virginia, newspapers (*Norfolk Day Book, Virginian, Ledger-Star* and *Southern Argus*); *Army and Navy Journal* issues from 1882, the year of Waller's entry into the Marine Corps, through 1902, when he returned from

the Philippines; various genealogies compiled by Waller descendants; and, finally, several books on plantation culture and daily life in Tidewater Virginia and Norfolk, which immersed me in the great political, social and economic forces that shaped Waller's formative years. Four were especially useful: Virginius Dabney, *Virginia: The New Dominion* (Garden City, NY: Doubleday & Company, 1971); Edward L. Ayers and John C. Willis, eds., *The Edge of the South: Life in Nineteenth-Century Virginia* (Charlottesville and London: University Press of Virginia, 1991); Paul Wilstach, *Tidewater Virginia* (New York: Tudor Publishing Co., 1964); and Susan Dunn, *Dominion of Memories: Jefferson, Madison, and the Decline of Virginia* (New York: Basic Books, 2007).

2　Waller's height and other physical characteristics are drawn from a May 6, 1909, document in his military personnel file, "Personal Description of Officers." The details about Waller's striking posture and commanding presence, as well as his horsemanship and the rakish manner in which he wore (and doffed) his hat are drawn from Smedley Butler's quasi-autobiography, written by Lowell Thomas: *Old Gimlet Eye: The Adventures of Smedley D. Butler as Told to Lowell Thomas* (1933; reprint, Quantico, VA: Marine Corps Association, 1981), 36–40. Waller's skill with a rifle is highlighted by an item in the *Army and Navy Journal* of November 10, 1883, which credits Waller with scoring the first hit on a wild boar in the hills of Morocco during a hunt with U.S. diplomats and fellow officers from the USS *Lancaster*. His vocal abilities were noted in an item in the May 12, 1883, *Army and Navy Journal*. Butler recalled Waller's vanity and his fondness for telling stories, especially about himself, in *Old Gimlet Eye*. A far more devastating critique of Waller's personality (with emphasis on his foibles) is an anonymous, undated, fifteen-page screed preserved in the personal papers of fellow Marine officer Ben H. Fuller at the USMCA.

3　See Smedley Butler's description of Waller in Thomas, *Old Gimlet Eye*, 36–40. Also see the anonymous essay in the Fuller personal papers. Waller's superior abilities as an officer are evidenced by the numerous letters of praise and commendations found in his personal papers and military personnel records, and the loyalty he commanded among his men in the Philippines and China. His willingness to share the hardships of his men is documented by a photograph taken in the field in China in the summer of 1900 (preserved in a photo album in Waller's personal papers), and in accounts of his expedition across Samar in early 1902. His penchant for drinking to excess is also well documented in his military records.

4　Butler quote from Thomas, *Old Gimlet Eye*, 37.

5　Waller's genealogy is reconstructed from the following sources: Lyon Gardiner Tyler, ed., *Encyclopedia of Virginia Biography*, vol. 4 (New York: Lewis Historical Publishing Company, 1915), 510–12; U.S. census records, including slave schedules documenting Matthew Waller's slave ownership; Norfolk newspaper archives; and Tazewell's *Waller Scrapbook*. According to Tony Waller's niece Fanny Waller Parker, the five Waller boys "were raised on the farm and at Williamsburg. When their father died, they came to the Tazewell House [in Norfolk], and were raised by [aunt] Sally Tazewell." See *Waller Scrapbook*, 66. Much has been written about Tony Waller's namesake and maternal grandfather, former Virginia governor and U.S.

senator Littleton Waller Tazewell. I consulted the following: Hugh Blair Grigsby, *Discourse on the Life and Character of the Hon. Littleton Waller Tazewell* (Norfolk, VA: J. D. Ghiselin, 1860); Norma Lois Peterson, *Littleton Waller Tazewell* (Charlottesville, VA: University Press of Virginia, 1983); and Tazewell's obituary, "Death of Ex-gov. Tazewell," printed in *The Southern Argus* on May 8, 1860.

6　My characterization of life in antebellum Norfolk is based on *Norfolk Day Book* coverage of daily events from October 1857 to March 1860; Edmund Ruffin, *The Diary of Edmund Ruffin*, vol.1 (Baton Rouge: Louisiana State University Press, 1972), 207–09; "The Perils of the Coast," *NYT*, February 9, 1857; "Affairs in Virginia," *NYT*, September 22, 1857; Dabney, 221–23; H. W. Burton, *The History of Norfolk, Virginia* (Norfolk, VA: Norfolk Virginian Printing, 1877), 20–42; Thomas Jefferson Wertenbaker, *Norfolk: Historic Southern Port* (Durham, NC: Duke University Press, 1962), 188–206; and Thomas C. Parramore with Peter C. Stewart and Tommy L. Bogger, *Norfolk: The First Four Centuries* (Charlottesville, VA: University Press of Virginia, 1994), 189–200.

7　Burton, 45–63.

8　See Tazewell, *Waller Scrapbook*, Waller family tree, entry twenty-six on Matthew Page Waller. Typhoid was a common cause of premature death in Norfolk in late 1861, especially as the city's population swelled with the influx of Confederate soldiers.

9　Various documents in Waller military personnel file, NPRC.

10　Millett and Shulimson, *Commandants*, 95–97.

11　*Daily Telegraph* dispatch quoted in "England and Egypt," *ANJ*, July 22, 1882, 1192.

12　Richard S. Collum, *History of the United States Marine Corps* (Philadelphia: L. R. Hamersly & Co., 1890), 218–19. For other accounts describing the scene in Alexandria and actions of the U.S. Marines see "Europeans Shockingly Mutilated," *Washington Evening Critic*, July 14, 1882; "American Marines in Service," *Washington Evening Critic*, July 14, 1882; "The War in Egypt," *The National Tribune*, July 22, 1882; "The War in Egypt," *The Sunday Herald*, July 16, 1882; and "Burning of Alexandria," *New York Sun*, July 15, 1882. Also see "A Court-martial for Major Waller," *NYT*, March 7, 1902, and Charles Royle, *The Egyptian Campaigns, 1882 to 1885* (London: Hurst and Blackett Ltd., 1900), 443.

13　Ibid.

14　Waller Court-martial Transcript, 437, GCM 30313, RG 153, NARA.

15　Medical records from Waller military personnel file, NPRC.

16　In a May 1, 1895, letter of commendation to the secretary of the Navy, the solicitor general praised Waller's written brief and oral argument before the Supreme Court. In the solicitor's words, Waller "met all the demands of the occasion with the readiness and skill of a trained advocate." The letter is in Waller's personnel file. Also see "An Important Question of Jurisdiction," *NYT*, April 2, 1895, and "Court-martial Sentences Stand," *NYT*, May 7, 1895.

17　Waller's intemperate words are quoted in a January 28, 1897, letter of reprimand from Secretary of the Navy H. A. Hebert, found in Waller's personnel file. Also see "Captain Waller Reprimanded," *NYT*, January 31, 1897.

18 Henry B. Russell, *The Story of Two Wars* (Hartford, CT: The Hartford Publishing Co., 1899), 316.

19 Ibid. The beginning of the U.S. Navy blockade of Cuba is also described by Captain F. E. Chadwick, skipper of the *New York*, in "The Navy in the War," *Scribner's Magazine*, Volume XXIV, July–December 1898 (New York, Charles Scribner's Sons, 1898), 530; by correspondent Richard Harding Davis, who was aboard the *New York*, in an April 26, 1898, letter addressed "Dear Family," reprinted in Charles Belmont Davis, ed., *Adventures and Letters of Richard Harding Davis* (New York: Charles Scribner's Sons, 1917), 228; and by Stephen Crane in "With the Blockade on Cuban Coast," *New York World*, May 9, 1898.

Chapter 4—Manila Bay

1 Ronald Spector, *Admiral of the New Empire: The Life and Career of George Dewey* (Baton Rouge, LA: Louisiana State University Press, 1974), 40.

2 Ibid., 56–57.

3 George Dewey, *Autobiography of George Dewey* (New York: Charles Scribner's Sons, 1913), 206.

4 Spector, 57.

5 Adelbert Dewey, *The Life and Letters of Admiral Dewey* (Akron, OH: The Werner Co., 1899), 172–79.

6 David Traxel, *1898* (New York: Alfred A. Knopf, 1998), 129.

7 Spector, *Admiral*, 31.

8 Ibid., 39.

9 Morris, *Rise*, 587. In his autobiography, Roosevelt would later explain that he liked Dewey's "willingness to accept responsibility" and "entire fearlessness." He also claimed that Dewey impressed him during an 1891 crisis in Chile by risking his career to make an emergency purchase of coal for his fleet in violation of Navy rules. That, however, was unlikely. Naval records place Dewey in Washington at that time. It seems more probable that Roosevelt's support reflected their Metropolitan Club friendship. Also, Roosevelt considered Dewey's rival, Commander John A. Howell, "irresolute" and "extremely afraid of responsibility."

10 "He Said 'Another Jag,'" *NYT*, October 10, 1899.

11 Spector, *Admiral*, 41.

12 TR to Henry Cabot Lodge, September 21, 1897, and TR to William W. Kimball, November 19, 1897, TR Letters, 1:690 and 716–17.

13 TR cablegram to George Dewey, February 25, 1898; Brands, *Letters*, 170–71.

14 Stanley Karnow, *In Our Image: America's Empire in the Philippines* (New York: Random House, 1989), 70–77.

15 David Haward Bain, *Sitting in Darkness: Americans in the Philippines* (Boston: Houghton Mifflin Co., 1984), 154–55.

16 Karnow, *In Our Image*, 76.

17 G. Dewey, *Autobiography*, 186. For more on Williams and how he became America's eyes and ears in Manila, see "Consul Oscar Williams," *NYT*, May 5, 1898, and "Memorial to O. F. Williams, '69," *Cornell Alumni News*, vol. 12, no. 12, December 15, 1909, 137.

18 Spector, *Admiral*, 46.

19 Ibid., 47.

20 Emilio Aguinaldo and Vicente Albano Pacis, *A Second Look at America* (New York: Robert Speller & Sons, Publishers Inc., 1957), 29–31.

21 Emilio Aguinaldo, *True Version of the Philippine Revolution* (Tarlac, Philippines: 1899), 9–12; Aguinaldo and Pacis, *A Second Look*, 33.

22 Aguinaldo and Pacis, *A Second Look*, 32–34; *Singapore Free Press*, May 4, 1898, quoted in 55th Congress, 3rd Session (1899), Senate Document 95, "Articles Relating to Islands, February 1, 1899."

23 Spector, *Admiral*, 56.

24 G. Dewey, *Autobiography*, 205.

25 Ibid., 192. Also see Thomas J. Vivian, *With Dewey at Manila* (New York: R. F. Fenno & Company, 1898), 27–28.

26 Ibid., 208–09. Also see Laurin Hall Healy and Luis Kutner, *The Admiral* (New York: Ziff-Davis, 1944), 174–75.

27 Vivian, *With Dewey*, 32–34.

28 Ibid., 35–36.

29 Ibid., 48–49.

30 Ibid., 48.

31 G. Dewey, *Autobiography*, 214.

32 Spector, *Admiral*, 59. Admiral Montojo's account of the battle can be found in "The Battle of Manila," *NYT*, June 24, 1898.

33 Vivian, *With Dewey*, 53. George Dewey's blow-by-blow of the battle is recounted in his autobiography, 212–20. Another eyewitness account is that of correspondent Joseph L. Stickney, who served as an aide to Dewey during the battle. See Stickney, *Admiral Dewey at Manila* (Chicago: Imperial Publishing Co., 1899), 42–56. For Captain Gridley's account of the action, see A. Dewey, *Life and Letters*, 321–22. The perspective of an enlisted man is related by *Olympia* stoker Charles H. Twitchell in A. Dewey, *Life and Letters*, 370–74.

34 G. Dewey, *Autobiography*, 225.

Chapter 5—Guantánamo Bay

1 Spector, *Admiral*, 64–67.

2 TR to Dewey, May 7, 1898, in Dewey Papers, LC; and Dewey to George Goodwin Dewey, June 16, 1898, quoted in Spector, *Admiral*, 67.

3 Charles H. Brown, *The Correspondents' War: Journalists in the Spanish-American War* (New York: Charles Scribner's Sons, 1967), 264–65.

4   Colonel Robert D. Heinl Jr., "How We Got Guantánamo," *American Heritage* 13 (February 1962): 18–21.

5   The scene in Guantánamo Bay on June 10, 1898, is described in Shulimson, et al., *Marines*, 34 and 68, and Trevor Plante, "New Glory to Its Already Gallant Record," *Prologue* 30 (Spring 1998), 23.

6   Shulimson, et al., *Marines*, 68. Also see "Our Flag Flies at Guantánamo," *NYT*, June 12, 1898.

7   Robert W. Huntington to son, June 18, 1898, Huntington Papers, USMCA.

8   Entry for June 10, 1898, "Journal of the Marine Battalion under Lt. Col. Robert W. Huntington, Apr.–Sept. 1898," 8, Record Group 127, NARA. Huntington's June 17, 1898, report on the First Marine Battalion's early days at Guantánamo provides a useful narrative framework. It is reprinted in "Services of the First Marine Battalion in Cuba," *The United Service* 2 (New York: L. R. Hamersly Co., 1903), 553–55, and will be hereafter referred to as the Huntington Report.

9   Colonel Robert Huntington's report and his "Journal of the First Marine Battalion" were invaluable in my reconstruction of the June 10–14 events at Guantánamo Bay (and my efforts to sort out discrepancies among the various accounts). Also helpful were the diary and letters of Henry Clay Cochrane and letters from other Marine participants in the events. The sources I consulted in describing the landing and subsequent events at Guantánamo Bay are: Colonel Huntington's report and journal; dispatches of Stephen Crane; dispatches of the Associated Press as printed in the *New York Times* on June 12–16; and Ralph D. Paine, *Roads of Adventure* (Boston: Houghton Mifflin Co., 1922), by a newspaper correspondent who witnessed the landing. Excellent contemporary accounts drawn from these sources and others include: Plante, "New Glory"; James Holden-Rhodes, "Crucible of the Corps," from *The Marines in the Spanish-American War: Anthology and Annotated Bibliography* (Washington, D.C.: History and Museums Division, Headquarters, U.S. Marine Corps, 1998); and Allan R. Millett's definitive *Semper Fidelis*, an excerpt of which was reprinted as "The Spanish-American War," in the aforementioned anthology.

10   Shulimson, et al., *Marines*, 83.

11   Charles Smith obituary, *Westminster Democratic Advocate*, June 18, 1898, reprinted in *Carroll County Times*, June 14, 1998.

12   From an undated article written by Olin Fay Johnson for the *National Tribune* of Washington, D.C.; also Huntington Journal, 8–9.

13   Eyewitness accounts quoted in C. Brown, *Correspondents' War*, 279–89.

14   "Our First Fight on Cuban Soil," *NYT*, June 13, 1898.

15   The physical description of Stephen Crane and quotes from Joseph Conrad and Richard Harding Davis are drawn from Betting L. Knapp, *Stephen Crane* (New York: Continuum Publishing, 1987), 27–30.

16   R. W. Stallman and E. R. Hagemann, eds., *The War Dispatches of Stephen Crane* (Westport, CT: Greenwood Press Publishers, 1977), 267–68.

17   Crane, Stephen, *Wounds in the Rain: War Stories* (New York: Frederick A. Stokes Company, 1900), 238. In "Marines Signaling under Fire at Guantánamo," *McClure's*

Magazine 12 (February 1899), Crane mistakenly recalled the death of Gibbs as occurring on the third night rather than the second.

18 Robert W. Huntington to son, June 18, 1898; Crane, "Marines Signaling under Fire," 332–36; also see "Our First Fight on Cuban Soil," *NYT*, June 13, 1898.

19 Smith obituary, *Westminster Democratic Advocate*, June 18, 1898.

20 Huntington Journal, 30–31; "Marines Repel Another Attack," AP dispatch in *NYT*, June 14, 1898; Holden-Rhodes, "Crucible," 71–72; C. Brown, *Correspondents' War*, 283; "Marines Repel Another Attack," AP dispatch in *NYT*, June 15, 1898.

21 Holden-Rhodes, "Crucible," 72.

22 Sources used in describing this attack are the AP account of the fighting in the *NYT*, June 15, 1898; Huntington Report; Huntington Journal, 9; and Holden-Rhodes, "Crucible," 72.

23 Crane, "Marines Signaling under Fire," 332.

24 Crane vividly described the attack on Cuzco Well in "The Red Badge of Courage Was His Wig-Wag Flag," *New York World*, July 1, 1898, and "Marines Signaling under Fire," 335–36; another contemporary account is "Sharp Fighting at Guantánamo," *NYT*, June 16, 1898; Captain George F. Elliott provided a detailed account of the operation in his report of June 15, 1898, reprinted in the above cited "Services of the First Marine Battalion in Cuba," 557–59; also see Holden-Rhodes, "Crucible," 74–76; Carolyn A. Tyson, ed., "The Journal of Frank Keeler, 1898," *Marine Corps Letter Series* 1 (1967), 17–18; and Plante, "New Glory," 24–26.

25 Ibid.

26 Ibid.

27 Crane, "Marines Signaling under Fire," 335–36.

28 Crane, "Wig-Wag Flag," *New York World*, July 1, 1898.

29 Millett, "The Spanish-American War," in *Marines*, 35.

Chapter 6—"It Was War, and It Was Magnificent"

1 Musicant, *Empire*, 354; Morris, *Rise*, 634; Theodore Roosevelt recalls the armada's journey from Florida to Cuba in his bestselling memoir of the war, *The Rough Riders* (New York: Charles Scribner's Sons, 1899), 64–69; Richard Harding Davis records his observations of the fleet's passage to Cuba in *The Cuban and Porto Rican Campaigns* (New York: Charles Scribner's Sons, 1898), 86–99.

2 George O'Toole, *The Spanish War* (New York: W. W. Norton & Co. 1984), 256.

3 "Our Landing Place in Cuba," *NYT*, July 10, 1898; O'Toole, *Spanish War*, 265–66; Morris, *Rise*, 634–36; Musicant, *Empire*, 366.

4 R. Davis, *Campaigns*, 116. Also see Associated Press dispatch, "The Landing of Shafter's Army," *BDE*, June 23, 1898.

5 Morris, *Rise*, 628.

6 R. Davis, *Campaigns*, 119. Another vivid account of the day's events at Daiquirí can be found in C. Brown, *Correspondents' War*, 303–08.

7   "The Landing of Shafter's Army," *BDE*, June 23, 1898; Roosevelt, *Rough Riders*, 74–75.

8   Roosevelt, *Rough Riders*, 76–77; Private Wells quoted in Musicant, *Empire*, 376.

9   Roosevelt, *Rough Riders*, 78–80.

10 Ibid., 80.

11 TR to Paul Dana, April 18, 1898, TR Letters, 2:816–17.

12 "Roosevelt Wants Kentuckians," *NYT*, April 27, 1898.

13 Morris, *Rise*, 620.

14 "The Cowboy Regiment," *NYT*, April 28, 1898.

15 Roosevelt, *Rough Riders*, 59–60.

16 Musicant, *Empire*, 378.

17 C. Brown, *Correspondents' War*, 315.

18 This account of the battle of Las Guásimas is based on the following: Roosevelt, *Rough Riders*, 83–101; Edward Marshall, "How It Feels to Be Shot," *Cosmopolitan* 25 (September 1898), 557–58; Stephen Crane's *New York World* dispatches of June 26 and 27, 1898; and Richard Harding Davis's dispatches of June 26 and 28 in the *New York Herald*, as well as his account in the September 1898 *Scribner's*, "The Rough Riders Fight at Guásimas," 259–73.

19 O'Toole, *Spanish War*, 298.

20 Ibid., 312.

21 Ibid., 313.

22 Roosevelt, *Rough Riders*, 122.

23 Ibid., 122–24.

24 Ibid., 126.

25 Ibid., 130.

26 R. Davis, *Campaigns*, 218; foreign military observers quoted in Stephen Crane, *Prose and Poetry* (New York: Literary Classics of the U.S., 1984), 1005.

27 Roosevelt, *Rough Riders*, 132.

28 Ibid., 155–56.

29 The war council is related by former secretary of war Russell Alger in his book *The Spanish-American War* (New York: Harper & Brothers, 1901), 176; also see Musicant, *Empire*, 428–29.

30 TR to Henry Cabot Lodge, July 3, 1898, TR Letters, 2:846.

Chapter 7—The Eagle Spreads Its Wings

1   McKinley's war room is described in Benjamin R. Beede, ed., *The War of 1898 and U.S. Interventions, 1898–1934: An Encyclopedia* (New York: Garland Publishing Inc., 1994), 579.

2   Leech, *McKinley*, 252.

3   Shafter cable to Adjutant General Henry C. Corbin, July 2, 1898, *Correspondence*, 1:72.

4   Alger, *Spanish-American War*, 172–73.

5   Ibid., 173; Leech, *McKinley*, 252–53.

6 Captain Henry C. Taylor, "The 'Indiana' at Santiago," from "The Story of the Captains: Personal Narratives of the Battle off Santiago by Officers of the American Fleet," *The Century Magazine* 58 (May 1899), 62.

7 Cervera background from Musicant, *Empire*, 279, and O'Toole, *Spanish War*, 120.

8 O'Toole, *Spanish War*, 288.

9 "The 'Indiana' a Wonder," *NYT*, October 19, 1895.

10 "Defects in Battleships," *NYT*, January 29, 1898.

11 Henry Taylor, "The 'Indiana' at Santiago," 64.

12 Ibid., 65.

13 O'Toole, *Spanish War*, 330.

14 Henry Taylor, "The 'Indiana' at Santiago," 69.

15 William G. Cassard, Chaplain, "Rescuing the Enemy," from "The Story of the Captains," 116–18; Richard Wainwright, Commander, U.S.N., "The 'Gloucester' at Santiago," from "The Story of the Captains," 81–85.

16 Captain Robley D. Evans, "The 'Iowa' at Santiago," from "The Story of the Captains," 62. Cervera and other prisoners from the destroyed Spanish fleet were taken to several locations in the United States pending the signing of an armistice. Cervera was held at Annapolis, where his heroic conduct at Santiago Bay and humanitarian treatment of U.S. sailors taken captive prior to the battle made him a national celebrity. Gifts and autograph requests poured in from across the United States. After the armistice was signed, Cervera embarked on a well-received speaking tour across America.

17 Karnow, *In Our Image*, 108.

18 William Sexton, *Soldiers in the Sun: An Adventure in Imperialism* (Harrisburg, PA: Military Service Publishing Co., 1939), 28–29; James Blount, *American Occupation of the Philippines, 1898–1912* (New York: G. P. Putnam's Sons, 1912), 20; John M. Gates, *Schoolbooks and Krags: The United States Army in the Philippines, 1898–1902* (Westport, CT: Greenwood Press Inc., 1973), 15.

19 Oscar Williams, May 12, 1898, report to the State Department. The Williams report was forwarded to the War Department by Secretary of State Day on July 6, 1898. Also see *Correspondence*, 718–19.

20 *Correspondence*, 807–08; Gates, *Schoolbooks*, 19.

21 Karnow, *In Our Image*, 122–23.

22 Linn, *Philippine War*, 25.

23 The Marines were fortunate to have been based in an arid stretch of the southeastern Cuban coast, which spared them from disease-carrying mosquitoes.

24 Millett and Shulimson, *Commandants*, 132–33.

Chapter 8—"White Man's Burden"

1 The account of Albert Beveridge's arrival at Tomlinson Hall on September 16, 1898, is primarily drawn from Claude G. Bowers, *Beveridge and the Progressive Era* (Boston: Houghton Mifflin Co., 1932), 73–76.

2 Ibid., 69.

3 Christner quoted in Richard A. Sauers, *Pennsylvania in the Spanish American War* (Harrisburg, PA: Capitol Preservation Committee, Commonwealth of Pennsylvania, 1998), 70–71.

4 James J. Martin quoted in Sauers, *Pennsylvania*, 71; Christner quoted in Karnow, *In Our Image*, 131.

5 Linn, *Philippine War*, 31.

6 Description of Elwell Otis, including MacArthur quote, from Karnow, *In Our Image*, 132; also see Stuart Creighton Miller, *"Benevolent Assimilation": The American Conquest of the Philippines, 1899–1903* (New Haven, CT: Yale University Press, 1982), 46.

7 Karnow, *In Our Image*, 132.

8 Otis to adjutant general, Washington, September 5, 1898, *Correspondence*, 2:787.

9 Ibid., September 7, 1898, *Correspondence*, 2:788–89.

10 Ibid., September 15, 1898, *Correspondence*, 2:790; also see Karnow, *In Our Image*, 132.

11 Otis to adjutant general, Washington, September 16, 1898, *Correspondence*, 2:791.

12 Mabini quoted in Karnow, *In Our Image*, 124.

13 Felipe Agoncillo's pilgrimage to Lincoln Park in Chicago is recounted in "Hopes of the Filipinos," *NYT*, September 27, 1898.

14 Agoncillo's background and revolutionary activities are described in "Felipe E. Agoncillo: First Filipino Diplomat," a two-page biography prepared by the Philippines National Historical Institute.

15 Leech, *McKinley*, 332; and Ernest R. May, *Imperial Democracy: The Emergence of America as a Great Power* (New York: Harper & Row, 1980), 251.

16 Agoncillo had laid out his views on the revolution's goals and its admiration of the U.S. system in "Hopes of the Filipinos," *NYT*, September 27, 1898. Agoncillo's meeting with McKinley is described in Karnow, *In Our Image*, 128.

17 Charles S. Olcott, *The Life of William McKinley*, vol. 2 (Boston: Houghton Mifflin Company, 1916), 2:110–11.

18 Leech, *McKinley*, 49.

19 E. May, *Imperial Democracy*, 248–49.

20 "Cheer for Roosevelt," *NYT*, October 6, 1898.

21 E. May, *Imperial Democracy*, 258–59.

22 Ibid. Also see "The President at Omaha," *NYT*, October 12, 1898, and "Mr. McKinley on the War," *NYT*, October 13, 1898.

23 Ibid., 252.

24 Karnow, *In Our Image*, 130.

25 "Agoncillo Is at Paris," *NYT*, October 18, 1898; and "Aguinaldo's Agent Angered," *NYT*, November 22, 1898.

26 "Agoncillo and the Treaty," *NYT*, December 16, 1898.

27 Richard E. Welch Jr., *Response to Imperialism: The United States and the Philippine-American War, 1899–1902* (Chapel Hill, NC: The University of North Carolina Press, 1979), 43.

28 TR to Henry Cabot Lodge, January 12, 1899, TR Letters, 2:909.

29 Welch, *Response*, 16.

30 Richard E. Welch Jr., *George Frisbie Hoar and the Half-Breed Republicans* (Cambridge, MA: Harvard University Press, 1971), 232–34.

31 Ibid., 237.

32 Ibid., 236.

Chapter 9—Spring Victories, Summer Stalemate

1 "Annual Report of Maj. Gen. E. S. Otis, U.S.V., Commanding Department of the Pacific and Eighth Army Corps, Military Governor in the Philippine Islands," August 31, 1899, from *WD*, 1899, 1:4:70.

2 Bain, *Sitting in Darkness*, 77.

3 Robert Crosbie to Dear Mother, February 24, 1899, quoted in Linn, *Philippine War*, 63.

4 Associated Press dispatch printed in the *Otago Witness* (New Zealand), March 23, 1899.

5 Otis Report, *WD*, 1899, 1:4:108–09.

6 Linn, *Philippine War*, 59.

7 "Report of General Hughes and Others Concerning the Fires at Manila and Accompanying Events—February 22–23, 1899," from *WD*, 1899, 1:5:6; "Manila Panic-Stricken," *NYT*, February 24, 1899.

8 Report of Major G. A. Goodale, 23rd U.S. Infantry, February 24, 1899, in *WD*, 1899, 1:5:9–10.

9 Ibid.

10 Linn, *Philippine War*, 61.

11 Hughes Diary, February 6, 1899, quoted in Linn, *Philippine War*, 64.

12 Linn, *Philippine War*, 64.

13 "Hearings Before the Senate Committee on the Philippines," United States Senate, 1902, Senate Document 331, 862.

14 Linn, *Philippine War*, 94–95.

15 "Manila Battle Renewed Today," *Chicago Daily Tribune*, March 26, 1899; "Enemy Surrounded," *Los Angeles Times*, March 26, 1899.

16 Bain, *Sitting in Darkness*, 80.

17 Funston report on 20th Kansas operations, April 9, 1899, in *WD*, 1899, 1:5:421–23; Frederick Funston, *Memories of Two Wars: Cuban and Philippine Experiences* (New York: Charles Scribner's Sons, 1911), 262–63; also see "Report of Brig. Gen. Harrison Gray Otis, U.S.V.," April 2, 1899, in *WD*, 1899, 1:5:27.

18 *WD*, 1899, 1:5:404–06, and Funston, *Memories*, 273–74.

19 The account of Funston's heroics at the Río Grande de Pampanga is drawn from three sources: Funston's after-action report of May 4, 1899, in *WD*, 1899, 1:5:423–25; Funston's *Memories*, 278–87; and Brigadier General Lloyd Wheaton's report of May 10, 1899, in *WD*, 1899, 1:5:416–18.

20 Linn, *Philippine War,* 110.
21 "Proclamation at Manila," *NYT,* April 5, 1899.
22 Linn, *Philippine War,* 117.
23 Sexton, *Soldiers,* 164–65.
24 Linn, *Philippine War,* 117.
25 *Indianapolis Journal,* December 26, 1899, quoted in Bowers, *Beveridge,* 102.
26 Bowers, *Beveridge,* 107.
27 Ibid.

Chapter 10—"The Filipino Republic Is Destroyed"

1 Quoted in Report of Maj. Gen. E. S. Otis, United States Army, Commanding Division of the Philippines, Military Governor, September 1, 1899, to May 5, 1900 (Washington: Government Printing Office, 1900), 206.
2 Sexton, *Soldiers,* 180.
3 Ibid., 184.
4 Ibid., 194–95; also see "Filipinos Now Guerrillas," *NYT,* November 27, 1899.
5 Orlino A. Ochosa, *The Tinio Brigade: Anti-American Resistance in the Ilocos Provinces, 1899–1901* (Quezon City, Philippines: New Day Publishers, 1989), 15–16.
6 Simeon Villa diary, November 15, 1899, in Senate, *Affairs,* 1987–88; also see "Young's Men in Distress," *NYT,* December 12, 1899.
7 Gregorio del Pilar diary entry of December 2, 1899, quoted in Moorfield Storey and Marcial P. Lichauco, *The Conquest of the Philippines by the United States, 1898–1925,* (1926; reprint, Mandaluyong, Philippines: Cacho Hermanos, Inc., 1985), 109.
8 March report, *WD,* 1900, 1:6:330–34.
9 Bain, *Sitting in Darkness,* 191.
10 March report, *WD,* 1900, 1:6:330–34. In 1903, Roosevelt promoted March to lieutenant general and later named him Army chief of staff.
11 "Captive in Aguinaldo's Hands," *NYT,* April 29, 1900.
12 MacArthur telegram to Otis, November 23, 1899, quoted in Sexton, *Soldiers,* 198.

Chapter 11—"A Nasty Little War"

1 "General Otis Leaves Manila," *BDE,* May 5, 1900.
2 Otis to Adjutant General Henry Corbin, November 24, 1899, *Correspondence,* 1107; November 25, 1899, ibid., 1108; November 27, 1899, ibid., 1109; December 12, 1899, ibid., 1120.
3 McKinley annual message, quoted in Gates, *Schoolbooks,* 114.
4 Gates, *Schoolbooks,* 68.
5 *WD,* 1900, 1:5:275–76.
6 Otis to adjutant general, December 6, 1899, *Correspondence,* 1113–14.

7 The circumstances of General Lawton's death are recounted in a June 7, 1900, report by Major W. D. Beach, in *WD*, 1900, 1:3:192–93; the War Department circular announcing Lawton's death and condolence statements from General Otis, President McKinley and Secretary of War Root can be found in *WD*, 1900, 1:3:187–90; also see "Lawton's Body in Manila," *NYT*, December 21, 1899; and "Order to the Army Issued," *NYT*, December 22, 1899. Lawton's body was returned to the United States, and his burial at Arlington National Cemetery on February 9, 1900, was a major Washington event attended by President McKinley, Cabinet members, senior military and political leaders, and foreign diplomats.

8 Gates, *Schoolbooks*, 110–11.

9 Otis to adjutant general, Washington, January 8–10, *Correspondence*, 1130–31.

10 Brian McAllister Linn, *The U.S. Army and Counterinsurgency in the Philippine War, 1899–1902* (Chapel Hill, NC: The University of North Carolina Press, 1989), 35.

11 Howze to adjutant general, March 17, 1900, quoted in Linn, *U.S. Army*, 46.

12 Howze to Captain John G. Ballance, May 20, 1900, quoted in Linn, *U.S. Army*, 38. Also see Ochosa, *Tinio Brigade*, 148–49.

13 Ochosa, *Tinio Brigade*, 153–54.

14 Linn, *U.S. Army*, 53–54.

15 Ochosa, *Tinio Brigade*, 156.

16 AP dispatch quoted in Root cable to Otis, April 9, 1900, in *Correspondence*, 1158.

17 Otis reply to Root, April 10, 1900, *Correspondence*, 1159.

18 "More Troops Needed in the Philippines," *NYT*, July 16, 1900.

19 Captain C. J. Rollis report of April 25, 1900, in *WD*, 1900, 1:7:225–28.

20 Linn, *U.S. Army*, 48.

21 Lyon to Mary P. Lyon, April 12, 1900, Lyon Papers, U.S. Army Military History Institute Manuscript Collection, Carlisle, Pennsylvania. Also see Linn, *U.S. Army*, 95.

22 Linn, *U.S. Army*, 102–03.

23 Ibid., 107.

24 Linn, *Philippine War*, 70.

25 Sexton, *Soldiers*, 199.

26 *WD*, 1900, 1:8:284–90.

27 Otis to Adjutant General Corbin, February 17, 1900, *Correspondence*, 1145; Otis to Corbin, March 26, 1900, *Correspondence*, 1153.

28 Linn, *U.S. Army*, 57.

29 Colonel Benjamin F. Cheatham to adjutant general, Department of Southern Luzon, May 29, 1900, quoted in Linn, *U.S. Army*, 139–40.

30 "General Funston Is Indignant," *NYT*, November 2, 1899.

31 Funston, *Memories*, 315.

32 Linn, *U.S. Army*, 78–79, 83.

33 *WD*, 1900, 1:4:783 and 1:8:167–69; Funston did not mention the incident in his autobiography.

34 Funston, *Memories*, 333.

35   J. Franklin Bell to Bisbee, March 30, 1900, quoted in Linn, *Philippine War*, 224.

36   Frederick Palmer, *With My Own Eyes: A Personal Story of Battle Years* (Indianapolis: The Bobbs-Merrill Co., 1932), 151.

37   Villa diary entry of April 12, 1900, in Senate, *Affairs*, 2030–31.

38   Ibid., 3:2036–37. As the official American translation of Villa's diary is extremely stilted, I have drawn the "hail of bullets" quote from the translation of Orlino Ochosa in *Tinio Brigade*, 181.

39   Villa diary entry of May 28, 1900, in Senate, *Affairs*, 3:2043; also see Ochosa, *Tinio Brigade*, 182.

40   "Desperate Fight with Rebels," *BDE*, May 3, 1900.

41   Otis quoted in *Leslie's Weekly*, June 16, 1900, 462.

42   The departure of General Otis is described in "General Otis Leaves Manila," *BDE*, May 5, 1900, and "Departure of Major-General E. S. Otis," *Manila Times*, May 7, 1900.

Chapter 12—"Men of a Bygone Age"

1   Leech, *McKinley*, 357.

2   Ibid., 361.

3   "Speech at Dinner of the Home Market Club, Boston, Feb. 16, 1899," William McKinley, *Speeches and Addresses of William McKinley* (New York: Doubleday & McLure Co., 1900), 185–93.

4   Leech, *McKinley*, 362–63.

5   Welch, *Response*, 44.

6   Welch, *George Frisbie Hoar*, 9.

7   Ibid., 22–23, 29.

8   Ibid., 132.

9   TR to Alfred Thayer Mahan, December 9, December 11 and December 13, 1897, TR Letters 1:725–26, 741.

10   Hoar to H. Y. J. Taylor, June 28, 1898, Hoar Papers; quoted in Welch, *George Frisbie Hoar*, 217.

11   "Appeal for the Filipinos," *NYT*, March 14, 1899.

12   For a more detailed discussion of Edward Atkinson and his anti-imperialist beliefs, see Welch, *Response*, 49–51.

13   "Edward Atkinson's Offense," *NYT*, May 6, 1899.

14   "Mr. Atkinson's Open Letter," *NYT*, May 7, 1899.

15   "Treated as Seditious; Atkinson's Anti-Imperialist Documents Taken from Mails," *Chicago Daily Tribune*, May 3, 1899; "Call Patriotic Mass Meeting," *Chicago Daily Tribune*, April 29, 1899; "An Uncompromising Radical," *Los Angeles Times*, May 9, 1899.

16   Welch, *Response*, 51.

17   Welch, *George Frisbie Hoar*, 253.

18 TR to Henry Cabot Lodge, February 7, 1899, TR Letters, 2:935, and TR to Maria Longworth Storer, February 17, 1899, TR Letters, 2:950.

19 Andrew Carnegie to Carl Schurz, December 27, 1898, Carnegie Papers, LC, quoted in Wayne H. Morgan, *America's Road to Empire: The War with Spain and Overseas Expansion* (New York: John Wiley and Sons, Inc., 1967), 103.

20 TR to Maria Longworth Storer, February 17, 1899, TR Letters, 2:950.

21 TR to Lodge, March 9, 1899, ibid., 2:958.

22 Roosevelt's "Strenuous Life" speech, delivered in Chicago on April 10, 1899, in Theodore Roosevelt, *The Strenuous Life: Essays and Addresses* (New York: Charles Scribner's Sons, 1906), 3–22.

23 TR to Leonard Wood, April 24, 1899, TR Letters, 2:994.

24 TR to Lodge, July 1, 1899, and TR to John Hay, July 1, 1899, TR Letters, 2:1024.

25 TR to John Hay, July 1, 1899; ibid., 2:1024.

26 TR to Samuel Baldwin Marks Young, September 18, 1899, ibid., 2:1076.

27 Welch, *Response*, 54.

28 "Boston Hears Roosevelt," *NYT*, November 1, 1899.

29 Welch, *Response*, 59.

30 "Father McKinnon on the War," *NYT*, October 25, 1899.

31 "Filipinos Unfit to Rule Themselves," *NYT*, November 3, 1899.

32 "Root Sees End of War," *NYT*, November 28, 1899.

33 "A 'Thanksgiving of Shame,'" *NYT*, November 30, 1899.

34 Bowers, *Beveridge*, 116.

35 George B. Cortelyou diary, December 23, 1899, and January 4, 1900, quoted in Braeman, *Albert J. Beveridge*, 43.

36 Bowers, *Beveridge*, 118.

37 *CR*, Senate, 56th Congress, 1st Session, January 9, 1900, 704–12; Bowers, *Beveridge*, 119.

38 Ibid.; also see Bowers, *Beveridge*, 119–22.

39 *CR*, Senate, 56th Congress, 1st Session, 712.

40 Welch, *George Frisbie Hoar*, 263.

41 Ibid., 265; "Senator Hoar Pleads for the Filipinos," *NYT*, April 18, 1900; for the full text of Hoar's speech see *CR*, 56th Congress, 1st Session, 4278–306.

Chapter 13—"Brave Hearts and Bright Weapons"

1 "Cavite Notes," *Manila Times*, December 18, 1899.

2 "Suspected of Being a Spy," *Manila Times*, January 18, 1900.

3 *Navy Department, Annual Report*, 1900, 1115 and 1143–46.

4 Special Order, February 17, 1900, Col. Robert L. Meade, Commander 1st Regiment USMC, Cavite, Philippines, in E 43, Records of Overseas Brigades, Battalions and Regiments 1889–1914, Box 4, RG 127, NARA.

5 *Navy Department, Annual Report*, 1900, 1066. Chronic tropical ailments were not the
   most common malady encountered by the Marines and sailors at Cavite: That distinction belonged to venereal diseases. In the last nine months of 1899, the Cavite
   naval hospital treated sixty-two cases of sexually transmitted diseases—more cases
   than gunshot wounds (forty-three), malaria (thirty-two), recurring fever (twenty-
   five), dysentery (nineteen) and rheumatism (fifteen).

6 Thomas, *Old Gimlet Eye*, 40.

7 John H. Clifford, *History of the Pioneer Marine Battalion at Guam, L.I., 1899, and the
   Campaign in Samar, P.I., 1901* (Portsmouth, NH: Chronicle Job Print, 1914), 11–12
   and 15; and the 1900 annual report of the Marine Corps commandant, in *Navy
   Department, Annual Report*, 1900, 1103.

8 Peter Fleming, *The Siege at Peking: The Boxer Rebellion*, (1959; reprint, New York: Dor-
   set Press, 1990), 106; Diana Preston, *The Boxer Rebellion: The Dramatic Story of China's
   War on Foreigners That Shook the World in the Summer of 1900* (New York: Walker &
   Company, 2000), 81–82; also see "Baron Ketteler's Career," *NYT*, May 7, 1896.

9 I drew additional background on the Boxers and the rise of antiforeigner sentiment
   in turn-of-the-century China from J. A. G. Roberts, *A Concise History of China* (Cambridge, MA: Harvard University Press, 1999), 200–03; and Jonathan D. Spence,
   The Search for Modern China (New York: W. W. Norton & Company, 1990), 230–35.

10 Morrison diary quoted in Preston, *The Boxer Rebellion*, 74.

11 "The Siege of Peking," by Rev. Gilbert Reid, in *The Boxer Rising: A History of the Boxer
   Trouble in China* (Shanghai: Shanghai Mercury Ltd., 1900), 100; G. E. Morrison's
   account, quoting von Ketteler's secretary, in *London Times*, October 13, 1900; and
   Preston, *Boxer Rebellion*, 82–83.

12 Preston, *Boxer Rebellion*, 85; also see September 26, 1900, report of John T. Myers,
   Captain, U.S.M.C., commander of the Marine guard at the U.S. Legation, Peking,
   China, in Navy Subject File, 1875–1900, Box 182 HJ, RG 45, NARA.

13 Fred R. Brown, *History of the Ninth U.S. Infantry, 1799–1909* (Chicago: RR Donnelley
   and Sons, 1909), 441.

14 Leech, *McKinley*, 516–18.

15 Waller Report of June 28, 1900, in *Navy Department, Annual Report*, 1900, 1150–52;
   "Cossack outriders" from Schmidt, *Maverick Marine*, 15; also see detailed account of
   the Marine operations in China in *Navy Department, Annual Report*, 1900, 1116–32.

16 Account of the June 21 fighting from Waller report of June 28, 1900, and *Navy
   Department, Annual Report*, 1900, 1116–17; also see Schmidt, *Maverick Marine*, 15–16.

17 Ibid., 15. The four enlisted men with Butler were awarded Medals of Honor. Butler,
   as an officer not eligible for the honor at the time, earned Waller's high praise for
   "saving a wounded man at the risk of his own life under a very severe fire."

18 Battle of June 21 described in *Navy Department, Annual Report*, 1900, 1148–50, and
   Waller's June 28, 1900, report; also see Schmidt, *Maverick Marine*, 15.

19 Thomas, *Old Gimlet Eye*, 53–54; Herbert Hoover, *The Memoirs of Herbert Hoover: Years
   of Adventure, 1874–1920* (New York: Macmillan, 1951), 52.

20 Waller report of June 28, 1900, in *Navy Department, Annual Report*, 1900, 1150–52.

21 Vice Admiral Seymour and Lieutenant Colonel Bower notes reprinted in Waller report of July 30, 1900.

22 Meade report on battle of Tientsin, July 16, 1900, in Navy Subject File, U.S. Navy, 1875–1900, Box 182 HJ, RG 45, NARA; F. Brown, *History of the Ninth*, 454.

23 Schmidt, *Maverick Marine*, 19.

24 Battle accounts from reports of Meade and Major G. Engelhardt, March 14, 1901, in Navy Subject File, U.S. Navy, 1875–1900, Box 182 HJ, RG 45, NARA.

25 F. Brown, *History of the Ninth*, 458.

26 Ibid., 458–60; also see various reports of 9th Infantry officers in *WD*, 1900, 1:9:17–25.

27 F. Brown, *History of the Ninth*, 464–65; *WD*, 1900, 1:9:17–25; also see "The Fighting at Tien-Tsin: Detailed Reports by Col. Meade and Major Waller," *NYT*, August 18, 1900.

28 Endorsements attached to Waller report of July 30, 1900, in Navy Subject File, U.S. Navy, 1875–1900, Box 182 HJ, RG 45, NARA.

29 Reuters, *London Daily* and *London Times* dispatches quoted in Preston, *Boxer Rebellion*, 164, 172–73.

30 The fighting and difficult conditions during the march to Peking are described by Chaffee and various line officers in *WD*, 1900, 1:9:37, 44–50, 52–59.

31 *WD*, 1900, 1:9:39–41, 59–84.

32 Schmidt, *Maverick Marine*, 23.

33 The scenes that greeted the Marines and other American troops in the foreign quarter of Peking are described by Chaffee in *WD*, 1900, 1:9:40.

34 Schmidt, *Maverick Marine*, 23.

35 Accounts of the battle for the Imperial City taken from *WD*, 1900, 1:9:13, 41, 59–84 (including Major Waller's report of August 20 on 82–83); and F. Brown, *History of the Ninth*, 494–95.

36 Schmidt, *Maverick Marine*, 25; Roberts, *Concise History*, 203; and Spence, *Modern China*, 235.

37 Jonathan D. Spence, *The Chan's Great Continent: China in Western Minds* (New York: W. W. Norton & Co., 1998), 151; Schmidt, *Maverick Marine*, 24.

38 F. Brown, *History of the Ninth*, 501–04.

Chapter 14—The Election of 1900

1 Lewis L. Gould, *The Presidency of William McKinley* (Lawrence, KS: The Regents Press of Kansas, 1980), 214.

2 "The Philippine War," *San Francisco Call*, May 9, 1900; Whitmarsh quote in "Is the Philippine War Over?" *Literary Digest* 20 (1900) 523–24.

3 "Carnegie Goes Abroad," *BDE*, May 2, 1900.

4 The story of Roosevelt's nomination is related in Henry F. Pringle, *Theodore Roosevelt: A Biography* (New York: Harcourt, Brace, 1956), 220; also see Morris, *Rise*, 721–28.

5 Roosevelt convention speech quoted in Morris, *Rise,* 729.

6 TR to Raymon Reyes Lala, June 27, 1900, TR Letters, 2:1343, and TR to Marcus Alonzo Hanna, June 27, 1900, ibid., 2:1342.

7 "Roosevelt Speaks to Republican Clubs," *NYT,* July 18, 1900.

8 For a fuller discussion of the contrasting philosophies of Roosevelt and Bryan, see Michael Kazin, *A Godly Hero: The Life of William Jennings Bryan* (New York: Alfred A. Knopf, 2006), 105–06.

9 Kazin, *Godly Hero,* 96.

10 For analysis of the Democratic platform and differences with Republicans, see Welch, *Response,* 64–65.

11 Ibid., 61–63, for discussion of the Democratic party's varied responses to the Philippine issue.

12 Bryan speech quoted in Leech, *McKinley,* 549–50, and Kazin, *Godly Hero,* 103.

13 Leech, *McKinley,* 550.

14 Kazin, *Godly Hero,* 103.

15 See *Correspondence,* 1133 and 1137.

16 Taft to Root, July 14, 1900, and September 13, 1900, Elihu Root Papers, LC; also see Welch, *Response,* 67.

17 Corporal Sam Gillis to his parents, excerpt reprinted in "Brave Corporal Gillis," *San Francisco Call,* April 15, 1899.

18 *Kingston Daily Post* (New York), May 8, 1899, quoted in Miller, *Benevolent Assimilation,* 88.

19 Miller, *Benevolent Assimilation,* 94.

20 "General Anderson Indignant," *NYT,* August 3, 1899; "Capt. Dyer Home at Melrose: Says the Philippine War Will Be Quickly Ended If the Anti-Imperialists Are Suppressed," *NYT,* July 5, 1899; "Manila Consul Returns," *NYT,* December 5, 1899; for a fuller discussion of Root's campaign see Miller, *Benevolent Assimilation,* 92.

21 Senate, *Affairs,* 637–39.

22 Welch, Response, 65; Leon Wolff, *Little Brown Brother: How the United States Purchased and Pacified the Philippine Islands at the Century's Turn* (Garden City, NY: Doubleday, 1961), 307.

23 For a discussion of MacArthur's early months in command of U.S. forces see Linn, *Philippine War,* 208–10.

24 MacArthur to adjutant general, Washington, August 31, 1900, in *Correspondence,* 1203–04.

25 Henry F. Pringle, *The Life and Times of William Howard Taft,* 2 vols. (New York: Farrar & Rinehart, 1939), 1:169.

26 Wolff, *Little Brown Brother,* 312.

27 Ibid., 313.

28 Statistics on U.S. casualties drawn from various Otis cables to adjutant general, Washington, in *Correspondence,* 1128–96.

29 Wolff, *Little Brown Brother,* 322; Gates, *Schoolbooks,* 163.

30 Linn, *U.S. Army,* 53.

31 Ibid., 52.

32 Gates, *Schoolbooks*, 176, 189–90; Samuel B. M. Young to TR, quoted in Linn, *Philippine War*, 211; Young recommendations are further discussed in Sexton, *Soldiers*, 251–52.

33 On MacArthur's desire to take a harder line before the election, see Linn, *Philippine War*, 213.

34 Kazin, *Godly Hero*, 106.

35 Leech, *McKinley*, 551–53.

36 For a broader discussion of Bryan's campaign in 1900, see Kazin, *Godly Hero*, 106–07, and Welch, *Response*, 67–68.

37 *Harper's Weekly*, October 13, 1900.

38 Roosevelt's words are quoted from his vice presidential nomination acceptance letter of September 15, 1900, which provided the framework for his campaign speeches. TR Letters, 2:1397–1405.

39 Gould, *William McKinley*, 228.

40 Welch, *Response*, 63.

41 Kazin, *Godly Hero*, 107.

42 TR to "My dear President Eliot," November 14, 1900, TR Letters, 2:1415; TR to H. K. Love, November 24, 1900, TR Letters, 2:1441.

Chapter 15—"War Without Limits"

1 Roosevelt, *Rough Riders*, 135–36.

2 John H. Parker to TR, November 18, 1900, Roosevelt Papers, LC.

3 Gates, *Schoolbooks*, 193.

4 Parker to TR, October 13, 1900, forwarded in TR letter to Root, November 24, 1900, Root Papers, LC.

5 Sexton, *Soldiers*, 252.

6 MacArthur quotes from *WD*, 1900, 1:5:61; Gates, *Schoolbooks*, 166.

7 Colonel Robert L. Bullard diary, quoted in Gates, *Schoolbooks*, 174; Wheaton quoted in ibid., 189. Gates is a pioneering scholar of the Philippine War who is generally sympathetic to the U.S. military effort in the Philippines. Yet even he has concluded that American troops by mid-1900 had begun using "water cure" and "other forms of terror" to counter the Filipino resistance. See Gates, *Schoolbooks*, 175.

8 Wolff, *Little Brown Brother*, 318–19; Colonel Arthur Murray of the 43rd Infantry, quoted in Gates, *Schoolbooks*, 188.

9 MacArthur's proclamation of December 20, 1900, and instructions to commanders, in *WD*, 1901, 1:4:91–93.

10 Quoted in "Facts about the Filipinos," vol. 1, no. 10 (September 15, 1901), Philippine Information Society, 41–42.

11 Linn, *Philippine War*, 170.

12 Annual report of Brigadier General Robert P. Hughes, in *WD*, 1900, 1:5:254.

13 Hughes diary of events on Panay, August 23–September 21, 1900, quoted in "Facts about the Filipinos," vol. 1, no. 10 (September 15, 1901), Philippine Information Society, 25.

14 Ibid.

15 Otis to Corbin, February 17, 1900, *Correspondence*, 1141.

16 Hughes testimony before the Senate Committee on the Philippines, Senate, *Affairs*, 545–47, 558–62.

17 Hughes testimony, Senate, *Affairs*, 541–42.

18 Linn, *Philippine War*, 222–23.

19 Biographical material on Edwin F. Glenn drawn from George W. Cullum, *Biographical Register of the Officers and Graduates of the U.S. Military Academy* (Cambridge, MA: The Riverside Press, 1901), 288. Also see Captain Edwin F. Glenn and Captain W. R. Abercrombie, "Report of Explorations to the Territory of Alaska" (Washington: Government Printing Office, 1899).

20 Alan E. Donant, *Colonel Arthur L. Conger* (Pasadena, CA: Theosophical University Press, 1999), accessed April 3, 2010, http://www.theosociety.org/pasadena/conger/alconger.htm.

21 The photograph of Conger is the frontispiece of his mother's memoir, Emily Bronson Conger, *An Ohio Woman in the Philippines* (Akron, OH: Press of Richard H. Leighton, 1904). For details of Conger's activities on Panay in June and July 1900, see "Report of Lt. A. L. Conger, Eighteenth U.S. Infantry, of operations of detachment of mounted infantry near Dumangas, Island of Panay, P.I., June 20 to July 5, 1900," in *WD*, 1900, 1:7:291–95.

22 Conger, *An Ohio Woman*, 61, 131–32.

23 Ibid., 160.

24 "Report of Maj. Robert H. Noble, assistant adjutant general, Department of the Visayas," *WD*, 1901, 1:6:9.

25 The events in Igbaras on November 27, 1900, are reconstructed from the U.S. Senate testimony of three soldiers—Charles S. Riley, William L. Smith and Edward J. Davis—and testimony from Edwin Glenn's court-martial in 1902 (referred to in the notes as Glenn GCM 34401). See Senate, *Affairs*, 1527–29, 1538–40 and 1726–35. Also see "Told of 'Water Cure' Given to Filipinos," *NYT*, April 15, 1902, and "Saw the 'Water Cure' Given," *NYT*, April 18, 1902.

26 Ibid.

27 Ibid.

28 Linn, *Philippine War*, 252.

29 Dean Worcester to Mrs. Henry W. Lawton, December 5, 1900, quoted in Gates, *Schoolbooks*, 174–78.

30 Taft to Root, December 27, 1900, Root Papers, LC.

31 Linn, *U.S. Army*, 56.

32 For a discussion of the impact of the Federal Party see Gates, *Schoolbooks*, 228–29, and Sexton, *Soldiers*, 258–59; for an account of the party speeches and mass surrenders in the Luzon town of Irocin, see *WD*, 1901, 1:6:435.

33 The scene was preserved for history by Spanish mercenary Lázaro Segovia and is described in Bain, *Sitting in Darkness*, 210.

34 Ibid., 95.

35 Details of Aguinaldo's capture are taken from Funston's after-action report on the expedition in *WD*, 1901, 1:5:123–30; also see "The Most Famous Feat of the New Century," *Leslie's Weekly*, April 13, 1901, and Bain, *Sitting in Darkness*, 361–74.

36 Aguinaldo proclamation "To the Filipino People," April 19, 1901, in *WD*, 1901, 1:4:100.

37 Linn, *U.S. Army*, 60–61; Linn, *Philippine War*, 258.

38 Linn, *U.S. Army*, 60.

39 Boston *Transcript*, March 4, 1902, quoted in Moorfield Storey and Julian Codman, *Secretary Root's Record: "Marked Severities" in Philippine Warfare* (Boston: George H. Ellis Co., 1902), 27.

Chapter 16—The Massacre at Balangiga

1 The welcome by Balangiga's president and residents as recalled by privates Henry W. Manire and Henry Mayer is quoted in Reynaldo H. Imperial, "Balangiga and After" (paper presented at the Balangiga Roundtable Conference, Tacloban, Philippines, November 27–28, 1998).

2 Ibid.

3 Ibid.; also see the testimony of Private William J. Gibbs in Senate, *Affairs*, 2284–2310.

4 Ibid. Private Gibbs, who survived the attack at Balangiga, testified before the U.S. Senate Committee on the Philippines that a native woman had reported to Captain Connell that she had been raped by a Company C soldier. Balangiga scholar Rolando Borrinaga argues that there is no evidence of a pattern of rapes by U.S. soldiers in the town, as some recent accounts have suggested. See Rolando O. Borrinaga, "100 Years of Balangiga Literature: A Review," *ICHTHUS* 2 (2001), 59–81.

5 The events at Balangiga on September 28, 1901, are reconstructed from the following: Captain Edwin Bookmiller's official report of October 1, 1901, in *WD*, 1902, 1594–96; F. Brown, *History of the Ninth*, 582–85, which includes the personal accounts of several Company C survivors; Private Gamlin's account, which is related in Gerald J. Wall, "What's Left of Company C," *Saga Magazine* (November 1953), 34–37 and 66–67; Imperial, "Balangiga and After"; and Borrinaga, "100 Years of Balangiga Literature"; the latter two sources provide valuable insights into the perspective of Filipino participants.

6 The inauguration scene and Roosevelt's words are described in Morris, *Theodore Rex*, 12.

7 In January 1901, the Missouri House of Representatives had given voice to the unrequited passions by passing a resolution extending "sympathy to the people of the Philippine archipelago, in their heroic struggle for freedom." See *Nation Magazine*, January 17, 1901, 39.

8 "Mr. McKinley Begins His Second Term: Rain Fails to Mar Inauguration," *NYT*, March 5, 1901.

9 Miller, *Benevolent Assimilation*, 174.

10 "Report of the United States Philippine Commission to the Secretary of War," 1901, 1:350.

11 Paul Kramer, *The Blood of Government: Race, Empire, the United States, and the Philippines* (Chapel Hill, NC: The University of North Carolina Press, 2006), 196–97.

12 W. H. Taft to J. B. Bishop, September 20, 1901, Taft Papers, LC; Taft to Root, September 26, 1901, Root Papers, LC; and Pringle, *William Howard Taft*, 210–11; also see Taft to Root, September 26, 1901, Root Papers, LC.

13 TR to William Henry Hunt, September 26, 1901, TR Letters, 3:151.

14 TR to Root, September 28, 1901, TR Letters, 3:153.

15 Corbin to MacArthur, April 30, 1901, *Correspondence*, 1273; MacArthur to Corbin, May 3, 1901, 1275.

16 Corbin to MacArthur, May 11, 1901, *Correspondence*, 1277; Corbin to MacArthur, June 8, 1901, *Correspondence*, 1284. In August 1902, President Roosevelt reversed the policy of mailing casualty lists after "many requests to let those at home know of the fate of the soldiers in the regular army." See "Thirteen Sat at President's Table," *NYT*, August 16, 1902.

17 Chaffee to Adjutant General Henry Corbin, July 11, 1901, *Correspondence*, 1289.

18 "Practicing Economy in the Philippines," *NYT*, July 23, 1901.

19 Lukbán background from "Vicente R. Lukbán: Freedom Fighter," National Historical Institute, Manila, Philippines; and Mona Lisa H. Quizon, "Vicente Lukbán: Luz del Oriente," National Historical Institute, Manila, Philippines. Also see Donald Chaput, "The American Press and General Vicente Lukbán, Hero of Samar," *Leyte-Samar Studies* 8 (1974), 21–31, and "Leyte Leadership in the Revolution: The Moxica-Lukbán Issue," *Leyte-Samar Studies* 9 (1975), 3–12.

20 NHI profiles of Lukbán. Also see Linn, *Philippine War*, 176, and Father John Schumacher, *Revolutionary Clergy: The Filipino Clergy and the Nationalist Movement, 1850–1903* (Quezon City, Philippines: Ateneo, 1981), 138, 141–43.

21 MacArthur cable to Adjutant General Henry Corbin, May 16, 1900, *Correspondence*, 1168–69; also see Gregory J. W. Urwin, *The United States Infantry: An Illustrated History, 1775–1918* (Norman, OK: University of Oklahoma Press, 1988), 145.

22 "Final Report of Brig. Gen. Robert P. Hughes, U.S. Army, Commanding the Department of the Visayas," November 30, 1901, *WD*, 1902, 1:9:594.

23 Report of 1st Lt. W. K. McCue, August 7, 1901, *WD*, 1902, 1:9:617; for another account of the crop and livestock destruction carried out by U.S. soldiers, see Andrew Pohman, *My Army Experiences* (New York: Broadway Publishing Co., 1906), 62–68.

24 Hughes Report, *WD*, 1902, 1:9:603–04.

25 Ibid., 609, 612.

26 Hughes to adjutant general, Division of the Philippines, September 24, 1901, in *WD*, 1902, 1:9:624.

27 Linn, *Philippine War*, 309–10.

28 Report of 2nd Lt. G. L. Townsend, 1st Infantry, July 25, 1901, *WD*, 1902, 1:9: 616–17.

29 Report of First Lieutenant Campbell King, September 12, 1901, *WD*, 1902, 1:9: 622–23.

30 Hughes report, *WD*, 1902, 1:9:604.

31 Quoted in John R. M. Taylor, *The Philippine Insurrection Against the United States* (Pasay City, Philippines: Eugenio Lopez Foundation, 1971), Exhibit 1350; also see Borrinaga, "100 Years of Balangiga Literature."

32 Scholar Reynaldo Imperial believes it was Abayan's intention all along to attack the Americans. Other scholars, notably Rolando Borrinaga and Bob Couttie, contend that oppressive actions by Captain Connell and his men pushed the mayor and his citizens to drastic action.

33 Imperial interview with Pedro Duran Jr., in Balangiga, Samar, on April 14, 1981, quoted in "Balangiga and After."

34 Lieutenant Bumpus to "my dear father," August, 28, 1901, in Everitt C. Bumpus, *In Memoriam* (Norwood, MA: Norwood Press, 1902), 81; Bumpus to "my dear father," September 6, 1901, ibid., 82–83.

35 Bumpus to "my dear father," September 6, 1901, E. Bumpus, *In Memoriam*, 82–83; saga of Private Scheetherly in Joseph L. Schott, *The Ordeal of Samar* (New York: Bobbs-Merrill, 1964), 27–28.

36 "Attack, men of Balangiga!" quote from Dominador V. Amano, "The Balangiga Encounter," *Sunday Inquirer Magazine* (Manila, Philippines), September 26, 1993.

37 Closson account reprinted in F. Brown, *History of the Ninth*, 583–84.

38 "The Horrible Massacre at Balangiga," *National Tribune*, October 16, 1926, quoted in Imperial, "Balangiga and After."

39 See Bookmiller report, *WD*, 1902, 1594–96; F. Brown, *History of the Ninth*, 582–85; Wall, "What's Left of Company C," 34–37 and 66–67; Imperial, "Balangiga and After"; and Borrinaga, "100 Years of Balangiga Literature."

40 Corporal Hickman was one of only four or five men uninjured in the attack. See. F. Brown, *History of the Ninth*, 587–88.

41 Ibid., 590–92.

42 Some American officers would claim that hundreds of Filipinos had died at Balangiga, but the first American officer on the scene, Captain Bookmiller, estimated about fifty Filipino dead in a mass grave. The figure of twenty-eight comes from Major Eugenio Daza, Lukbán's district commander. Also, various accounts have accused the Filipinos of mutilating the American dead, but Bookmiller makes no mention of this. The most sensational mutilation claims came years after the fact. In a 1935 affidavit, Major Daza denied these allegations. "The Filipino believes that the profanation of the dead necessarily brings bad luck and misfortune," he wrote. In any event, he added, "there was no time to lose for such acts" after the attack. Quoted in Borrinaga, "100 Years of Balangiga Literature."

Chapter 17—Hell-roaring Jake

1 General Chaffee to "My Dear General Hughes," September 30, 1901, in Senate, *Affairs*, 1591–92.
2 Taft to Root, September 26, 1901, Root Papers.
3 Chaffee to Corbin, September 30, 1901, Corbin Papers, LC.
4 "Major Waller Testifies," *NYT*, April 9, 1902; Karnow, *In Our Image*, 191.
5 Account of Smith's wounding, from Jacob H. Smith, "Three Weeks Prior, During and Ten Days After the Battle of Shiloh: A Paper Read Before the Commandery of the State of Michigan, Military Order of the Loyal Legion of the United States," January 4, 1894 (Detroit: Winn and Hammond Printers, 1894).
6 Details on Smith's wartime activities drawn from various documents in adjutant general's office file S293CB1867, RG 94, NARA, including Smith's deposition of January 5–7, 1869, and his letter to Secretary of War William W. Belknap of December 25, 1869. Also see David L. Fritz, "Before the 'Howling Wilderness': The Military Career of Jacob Hurd Smith," *Military Affairs* 43 (December 1979), 186–90. Background on Louisville, Kentucky, during the war from "Confederate Kentucky—The State That Almost Was," *Civil War Times Illustrated*, April 1973, 12–21.
7 Details of Smith's deposition and other documents relating to the withdrawal of his judge advocate's nomination from adjutant general's office file S293CB1867, RG 94, NARA.
8 Smith's actions in the fighting before Santiago, Cuba, on July 1, 1898, are related in two army reports dated July 5, 1898: one written by Smith, and the other by Lieutenant Colonel William M. Wherry, commander of the 2nd Infantry, found in *WD*, 1898, 1:2:393–97. Smith was not involved in the fighting at El Caney, as some accounts have erroneously stated.
9 "Aided the Insurgents," *Washington Post*, August 28, 1899; Smith after-action reports of September 1, 1899, and November 11, 1899, RG 395, NARA.
10 "An Ambush Is Frustrated," *Manila Times*, February 17, 1900.
11 "Gen. Montenegro Is a Prisoner," *Manila Times*, April 17, 1900, and "Gen. Montenegro Gives Up," *Washington Post*, April 18, 1900.
12 "Delightful Excursion to Dagupan," *Manila Times*, December 10, 1900.
13 Taft to Elihu Root, February 23, 1901, AGO File 366708A, RG 94, NARA.
14 For initial reports on attack on Company E, 9th U.S. Infantry, see Chaffee to Adjutant General Corbin, October 18 and 19, 1901, *Correspondence*, 1298–99; also "Cut Down by Bolomen," *Washington Post*, October 19, 1901.
15 See "Repression in Samar," *Washington Post*, October 28, 1901, and "Samar Seething Ferment of Revolt," *Manila Times*, October 20, 1901.

Chapter 18—"Kill and Burn!"

1 Chaffee's recollection of the instructions he gave Smith are from his annual report of September 30, 1902, in *WD*, 1902, 1:9:188.

2 The suspension is noted in Waller's military personnel file. Details of the incident are found in an anonymous, undated, fifteen-page screed preserved in the personal papers of fellow Marine officer Ben H. Fuller at the USMCA in Quantico, Virginia.

3 Smith's instructions to Waller are reconstructed from the testimony of Waller and Smith in their respective courts-martial: Waller GCM 30313 and Smith GCM 30739.

4 Ibid. The briefing aboard the *New York* on October 23, 1902, was the first of three meetings in which Smith instructed Waller on the harsh nature of the campaign he was to conduct. The second meeting was at Balangiga the following day. A third meeting occurred several days later at Smith's headquarters in Tacloban. Admiral Fred Rodgers was present at the *New York* briefing, but was never called to testify about what he heard and never publicly gave his account. Two other Marines— Captain David D. Porter and Second Lieutenant Frank Halford—testified that they were present at Balangiga when Smith reiterated his instructions to "kill and burn." Waller and Smith are in general agreement on the severity of the campaign that Smith desired, but Smith disputes some particulars. At Waller's trial, Smith testified that he did not intend for Waller to execute prisoners, but merely avoid taking prisoners. He also testified that he intended Waller to "punish treachery summarily" as prescribed by the Civil War guideline known as General Orders 100 and not necessarily by summary execution. Smith did not testify at his subsequent trial.

5 Waller orders of October 23, 1901, reprinted in Waller report of May 24, 1902.

6 Testimony of Littleton W. T. Waller and David Dixon Porter in Waller GCM 30313 and Smith GCM 30739.

7 "Samar Seething Ferment of Revolt," *Manila Times*, October 20, 1901; "Repression in Samar," *Washington Post*, October 28, 1901; after the mid-October attack on 9th Infantry soldiers along the Gandara River, Army Adjutant General Corbin had cabled Chaffee: "What is the situation and what steps have been taken [to] suppress disturbance Samar?" Chaffee assured Corbin the War Department "need not feel further apprehension [of] serious loss [on] Samar." Chaffee to Corbin, October 23, 1901, *Correspondence*, 1299.

8 Hughes report, *WD*, 1902, 1:9:612.

9 Ibid. For Glenn's intelligence operations see reports on October 1902 naval operations in Samar campaign in ibid., 435–55. A court-martial later convicted Lieutenant Gaujot of torturing Father Guimbaolibot. See "Trials or Court-martials in the Philippines as a Consequence of Certain Instructions," Senate Document 213, 57th Congress, 1st Session, 14.

10 Smith circular of October 21, 1901, *WD*, 1902, 1:9:206.

11 Smith to Chaffee, October 29, 1901, *WD*, 1:9:222; ibid., 1:9:207.

12 Pohlman, *My Army Experiences*, 99.

13 Capt. M. S. Jarvis, report of operations for the month of October 1901, *WD*, 1902, 1:9:447.

14 Report of 2nd Lt. Ward Dabney of 1st Infantry, October 25, 1901, *WD*, 1902, 1:9:451.

15 Biographical details for Loveman Noa from "Naval Cadet Noa Is Shot: He Is Also Boloed by Insurgents on South Samar Island," *NYT*, October 28, 1901; "Loveman Noa Was Maritime Hero," *The Chattanoogan*, February 14, 2007; and "How *Noa* Got Her Name: Ship That Recovered Glenn Honors Officer Killed in '01," *NYT*, February 22, 1962.

16 David Dixon Porter testimony, Waller GCM 30313; Brian M. Linn, "We Will Go Heavily Armed: The Marines' Small War on Samar, 1901–1902," in William R. Roberts and Jack Sweetman, eds., *New Interpretations in Naval History: Selected Papers from the Ninth Naval History Symposium* (Annapolis, MD: Naval Institute Press, 1991), 280.

17 See Report of Ensign C. H. Fischer on USS *Villalobos* operations off Samar, October 31, 1902, in *WD*, 1902, 1:9:435–36.

18 Waller Report.

19 Porter report of operations near Balangiga, Samar, November 12, 1901, in Waller Report; Porter testimony, Waller GCM 30313.

20 The Marine expedition of November 6, 1901, is reconstructed from Waller's after-action report and the report of U.S. Navy Lieutenant Commander J. H. Glennon, November 17, 1901, in *WD*, 1902, 1:9:436–38.

21 See Waller Report for the results of Marine operations on Samar. Waller typically described any men killed on Samar as "bolomen," although the knives were carried by nearly every fisherman and farmer. That was still the case more than eighty years later when I traveled through the Samar countryside.

22 Undated statement of Arthur N. Sager from Hiram Bearss Papers at USMCA; biographical details on Bearss from George B. Clark, *His Road to Glory: The Life and Times of "Hiking Hiram" Bearss, Hoosier Marine* (Pike, NH: The Brass Hat, 2000), 10–12.

23 Waller Report.

24 The attack on Sohoton is reconstructed from Waller's field reports and the 1934 Medal of Honor citation honoring Porter and Bearss; some published accounts have described hand-to-hand combat at Sohoton, but as there is no mention of this in official reports I have concluded these details were likely embellished.

25 Waller Report.

Chapter 19—Death in the Jungle

1 Harold Kinman to sister, December 23, 1901, Kinman Papers, USMCA.

2 Waller Report, 38.

3   General Jacob Smith's Circular No. 6, December 24, 1901, *WD*, 1902, 1:9: 208–11.

4   Waller Report, 49.

5   Waller Report, 42.

6   Pohlman, *My Army Experiences*, 61–63.

7   Waller Report, 43 and 49.

8   Letter from Captain J. Pickering to adjutant general, 6th Separate Brigade, January 19, 1902, RG 395, NARA.

9   Waller Report, 49–50.

10 Ibid., 50.

11 Waller Report, 51.

12 The river scenes are based on the author's own travels by canoe in Eastern Samar. Descriptions of the forests through which the expedition traveled are found in *Annual Report of the Director of Forestry of the Philippine Islands,* 1916, 65.

13 Waller Report, 52.

14 Roosevelt quoted in Candice Millard, *The River of Doubt: Theodore Roosevelt's Darkest Journey* (New York: Doubleday, 2005), 180.

15 Waller Report, 52.

16 Ibid., 53.

17 Ibid., 53–54.

18 Ibid., 54–55.

19 There are some minor discrepancies in the accounts of Waller, Porter and Williams as to the day or hour when certain events took place. Waller's account in particular is muddled as to when certain movements occurred. In this case, Porter stated in his account that he left Williams at eight thirty a.m. on January 3, 1902. Given all the events that had already taken place that morning, including the exchange of messengers, the departure of Bearss and the meeting between Porter and Williams to determine their plan, it is logical to conclude that Porter left some hours later. I have applied similar analysis and logic in resolving other such discrepancies.

20 Waller to adjutant general, 6th Separate Brigade, Samar, Philippine Islands, January 7, 1902, in Waller Papers, USMCA.

21 Report of Lieutenant Kenneth P. Williams, January 19, 1902, in *WD*, 1902, 1:9:446.

22 Ibid.

23 Ibid.

24 Waller GCM 30313.

25 Smith testified to the January 23 exchange with General Chaffee during Waller's court-martial. See Waller GCM 30313.

Chapter 20—"Deeds of Hideous Cruelty"

1   "Uniforms in Line at the White House: Army and Navy Reception a Brilliant Event," *Washington Times,* January 31, 1902.

2 "Flag Being Blotted by the Methods Used to Subdue Filipinos," *Atlanta Constitution*, January 15, 1902.

3 "Uniforms in Line at the White House: Army and Navy Reception a Brilliant Event," *Washington Times*, January 31, 1902.

4 "Gov. Taft Talks Before Philippine Committee," *Washington Post*, February 1, 1902.

5 "Exciting Discussion on Floor of Senate," *Washington Times*, January 29, 1902.

6 Taft testimony in Senate, *Affairs*, 74.

7 Senate, *Affairs*, 411–12.

8 TR to Elihu Root, February 18, 1902, TR Letters, 2:232; Storey and Codman, *Marked Severities*, 87–88.

9 TR to Root, February 18, 1902, TR Letters, 2:232–33.

10 Philip C. Jessup, *Elihu Root* (New York: Dodd, Mead & Co., 1938), 1:342.

11 TR to William Bayard Cutting, April 17, 1899, TR Letters, 2:991.

12 Miller, *Benevolent Assimilation*, 89.

13 For a discussion of the Brenner case see Storey and Codman, *Marked Severities*, 11–21; also see Miller, *Benevolent Assimilation*, 89.

14 Taft to Root, August 19, 1900, Root Papers, LC.

15 Taft to Root, February 24, 1901, Root Papers, LC.

16 Jessup, *Root*, 1:340.

17 Biographer Edmund Morris notes that Roosevelt's "documentary caution extended to tracking down letters of his youth, and asking owners to keep them private." See Morris, *Theodore Rex*, 82.

18 See Linn, *U.S. Army*, 145.

19 Cornelius Gardener report, in Senate, *Affairs*, 881–85.

20 Taft to Elihu Root, February 7, 1902, Root Papers, LC; General Henry Corbin to General Adna Chaffee, February 19, 1902; Senate, *Affairs*, 886–87.

21 For a concise discussion of the trust issue and the Northern Securities case see Brands, *Last Romantic*, 434–39.

22 Morris, *Theodore Rex*, 95.

23 Senate, *Affairs*, 556.

24 Ibid., 560.

25 Ibid., 654.

26 Ibid., 655.

27 Ibid., 655.

28 Corbin to Chaffee, February 17, 1902, *Correspondence*, 1317.

29 Root to Chaffee, March 4, 1902, *Correspondence*, 1319.

Chapter 21—The Trial of Major Waller

1 Waller GCM 30313.

2 Waller described the scene in Manila Bay in his closing argument before the Manila court-martial on April 11, 1902, Waller GCM 30313.

3 "A Court-martial for Major Waller," *NYT*, March 7, 1902; "Truly Atrocious," *Arlington Journal* (Texas), March 13, 1902; "Maj. Waller: May Be Tried for Torturing and Murdering Natives While in Samar," *Manila Times*, March 7, 1902.

4 Morris, *Theodore Rex*, 97.

5 "Major Waller's Case," *Manila Times*, March 7, 1902.

6 Kingsbury biographical material is drawn from *Biographical Register of the Officers and Graduates of the U.S. Military Academy* (Saginaw, MI: Seemann & Peters, Printers, 1910), 180, and from "Wed Yesterday: Marriage of Capt. Kingsbury and Miss Slocum in Brooklyn," *NYT*, June 12, 1889.

7 The seven Army officers on the panel were: Brigadier General William H. Bisbee, Colonel Cyrus S. Roberts, Lieutenant Colonel Allen Smith, Lieutenant George S. Anderson, Major Edgar S. Steever, Major Edgard B. Robertson, and Captain Samson L. Faison. The Marine members were Colonel James Forney, Lieutenant Colonel Mancil C. Goodrell, Lieutenant Colonel Otway C. Berryman, Major William P. Biddle, Captain Eli K. Cole, and Captain Robert M. Gilson.

8 In his memoirs, *Through Four American Wars*, Bisbee scoffed at the "cruelty" allegations leveled against the U.S. military in the Philippines. For more on Bisbee's use of extralegal tactics in Central Luzon, see J. Franklin Bell to "My dear Colonel" (William) Bisbee, March 30, LS 69, LSB I, E2206, RG 395, NARA.

9 Waller GCM 30313.

10 An October 15, 1899, report by Major George Elliott to Brigadier General Charles Heywood on the performance of his men in the battle of Novaleta speaks to Lieutenant Day's deficiencies in combat.

11 Waller GCM 30313.

12 "Bit and Stabbed Lieutenant Williams," *Manila Times*, March 26, 1902.

13 Waller GCM 30313.

14 Ibid.; also see "Scout 'Smoke' Tells His Story," *Manila Times*, March 28, 1902.

15 Waller GCM 30313.

16 "Marine Shoots Himself," *Manila Times*, April 2, 1902.

17 Waller GCM 30313; also see "The Waller Trial," *Manila Times*, April 1, 1902.

18 "Dread Cholera Is Now with Us," *Manila Times*, March 23, 1902; "Cholera Mortalities Are Still on Decrease," *Manila Times*, March 27, 1902; also see "More Cheerful Reports from Board of Health," *Manila Times*, April 1, 1902; "Feared That Cholera May Take a More Serious Turn," *Manila Times*, April 2, 1902; "The Latest Returns," *Manila Times*, April 3, 1902.

19 Waller GCM 30313.

20 Ibid.; also see "Gen. 'Jakey' Smith Testifies," *Manila Times*, April 8, 1902.

21 Waller's closing argument in Waller GCM 30313.

22 Kingsbury's closing argument in Waller GCM 30313; also see "Raffle of Death," *Manila Times*, April 13, 1902.

Chapter 22—"The President Desires All the Facts"

1   "Rebuff for Miles," *Washington Post*, March 17, 1902; Morris, *Theodore Rex*, 97.

2   Morris, *Theodore Rex*, 97.

3   "Miles Charges Defects in Mr. Root's New Army Bill," *The Evening Times* (Washington, D.C.), March 20, 1902.

4   "Gen. Miles' Retirement Has Been Decided Upon," *Evening Times*, March 22, 1902.

5   "Gen. Miles' Philippine Plan and the Correspondence," *Evening Times*, March 29, 1902.

6   "Republicans at Sea," *Washington Post*, March 15, 1902.

7   Senate, *Affairs*, 738–39.

8   Ibid., 738.

9   Ibid., 787.

10 "Charleston Warmly Greets President," *Washington Times*, April 9, 1902.

11 "Roosevelt Wins the South," *The New York Sun*, April 10, 1902. As Roosevelt spoke of spreading liberty to the Philippines, American authorities in Manila that same day were arresting three editors of an American-owned newspaper. The editors were charged with publishing a seditious attack on Governor Taft's civil government, joining two other editors of another paper who had been arrested for criticizing an American judge who had convicted another outspoken expatriate journalist of libel. See "Manila Editors Arrested," *The New York Sun*, April 11, 1902.

12 Senate, *Affairs*, 850.

13 Ibid., 851.

14 Ibid., 857.

15 Ibid., 853.

16 "President's Visit Ended," *NYT*, April 11, 1902.

17 "Brig. Gen. Smith Urged Generosity," *Washington Times*, April 10, 1902; "Enjoined Kind Treatment," *Washington Post*, April 10, 1902.

18 Florencio R. Caedo to William Howard Taft, Senate, *Affairs*, 887–88; also see "Batangas Province in Desperate Straits," *Washington Times*, April 12, 1902.

19 "Marked Severity of War: General Miles Says His Charges Are Verified," *San Francisco Call*, April 10, 1902.

20 "Philippines War Most Humane Ever Fought," *Washington Times*, April 11, 1902.

21 Editorial from London's *St. James's Gazette*, quoted in "Comment on Waller Case," *NYT*, April 11, 1902.

22 "Our Soldiers Cruel—Dr. Adler," *The New York Sun*, April 14, 1902.

23 Welch, *Response*, 135–36.

24 Senate, *Affairs*, 1535.

25 Ibid., 1540.

26 Ibid., 1540–41.

27 Ibid., 1547; also see "Told of 'Water Cure' Given to Filipinos," *NYT*, April 14, 1902.

28 "More Rigid Army Inquiry: Prompt Action after a Cabinet Discussion," *The New York Sun*, April 16, 1902.

29 Elihu Root cable to General Adna Chaffee, April 15, 1902, *Correspondence*, 1328. Also see "By Court-martial: Tales of Torture in Philippines to Be Probed," *Washington Post*, April 16, 1902; "More Courts-martial in the Philippines," *NYT*, April 16, 1902; "Cruelty and Barbarity Will Be Investigated," *Atlanta Constitution*, April 16, 1902.

30 "Cruelty and Barbarity Will Be Investigated," *Atlanta Constitution*, April 16.

31 Tom Reed to Thomas Gifford, April 17, 1902, quoted in Evan Thomas, *The War Lovers: Roosevelt, Lodge, Hearst and the Rush to Empire, 1898* (New York: Little, Brown and Co., 2010), 497.

Chapter 23—"Blood Grown Hot"

1 Adjutant General Henry Corbin cable to General Adna Chaffee, April 2, 1902, *Correspondence*, 1324; Corbin to Chaffee, April 7, 1902, ibid., 1325; and Chaffee to Corbin, April 10, 1902, ibid., 1326.

2 Chaffee cable to Corbin, April 19, 1902, *Correspondence*, 1329.

3 "General Jacob Smith and Major Glenn to Be Tried," *Manila Times*, April 20, 1902.

4 "Rebuke for Court," *Manila Times*, April 22, 1902.

5 "A Strong Protest," *Manila Times*, April 23, 1902.

6 Chaffee cable to Corbin, April 15, 1902, *Correspondence*, 1327.

7 Chaffee cable to Corbin, April 19, 1902, *Correspondence*, 1329.

8 See "Halts Our Troops: President Orders Withdrawal from Mindanao," *Washington Post*, April 23, 1902; Chaffee cable to Corbin, April 22, 1902, *Correspondence*, 1330–31.

9 "Chaffee Turned Down," *Manila Times*, April 23, 1902.

10 Ibid.

11 "Determined to Push War Against Moros," *Washington Times*, April 23, 1902.

12 "Smith Court Ordered," *Manila Times*, April 22, 1902.

13 Smith GCM 30739; also see "General Smith Admits Truth of Accusations," *Washington Times*, April 26, 1902; "Smith Admits All," *Washington Post*, April 26, 1902.

14 Ibid.

15 Ibid.

16 Smith GCM 30739; also see "More Witnesses Heard in the Smith Court-martial," *Washington Post*, April 30, 1902.

17 "Col. Woodruff's Speech in Defense of Gen. Smith," *Washington Post*, May 4, 1902.

18 "Lt. Flint Tells of Water Cure," *Washington Times*, April 22, 1902.

19 Welch, *Response*, 138.

20 Ibid., 140.

21 Ibid., 141.

22 "Sharp Comment on the Philippines," *Washington Times*, April 26, 1902.

23 Ibid.

24 "Gen. J. H. Smith Severely Criticized: Mr. Sibley Declares Him a Disgrace to the Uniform He Wears," *NYT*, April 29, 1902; "Smith Likened to King Herod," April

29, 1902, *Chicago Daily Tribune*; "Smith's Cruel Order: Subject of Warm Discussion in the Senate," *Washington Post*, April 30, 1902.

25 "Republicans Try to Lay Burn and Kill Tempest," *Atlanta Constitution*, May 1, 1902.

26 "War Department Distances Itself from Smith," *Washington Post*, May 1, 1902.

27 "Will Reply to the Minority Attacks," *Washington Times*, May 4, 1902.

28 *CR*, 57th Congress, 1st Session, May 5, 1902, 4030–40; also see "Senator Lodge Eloquent in Defense of Our Army," *Washington Times*, May 6, 1902, and "Senator Lodge's Speech," *NYT*, May 6, 1902.

29 Ibid.

30 Welch, *Response*, 144.

31 Joseph Bucklin Bishop, *Theodore Roosevelt and His Time: Shown in His Own Letters*, vol. 1 (New York: Charles Scribner's Sons, 1920), 191–92.

32 "Instance of Cruelty to a Filipino Cited," *Washington Times*, May 7, 1902.

33 "Mr. Hoar's Speech on the Philippines," *NYT*, May 23, 1902.

34 See Morris, *Theodore Rex*, 110.

35 "Army of Living Honor Dead at Arlington," *Washington Times*, May 31, 1902, and "President's Notable Oration at Beautiful Arlington," ibid.

36 Theodore Roosevelt, *Presidential Addresses and State Papers*, vol. 1 (New York: The Review of Reviews Co., 1910), 56–67.

37 Ibid.

38 For a discussion of the impact of Roosevelt's counterattack on the military misconduct issue see Welch, *Response*, 145–46.

39 Morris, *Theodore Rex*, 119.

Chapter 24—Homecoming

1 Brigadier General Charles Heywood to Mr. George W. Sullivan, April 24, 1902, in USMC, Office of the Commandant, Letters Sent, Vol. 97, RG 127, NARA. The Sullivan family's decision is nowhere to be found in Marine Corps records.

2 Violet Foster to Littleton Waller Tazewell Waller, March 14, 1902, Waller Papers, USMCA; Aaron Ward to Major L. W. T. Waller, May 1, 1902, in ibid.

3 "Society Notes and Events," *Manila Times*, May 4, 1902.

4 See Adjutant General Henry Corbin's cable to General Chaffee, May 22, 1902, *Correspondence*, 1340; also see "The Brooklyn Home Again," *NYT*, May 2, 1902.

5 The departure of the *Warren* was reported in "Society Notes and Events," *Manila Times*, May 16, 1902.

6 "Glenn Court Sails Today," *Manila Times*, May 15, 1902; "Society Notes and Events," *Manila Times*, May 16, 1902.

7 General Chaffee cable to Adjutant General Henry Corbin, April 26, 1902, *Correspondence*, 1329; Corbin cable to Chaffee, April 28, 1902, ibid., 1333.

8 Glenn GCM 34401; also see "The Trial of Major Glenn for Water-Curing the Presidente of Igbaras Is Now Ended," *Manila Times*, June 7, 1902.

9 Glenn GCM 34401; also see "Glenn's Testimony," *Manila Times,* June 8, 1902, and "The Glenn Court-martial," *NYT,* June 11, 1902.

10 Glenn GCM 34401; also see "Defended the Water Cure," *NYT,* July 26, 1902.

11 Glenn GCM 34401; also see "Court-martial Findings," *NYT,* July 27, 1902.

12 "Investigation of Maj. Gardener," *Manila Times,* June 15, 1902.

13 "The Gardener Case," *Manila Times,* June 21, 1902.

14 "In His Own Behalf," *Manila Times,* June 28, 1902.

15 Gardener to the Gov. General, Manila, July 10, 1901, from Cornelius Gardener military personnel file, NARA.

16 See "Beginning of the End," *Manila Times,* July 8, 1902.

17 "Gardener Ordered Home," *Manila Times,* July 13, 1902.

18 Life aboard the U.S.-bound transports in the spring of 1902 is described by 9th U.S. Infantry veteran Ernest Uriah Ralston in his unpublished diary. A copy was made available to the author by Jeanne Wall, daughter of Balangiga survivor Adolph Gamelin.

19 "Major Waller Has Returned," *NYT,* June 14, 1902.

20 "Rebuke Given Major Waller," *Atlanta Constitution,* June 17, 1902; "Major Waller's Marines Talk of the Water Cure," *Brooklyn Daily Eagle,* June 22, 1902.

21 "Rebuke Given Major Waller," *Atlanta Constitution,* June 17, 1902.

22 "Marines Return from the Philippines," *NYT,* June 21, 1902; "Waller Is at Navy Yard," *BDE,* June 20, 1902.

23 "Major Waller's Marines Talk of the Water Cure," *BDE,* June 22, 1902.

24 "Major Waller Sees Secretary Moody," *NYT,* June 22, 1902; "Major Waller Gone to Norfolk," *Washington Post,* June 22, 1902.

25 The scene is described in Morris, *Theodore Rex,* 121.

26 Ibid., 123–24; also see "Oyster Bay's Boom," *Washington Post,* July 13, 1902.

27 Morris, *Theodore Rex,* 145.

28 "Root Sees the President," *New York Tribune,* July 13, 1902.

29 Roosevelt quotes taken from a letter he wrote to his friend Hermann Speck von Sternberg, July 19, 1902, TR Letters, 2:297–98.

30 "President Retires Gen. Jacob H. Smith," *NYT,* July 17, 1902; "Gen. Smith Is Retired," *Washington Post,* July 17, 1902; also see Elihu Root's July 12, 1902, letter to President Theodore Roosevelt that accompanied the Smith trial transcript in Smith GCM 30739.

31 "Guilt of the Army," *Washington Post,* July 28, 1902; and "Anti-Imperialists to the President," *NYT,* July 28, 1902.

32 Charles Francis Adams to Carl Schurz, August 4, 1902, and August 21, 1902, quoted in Morris, *Theodore Rex,* 129.

33 "Gen. Smith in America," *NYT,* June 14, 1902.

34 *Correspondence,* 1336; Chaffee letter to Root, Root Papers, LC.

35 *Correspondence,* 1347–48.

36 "Back from Samar: Gen. Smith First Hears of His Forced Retirement," *Washington Post,* August 2, 1902; "Gen. Smith on Samar," *Washington Post,* August 4, 1902; "Gen. Smith Says He Was Not Severe," *NYT,* August 4, 1902.

37 "Welcome for Gen. Smith," *Washington Post,* August 11, 1902; "Gen. Smith's Future," *Washington Post,* August 13, 1902.

38 "Gen. Jacob H. Smith Honored," *NYT,* August 20, 1902.

39 "Praise for the Splendid Example Set by Gen. Jacob H. Smith," *Washington Post,* August 24, 1902.

Chapter 25—"Where Is the Line to Be Drawn?"

1 TR to Hermann Speck von Sternberg, July 19, 1902, TR Letters, 2:297–98.

2 Ibid.

3 "President Gives Praise to Work Done in the Islands," *Washington Times,* August 23, 1902.

4 Storey and Codman, *Marked Severities,* 3.

5 "Trusts Again the President's Theme," *Washington Times,* August 26, 1902.

6 For a discussion of the 1903 midterm election results see Morris, *Theodore Rex,* 171.

7 Chaffee annual report in *WD,* 1902, 1:9:189–92; also see "Gen. Chaffee's Report on the Philippines," *NYT,* November 15, 1902.

8 *WD,* 1902, 1:9:188.

9 "Defends Gen. Smith," *Washington Post,* April 12, 1906.

10 Summary of the court-martial of Captain James A. Ryan, published as "General orders, No. 100, Headquarters of the Army, Adjutant General's Office, Washington, September 8, 1902," in *General Orders and Circulars, Adjutant General's Office, 1902* (Washington: Government Printing Office, 1903).

11 "May Summon Gen. Chaffee," *NYT,* December 14, 1902; "The Maj. Glenn Court-martial Will Summon Generals Chaffee and Smith to Manila as Witnesses," *NYT,* December 16, 1902; "Maj. Glenn on Trial," *Lewiston Daily Sun,* January 7, 1903; also see Mark Oswald, "The 'Howling Wilderness' Courts-martial of 1902," U.S. Army War College, Carlisle Barracks, Pennsylvania.

12 Chaffee to Henry C. Corbin, January 10, 1902, Corbin Papers, LC.

13 "Gen. Chaffee Explains," *NYT,* January 9, 1903.

14 "Glenn Court-martial Ends," *NYT,* January 25, 1903.

15 Glenn GCM 34401; also see "Maj. Glenn Acquitted," January 30, 1903; "The Case of Maj. Glenn," *NYT,* February 19, 1903; "Censure for Maj. Glenn," *Chicago Daily Tribune,* February 19, 1903.

16 Edwin F. Glenn to Matthew F. Steele, February 10, 1903, Steele Papers, U.S. Army Military Historic Institute, Carlisle Barracks, Pennsylvania, quoted in Linn, *Philippine War,* 321.

17 Glenn GCM 33401.

18 "Proceedings in Congress," *NYT,* January 29, 1903.

19 "Cruelty in the Philippines," *NYT,* February 26, 1903; "Cruelty in the Philippines: No Further Evidence Will Be Taken by Republicans," *Atlanta Constitution,* February 24, 1903.

20 "Tales of Torture in the Philippines," *Boston Daily Globe*, March 20, 1903.

21 "Home Market Club Banquet," AP dispatch reprinted in *Deseret Evening News*, April 3, 1903.

22 "Miles Starts Inquiries," *NYT*, December 25, 1902.

23 "Gen. Miles's Report on Philippines Army: His Criticism of Various Conditions Made Public," *NYT*, April 28, 1903; "Miles' Tales of Army Cruelties," *Boston Daily Globe*, April 28, 1903.

24 "Col. Howze Again Exonerated: Secretary Root Says Charges of Cruelty Appear to Be Unfounded," *NYT*, April 2, 1903; "Secretary of War Acquits Major Howze," *NYT*, May 29, 1903; "Searchlight on Luzon Cruelties," *Chicago Daily Tribune*, May 29, 1903; "Major Howze Exonerated," *NYT*, October 31, 1903.

25 Welch, *Response*, 146.

26 Miller, *Benevolent Assimilation*, 251–52.

27 Davis to Secretary of War Root, July 18, 1902, quoted in Frederic L. Borch, "From Frontier Cavalryman to the World Stage: The Career of Army Judge Advocate General George B. Davis," *Army History* (Winter 2010), 14.

28 Davis to Secretary Root, September 17, 1902, *Trials or Courts-martial in the Philippine Islands in Consequence of Certain Instructions*, 57th Congress, 2nd Session, 1903, Senate Document 213, 42–43.

29 Davis to Root, September 17, 1902, in ibid.; also see Paul Kramer, "The Water Cure," *The New Yorker*, February 25, 2008.

30 Scholar Mark Oswald concludes that Roosevelt had made "improper use of the military justice system to deflect political and public criticism over the conduct and objectives of the lingering war while at the same time minimizing the consequences of judicial action upon the officers concerned. Not only did Roosevelt direct, through Root, the initiation of highly public war crimes–like charges, White House influence manipulated the composition of court panels, overruled valid exculpatory motions, restricted convening authority liberties and skillfully exploited inter- and intra-service rivalries." See Oswald, "The 'Howling-Wilderness' Courts-martial of 1902," 15–16.

31 Miller, *Benevolent Assimilation*, 253.

32 Morrison, *Theodore Rex*, 205.

33 Ibid., 255 and 274; also see TR Letters, 3:599.

34 Morris, *Theodore Rex*, 295.

35 TR to Navy Secretary Moody, December 21, 1903, quoted in Morris, *Theodore Rex*, 673.

36 TR to Albert Shaw, November 6, 1903; TR to Arthur Lee, December 7, 1903, quoted in Brands, *TR: The Last Romantic*, 486–87.

37 Butler, *Across the Busy Years: Recollections and Reflections*, 1:318; Jessup, *Elihu Root*, 1:404–05.

38 H. W. Brands, *The Reckless Decade: America in the 1890s* (New York: St. Martin's Press, 1995), 338.

Epilogue

1　Kramer, *The Blood of Government,* 257 and 267.

2　Ibid., 278–79.

3　Beveridge to TR, October 1, 1906, Beveridge Papers, LC; also see Braeman, 66–67.

4　TR to Taft, October 4, 1906, Roosevelt Papers, LC.

5　See Kramer, *Blood of Government,* 219–20.

6　Ibid., 220.

7　David D. Porter personnel file, NPRC.

8　Hiram Bearss personnel file, NPRC.

9　Various documents in the Alexander S. Williams personnel file, NPRC.

10　John H. A. Day personnel file, NPRC.

11　John H. Quick personnel file, NPRC.

12　Waller Papers, USMCA.

13　Jim Zwick, "Mark Twain's Anti-Imperialist Writings in the 'American Century,'" in *Vestiges of War: The Philippine-American War and the Aftermath of an Imperial Dream, 1899–1999,* Angel Velasco Shaw and Luis H. Francia., eds. (New York: New York University Press, 2002), 43.

14　Mark Twain, "A Defence of General Funston," *North American Review* 174 (May 1902), 623.

15　Zimmerman, *First Great Triumph,* 478–79.

16　Ibid., 478–80.

17　Ibid., 487–88.

18　"America Powerless to Investigate Congo," *NYT,* February 26, 1906; "Atrocities on the Congo," *Los Angeles Times,* December 11, 1906; "Appeal to Root to Help End Congo Abuses," *NYT,* December 26, 1906; "Root Demands on Belgium," *NYT,* January 29, 1909; also see Adam Hochschild, *King Leopold's Ghost: A Story of Greed, Terror and Heroism in Colonial Africa* (Boston: Houghton Mifflin Co., 1998), 248–49.

19　Zimmerman, *First Great Triumph,* 486–87.

20　Ibid., 487–88.

21　TR to William Howard Taft, August 21, 1907, Taft Papers, LC.

INDEX

- Spanish American War
4/18/98 to 8/1/1898
- Phillepiec War
2/1899 2/18 99 to 7/1/1902